Buffy the vampire slayer™

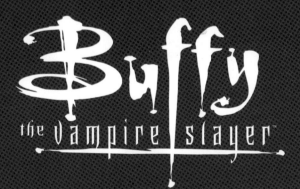

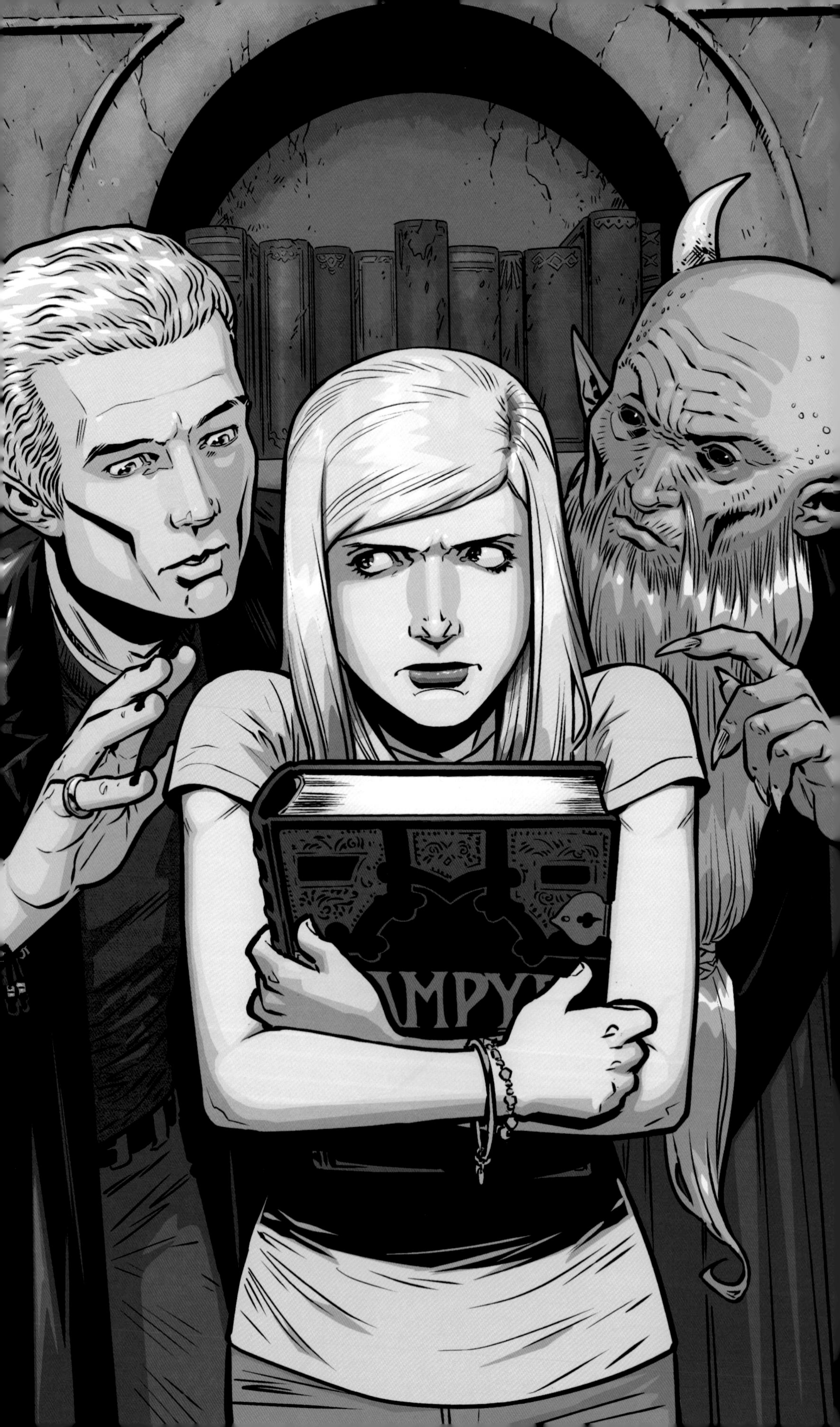

Buffy the Vampire Slayer™

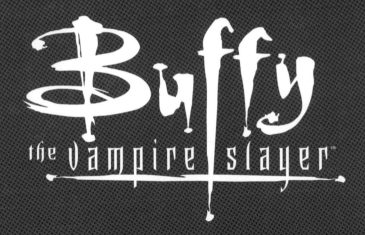

SEASON 10 · VOLUME 6

OWN IT

SCRIPT
CHRISTOS GAGE

ART · CHAPTERS 1–5
REBEKAH ISAACS

ART · CHAPTER 6
JUANAN RAMÍREZ

COLORS DAN JACKSON
LETTERS RICHARD STARKINGS & COMICRAFT'S JIMMY BETANCOURT
COVER AND CHAPTER BREAK ART STEVE MORRIS

EXECUTIVE PRODUCER JOSS WHEDON

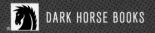

DARK HORSE BOOKS

PRESIDENT & PUBLISHER: MIKE RICHARDSON · EDITORS: FREDDYE MILLER & JIM GIBBONS
COLLECTION DESIGNER: JUSTIN COUCH · DIGITAL ART TECHNICIAN: CHRISTIANNE GOUDREAU

Special thanks to NICOLE SPIEGEL *and* JOSH IZZO *at* TWENTIETH CENTURY FOX, DANIEL
KAMINSKY, BECCA J. SADOWSKY, SCOTT ALLIE, SPENCER CUSHING, SIERRA HAHN, *and*
RANDY STRADLEY.

The art on page 2 is the variant cover for *Buffy* Season 10 #26, by Rebekah Isaacs with Dan Jackson.

This volume reprints the comic book series *Buffy the Vampire Slayer* Season 10 #26–#30 and
"Buffy the Vampire Slayer Season 10: Where Are They Now?," originally printed in
Dark Horse Day Sampler 2016 from Dark Horse Comics.

DARKHORSE.COM

First edition: December 2016
ISBN 978-1-50670-034-2

1 3 5 7 9 10 8 6 4 2
Printed in China

Published by Dark Horse Books, a division of Dark Horse Comics, Inc.
10956 SE Main Street, Milwaukie, OR 97222

BUFFY THE VAMPIRE SLAYER SEASON 10 VOLUME 6: OWN IT

This volume reprints the comic book series *Buffy the Vampire Slayer* Season 10 #26–#30, from Dark Horse
Comics.

Library of Congress Cataloging-in-Publication Data

Names: Gage, Christos, author. | Isaacs, Rebekah, artist. | Ramírez, Juanan,
 artist. | Jackson, Dan, 1971- colorist. | Starkings, Richard, letterer. |
 Betancourt, Jimmy, letterer. | Morris, Steven, artist.
Title: Buffy the Vampire Slayer. Season 10. Volume 6, Own it / script,
 Christos Gage ; art (chapters 1-5), Rebekah Isaacs ; art (chapter 6),
 Juanan Ramírez ; colors, Dan Jackson ; letters, Richard Starkings &
 Comicraft's Jimmy Betancourt ; cover and chapter break art, Steve Morris.
Other titles: Own it
Description: First edition. | Milwaukie, OR : Dark Horse Books, 2016.
Identifiers: LCCN 2016034416 | ISBN 9781506700342 (paperback)
Subjects: LCSH: Comic books, strips, etc. | BISAC: COMICS & GRAPHIC NOVELS /
 Horror.
Classification: LCC PN6728.B84 G39 2016 | DDC 741.5/973--dc23
LC record available at https://lccn.loc.gov/2016034416

To find a comics shop in your area, call the Comic Shop Locator Service toll-free at
(888) 266-4226. International Licensing: 503-905-2377.

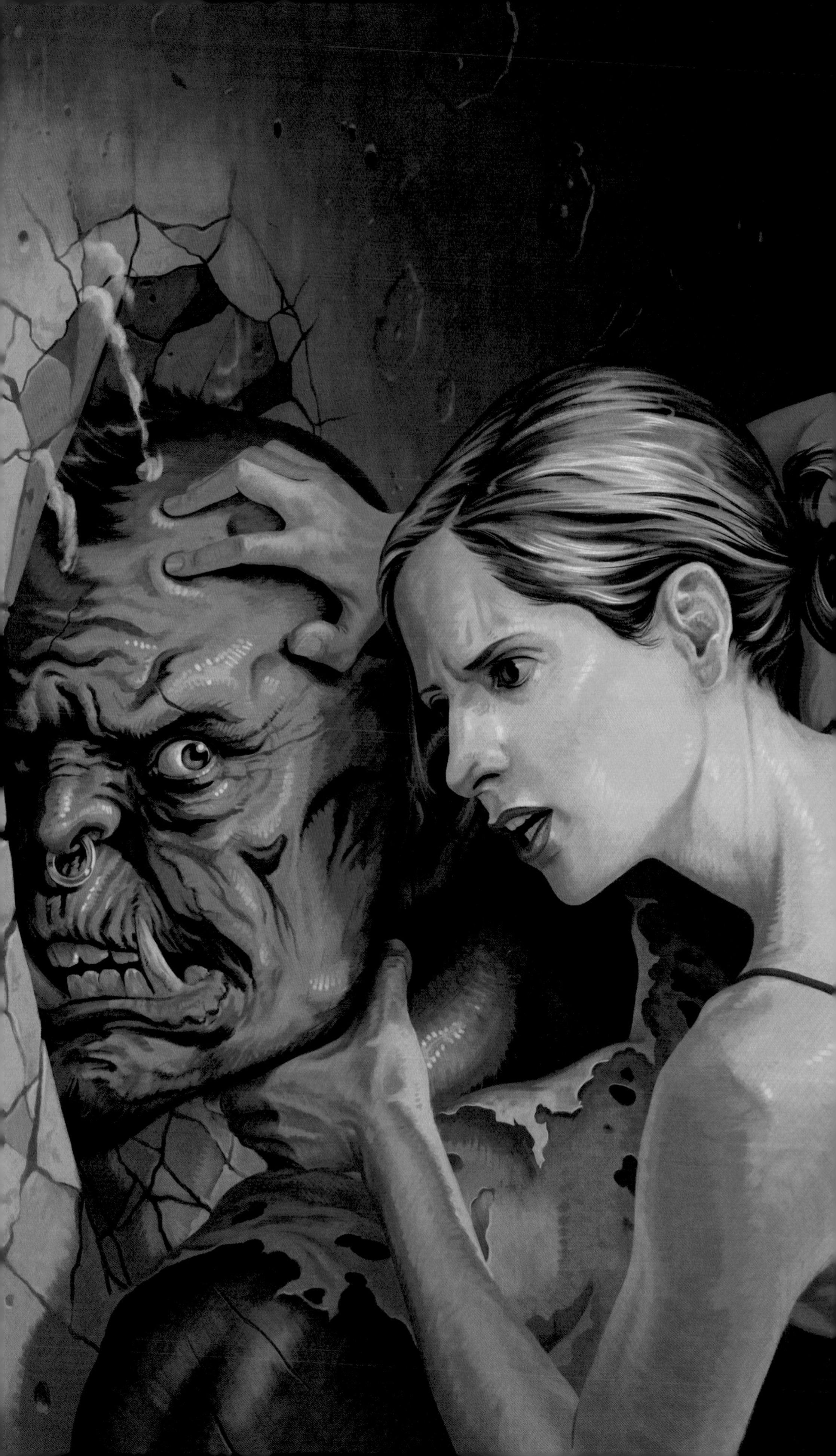

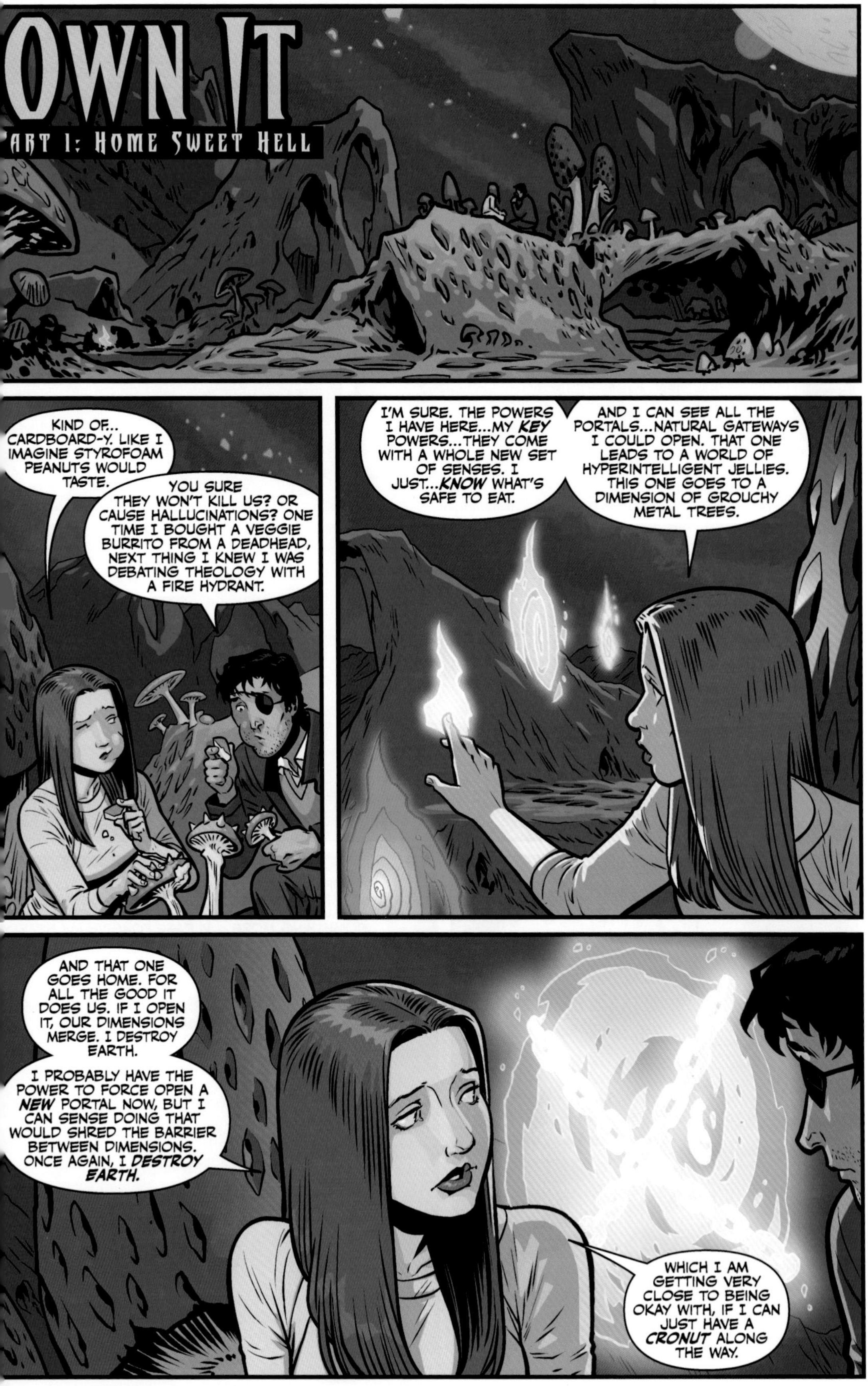
OWN IT
ART 1: HOME SWEET HELL
KIND OF... CARDBOARD-Y. LIKE I IMAGINE STYROFOAM PEANUTS WOULD TASTE.
YOU SURE THEY WON'T KILL US? OR CAUSE HALLUCINATIONS? ONE TIME I BOUGHT A VEGGIE BURRITO FROM A DEADHEAD, NEXT THING I KNEW I WAS DEBATING THEOLOGY WITH A FIRE HYDRANT.
I'M SURE. THE POWERS I HAVE HERE...MY KEY POWERS...THEY COME WITH A WHOLE NEW SET OF SENSES. I JUST...KNOW WHAT'S SAFE TO EAT.
AND I CAN SEE ALL THE PORTALS...NATURAL GATEWAYS I COULD OPEN. THAT ONE LEADS TO A WORLD OF HYPERINTELLIGENT JELLIES. THIS ONE GOES TO A DIMENSION OF GROUCHY METAL TREES.
AND THAT ONE GOES HOME. FOR ALL THE GOOD IT DOES US. IF I OPEN IT, OUR DIMENSIONS MERGE. I DESTROY EARTH.
I PROBABLY HAVE THE POWER TO FORCE OPEN A NEW PORTAL NOW, BUT I CAN SENSE DOING THAT WOULD SHRED THE BARRIER BETWEEN DIMENSIONS. ONCE AGAIN, I DESTROY EARTH.
WHICH I AM GETTING VERY CLOSE TO BEING OKAY WITH, IF I CAN JUST HAVE A CRONUT ALONG THE WAY.

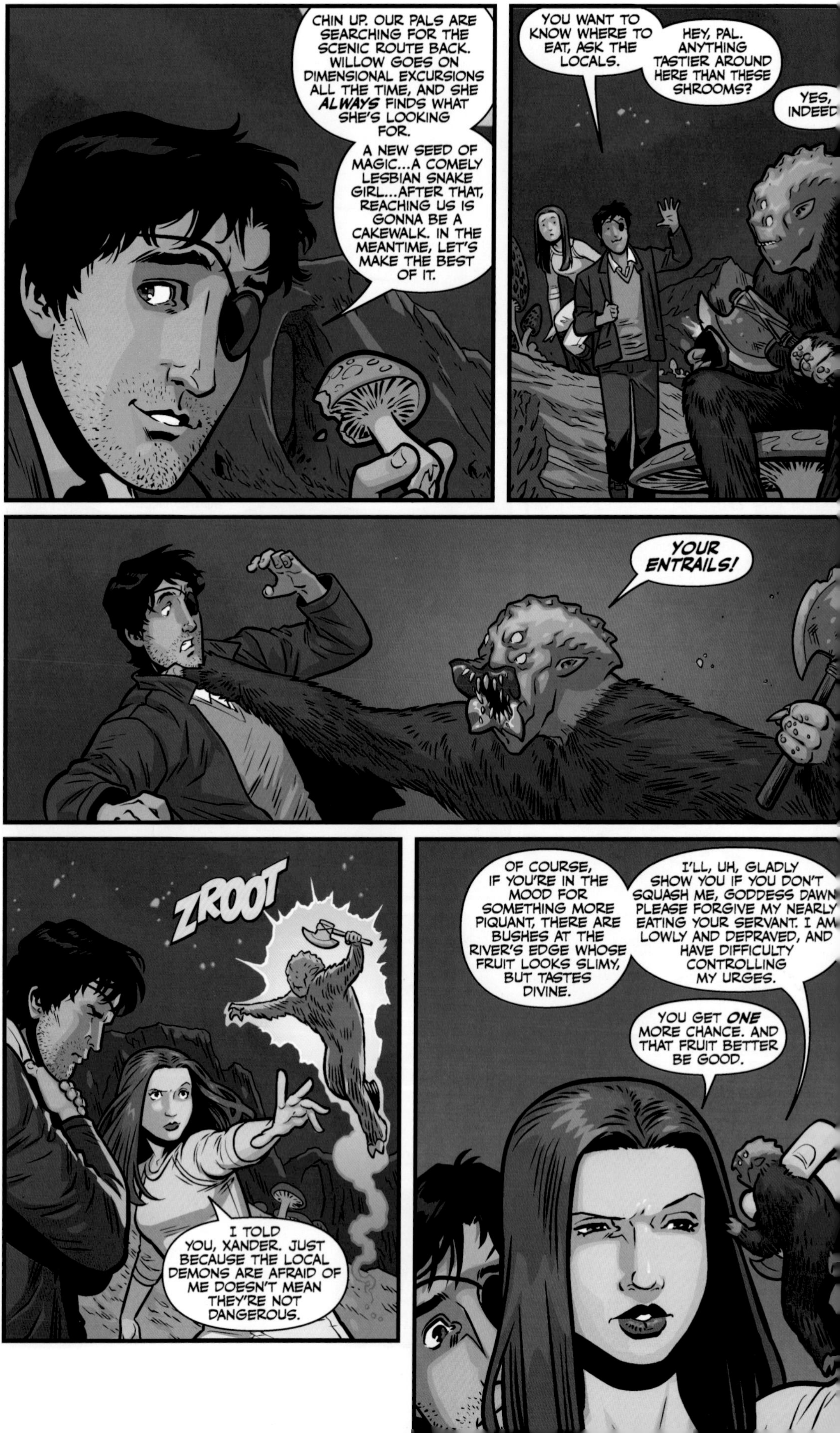
CHIN UP. OUR PALS ARE SEARCHING FOR THE SCENIC ROUTE BACK. WILLOW GOES ON DIMENSIONAL EXCURSIONS ALL THE TIME, AND SHE *ALWAYS* FINDS WHAT SHE'S LOOKING FOR.
A NEW SEED OF MAGIC...A COMELY LESBIAN SNAKE GIRL...AFTER THAT, REACHING US IS GONNA BE A CAKEWALK. IN THE MEANTIME, LET'S MAKE THE BEST OF IT.
YOU WANT TO KNOW WHERE TO EAT, ASK THE LOCALS.
HEY, PAL. ANYTHING TASTIER AROUND HERE THAN THESE SHROOMS?
YES, INDEED
YOUR ENTRAILS!
ZROOT
I TOLD YOU, XANDER. JUST BECAUSE THE LOCAL DEMONS ARE AFRAID OF ME DOESN'T MEAN THEY'RE NOT DANGEROUS.
OF COURSE, IF YOU'RE IN THE MOOD FOR SOMETHING MORE PIQUANT, THERE ARE BUSHES AT THE RIVER'S EDGE WHOSE FRUIT LOOKS SLIMY, BUT TASTES DIVINE.
I'LL, UH, GLADLY SHOW YOU IF YOU DON'T SQUASH ME, GODDESS DAWN PLEASE FORGIVE MY NEARLY EATING YOUR SERVANT. I AM LOWLY AND DEPRAVED, AND HAVE DIFFICULTY CONTROLLING MY URGES.
YOU GET *ONE* MORE CHANCE. AND THAT FRUIT BETTER BE GOOD.

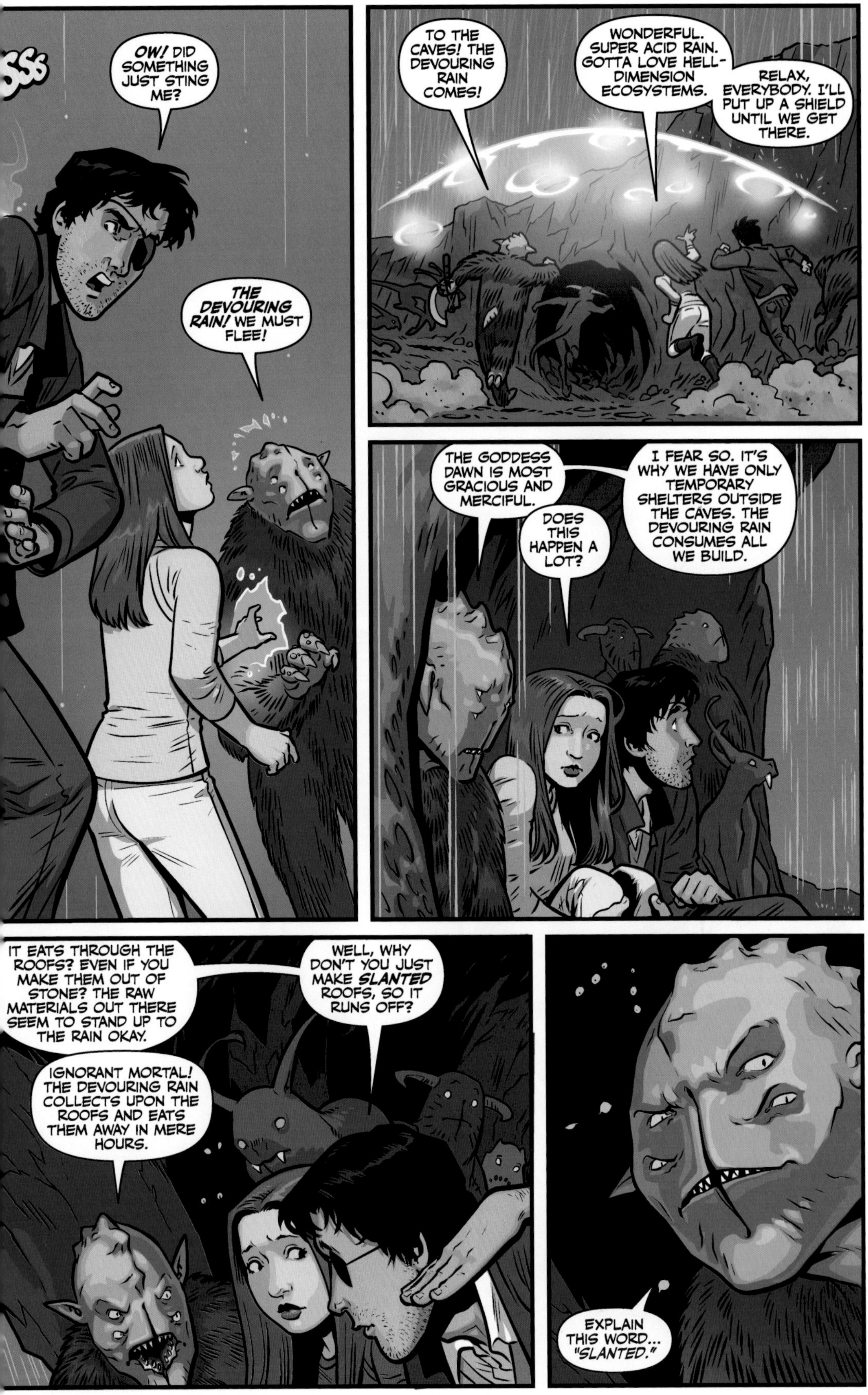
SSS
OW! DID SOMETHING JUST STING ME?
THE DEVOURING RAIN! WE MUST FLEE!
TO THE CAVES! THE DEVOURING RAIN COMES!
WONDERFUL. SUPER ACID RAIN. GOTTA LOVE HELL-DIMENSION ECOSYSTEMS.
RELAX, EVERYBODY. I'LL PUT UP A SHIELD UNTIL WE GET THERE.
THE GODDESS DAWN IS MOST GRACIOUS AND MERCIFUL.
DOES THIS HAPPEN A LOT?
I FEAR SO. IT'S WHY WE HAVE ONLY TEMPORARY SHELTERS OUTSIDE THE CAVES. THE DEVOURING RAIN CONSUMES ALL WE BUILD.
IT EATS THROUGH THE ROOFS? EVEN IF YOU MAKE THEM OUT OF STONE? THE RAW MATERIALS OUT THERE SEEM TO STAND UP TO THE RAIN OKAY.
WELL, WHY DON'T YOU JUST MAKE SLANTED ROOFS, SO IT RUNS OFF?
IGNORANT MORTAL! THE DEVOURING RAIN COLLECTS UPON THE ROOFS AND EATS THEM AWAY IN MERE HOURS.
EXPLAIN THIS WORD... "SLANTED."

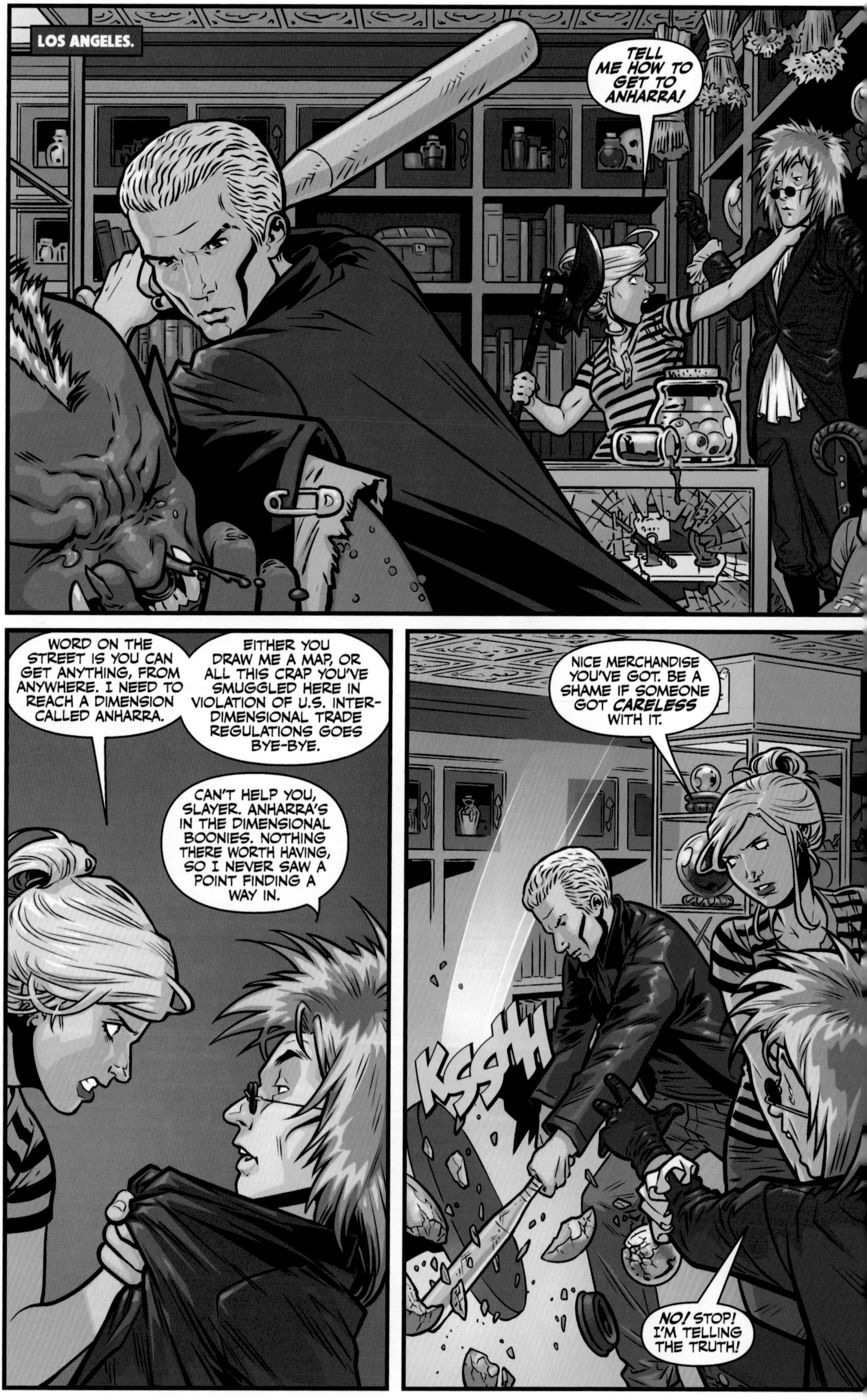
LOS ANGELES.
TELL ME HOW TO GET TO ANHARRA!
WORD ON THE STREET IS YOU CAN GET ANYTHING, FROM ANYWHERE. I NEED TO REACH A DIMENSION CALLED ANHARRA.
EITHER YOU DRAW ME A MAP, OR ALL THIS CRAP YOU'VE SMUGGLED HERE IN VIOLATION OF U.S. INTER-DIMENSIONAL TRADE REGULATIONS GOES BYE-BYE.
CAN'T HELP YOU, SLAYER. ANHARRA'S IN THE DIMENSIONAL BOONIES. NOTHING THERE WORTH HAVING, SO I NEVER SAW A POINT FINDING A WAY IN.
NICE MERCHANDISE YOU'VE GOT. BE A SHAME IF SOMEONE GOT CARELESS WITH IT.
KSSHH
NO! STOP! I'M TELLING THE TRUTH!

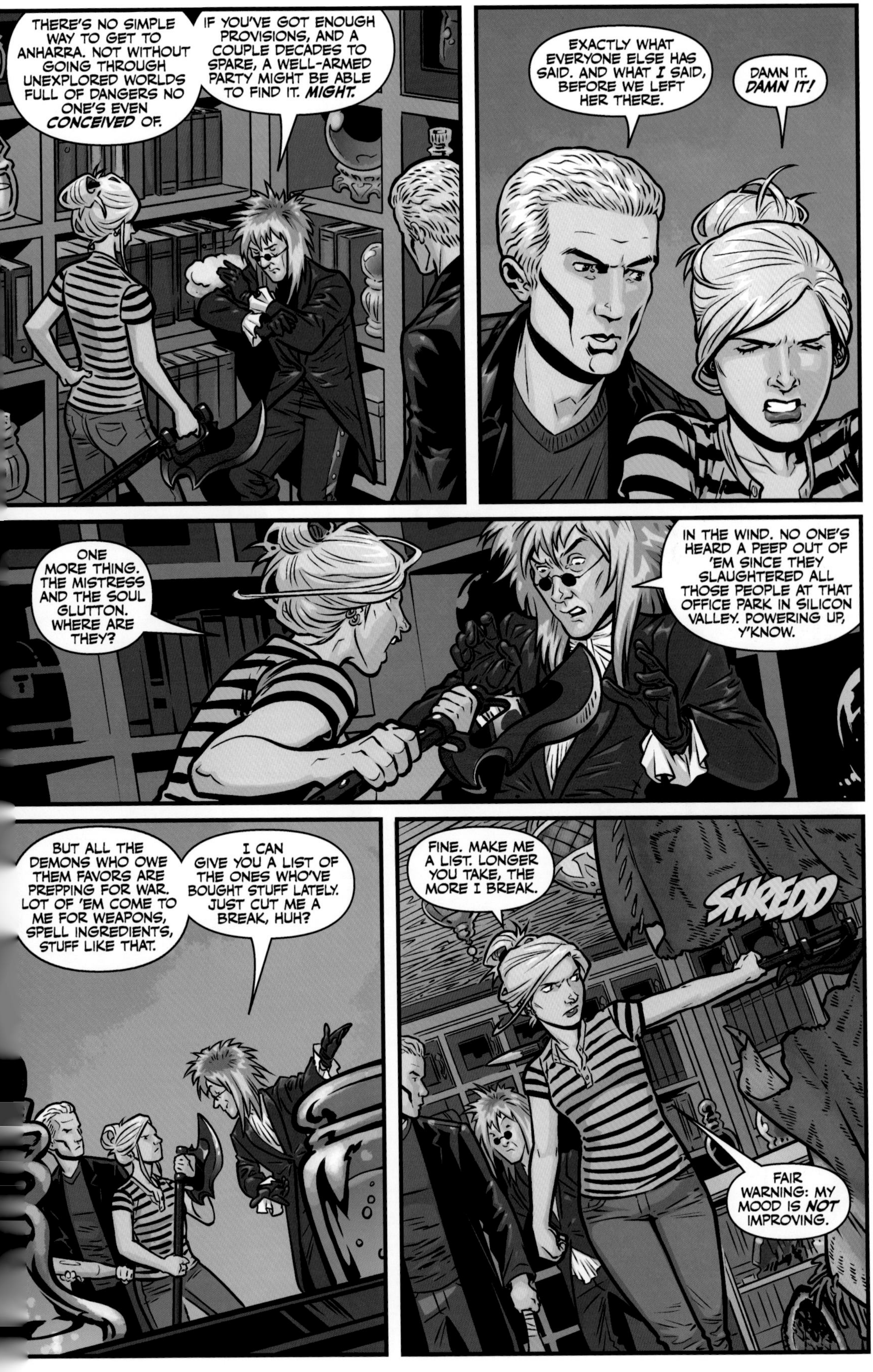
THERE'S NO SIMPLE WAY TO GET TO ANHARRA. NOT WITHOUT GOING THROUGH UNEXPLORED WORLDS FULL OF DANGERS NO ONE'S EVEN *CONCEIVED* OF.
IF YOU'VE GOT ENOUGH PROVISIONS, AND A COUPLE DECADES TO SPARE, A WELL-ARMED PARTY MIGHT BE ABLE TO FIND IT. *MIGHT.*
EXACTLY WHAT EVERYONE ELSE HAS SAID. AND WHAT *I* SAID, BEFORE WE LEFT HER THERE.
DAMN IT. *DAMN IT!*
ONE MORE THING. THE MISTRESS AND THE SOUL GLUTTON. WHERE ARE THEY?
IN THE WIND. NO ONE'S HEARD A PEEP OUT OF 'EM SINCE THEY SLAUGHTERED ALL THOSE PEOPLE AT THAT OFFICE PARK IN SILICON VALLEY. POWERING UP, Y'KNOW.
BUT ALL THE DEMONS WHO OWE THEM FAVORS ARE PREPPING FOR WAR. LOT OF 'EM COME TO ME FOR WEAPONS, SPELL INGREDIENTS, STUFF LIKE THAT.
I CAN GIVE YOU A LIST OF THE ONES WHO'VE BOUGHT STUFF LATELY. JUST CUT ME A BREAK, HUH?
FINE. MAKE ME A LIST. LONGER YOU TAKE, THE MORE I BREAK.
SHREDD
FAIR WARNING: MY MOOD IS *NOT* IMPROVING.

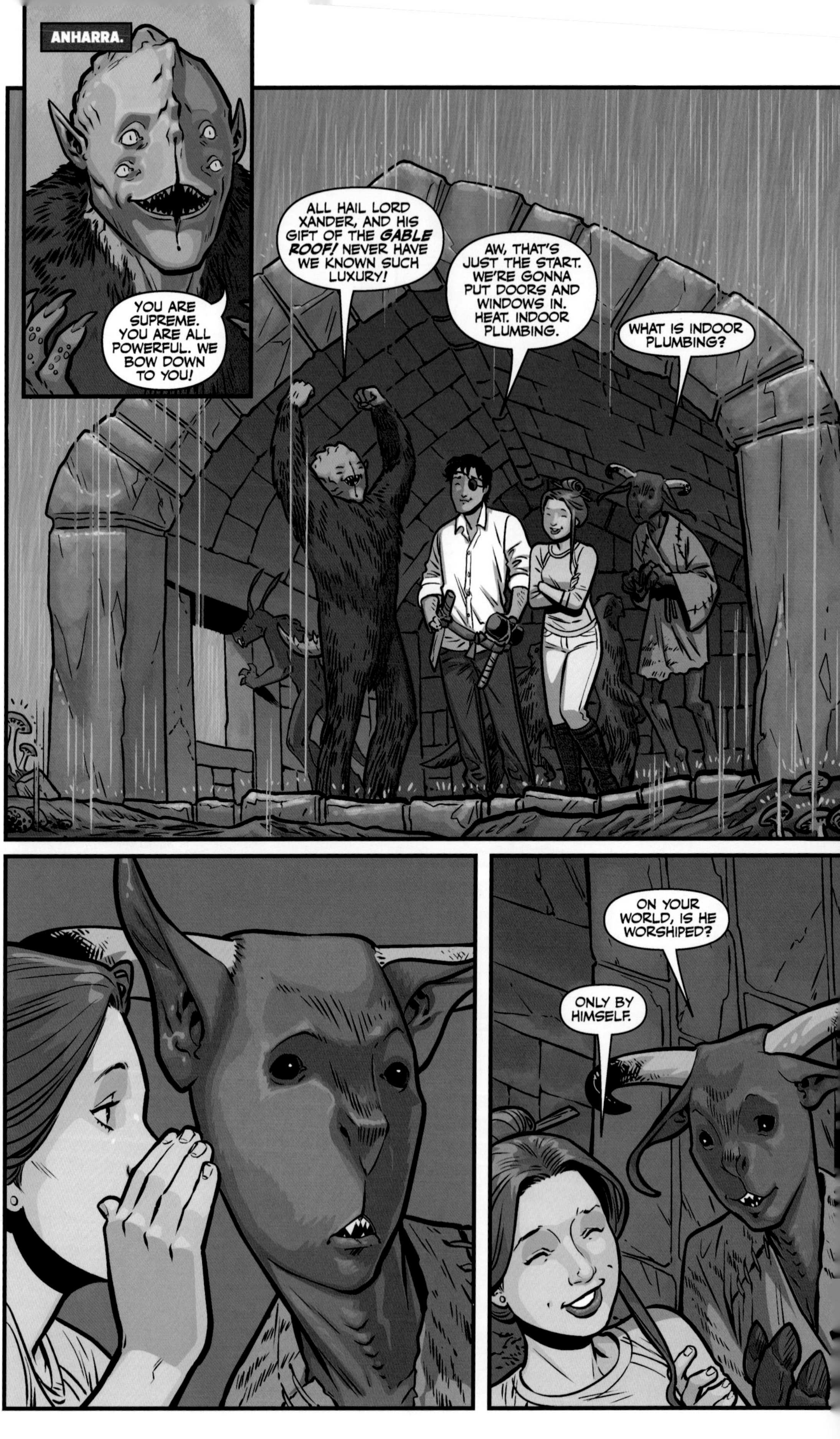
ANHARRA.
YOU ARE SUPREME. YOU ARE ALL POWERFUL. WE BOW DOWN TO YOU!
ALL HAIL LORD XANDER, AND HIS GIFT OF THE *GABLE ROOF!* NEVER HAVE WE KNOWN SUCH LUXURY!
AW, THAT'S JUST THE START. WE'RE GONNA PUT DOORS AND WINDOWS IN. HEAT. INDOOR PLUMBING.
WHAT IS INDOOR PLUMBING?
ON YOUR WORLD, IS HE WORSHIPED?
ONLY BY HIMSELF.

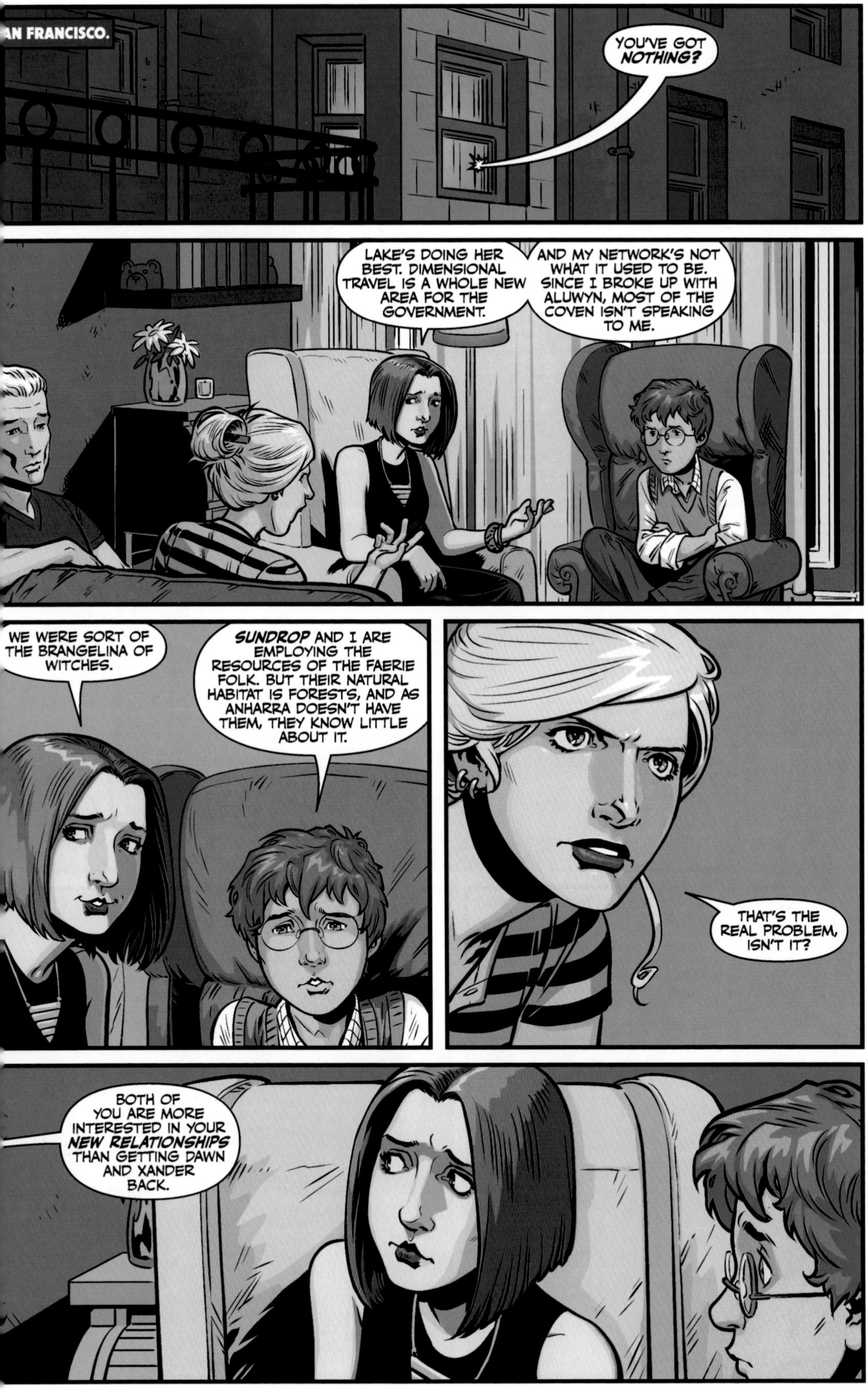
AN FRANCISCO.
YOU'VE GOT NOTHING?
LAKE'S DOING HER BEST. DIMENSIONAL TRAVEL IS A WHOLE NEW AREA FOR THE GOVERNMENT.
AND MY NETWORK'S NOT WHAT IT USED TO BE. SINCE I BROKE UP WITH ALUWYN, MOST OF THE COVEN ISN'T SPEAKING TO ME.
WE WERE SORT OF THE BRANGELINA OF WITCHES.
SUNDROP AND I ARE EMPLOYING THE RESOURCES OF THE FAERIE FOLK. BUT THEIR NATURAL HABITAT IS FORESTS, AND AS ANHARRA DOESN'T HAVE THEM, THEY KNOW LITTLE ABOUT IT.
THAT'S THE REAL PROBLEM, ISN'T IT?
BOTH OF YOU ARE MORE INTERESTED IN YOUR NEW RELATIONSHIPS THAN GETTING DAWN AND XANDER BACK.

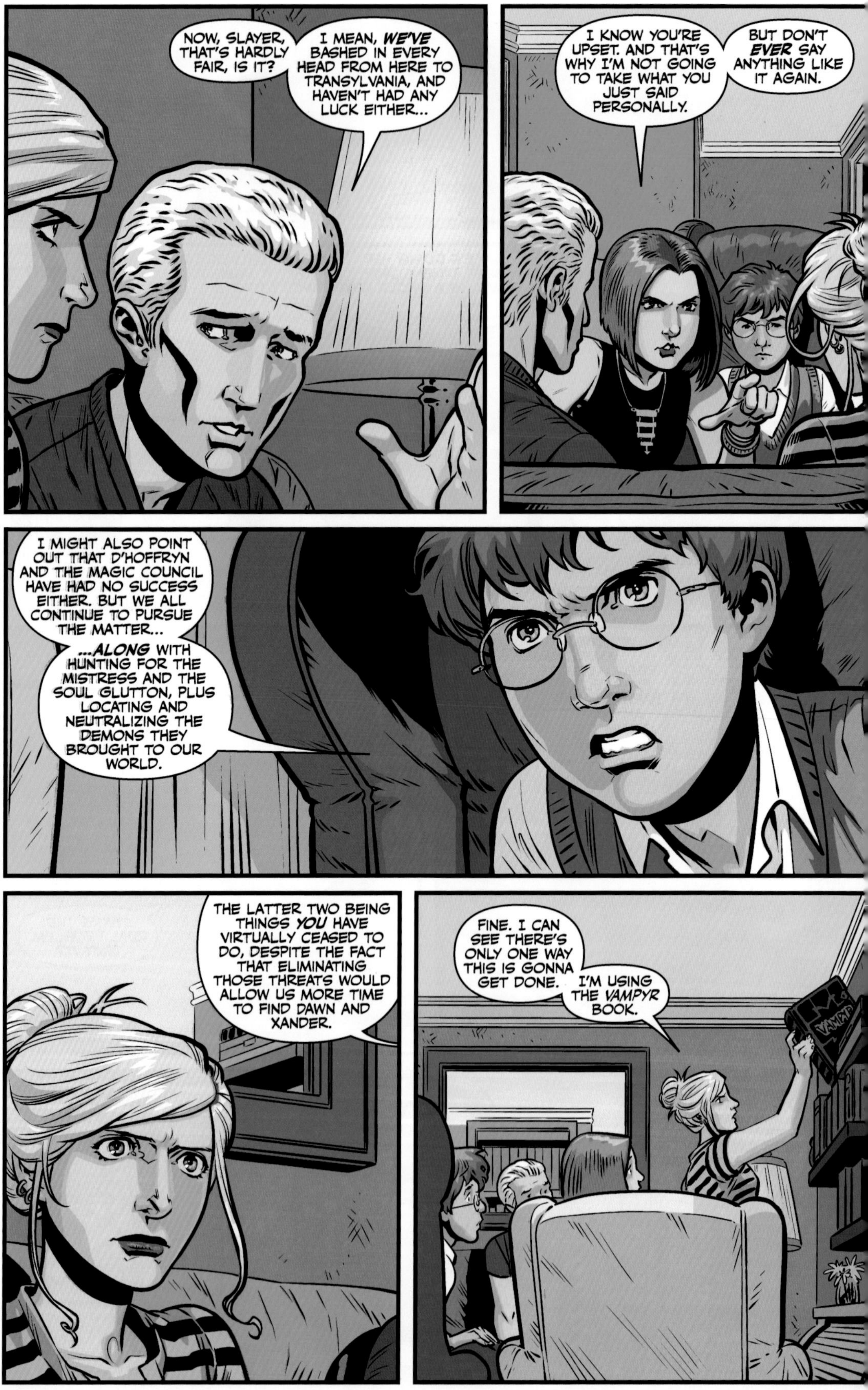
NOW, SLAYER, THAT'S HARDLY FAIR, IS IT?
I MEAN, WE'VE BASHED IN EVERY HEAD FROM HERE TO TRANSYLVANIA, AND HAVEN'T HAD ANY LUCK EITHER...
I KNOW YOU'RE UPSET. AND THAT'S WHY I'M NOT GOING TO TAKE WHAT YOU JUST SAID PERSONALLY.
BUT DON'T EVER SAY ANYTHING LIKE IT AGAIN.
I MIGHT ALSO POINT OUT THAT D'HOFFRYN AND THE MAGIC COUNCIL HAVE HAD NO SUCCESS EITHER. BUT WE ALL CONTINUE TO PURSUE THE MATTER...
...ALONG WITH HUNTING FOR THE MISTRESS AND THE SOUL GLUTTON, PLUS LOCATING AND NEUTRALIZING THE DEMONS THEY BROUGHT TO OUR WORLD.
THE LATTER TWO BEING THINGS YOU HAVE VIRTUALLY CEASED TO DO, DESPITE THE FACT THAT ELIMINATING THOSE THREATS WOULD ALLOW US MORE TIME TO FIND DAWN AND XANDER.
FINE. I CAN SEE THERE'S ONLY ONE WAY THIS IS GONNA GET DONE.
I'M USING THE VAMPYR BOOK.
VAMPYR

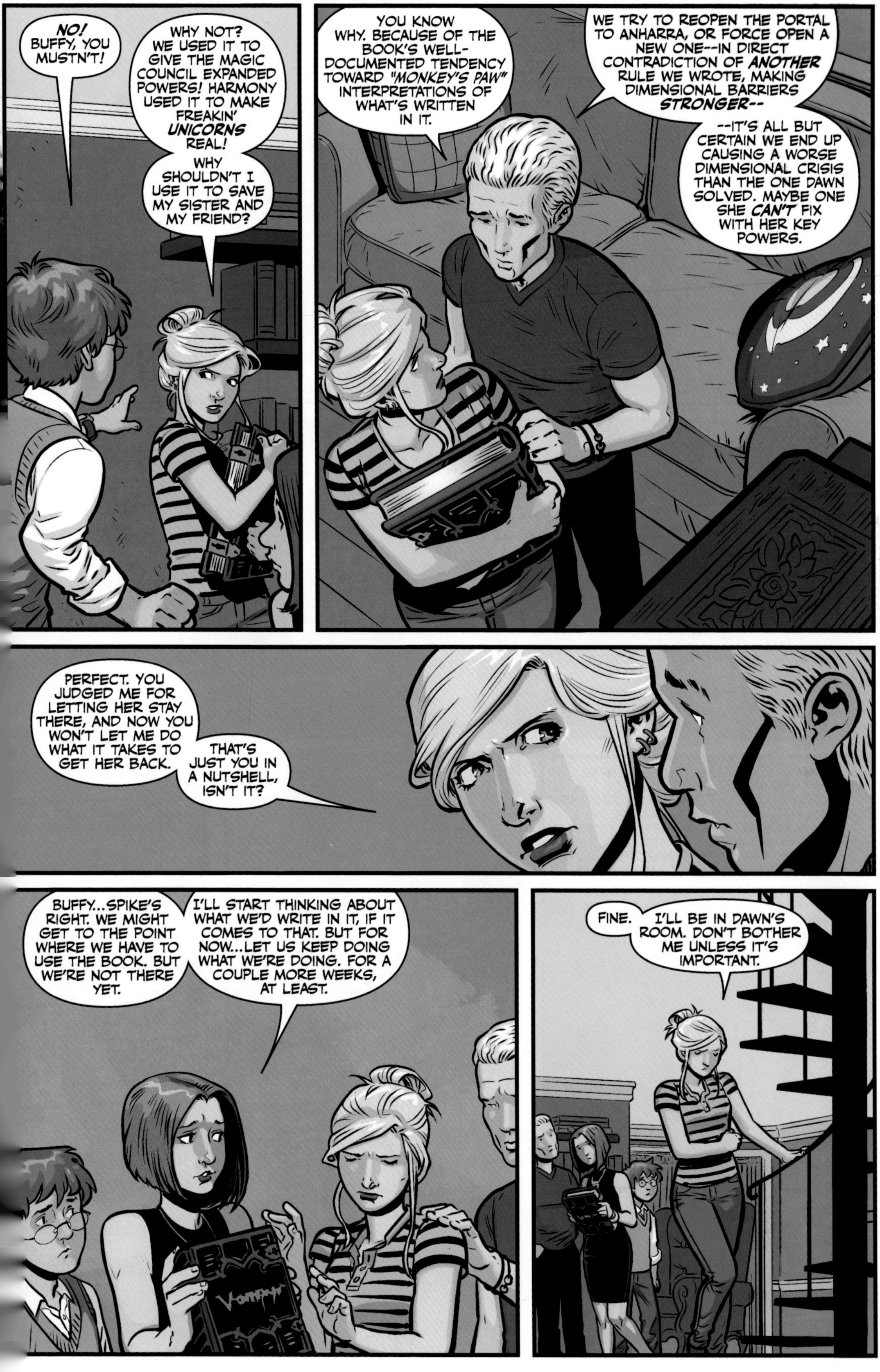
NO! BUFFY, YOU MUSTN'T!
WHY NOT? WE USED IT TO GIVE THE MAGIC COUNCIL EXPANDED POWERS! HARMONY USED IT TO MAKE FREAKIN' UNICORNS REAL!
WHY SHOULDN'T I USE IT TO SAVE MY SISTER AND MY FRIEND?
YOU KNOW WHY. BECAUSE OF THE BOOK'S WELL-DOCUMENTED TENDENCY TOWARD "MONKEY'S PAW" INTERPRETATIONS OF WHAT'S WRITTEN IN IT.
WE TRY TO REOPEN THE PORTAL TO ANHARRA, OR FORCE OPEN A NEW ONE--IN DIRECT CONTRADICTION OF ANOTHER RULE WE WROTE, MAKING DIMENSIONAL BARRIERS STRONGER--
--IT'S ALL BUT CERTAIN WE END UP CAUSING A WORSE DIMENSIONAL CRISIS THAN THE ONE DAWN SOLVED. MAYBE ONE SHE CAN'T FIX WITH HER KEY POWERS.
PERFECT. YOU JUDGED ME FOR LETTING HER STAY THERE, AND NOW YOU WON'T LET ME DO WHAT IT TAKES TO GET HER BACK.
THAT'S JUST YOU IN A NUTSHELL, ISN'T IT?
BUFFY...SPIKE'S RIGHT. WE MIGHT GET TO THE POINT WHERE WE HAVE TO USE THE BOOK. BUT WE'RE NOT THERE YET.
I'LL START THINKING ABOUT WHAT WE'D WRITE IN IT, IF IT COMES TO THAT. BUT FOR NOW...LET US KEEP DOING WHAT WE'RE DOING. FOR A COUPLE MORE WEEKS, AT LEAST.
FINE.
I'LL BE IN DAWN'S ROOM. DON'T BOTHER ME UNLESS IT'S IMPORTANT.

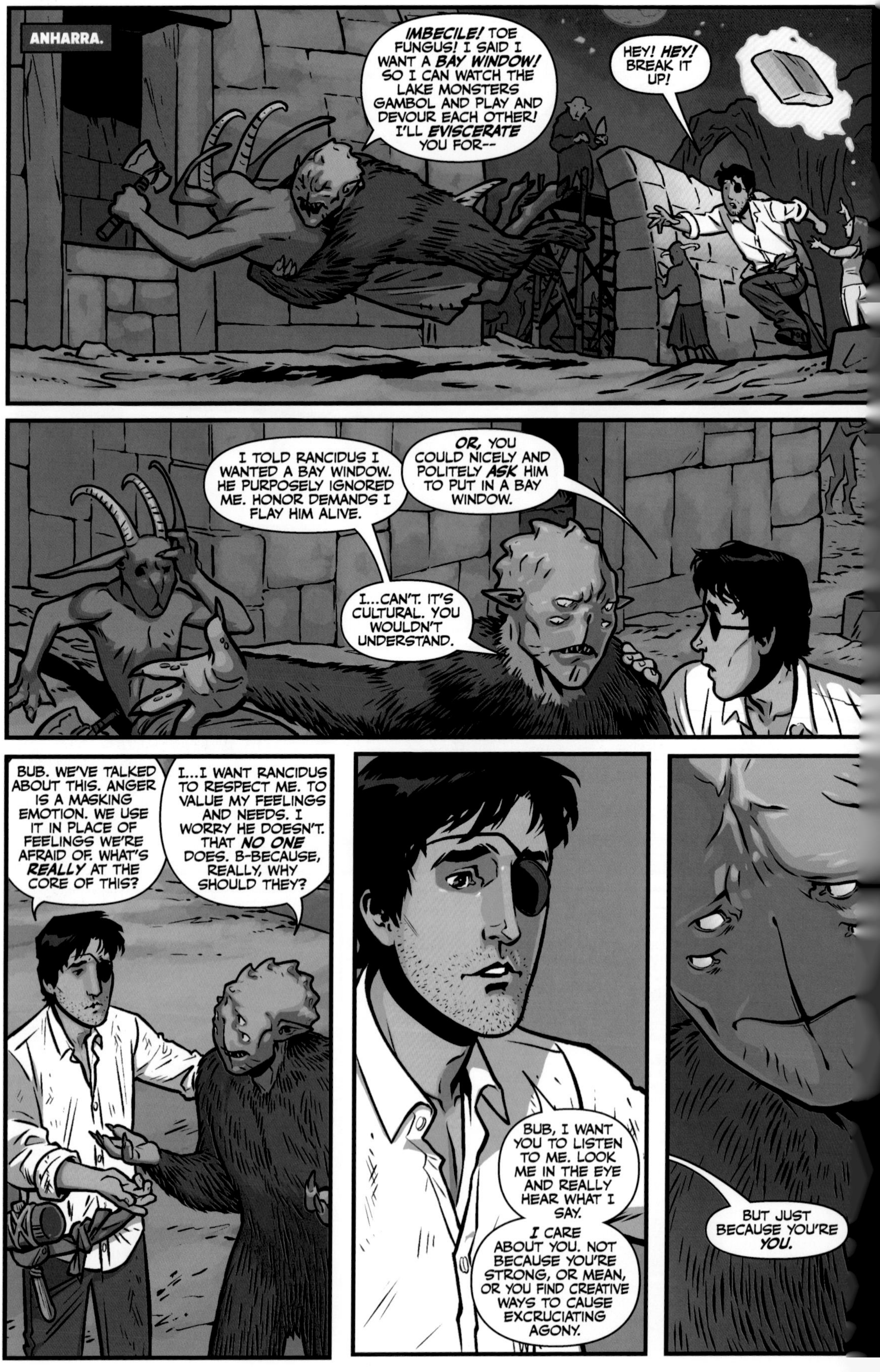
ANHARRA.
IMBECILE! TOE FUNGUS! I SAID I WANT A BAY WINDOW! SO I CAN WATCH THE LAKE MONSTERS GAMBOL AND PLAY AND DEVOUR EACH OTHER! I'LL EVISCERATE YOU FOR--
HEY! HEY! BREAK IT UP!
I TOLD RANCIDUS I WANTED A BAY WINDOW. HE PURPOSELY IGNORED ME. HONOR DEMANDS I FLAY HIM ALIVE.
OR, YOU COULD NICELY AND POLITELY ASK HIM TO PUT IN A BAY WINDOW.
I...CAN'T. IT'S CULTURAL. YOU WOULDN'T UNDERSTAND.
BUB. WE'VE TALKED ABOUT THIS. ANGER IS A MASKING EMOTION. WE USE IT IN PLACE OF FEELINGS WE'RE AFRAID OF. WHAT'S REALLY AT THE CORE OF THIS?
I...I WANT RANCIDUS TO RESPECT ME. TO VALUE MY FEELINGS AND NEEDS. I WORRY HE DOESN'T. THAT NO ONE DOES. B-BECAUSE, REALLY, WHY SHOULD THEY?
BUB, I WANT YOU TO LISTEN TO ME. LOOK ME IN THE EYE AND REALLY HEAR WHAT I SAY.
I CARE ABOUT YOU. NOT BECAUSE YOU'RE STRONG, OR MEAN, OR YOU FIND CREATIVE WAYS TO CAUSE EXCRUCIATING AGONY.
BUT JUST BECAUSE YOU'RE YOU.

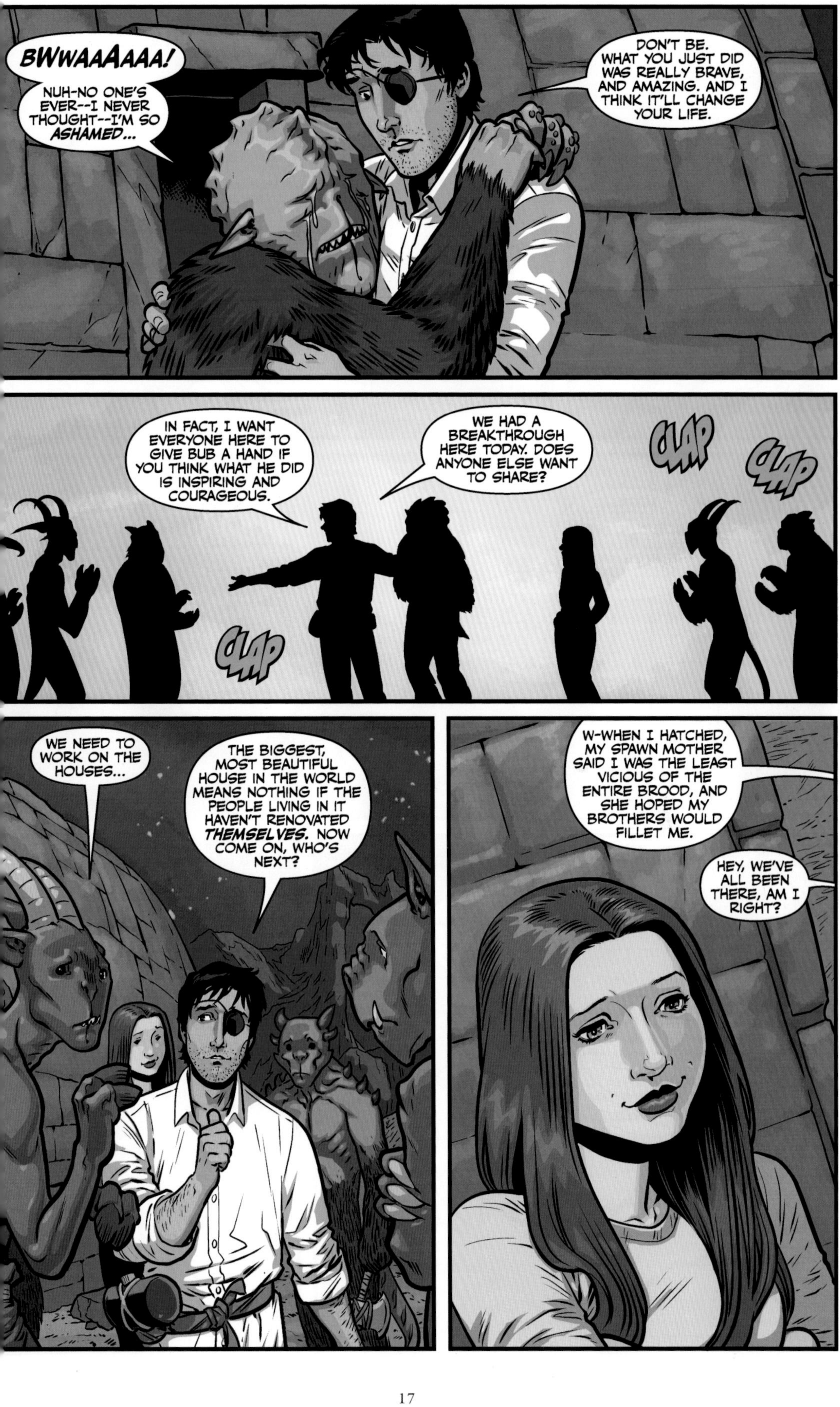

BWWAAAAAA!
NUH-NO ONE'S EVER--I NEVER THOUGHT--I'M SO ASHAMED...
DON'T BE. WHAT YOU JUST DID WAS REALLY BRAVE, AND AMAZING. AND I THINK IT'LL CHANGE YOUR LIFE.
IN FACT, I WANT EVERYONE HERE TO GIVE BUB A HAND IF YOU THINK WHAT HE DID IS INSPIRING AND COURAGEOUS.
WE HAD A BREAKTHROUGH HERE TODAY. DOES ANYONE ELSE WANT TO SHARE?
CLAP
CLAP
CLAP
WE NEED TO WORK ON THE HOUSES...
THE BIGGEST, MOST BEAUTIFUL HOUSE IN THE WORLD MEANS NOTHING IF THE PEOPLE LIVING IN IT HAVEN'T RENOVATED THEMSELVES. NOW COME ON, WHO'S NEXT?
W-WHEN I HATCHED, MY SPAWN MOTHER SAID I WAS THE LEAST VICIOUS OF THE ENTIRE BROOD, AND SHE HOPED MY BROTHERS WOULD FILLET ME.
HEY, WE'VE ALL BEEN THERE, AM I RIGHT?

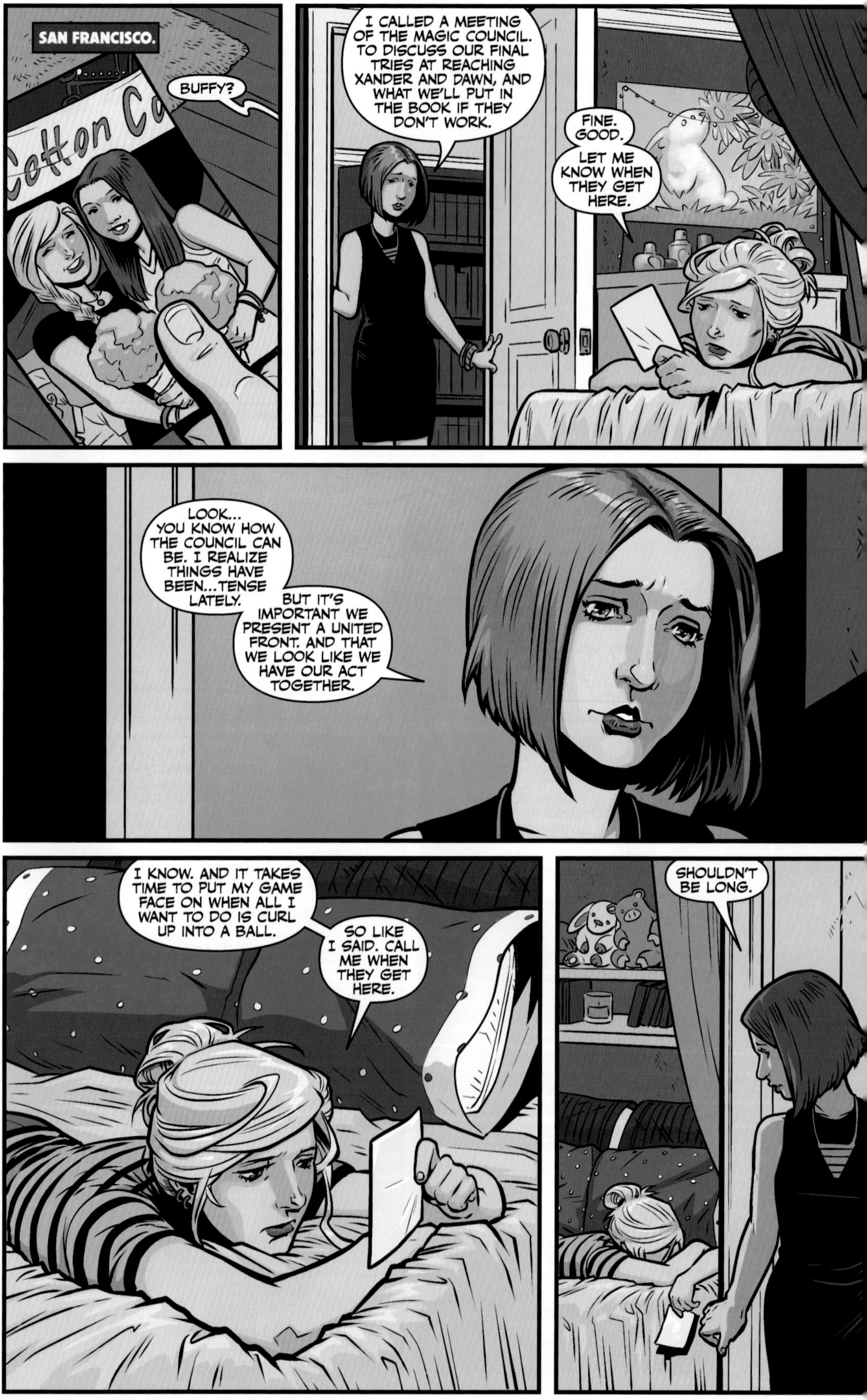
SAN FRANCISCO.
BUFFY?
Cotton Co
I CALLED A MEETING OF THE MAGIC COUNCIL. TO DISCUSS OUR FINAL TRIES AT REACHING XANDER AND DAWN, AND WHAT WE'LL PUT IN THE BOOK IF THEY DON'T WORK.
FINE. GOOD.
LET ME KNOW WHEN THEY GET HERE.
LOOK... YOU KNOW HOW THE COUNCIL CAN BE. I REALIZE THINGS HAVE BEEN...TENSE LATELY.
BUT IT'S IMPORTANT WE PRESENT A UNITED FRONT. AND THAT WE LOOK LIKE WE HAVE OUR ACT TOGETHER.
I KNOW. AND IT TAKES TIME TO PUT MY GAME FACE ON WHEN ALL I WANT TO DO IS CURL UP INTO A BALL.
SO LIKE I SAID. CALL ME WHEN THEY GET HERE.
SHOULDN'T BE LONG.

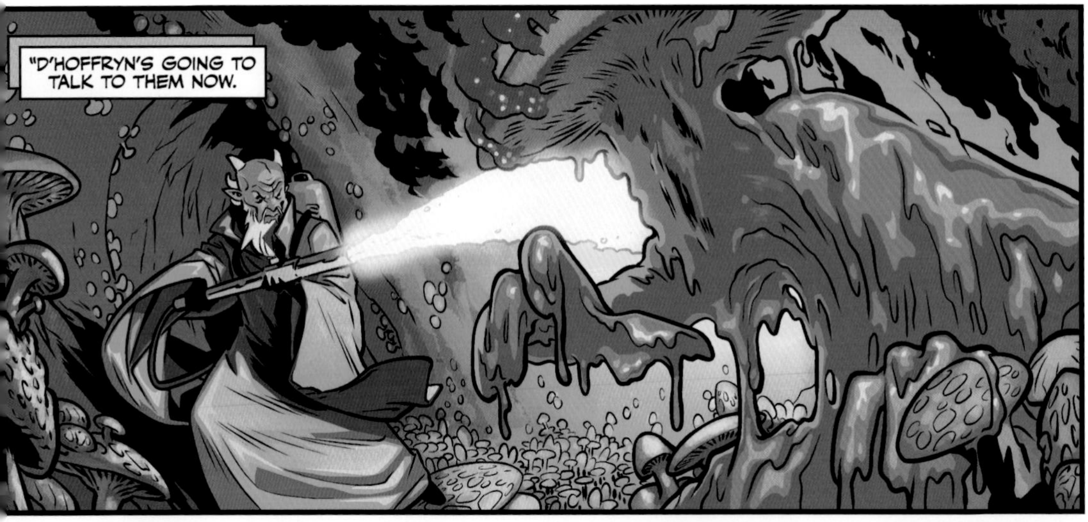
"D'HOFFRYN'S GOING TO TALK TO THEM NOW.

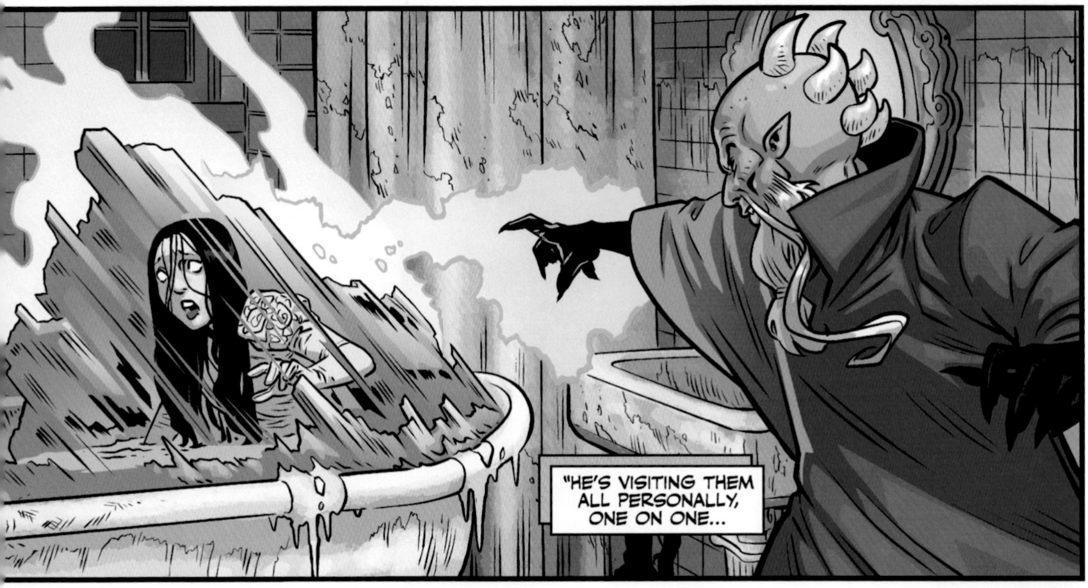
"HE'S VISITING THEM ALL PERSONALLY, ONE ON ONE...

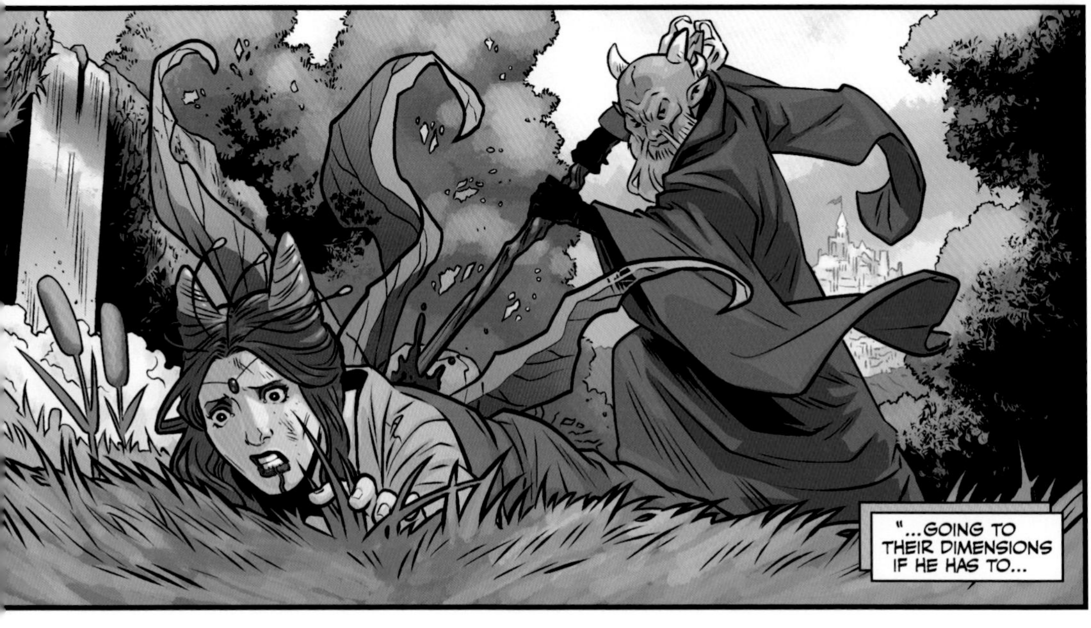
"...GOING TO THEIR DIMENSIONS IF HE HAS TO...

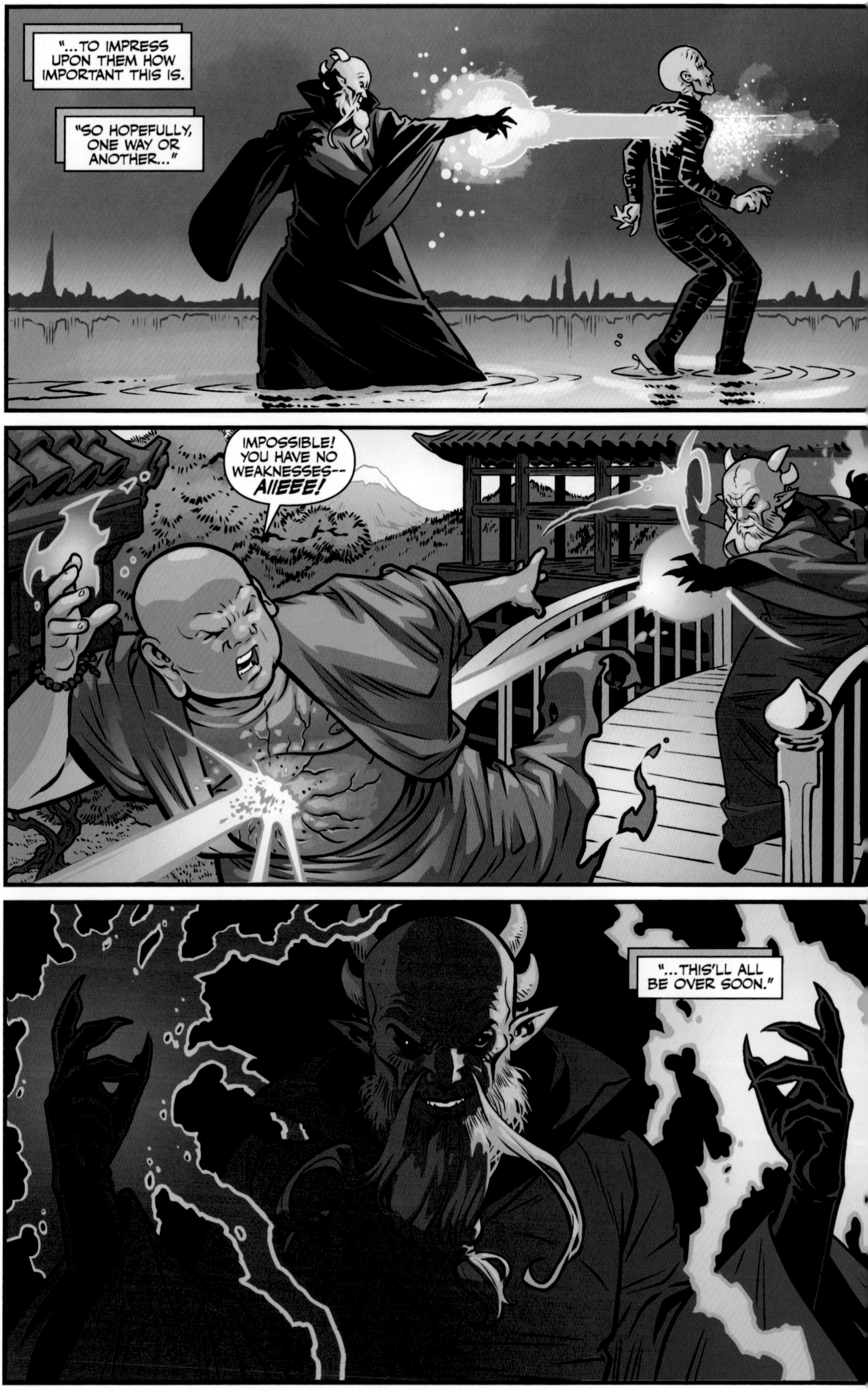
"...TO IMPRESS UPON THEM HOW IMPORTANT THIS IS.
"SO HOPEFULLY, ONE WAY OR ANOTHER..."
IMPOSSIBLE! YOU HAVE NO WEAKNESSES-- AIIEEE!
"...THIS'LL ALL BE OVER SOON."

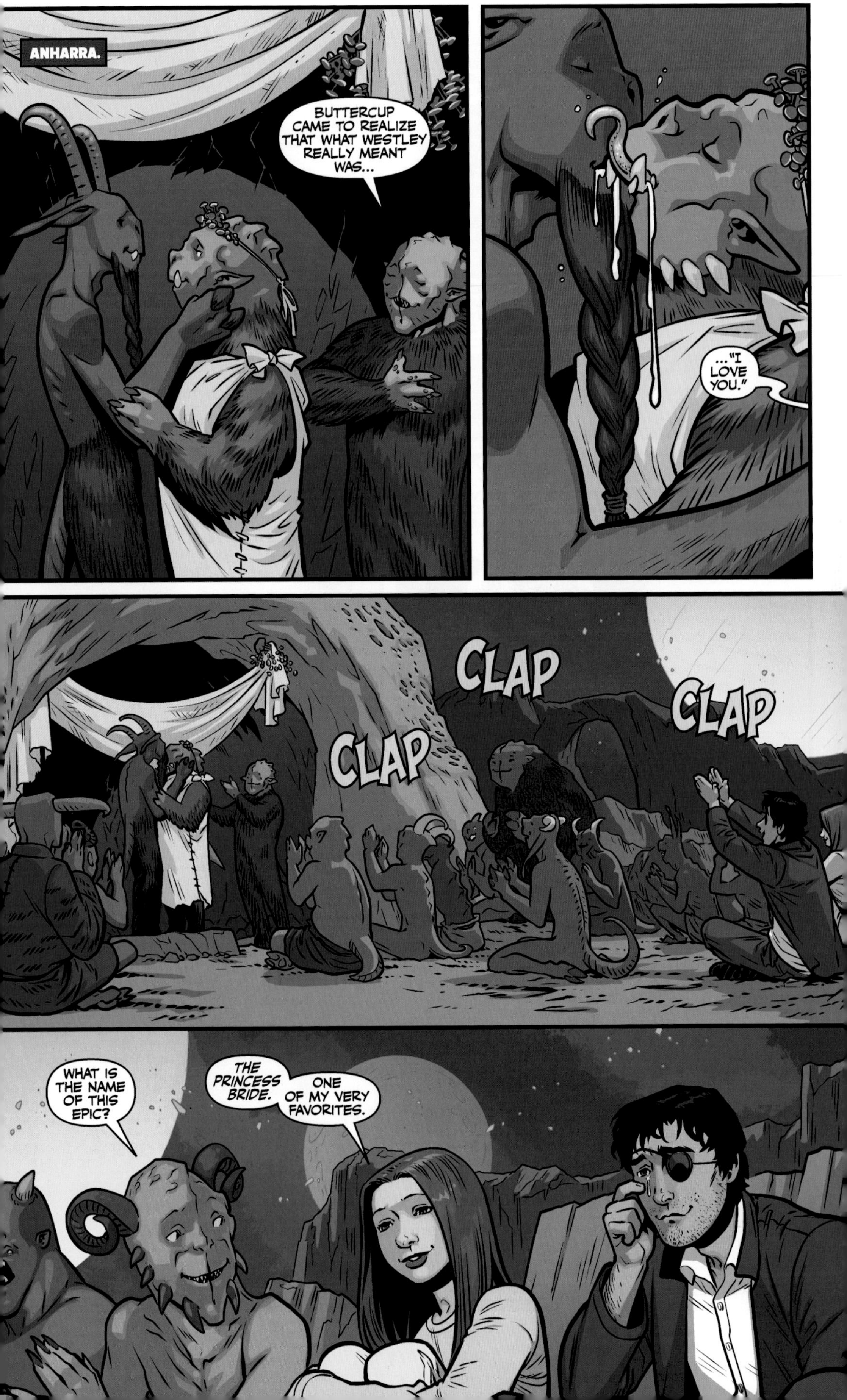
ANHARRA.
BUTTERCUP CAME TO REALIZE THAT WHAT WESTLEY REALLY MEANT WAS...
..."I LOVE YOU."
CLAP
CLAP
CLAP
WHAT IS THE NAME OF THIS EPIC?
THE PRINCESS BRIDE.
ONE OF MY VERY FAVORITES.

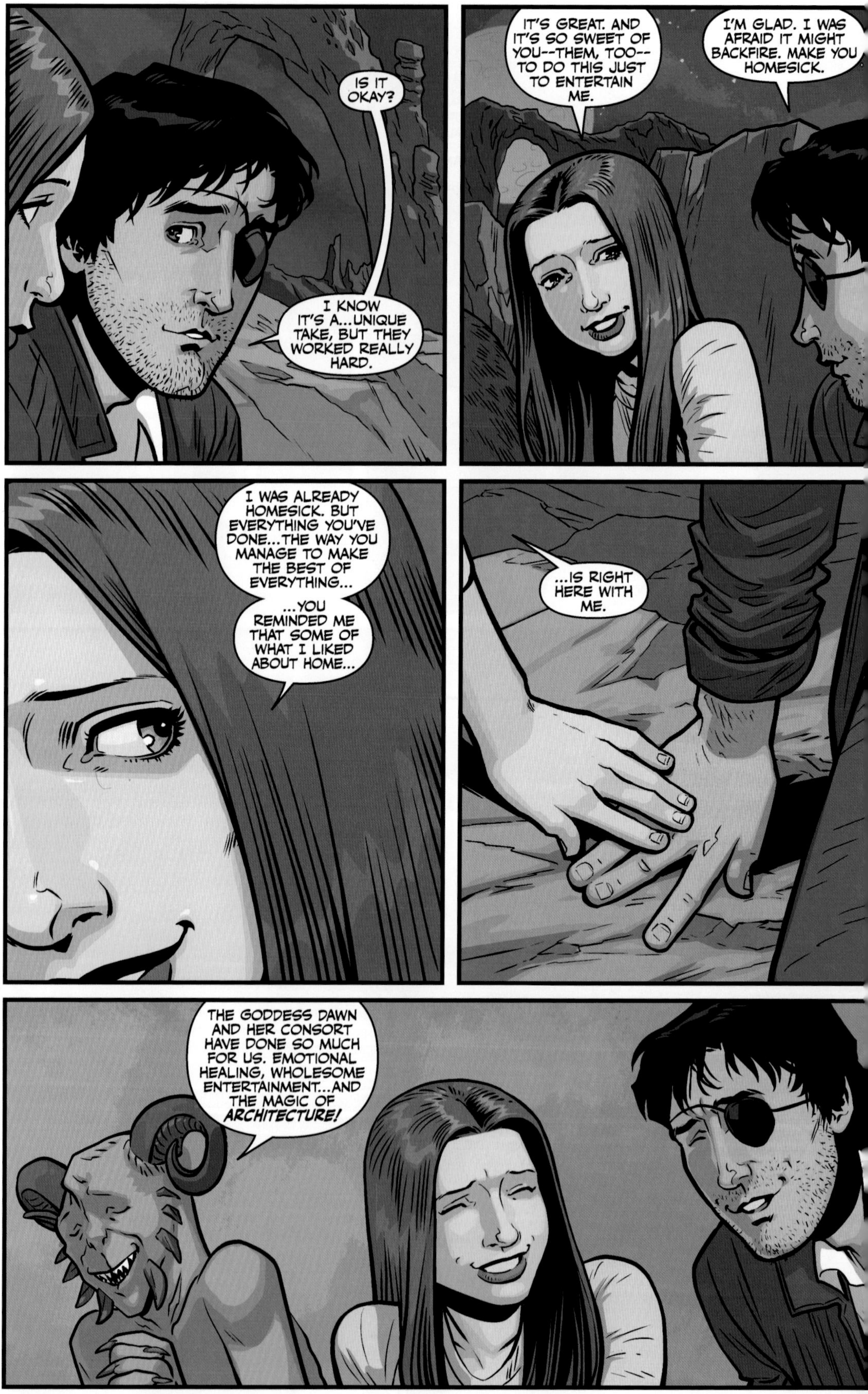
IS IT OKAY?
I KNOW IT'S A...UNIQUE TAKE, BUT THEY WORKED REALLY HARD.
IT'S GREAT. AND IT'S SO SWEET OF YOU--THEM, TOO--TO DO THIS JUST TO ENTERTAIN ME.
I'M GLAD. I WAS AFRAID IT MIGHT BACKFIRE. MAKE YOU HOMESICK.
I WAS ALREADY HOMESICK. BUT EVERYTHING YOU'VE DONE...THE WAY YOU MANAGE TO MAKE THE BEST OF EVERYTHING...
...YOU REMINDED ME THAT SOME OF WHAT I LIKED ABOUT HOME...
...IS RIGHT HERE WITH ME.
THE GODDESS DAWN AND HER CONSORT HAVE DONE SO MUCH FOR US. EMOTIONAL HEALING, WHOLESOME ENTERTAINMENT...AND THE MAGIC OF ***ARCHITECTURE!***

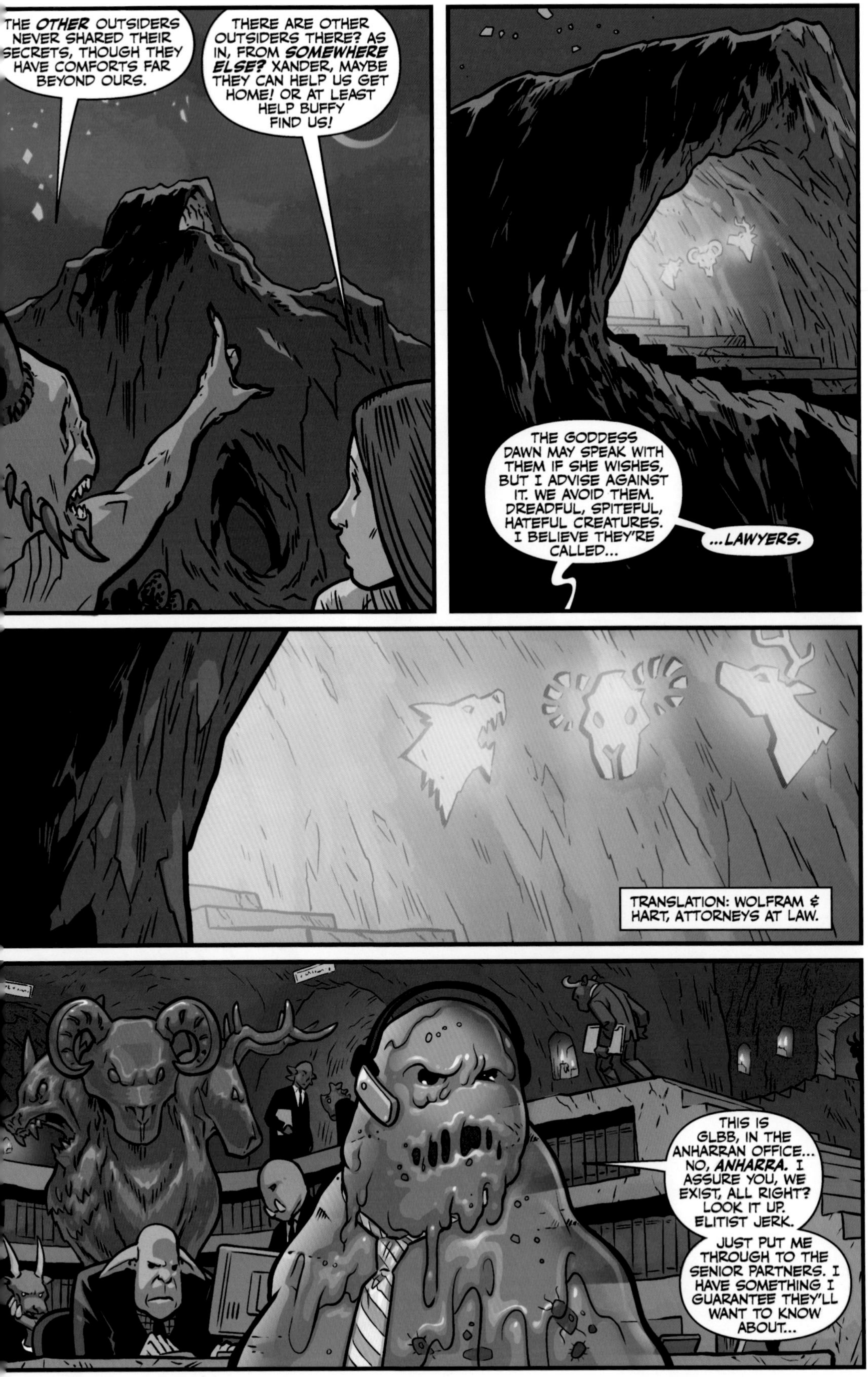

THE *OTHER* OUTSIDERS NEVER SHARED THEIR SECRETS, THOUGH THEY HAVE COMFORTS FAR BEYOND OURS.
THERE ARE OTHER OUTSIDERS THERE? AS IN, FROM *SOMEWHERE ELSE?* XANDER, MAYBE THEY CAN HELP US GET HOME! OR AT LEAST HELP BUFFY FIND US!
THE GODDESS DAWN MAY SPEAK WITH THEM IF SHE WISHES, BUT I ADVISE AGAINST IT. WE AVOID THEM. DREADFUL, SPITEFUL, HATEFUL CREATURES. I BELIEVE THEY'RE CALLED...
...LAWYERS.
TRANSLATION: WOLFRAM & HART, ATTORNEYS AT LAW.
THIS IS GLBB, IN THE ANHARRAN OFFICE... NO, *ANHARRA.* I ASSURE YOU, WE EXIST, ALL RIGHT? LOOK IT UP. ELITIST JERK.
JUST PUT ME THROUGH TO THE SENIOR PARTNERS. I HAVE SOMETHING I GUARANTEE THEY'LL WANT TO KNOW ABOUT...

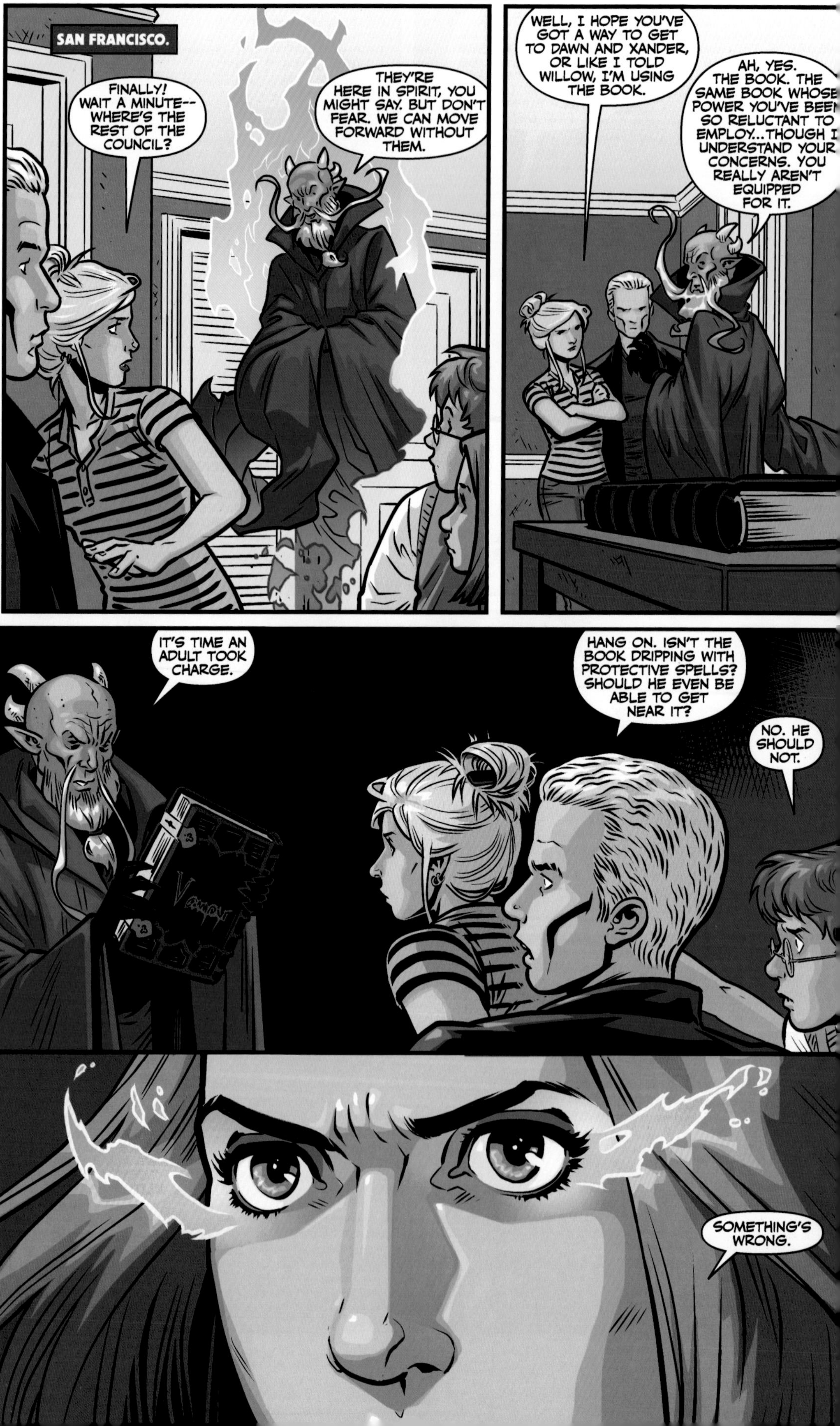

SAN FRANCISCO.
FINALLY! WAIT A MINUTE-- WHERE'S THE REST OF THE COUNCIL?
THEY'RE HERE IN SPIRIT, YOU MIGHT SAY. BUT DON'T FEAR. WE CAN MOVE FORWARD WITHOUT THEM.
WELL, I HOPE YOU'VE GOT A WAY TO GET TO DAWN AND XANDER, OR LIKE I TOLD WILLOW, I'M USING THE BOOK.
AH, YES. THE BOOK. THE SAME BOOK WHOSE POWER YOU'VE BEEN SO RELUCTANT TO EMPLOY...THOUGH I UNDERSTAND YOUR CONCERNS. YOU REALLY AREN'T EQUIPPED FOR IT.
IT'S TIME AN ADULT TOOK CHARGE.
HANG ON. ISN'T THE BOOK DRIPPING WITH PROTECTIVE SPELLS? SHOULD HE EVEN BE ABLE TO GET NEAR IT?
NO. HE SHOULD NOT.
SOMETHING'S WRONG.

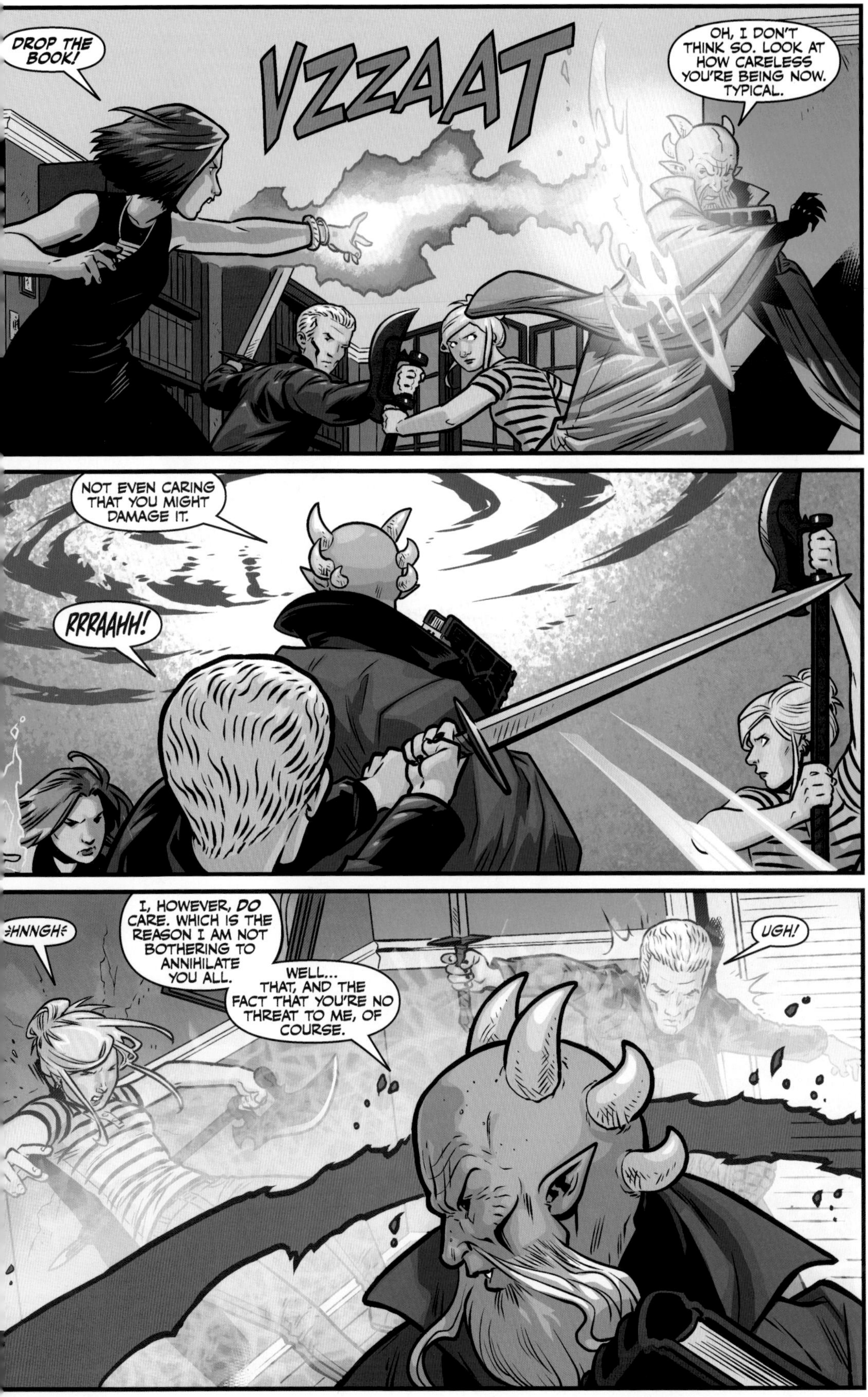
DROP THE BOOK!
VZZAAT
OH, I DON'T THINK SO. LOOK AT HOW CARELESS YOU'RE BEING NOW. TYPICAL.
NOT EVEN CARING THAT YOU MIGHT DAMAGE IT.
RRRAAHH!
HNNGH
I, HOWEVER, DO CARE. WHICH IS THE REASON I AM NOT BOTHERING TO ANNIHILATE YOU ALL.
WELL... THAT, AND THE FACT THAT YOU'RE NO THREAT TO ME, OF COURSE.
UGH!

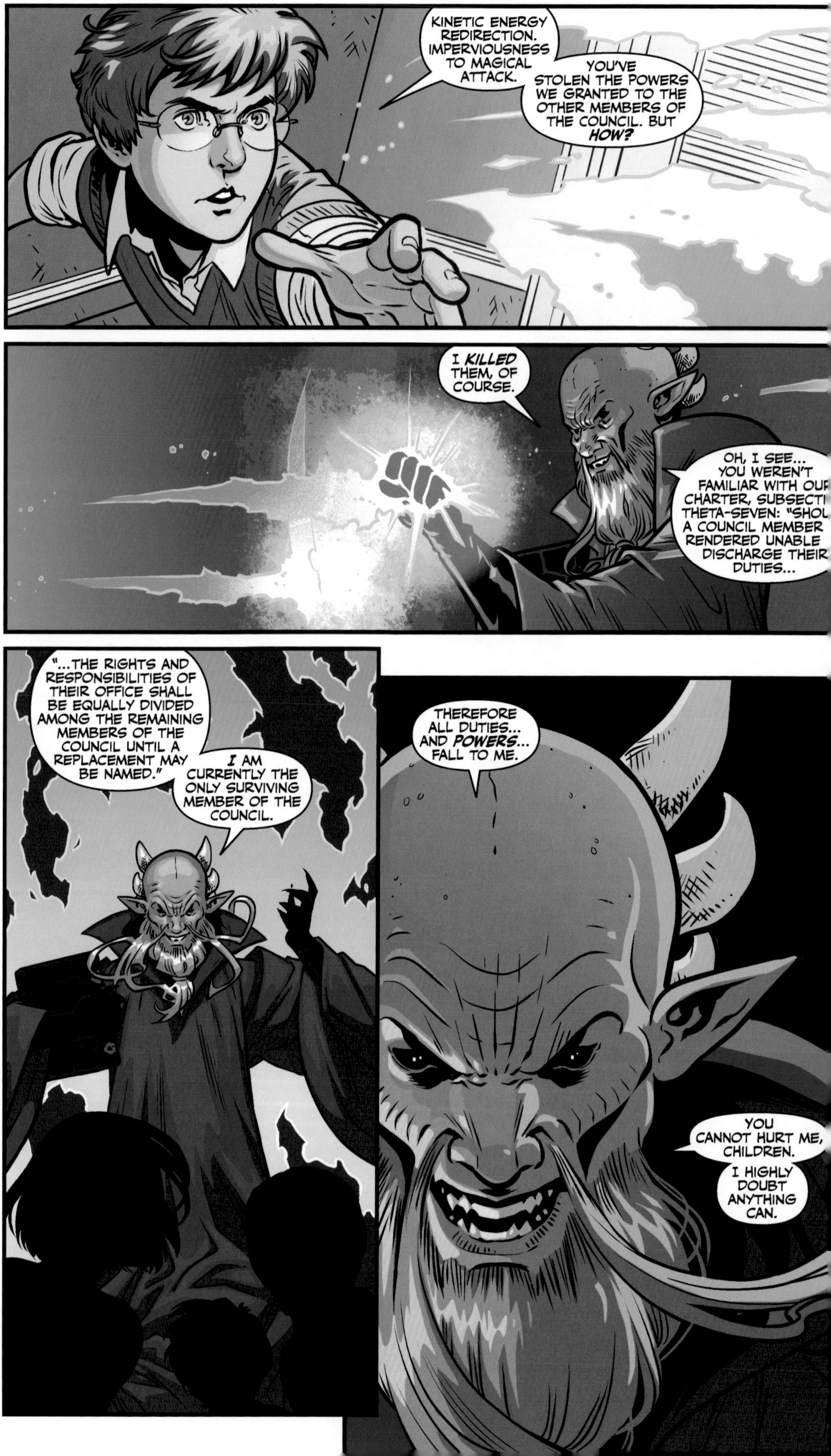

KINETIC ENERGY REDIRECTION. IMPERVIOUSNESS TO MAGICAL ATTACK.
YOU'VE STOLEN THE POWERS WE GRANTED TO THE OTHER MEMBERS OF THE COUNCIL. BUT *HOW?*
I *KILLED* THEM, OF COURSE.
OH, I SEE... YOU WEREN'T FAMILIAR WITH OU CHARTER, SUBSECT THETA-SEVEN: "SHO A COUNCIL MEMBER RENDERED UNABLE DISCHARGE THEIR DUTIES...
"...THE RIGHTS AND RESPONSIBILITIES OF THEIR OFFICE SHALL BE EQUALLY DIVIDED AMONG THE REMAINING MEMBERS OF THE COUNCIL UNTIL A REPLACEMENT MAY BE NAMED."
I AM CURRENTLY THE ONLY SURVIVING MEMBER OF THE COUNCIL.
THEREFORE ALL DUTIES... AND *POWERS*... FALL TO ME.
YOU CANNOT HURT ME, CHILDREN.
I HIGHLY DOUBT ANYTHING CAN.

YOU PLAYED US.

ALL THAT TIME YOU PRETENDED TO BE OUR OBI-WAN KENOBI, GIVING US ADVICE LIKE SOME WISE SENSEI, YOU WERE TRICKING US INTO DOING WHAT YOU WANTED.

OF COURSE. AND YOU COMPLIED LIKE DULL-WITTED SHEEP. IF ONLY YOU'D KNOWN I WAS A SOULLESS DEMON WHOSE REASON FOR BEING IS REVENGE...OH, WAIT. YOU DID.

I ASK YOU, SHOULD SOMEONE SO INEPT CONTROL A BOOK THAT CAN SHAPE THE FUNDAMENTAL FORCES OF AN ENTIRE UNIVERSE?

I'M DOING YOU A *FAVOR*, YOU POOR, SAD DILETTANTES. I AM ACCEPTING THE RESPONSIBILITY YOU HAD NEITHER THE DESIRE NOR ABILITY TO SHOULDER.

IF YOU THINK WE'LL GO DOWN WITHOUT A SCRAP--

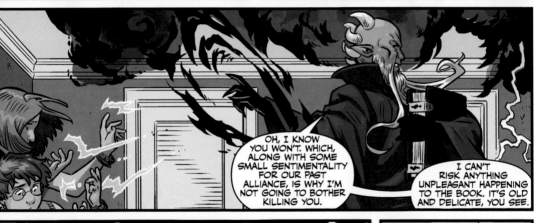

OH, I KNOW YOU WON'T. WHICH, ALONG WITH SOME SMALL SENTIMENTALITY FOR OUR PAST ALLIANCE, IS WHY I'M NOT GOING TO BOTHER KILLING YOU.

I CAN'T RISK ANYTHING UNPLEASANT HAPPENING TO THE BOOK. IT'S OLD AND DELICATE, YOU SEE.

RRNCCH

YOU ARE *FREE*, CHILDREN. FREE OF A RESPONSIBILITY YOU NEVER WANTED.

CONTINUE WITH YOUR SMALL, SELF-ABSORBED LIVES...YOUR ROMANTIC TRAVAILS AND DRAMATIC OUTBURSTS...YOUR GRANDIOSE WEEPING AND WAILING.

THIS WORLD IS IN GOOD HANDS.

MINE.

27

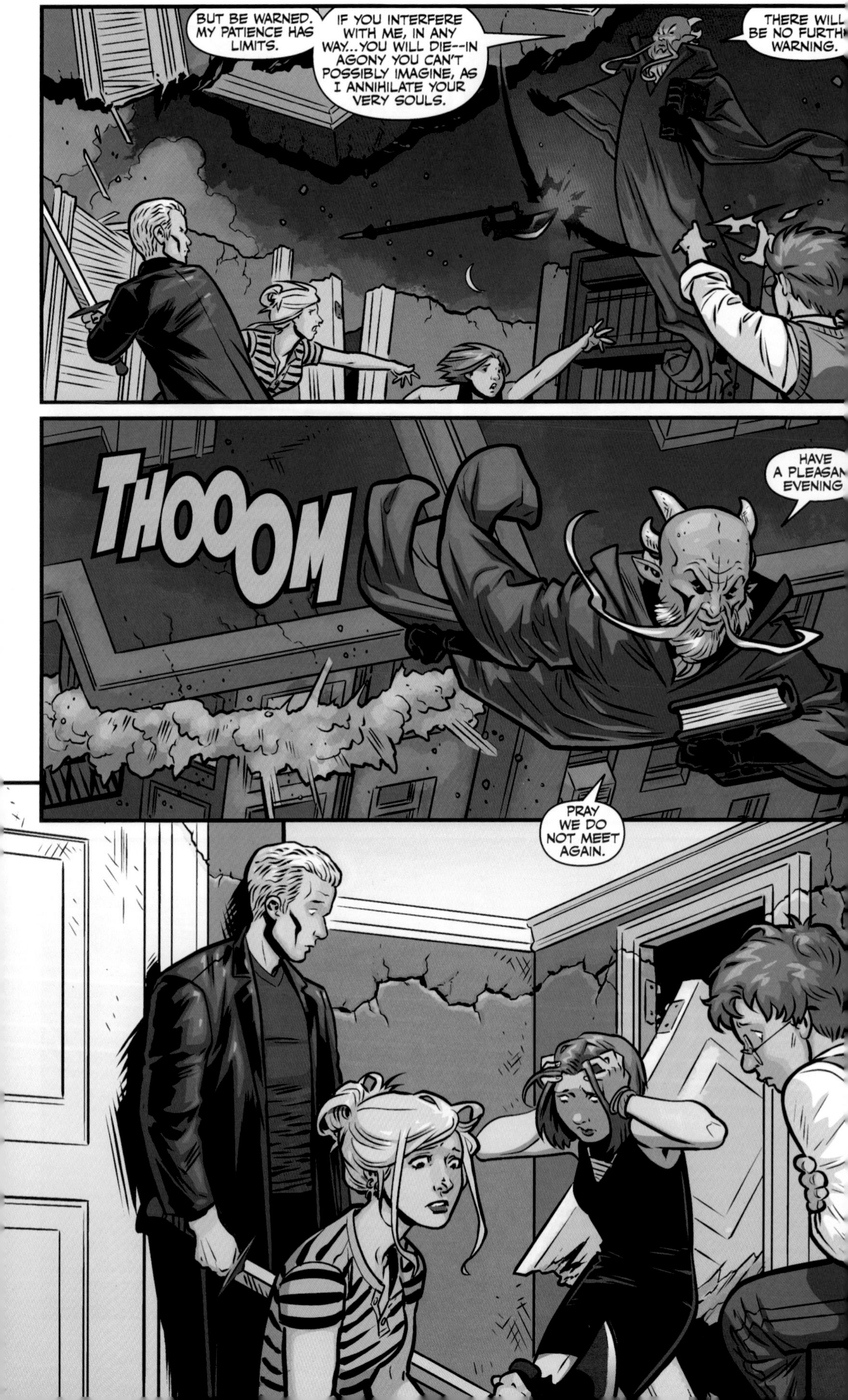
BUT BE WARNED. MY PATIENCE HAS LIMITS.
IF YOU INTERFERE WITH ME, IN ANY WAY...YOU WILL DIE--IN AGONY YOU CAN'T POSSIBLY IMAGINE, AS I ANNIHILATE YOUR VERY SOULS.
THERE WILL BE NO FURTH WARNING.
THOOOM
HAVE A PLEASAN EVENING
PRAY WE DO NOT MEET AGAIN.

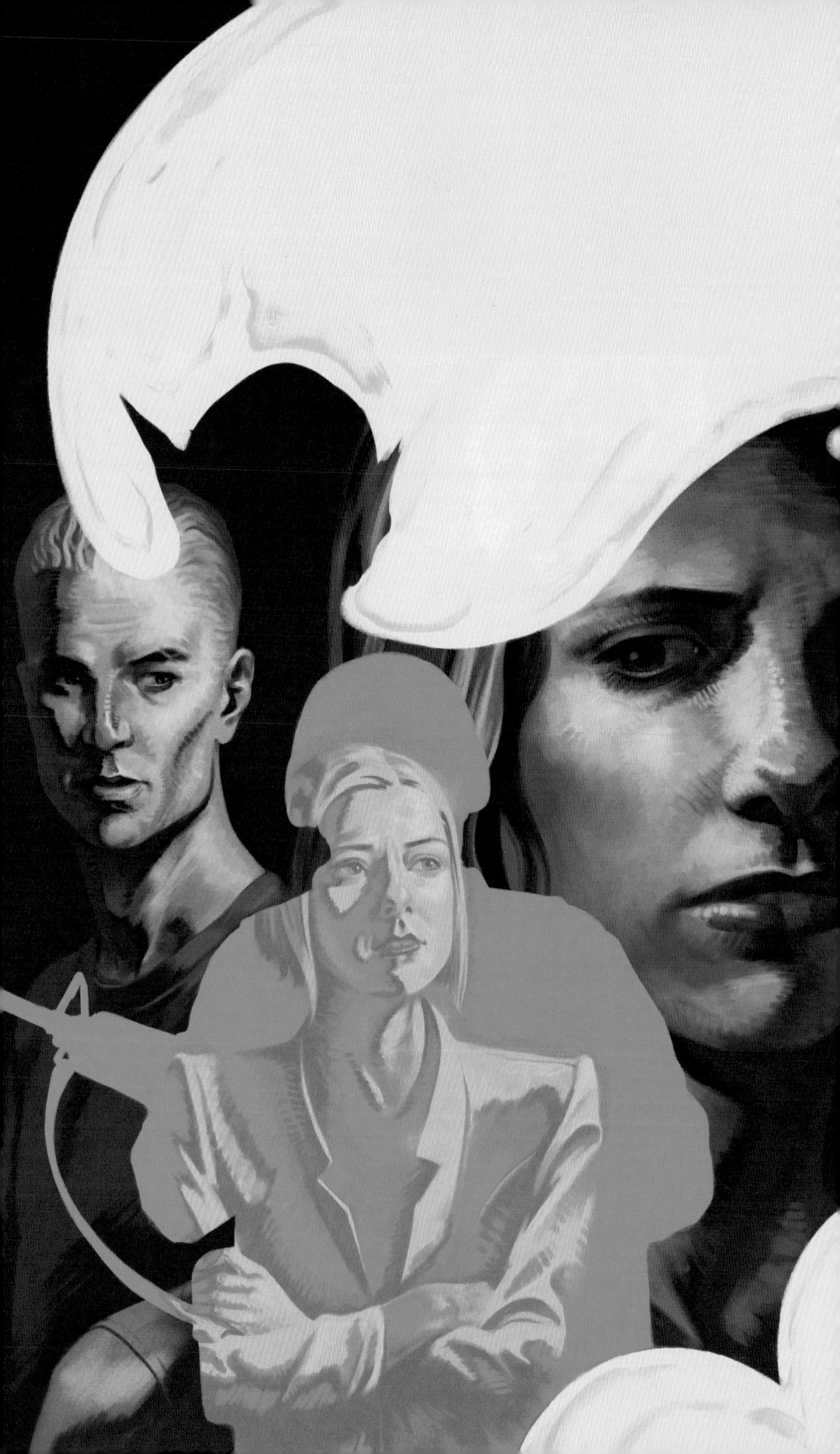

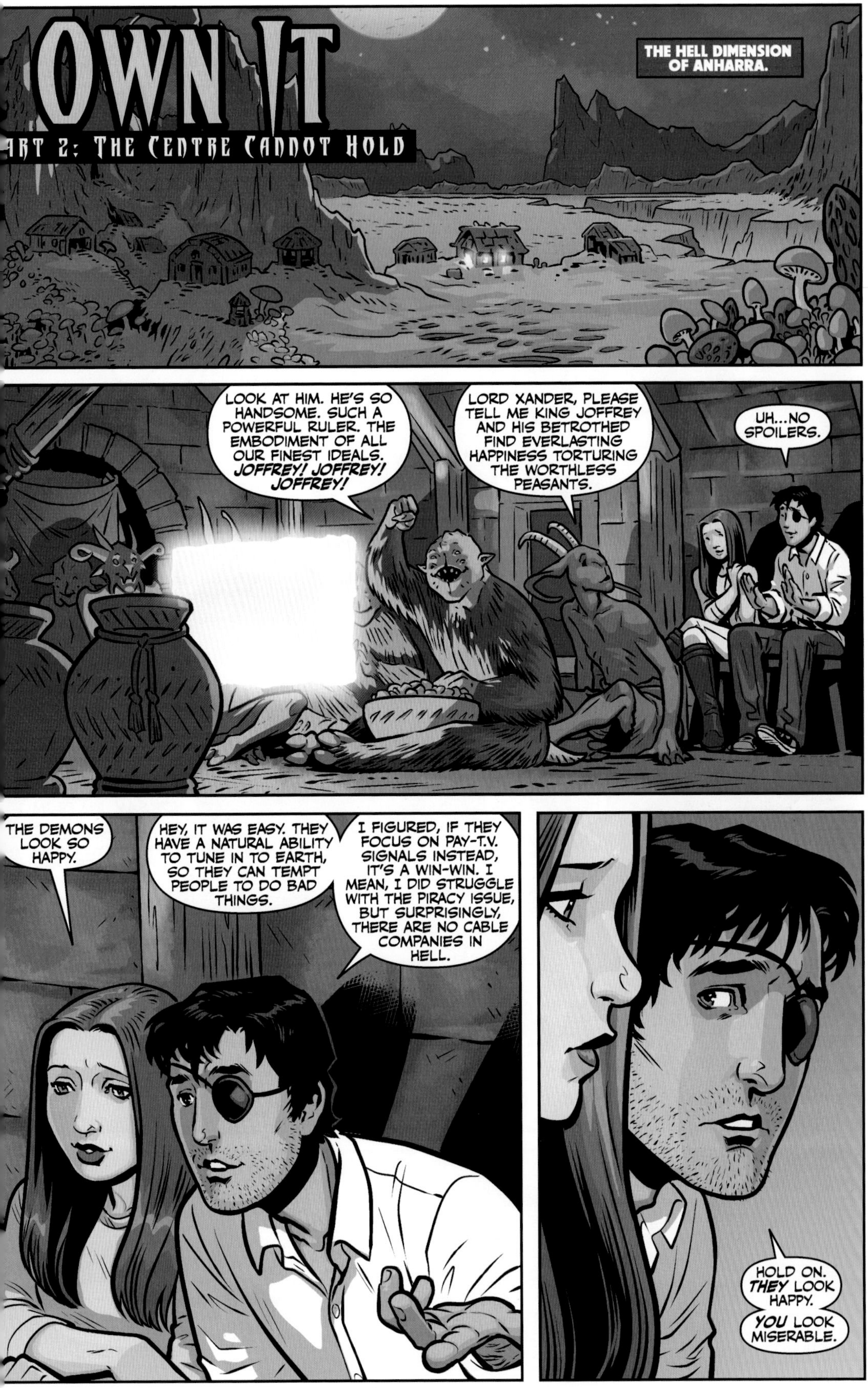
OWN IT
ART 2: THE CENTRE CANNOT HOLD
THE HELL DIMENSION OF ANHARRA.
LOOK AT HIM. HE'S SO HANDSOME. SUCH A POWERFUL RULER. THE EMBODIMENT OF ALL OUR FINEST IDEALS. JOFFREY! JOFFREY! JOFFREY!
LORD XANDER, PLEASE TELL ME KING JOFFREY AND HIS BETROTHED FIND EVERLASTING HAPPINESS TORTURING THE WORTHLESS PEASANTS.
UH...NO SPOILERS.
THE DEMONS LOOK SO HAPPY.
HEY, IT WAS EASY. THEY HAVE A NATURAL ABILITY TO TUNE IN TO EARTH, SO THEY CAN TEMPT PEOPLE TO DO BAD THINGS.
I FIGURED, IF THEY FOCUS ON PAY-T.V. SIGNALS INSTEAD, IT'S A WIN-WIN. I MEAN, I DID STRUGGLE WITH THE PIRACY ISSUE, BUT SURPRISINGLY, THERE ARE NO CABLE COMPANIES IN HELL.
HOLD ON. THEY LOOK HAPPY.
YOU LOOK MISERABLE.

YOU'VE DONE SO MUCH TO TRY TO MAKE ME HAPPY HERE. AND SO HAVE THE DEMONS. THEY LITERALLY WORSHIP ME.

BUT I MISS HOME. I MISS BUFFY, WILLOW, AND SCHOOL...

I KNOW WILLOW SAID TO STAY HERE UNTIL THEY COME BACK FOR US. BUT I CAN SEE ALL THESE PORTALS, JUST FLOATING THERE.

I'M *THE KEY.* OPENING DIMENSIO DOORS IS WHAT DO. HOW HARD C IT BE TO FIND TH WAY HOME?

ACCORDING TO WILLOW, *VERY.* SHE SAID WE COULD GET HOPELESSLY LOST.

YOU'RE THE KEY, NOT THE MAP. WE'D HAVE NO IDEA WHERE WE'RE GOING.

THEN IT'S A GOOD THING I DO.

WHO THE HELL ARE YOU, LADY?

MY NAME'S *LILAH MORGAN.* I'M FROM EARTH, LIKE YOU TWO. AND IT'S COME TO MY ATTENTION YOU WANT NOTHING MORE THAN TO GO BACK THERE.

WELL, GREAT NEWS. MY EMPLOYERS AT *WOLFRAM & HART* WANT NOTHING MORE THAN TO SHOW YOU THE WAY HOME...

...IF WE CAN COME TO A MUTUALLY BENEFICIAL ARRANGEMENT.

NOT A CHANCE. WE KNOW ALL ABOUT YOUR EVIL LAW FIRM.

THAT'S A COMMONLY MISUSED TERM. PEOPLE THINK WE'RE AN "EVIL LAW FIRM" WHEN ITS JUST THAT "EVIL LAW" IS A SUBSPECIALTY WE HAPPEN TO BE VERY GOOD AT.

OH YEAH? THEN WHAT EXACTLY WOULD WE HAVE TO DO TO GET HOME?

OH, THERE'S A WIDE RANGE OF POSSIBILITIES. OPENING AND CLOSING THE RIGHT PORTALS, FOR A START. THE BARRIERS BACK TO EARTH ARE A LOT TOUGHER THAN THEY USED TO BE.

AND I UNDERSTAND YOUR SISTER'S GOT SOME INFLUENCE IN WRITING EARTH'S NEW RULES OF MAGIC. A WORD HERE, A COMMA THERE...

NO. HELL NO.

YOU HEARD HER. HIT THE BRICKS. AND I WAS *TOTALLY* NOT STARING AT YOUR BOOBS! IT'S THAT MASSIVE SCAR ON YOUR NECK, IT DRAWS THE EYE.

GNORE THAT. SUALLY WEAR RVES, BUT IT'S DICULOUSLY UMID HERE.

BUT I'M SURE YOU'VE NOTICED THAT. ALONG WITH THE FOUL-TASTING FOOD, ACID RAIN, AND GENERAL HIGH MISERY INDEX.

I'LL BE AT THE LOCAL OFFICE. WHICH IS A HOVEL, BUT AT LEAST HAS AIR CONDITIONING. THINK ABOUT MY OFFER.

BUT DON'T TAKE TOO LONG. BECAUSE I CAN'T ABIDE BEING HERE FOR MORE THAN A FEW DAYS...

...AND I ASSUME YOU WANT TO SEE YOUR SISTER AGAIN. WITH THE LIFE EXPECTANCY OF A SLAYER, YOU NEVER KNOW HOW SHORT A WINDOW YOU HAVE, DO YOU?

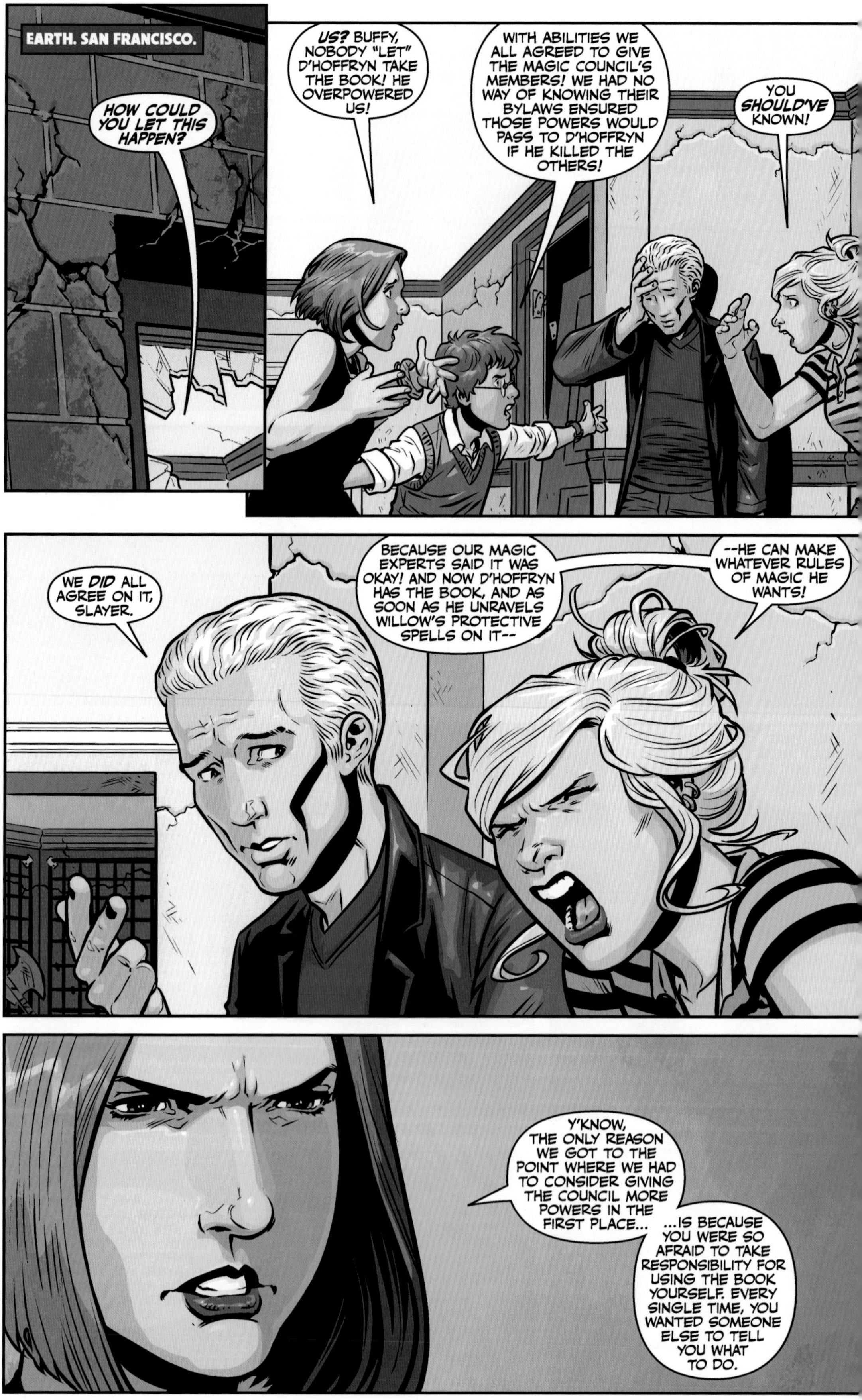
EARTH. SAN FRANCISCO.
HOW COULD YOU LET THIS HAPPEN?
US? BUFFY, NOBODY "LET" D'HOFFRYN TAKE THE BOOK! HE OVERPOWERED US!
WITH ABILITIES WE ALL AGREED TO GIVE THE MAGIC COUNCIL'S MEMBERS! WE HAD NO WAY OF KNOWING THEIR BYLAWS ENSURED THOSE POWERS WOULD PASS TO D'HOFFRYN IF HE KILLED THE OTHERS!
YOU SHOULD'VE KNOWN!
WE DID ALL AGREE ON IT, SLAYER.
BECAUSE OUR MAGIC EXPERTS SAID IT WAS OKAY! AND NOW D'HOFFRYN HAS THE BOOK, AND AS SOON AS HE UNRAVELS WILLOW'S PROTECTIVE SPELLS ON IT--
--HE CAN MAKE WHATEVER RULES OF MAGIC HE WANTS!
Y'KNOW, THE ONLY REASON WE GOT TO THE POINT WHERE WE HAD TO CONSIDER GIVING THE COUNCIL MORE POWERS IN THE FIRST PLACE...
...IS BECAUSE YOU WERE SO AFRAID TO TAKE RESPONSIBILITY FOR USING THE BOOK YOURSELF. EVERY SINGLE TIME, YOU WANTED SOMEONE ELSE TO TELL YOU WHAT TO DO.

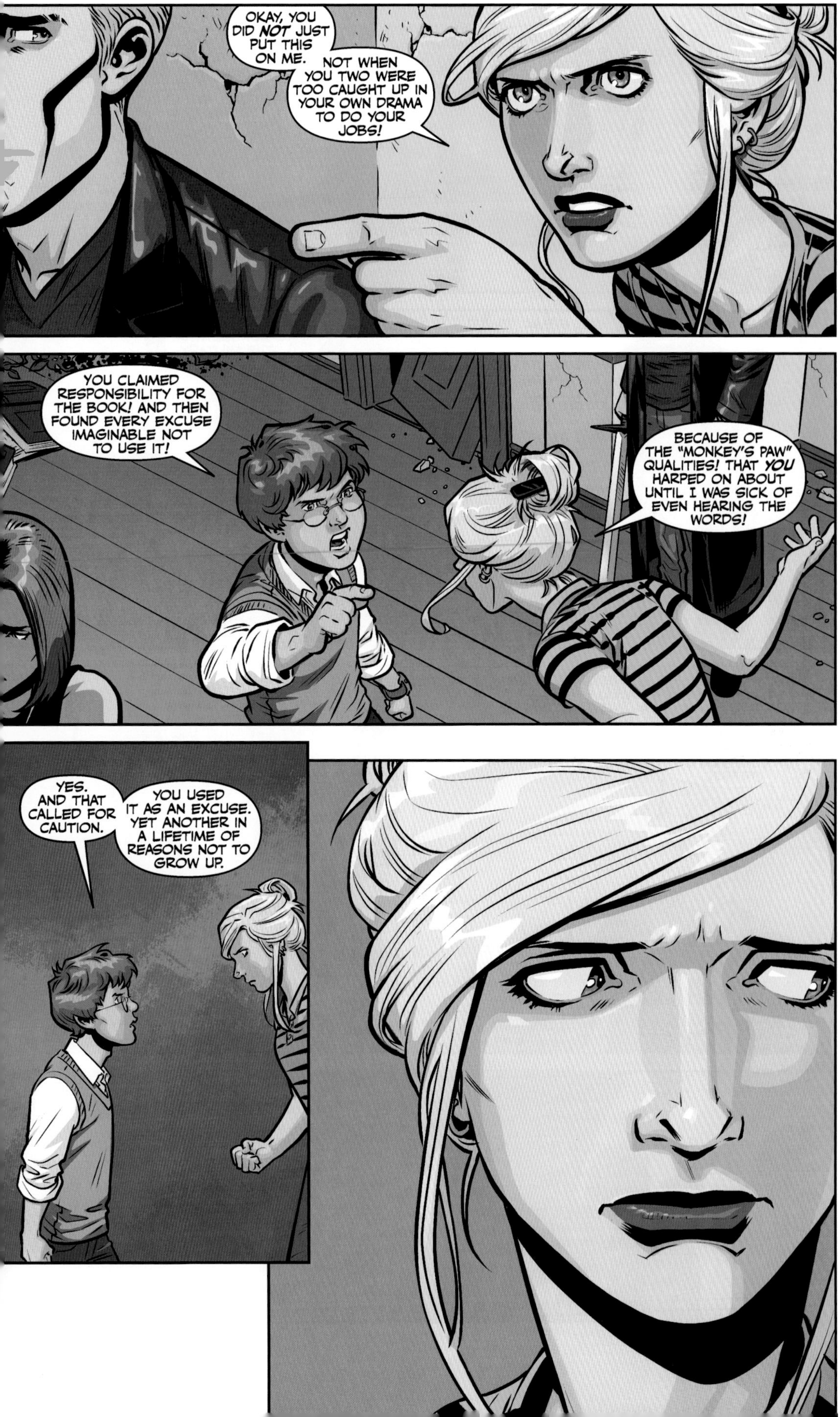
OKAY, YOU DID NOT JUST PUT THIS ON ME.
NOT WHEN YOU TWO WERE TOO CAUGHT UP IN YOUR OWN DRAMA TO DO YOUR JOBS!
YOU CLAIMED RESPONSIBILITY FOR THE BOOK! AND THEN FOUND EVERY EXCUSE IMAGINABLE NOT TO USE IT!
BECAUSE OF THE "MONKEY'S PAW" QUALITIES! THAT YOU HARPED ON ABOUT UNTIL I WAS SICK OF EVEN HEARING THE WORDS!
YES. AND THAT CALLED FOR CAUTION.
YOU USED IT AS AN EXCUSE. YET ANOTHER IN A LIFETIME OF REASONS NOT TO GROW UP.

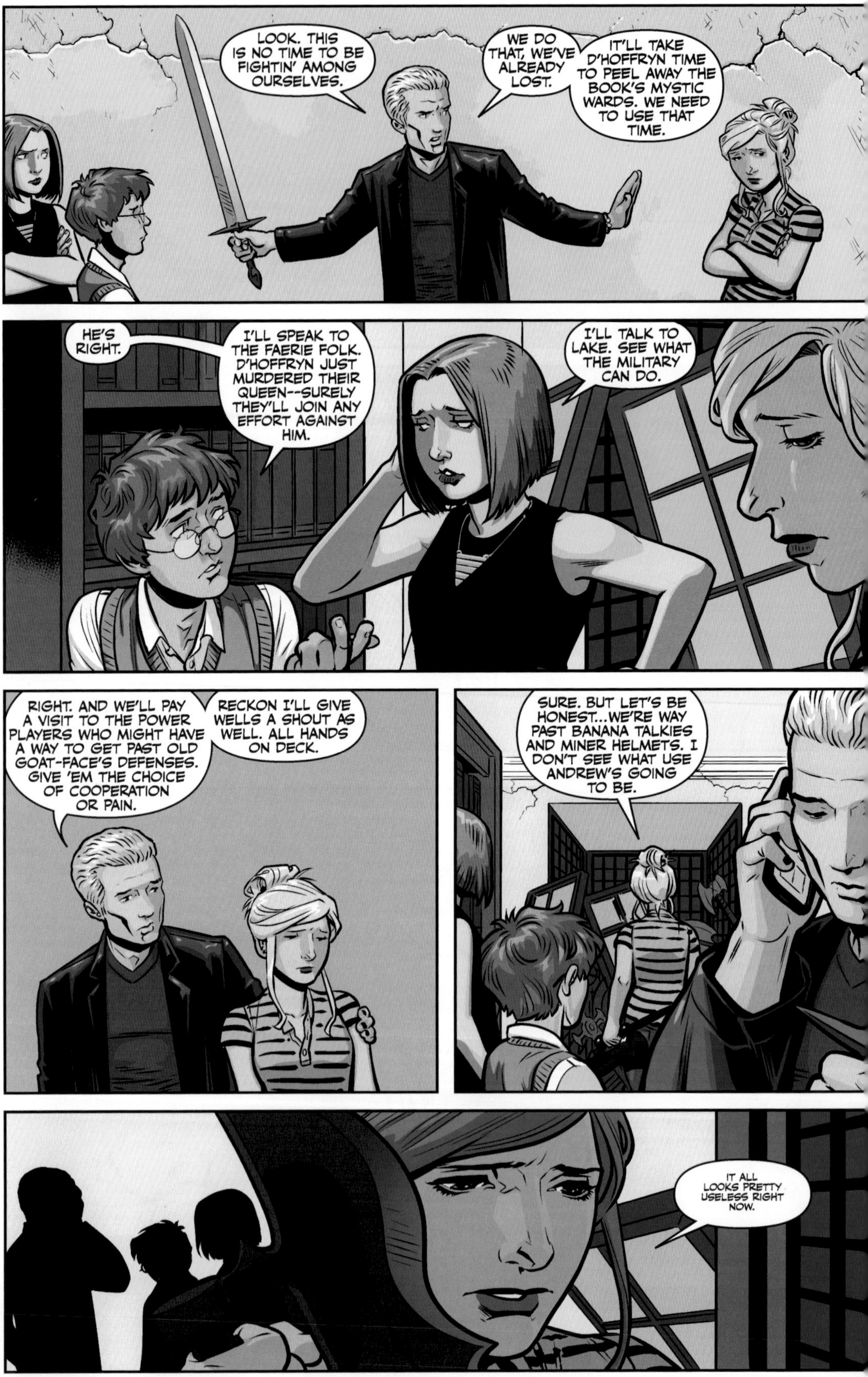
LOOK. THIS IS NO TIME TO BE FIGHTIN' AMONG OURSELVES.
WE DO THAT, WE'VE ALREADY LOST.
IT'LL TAKE D'HOFFRYN TIME TO PEEL AWAY THE BOOK'S MYSTIC WARDS. WE NEED TO USE THAT TIME.
HE'S RIGHT.
I'LL SPEAK TO THE FAERIE FOLK. D'HOFFRYN JUST MURDERED THEIR QUEEN--SURELY THEY'LL JOIN ANY EFFORT AGAINST HIM.
I'LL TALK TO LAKE. SEE WHAT THE MILITARY CAN DO.
RIGHT. AND WE'LL PAY A VISIT TO THE POWER PLAYERS WHO MIGHT HAVE A WAY TO GET PAST OLD GOAT-FACE'S DEFENSES. GIVE 'EM THE CHOICE OF COOPERATION OR PAIN.
RECKON I'LL GIVE WELLS A SHOUT AS WELL. ALL HANDS ON DECK.
SURE. BUT LET'S BE HONEST...WE'RE WAY PAST BANANA TALKIES AND MINER HELMETS. I DON'T SEE WHAT USE ANDREW'S GOING TO BE.
IT ALL LOOKS PRETTY USELESS RIGHT NOW.

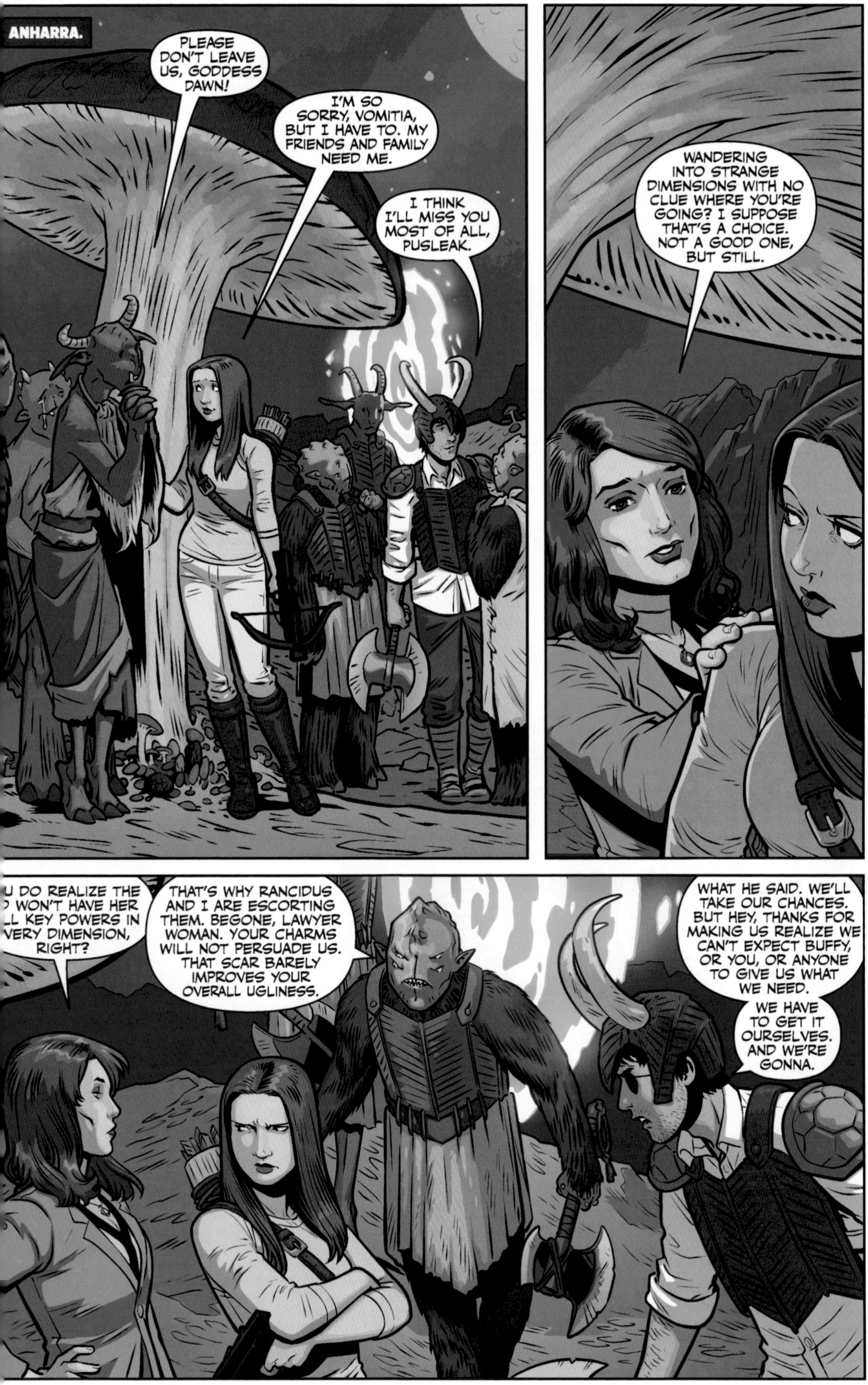
ANHARRA.
PLEASE DON'T LEAVE US, GODDESS DAWN!
I'M SO SORRY, VOMITIA, BUT I HAVE TO. MY FRIENDS AND FAMILY NEED ME.
I THINK I'LL MISS YOU MOST OF ALL, PUSLEAK.
WANDERING INTO STRANGE DIMENSIONS WITH NO CLUE WHERE YOU'RE GOING? I SUPPOSE THAT'S A CHOICE. NOT A GOOD ONE, BUT STILL.
U DO REALIZE THE D WON'T HAVE HER LL KEY POWERS IN VERY DIMENSION, RIGHT?
THAT'S WHY RANCIDUS AND I ARE ESCORTING THEM. BEGONE, LAWYER WOMAN. YOUR CHARMS WILL NOT PERSUADE US. THAT SCAR BARELY IMPROVES YOUR OVERALL UGLINESS.
WHAT HE SAID. WE'LL TAKE OUR CHANCES. BUT HEY, THANKS FOR MAKING US REALIZE WE CAN'T EXPECT BUFFY, OR YOU, OR ANYONE TO GIVE US WHAT WE NEED.
WE HAVE TO GET IT OURSELVES. AND WE'RE GONNA.

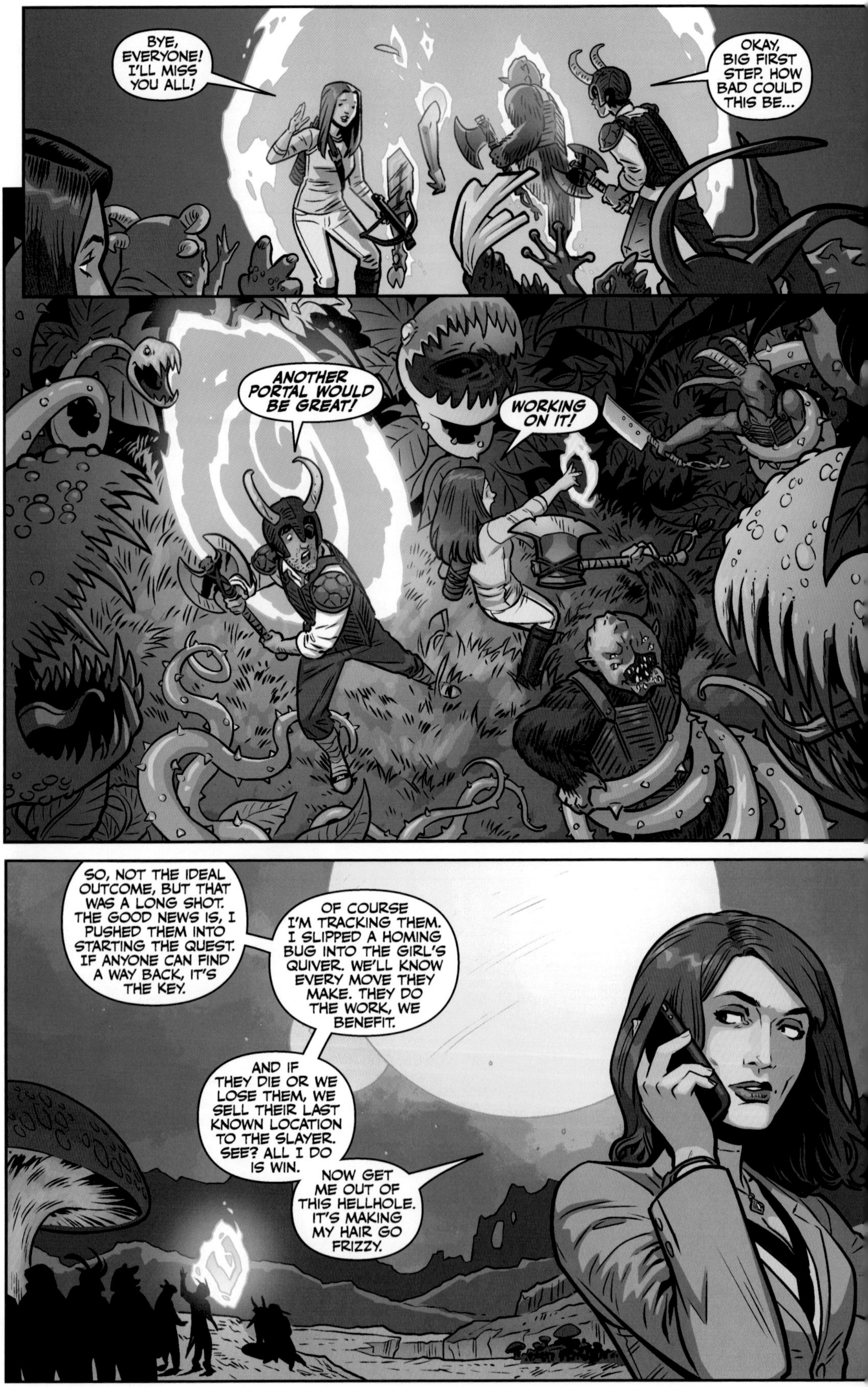
BYE, EVERYONE! I'LL MISS YOU ALL!
OKAY, BIG FIRST STEP. HOW BAD COULD THIS BE...
ANOTHER PORTAL WOULD BE GREAT!
WORKING ON IT!
SO, NOT THE IDEAL OUTCOME, BUT THAT WAS A LONG SHOT. THE GOOD NEWS IS, I PUSHED THEM INTO STARTING THE QUEST. IF ANYONE CAN FIND A WAY BACK, IT'S THE KEY.
OF COURSE I'M TRACKING THEM. I SLIPPED A HOMING BUG INTO THE GIRL'S QUIVER. WE'LL KNOW EVERY MOVE THEY MAKE. THEY DO THE WORK, WE BENEFIT.
AND IF THEY DIE OR WE LOSE THEM, WE SELL THEIR LAST KNOWN LOCATION TO THE SLAYER. SEE? ALL I DO IS WIN.
NOW GET ME OUT OF THIS HELLHOLE. IT'S MAKING MY HAIR GO FRIZZY.

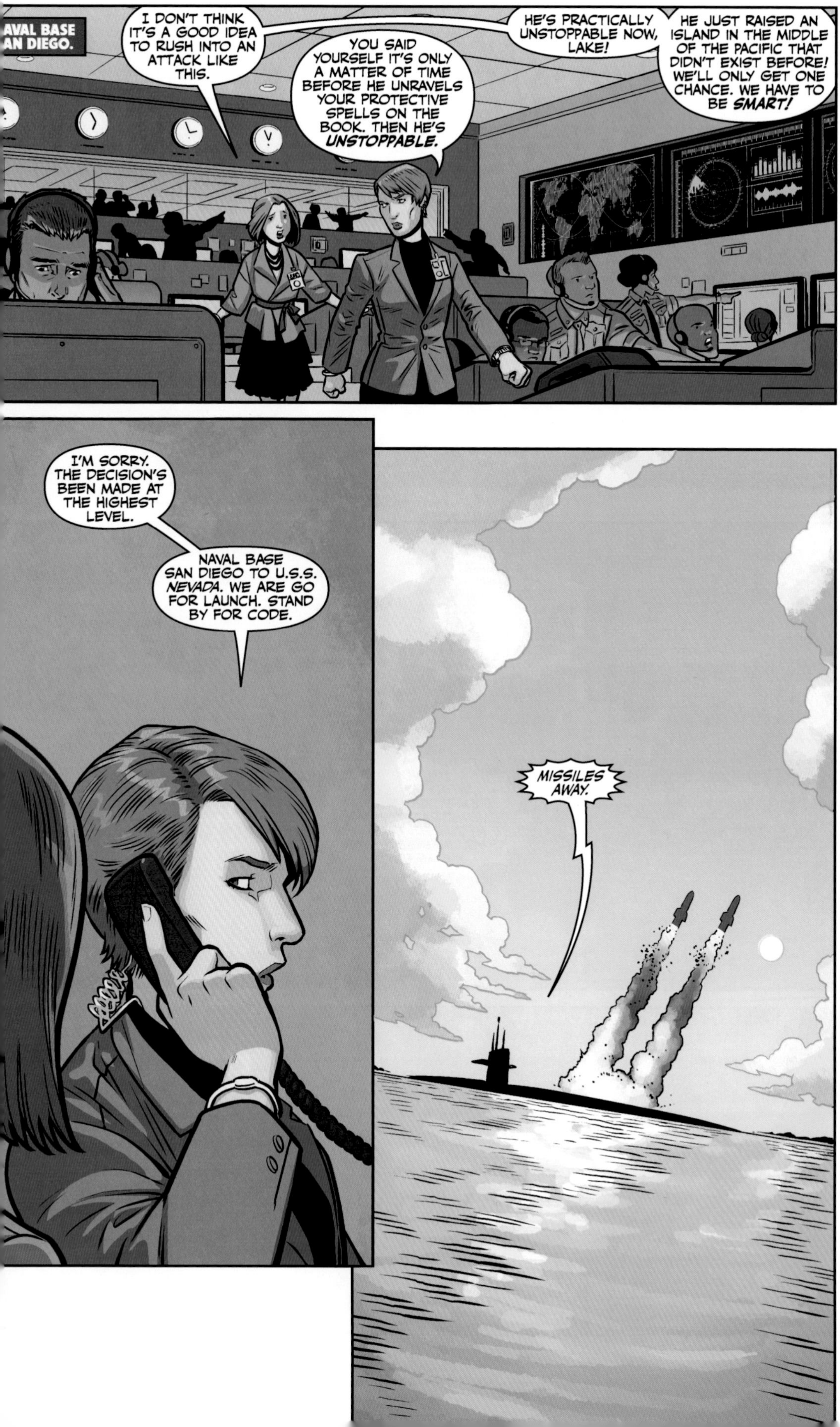
AVAL BASE
AN DIEGO.
I DON'T THINK IT'S A GOOD IDEA TO RUSH INTO AN ATTACK LIKE THIS.
YOU SAID YOURSELF IT'S ONLY A MATTER OF TIME BEFORE HE UNRAVELS YOUR PROTECTIVE SPELLS ON THE BOOK. THEN HE'S UNSTOPPABLE.
HE'S PRACTICALLY UNSTOPPABLE NOW, LAKE!
HE JUST RAISED AN ISLAND IN THE MIDDLE OF THE PACIFIC THAT DIDN'T EXIST BEFORE! WE'LL ONLY GET ONE CHANCE. WE HAVE TO BE SMART!
I'M SORRY. THE DECISION'S BEEN MADE AT THE HIGHEST LEVEL.
NAVAL BASE SAN DIEGO TO U.S.S. NEVADA. WE ARE GO FOR LAUNCH. STAND BY FOR CODE.
MISSILES AWAY.

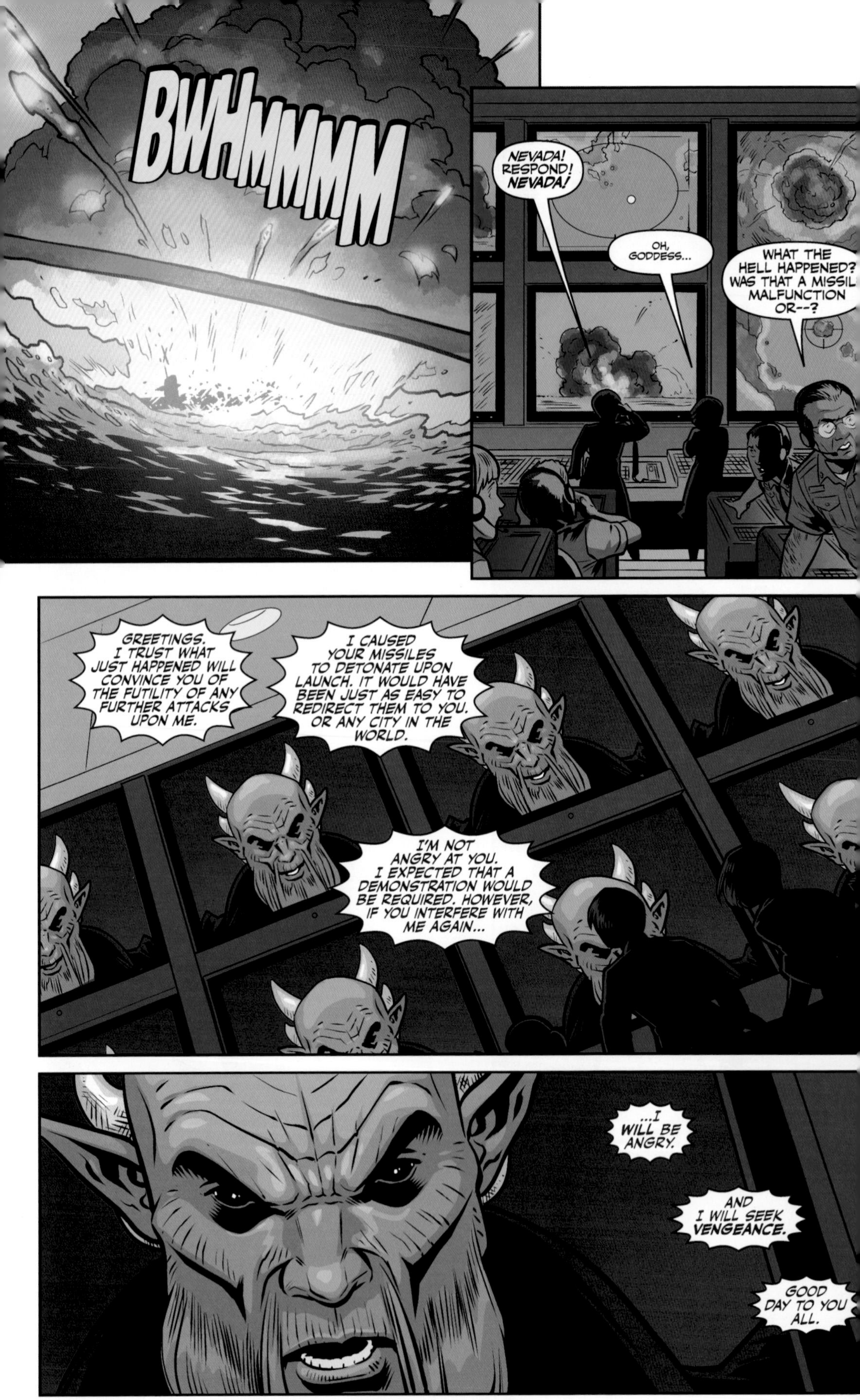
BWHMMMM
NEVADA! RESPOND! NEVADA!
OH, GODDESS...
WHAT THE HELL HAPPENED? WAS THAT A MISSIL MALFUNCTION OR--?
GREETINGS. I TRUST WHAT JUST HAPPENED WILL CONVINCE YOU OF THE FUTILITY OF ANY FURTHER ATTACKS UPON ME.
I CAUSED YOUR MISSILES TO DETONATE UPON LAUNCH. IT WOULD HAVE BEEN JUST AS EASY TO REDIRECT THEM TO YOU. OR ANY CITY IN THE WORLD.
I'M NOT ANGRY AT YOU. I EXPECTED THAT A DEMONSTRATION WOULD BE REQUIRED. HOWEVER, IF YOU INTERFERE WITH ME AGAIN...
...I WILL BE ANGRY.
AND I WILL SEEK VENGEANCE.
GOOD DAY TO YOU ALL.

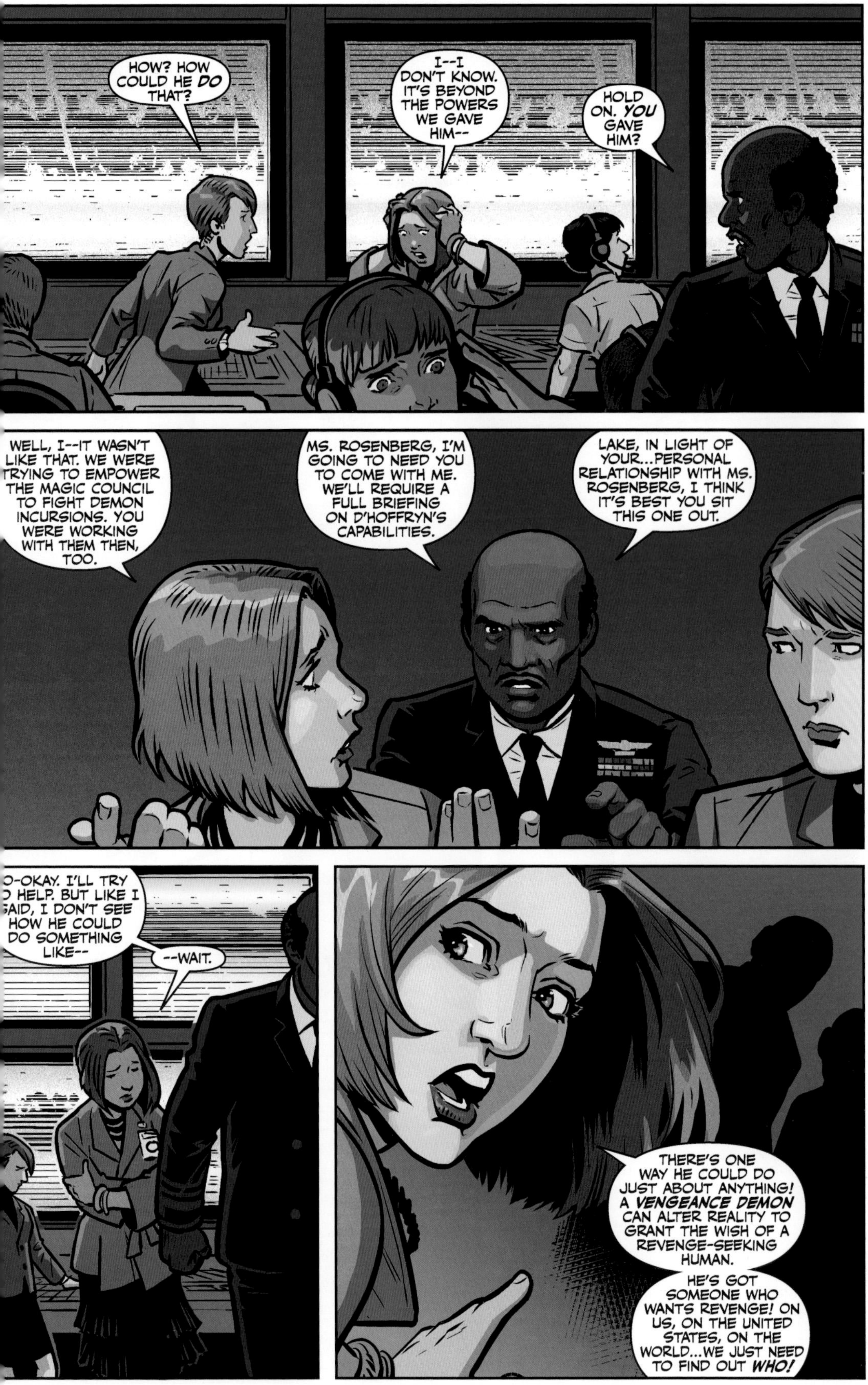
HOW? HOW COULD HE *DO* THAT?
I--I DON'T KNOW. IT'S BEYOND THE POWERS WE GAVE HIM--
HOLD ON. *YOU* GAVE HIM?
WELL, I--IT WASN'T LIKE THAT. WE WERE TRYING TO EMPOWER THE MAGIC COUNCIL TO FIGHT DEMON INCURSIONS. YOU WERE WORKING WITH THEM THEN, TOO.
MS. ROSENBERG, I'M GOING TO NEED YOU TO COME WITH ME. WE'LL REQUIRE A FULL BRIEFING ON D'HOFFRYN'S CAPABILITIES.
LAKE, IN LIGHT OF YOUR...PERSONAL RELATIONSHIP WITH MS. ROSENBERG, I THINK IT'S BEST YOU SIT THIS ONE OUT.
O-OKAY. I'LL TRY TO HELP. BUT LIKE I SAID, I DON'T SEE HOW HE COULD DO SOMETHING LIKE--
--WAIT.
THERE'S ONE WAY HE COULD DO JUST ABOUT ANYTHING! A *VENGEANCE DEMON* CAN ALTER REALITY TO GRANT THE WISH OF A REVENGE-SEEKING HUMAN.
HE'S GOT SOMEONE WHO WANTS REVENGE! ON US, ON THE UNITED STATES, ON THE WORLD...WE JUST NEED TO FIND OUT *WHO!*

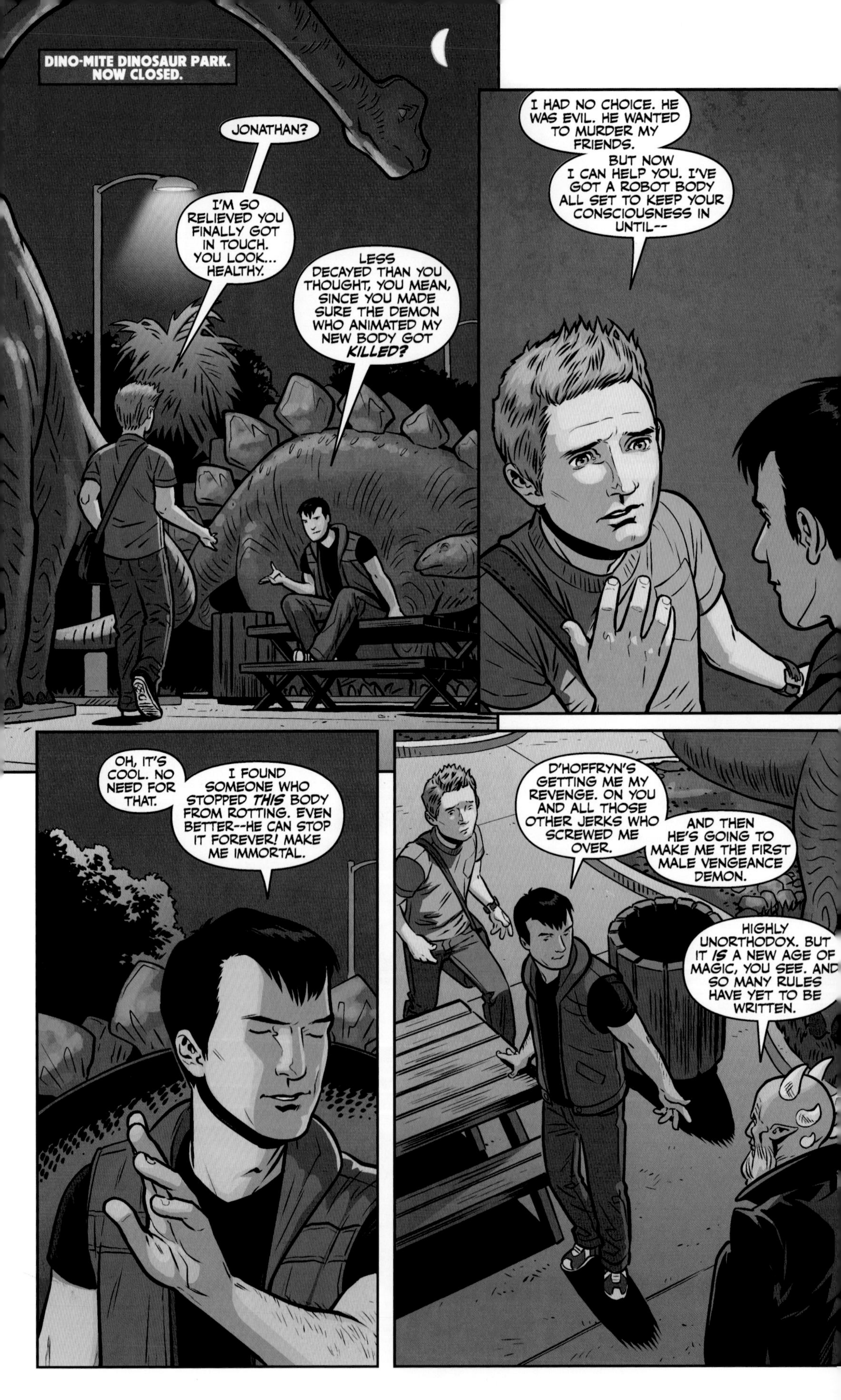
DINO-MITE DINOSAUR PARK. NOW CLOSED.
JONATHAN?
I'M SO RELIEVED YOU FINALLY GOT IN TOUCH. YOU LOOK... HEALTHY.
LESS DECAYED THAN YOU THOUGHT, YOU MEAN, SINCE YOU MADE SURE THE DEMON WHO ANIMATED MY NEW BODY GOT *KILLED?*
I HAD NO CHOICE. HE WAS EVIL. HE WANTED TO MURDER MY FRIENDS.
BUT NOW I CAN HELP YOU. I'VE GOT A ROBOT BODY ALL SET TO KEEP YOUR CONSCIOUSNESS IN UNTIL--
OH, IT'S COOL. NO NEED FOR THAT.
I FOUND SOMEONE WHO STOPPED *THIS* BODY FROM ROTTING. EVEN BETTER--HE CAN STOP IT FOREVER! MAKE ME IMMORTAL.
D'HOFFRYN'S GETTING ME MY REVENGE. ON YOU AND ALL THOSE OTHER JERKS WHO SCREWED ME OVER.
AND THEN HE'S GOING TO MAKE ME THE FIRST MALE VENGEANCE DEMON.
HIGHLY UNORTHODOX. BUT IT *IS* A NEW AGE OF MAGIC, YOU SEE. AND SO MANY RULES HAVE YET TO BE WRITTEN.

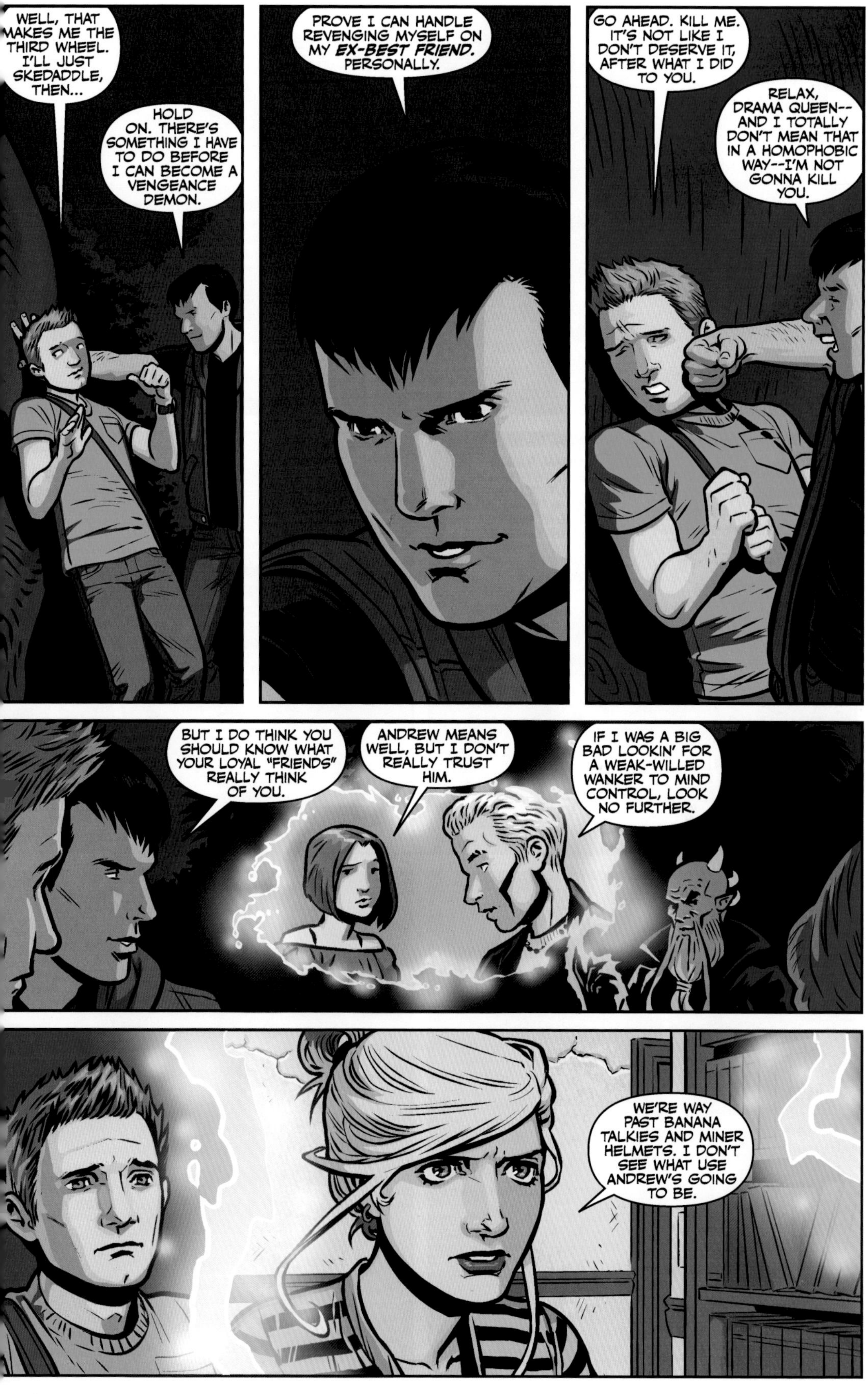
WELL, THAT MAKES ME THE THIRD WHEEL. I'LL JUST SKEDADDLE, THEN...
HOLD ON. THERE'S SOMETHING I HAVE TO DO BEFORE I CAN BECOME A VENGEANCE DEMON.
PROVE I CAN HANDLE REVENGING MYSELF ON MY *EX-BEST FRIEND.* PERSONALLY.
GO AHEAD. KILL ME. IT'S NOT LIKE I DON'T DESERVE IT, AFTER WHAT I DID TO YOU.
RELAX, DRAMA QUEEN--AND I TOTALLY DON'T MEAN THAT IN A HOMOPHOBIC WAY--I'M NOT GONNA KILL YOU.
BUT I DO THINK YOU SHOULD KNOW WHAT YOUR LOYAL "FRIENDS" REALLY THINK OF YOU.
ANDREW MEANS WELL, BUT I DON'T REALLY TRUST HIM.
IF I WAS A BIG BAD LOOKIN' FOR A WEAK-WILLED WANKER TO MIND CONTROL, LOOK NO FURTHER.
WE'RE WAY PAST BANANA TALKIES AND MINER HELMETS. I DON'T SEE WHAT USE ANDREW'S GOING TO BE.

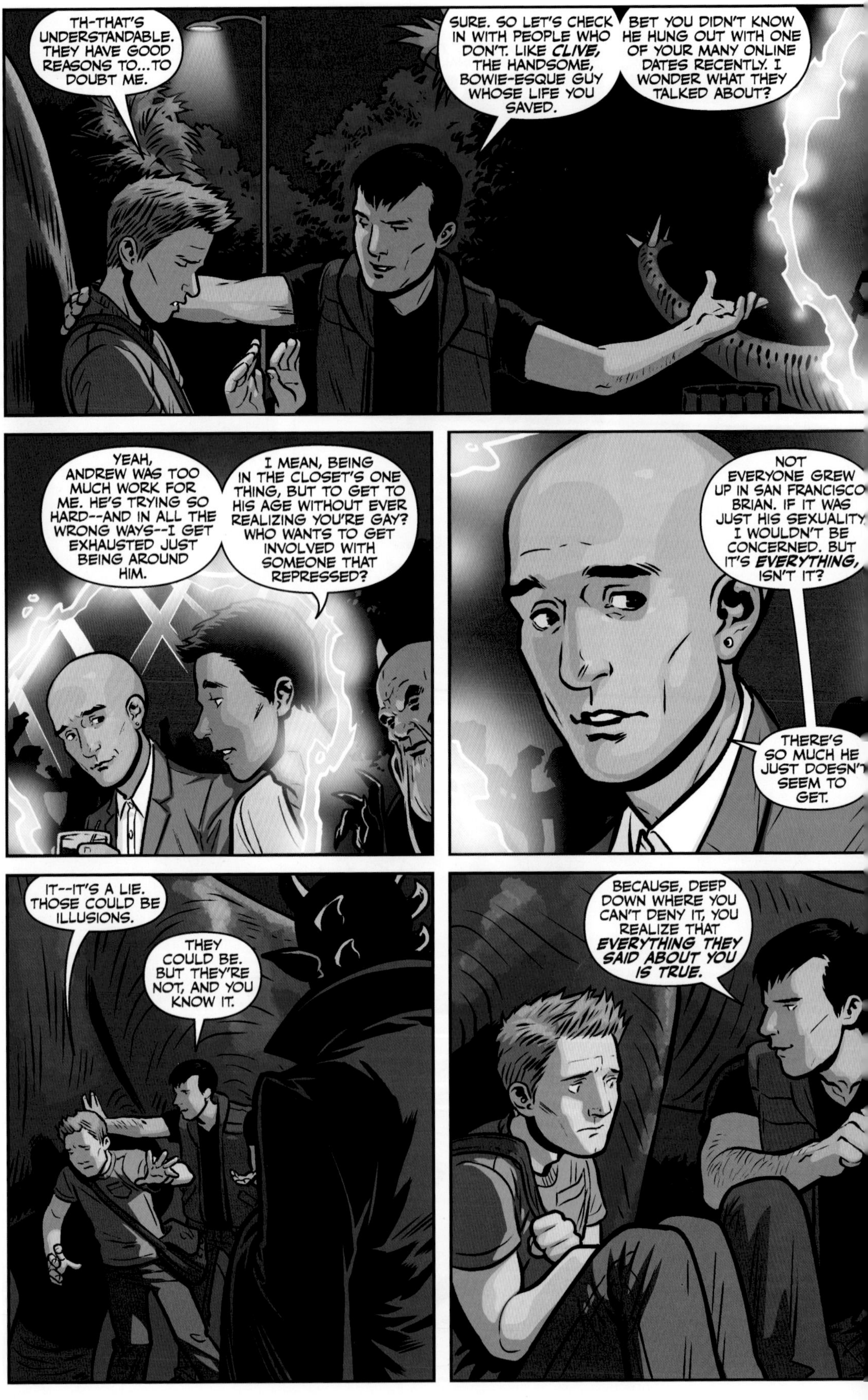
TH-THAT'S UNDERSTANDABLE. THEY HAVE GOOD REASONS TO...TO DOUBT ME.
SURE. SO LET'S CHECK IN WITH PEOPLE WHO DON'T. LIKE *CLIVE,* THE HANDSOME, BOWIE-ESQUE GUY WHOSE LIFE YOU SAVED.
BET YOU DIDN'T KNOW HE HUNG OUT WITH ONE OF YOUR MANY ONLINE DATES RECENTLY. I WONDER WHAT THEY TALKED ABOUT?
YEAH, ANDREW WAS TOO MUCH WORK FOR ME. HE'S TRYING SO HARD--AND IN ALL THE WRONG WAYS--I GET EXHAUSTED JUST BEING AROUND HIM.
I MEAN, BEING IN THE CLOSET'S ONE THING, BUT TO GET TO HIS AGE WITHOUT EVER REALIZING YOU'RE GAY? WHO WANTS TO GET INVOLVED WITH SOMEONE THAT REPRESSED?
NOT EVERYONE GREW UP IN SAN FRANCISCO BRIAN. IF IT WAS JUST HIS SEXUALITY I WOULDN'T BE CONCERNED. BUT IT'S *EVERYTHING,* ISN'T IT?
THERE'S SO MUCH HE JUST DOESN'T SEEM TO GET.
IT--IT'S A LIE. THOSE COULD BE ILLUSIONS.
THEY COULD BE. BUT THEY'RE NOT, AND YOU KNOW IT.
BECAUSE, DEEP DOWN WHERE YOU CAN'T DENY IT, YOU REALIZE THAT ***EVERYTHING THEY SAID ABOUT YOU IS TRUE.***

I THINK WE'RE DONE HERE.

MASTERFULLY EXECUTED, MR. LEVINSON. A *VERY* PROMISING START.

AS I ALWAYS TOLD MY VENGEANCE DEMONS-- NEVER GO FOR THE KILL WHEN YOU CAN GO FOR THE PAIN.

SO YOU'RE NOT GOING TO KILL THE SLAYER AND HER GANG OF IDIOTS?

NOT UNLESS THEY FORCE MY HAND. BUT IF THEY CONTINUE TO INTERFERE, AFTER I WARNED THEM NOT TO, I MIGHT HAVE NO OTHER CHOICE.

THEN AGAIN, WITH THAT GROUP, JUST KILLING THE *RIGHT* ONES CAN BE MOST EFFECTIVE OF ALL.

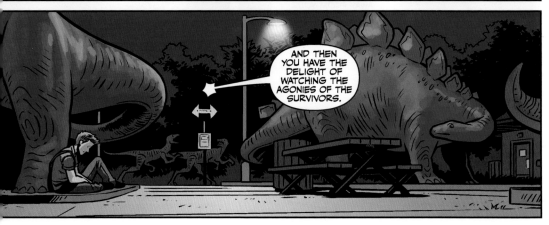

AND THEN YOU HAVE THE DELIGHT OF WATCHING THE AGONIES OF THE SURVIVORS.

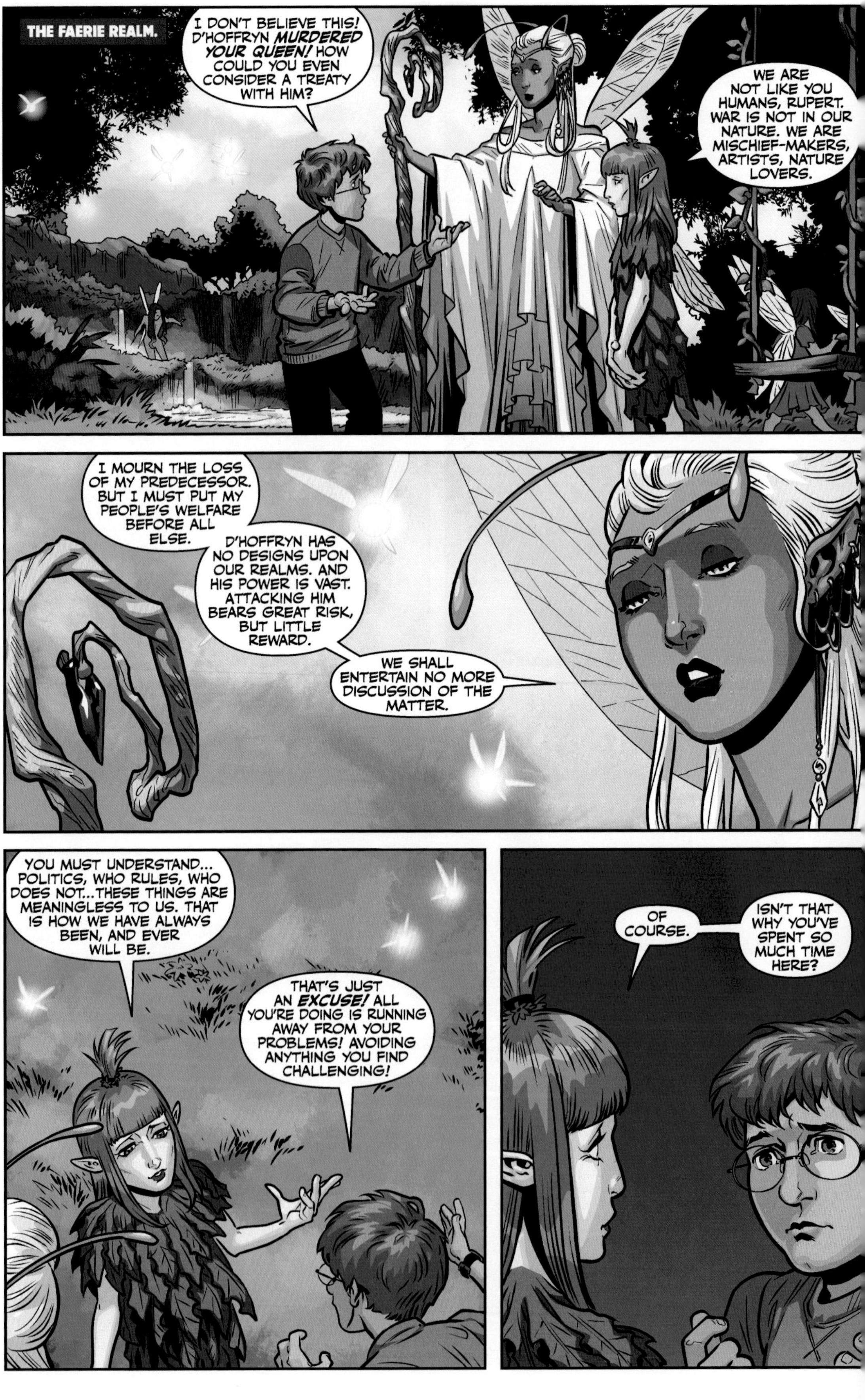

THE FAERIE REALM.
I DON'T BELIEVE THIS! D'HOFFRYN MURDERED YOUR QUEEN! HOW COULD YOU EVEN CONSIDER A TREATY WITH HIM?
WE ARE NOT LIKE YOU HUMANS, RUPERT. WAR IS NOT IN OUR NATURE. WE ARE MISCHIEF-MAKERS, ARTISTS, NATURE LOVERS.
I MOURN THE LOSS OF MY PREDECESSOR. BUT I MUST PUT MY PEOPLE'S WELFARE BEFORE ALL ELSE.
D'HOFFRYN HAS NO DESIGNS UPON OUR REALMS. AND HIS POWER IS VAST. ATTACKING HIM BEARS GREAT RISK, BUT LITTLE REWARD.
WE SHALL ENTERTAIN NO MORE DISCUSSION OF THE MATTER.
YOU MUST UNDERSTAND... POLITICS, WHO RULES, WHO DOES NOT...THESE THINGS ARE MEANINGLESS TO US. THAT IS HOW WE HAVE ALWAYS BEEN, AND EVER WILL BE.
THAT'S JUST AN EXCUSE! ALL YOU'RE DOING IS RUNNING AWAY FROM YOUR PROBLEMS! AVOIDING ANYTHING YOU FIND CHALLENGING!
OF COURSE.
ISN'T THAT WHY YOU'VE SPENT SO MUCH TIME HERE?

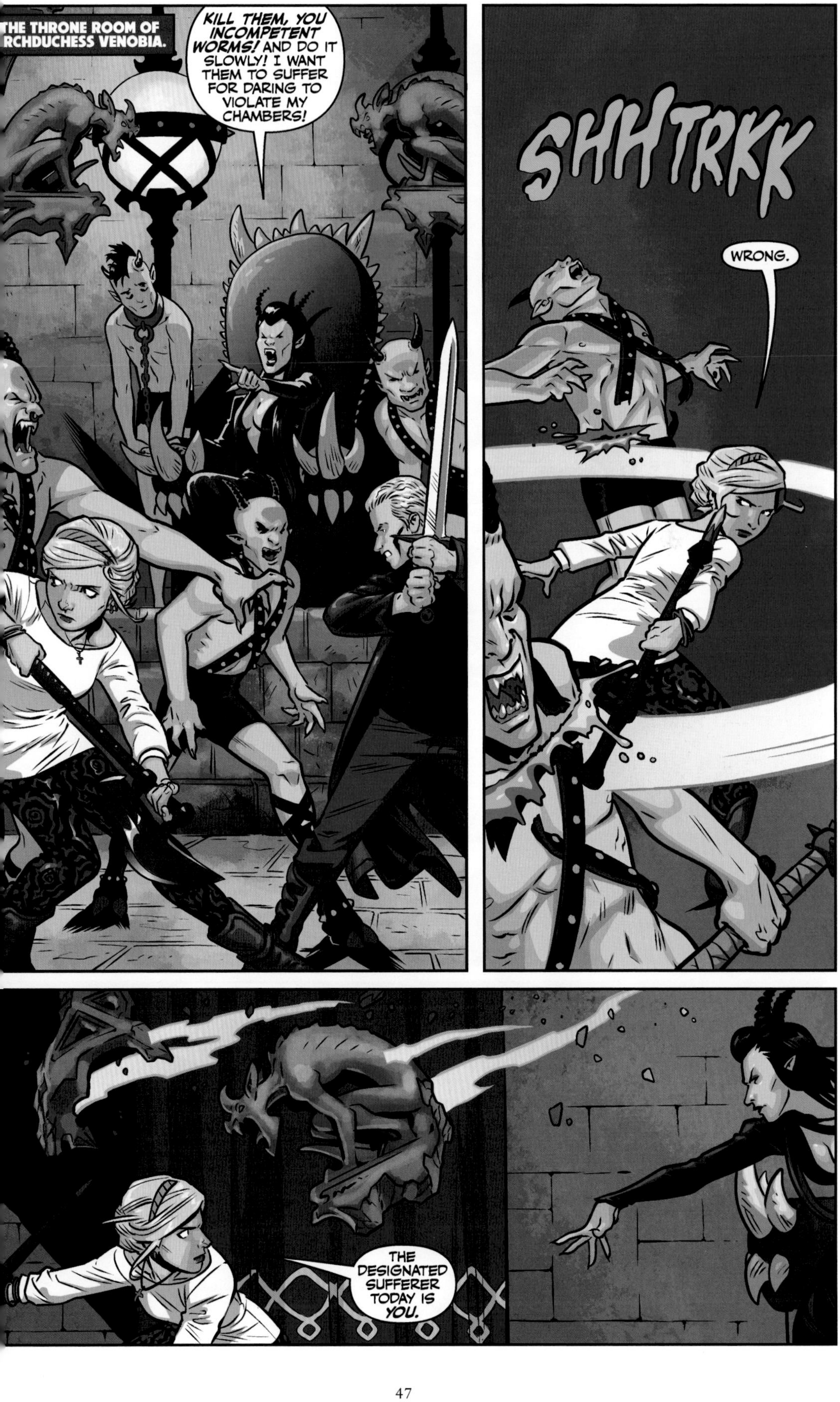
THE THRONE ROOM OF ARCHDUCHESS VENOBIA.
KILL THEM, YOU INCOMPETENT WORMS! AND DO IT SLOWLY! I WANT THEM TO SUFFER FOR DARING TO VIOLATE MY CHAMBERS!
SHHTRKK
WRONG.
THE DESIGNATED SUFFERER TODAY IS YOU.

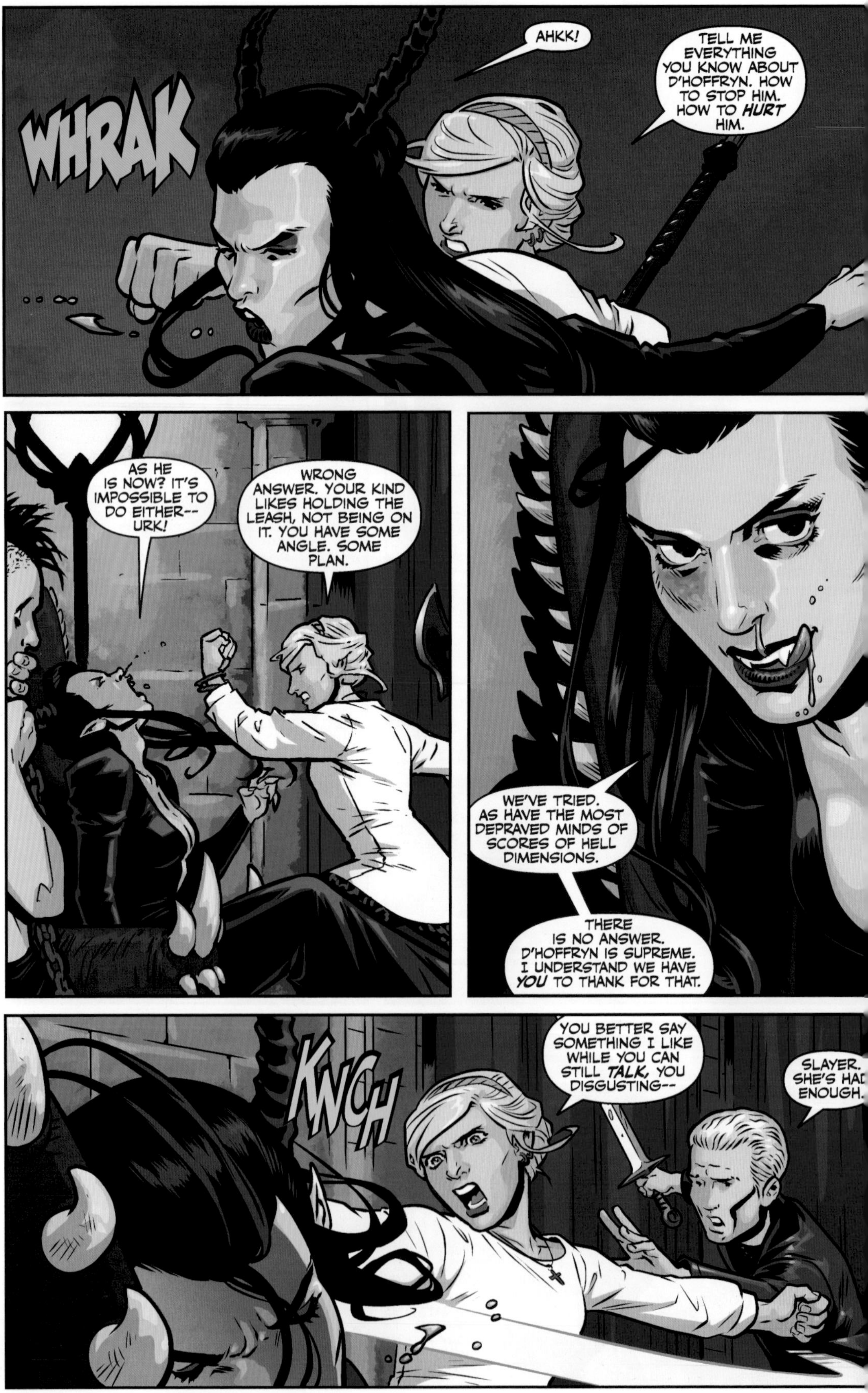
WHRAK
AHKK!
TELL ME EVERYTHING YOU KNOW ABOUT D'HOFFRYN. HOW TO STOP HIM. HOW TO *HURT* HIM.
AS HE IS NOW? IT'S IMPOSSIBLE TO DO EITHER-- URK!
WRONG ANSWER. YOUR KIND LIKES HOLDING THE LEASH, NOT BEING ON IT. YOU HAVE SOME ANGLE. SOME PLAN.
WE'VE TRIED. AS HAVE THE MOST DEPRAVED MINDS OF SCORES OF HELL DIMENSIONS.
THERE IS NO ANSWER. D'HOFFRYN IS SUPREME. I UNDERSTAND WE HAVE *YOU* TO THANK FOR THAT.
KNCH
YOU BETTER SAY SOMETHING I LIKE WHILE YOU CAN STILL *TALK*, YOU DISGUSTING--
SLAYER. SHE'S HAD ENOUGH.

SHE'S LYING! SHE'S MEMBER OF THE ?LE OF THE BLACK ?RN, THE FIRST THE FALLEN, THE ?ROTHERHOOD OF ULTIMATE PERVERSION!

IF ANYONE KNOWS HOW TO STOP D'HOFFRYN, IT'S HER!

WE'VE BEEN BRUTALIZING MEMBERS OF THOSE ORGANIZATIONS ALL DAY. AND WE KEEP GETTING THE SAME ANSWER.

NOT SAYING THEY DON'T DESERVE A THUMPING, FOR ALL MANNER OF REASONS. BUT PERHAPS IT'S TIME WE ADMIT THEY'RE TELLING THE TRUTH.

AND ALL WE'RE REALLY DOING IS MAKING OURSELVES FEEL BETTER ABOUT THE ROYAL COCK-UP WE'VE MADE OF THINGS.

ALL I'VE BEEN DOING SINCE THIS STARTED IS TRYING TO FIX IT! AND ALL *YOU'VE* BEEN DOING IS TELLING ME HOW BAD I SCREWED UP!

NO, ALL YOU'VE BEEN DOING IS ATTACKING *ME*! BLOODY HELL, SLAYER, I'M NOT YOUR ENEMY! I'M TRYING TO COME UP WITH ACTUAL SOLUTIONS HERE!

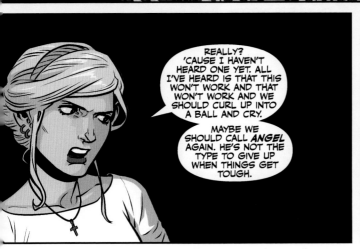

REALLY? 'CAUSE I HAVEN'T HEARD ONE YET. ALL I'VE HEARD IS THAT THIS WON'T WORK AND THAT WON'T WORK AND WE SHOULD CURL UP INTO A BALL AND CRY.

MAYBE WE SHOULD CALL *ANGEL* AGAIN. HE'S NOT THE TYPE TO GIVE UP WHEN THINGS GET TOUGH.

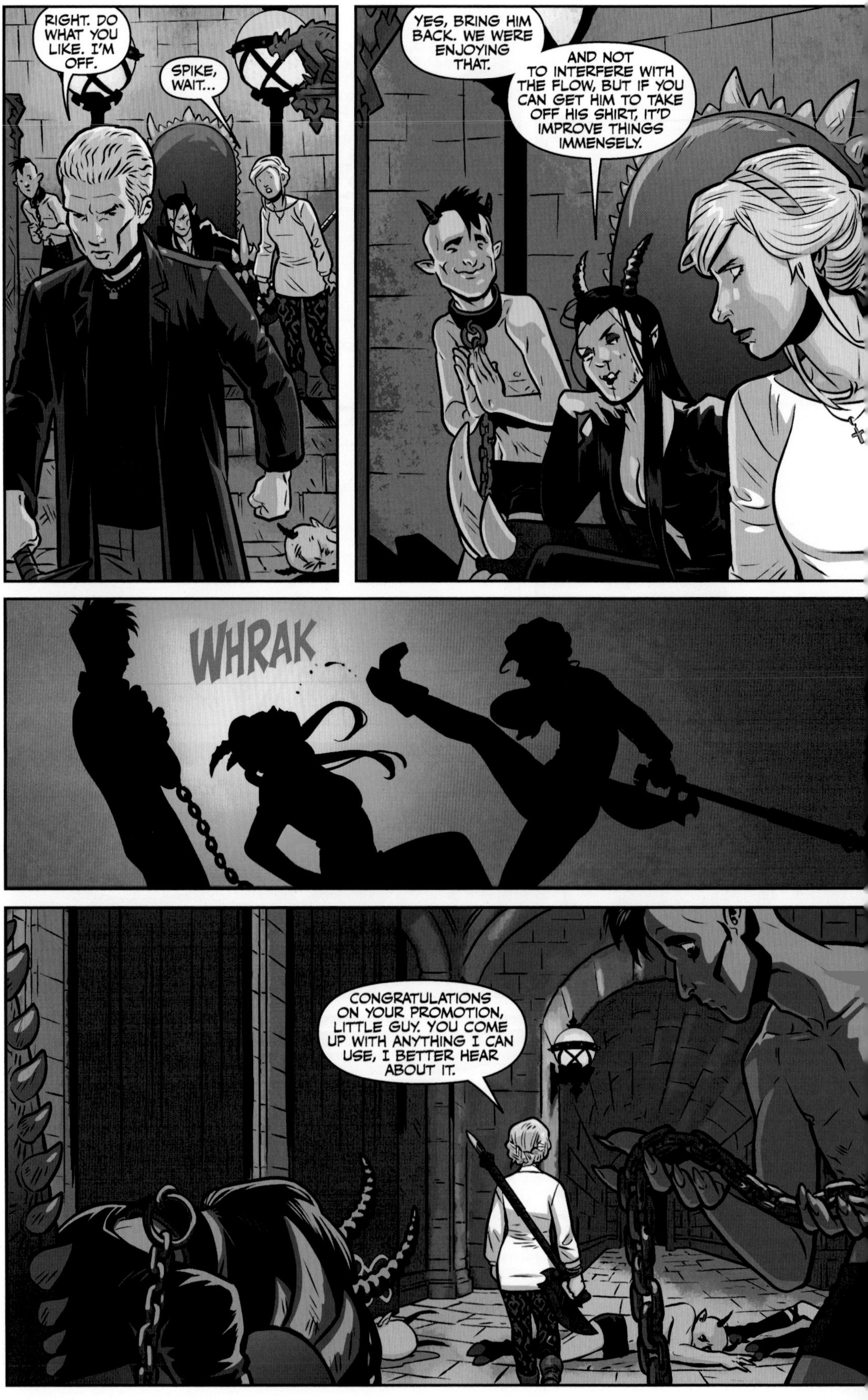

RIGHT. DO WHAT YOU LIKE. I'M OFF.
SPIKE, WAIT...
YES, BRING HIM BACK. WE WERE ENJOYING THAT.
AND NOT TO INTERFERE WITH THE FLOW, BUT IF YOU CAN GET HIM TO TAKE OFF HIS SHIRT, IT'D IMPROVE THINGS IMMENSELY.
WHRAK
CONGRATULATIONS ON YOUR PROMOTION, LITTLE GUY. YOU COME UP WITH ANYTHING I CAN USE, I BETTER HEAR ABOUT IT.

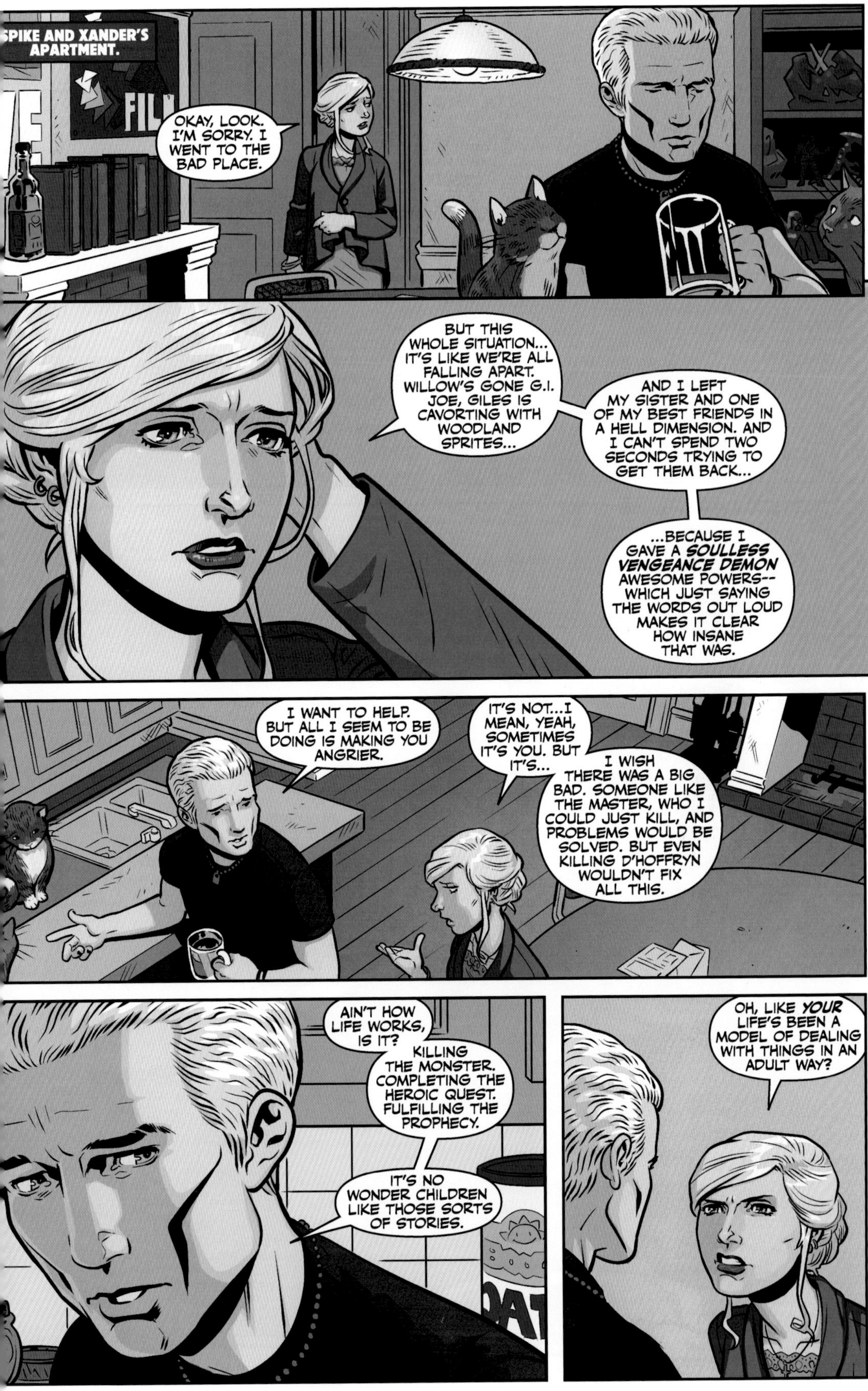
SPIKE AND XANDER'S APARTMENT.
FILM
OKAY, LOOK. I'M SORRY. I WENT TO THE BAD PLACE.
BUT THIS WHOLE SITUATION... IT'S LIKE WE'RE ALL FALLING APART. WILLOW'S GONE G.I. JOE, GILES IS CAVORTING WITH WOODLAND SPRITES...
AND I LEFT MY SISTER AND ONE OF MY BEST FRIENDS IN A HELL DIMENSION. AND I CAN'T SPEND TWO SECONDS TRYING TO GET THEM BACK...
...BECAUSE I GAVE A ***SOULLESS VENGEANCE DEMON*** AWESOME POWERS-- WHICH JUST SAYING THE WORDS OUT LOUD MAKES IT CLEAR HOW INSANE THAT WAS.
I WANT TO HELP. BUT ALL I SEEM TO BE DOING IS MAKING YOU ANGRIER.
IT'S NOT...I MEAN, YEAH, SOMETIMES IT'S YOU. BUT IT'S...
I WISH THERE WAS A BIG BAD. SOMEONE LIKE THE MASTER, WHO I COULD JUST KILL, AND PROBLEMS WOULD BE SOLVED. BUT EVEN KILLING D'HOFFRYN WOULDN'T FIX ALL THIS.
AIN'T HOW LIFE WORKS, IS IT?
KILLING THE MONSTER. COMPLETING THE HEROIC QUEST. FULFILLING THE PROPHECY.
IT'S NO WONDER CHILDREN LIKE THOSE SORTS OF STORIES.
OAT
OH, LIKE ***YOUR*** LIFE'S BEEN A MODEL OF DEALING WITH THINGS IN AN ADULT WAY?

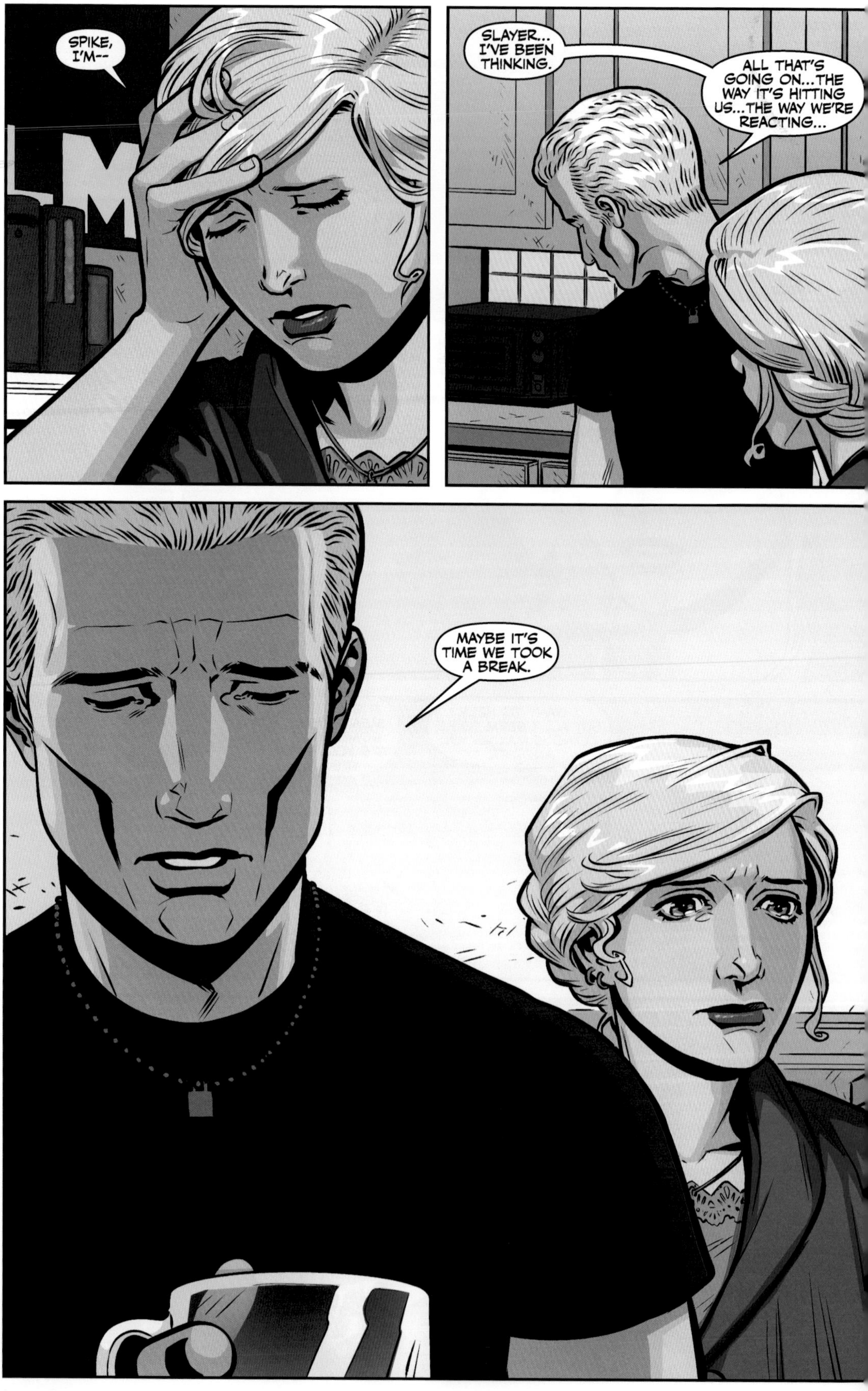
SPIKE, I'M--
SLAYER... I'VE BEEN THINKING.
ALL THAT'S GOING ON...THE WAY IT'S HITTING US...THE WAY WE'RE REACTING...
MAYBE IT'S TIME WE TOOK A BREAK.

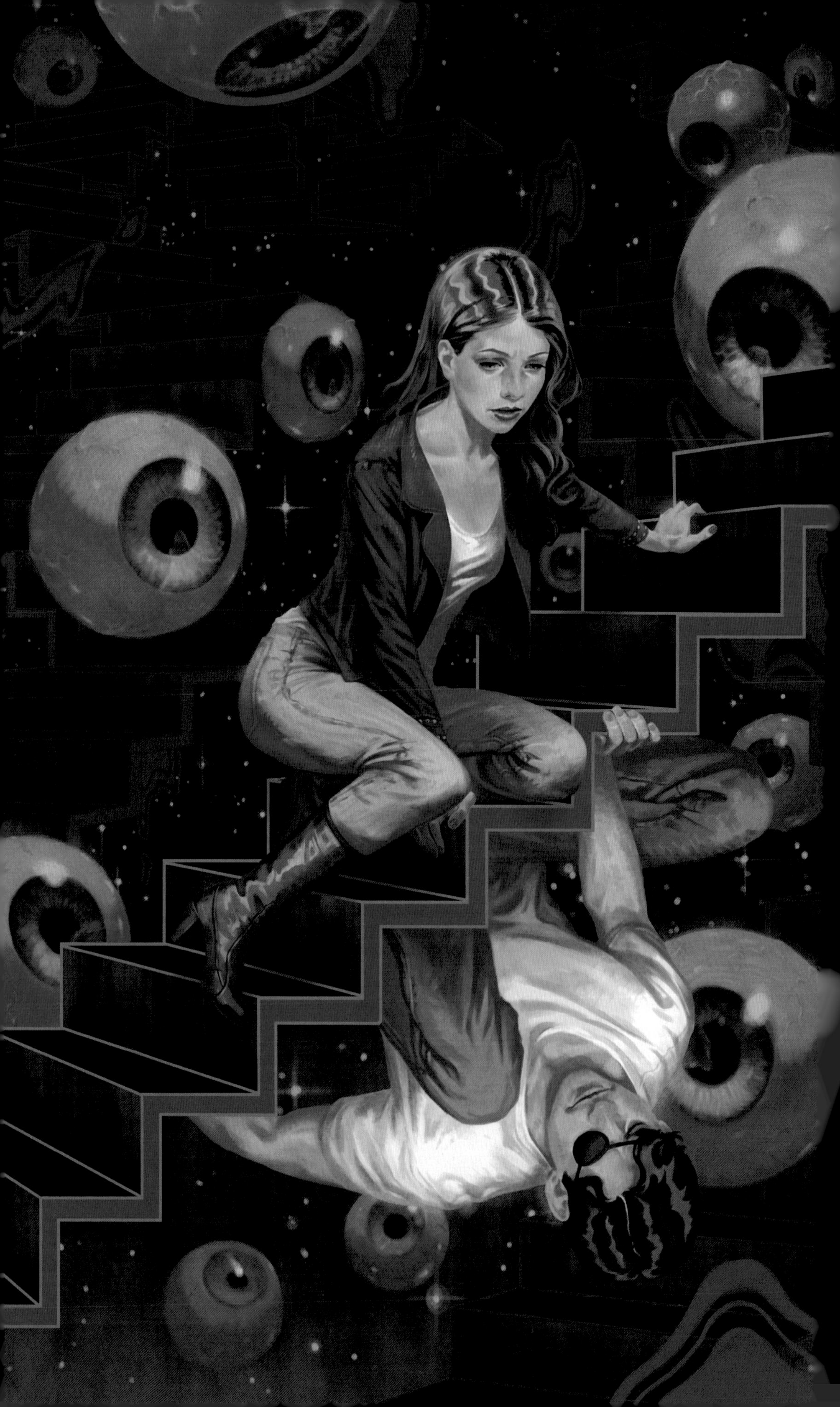

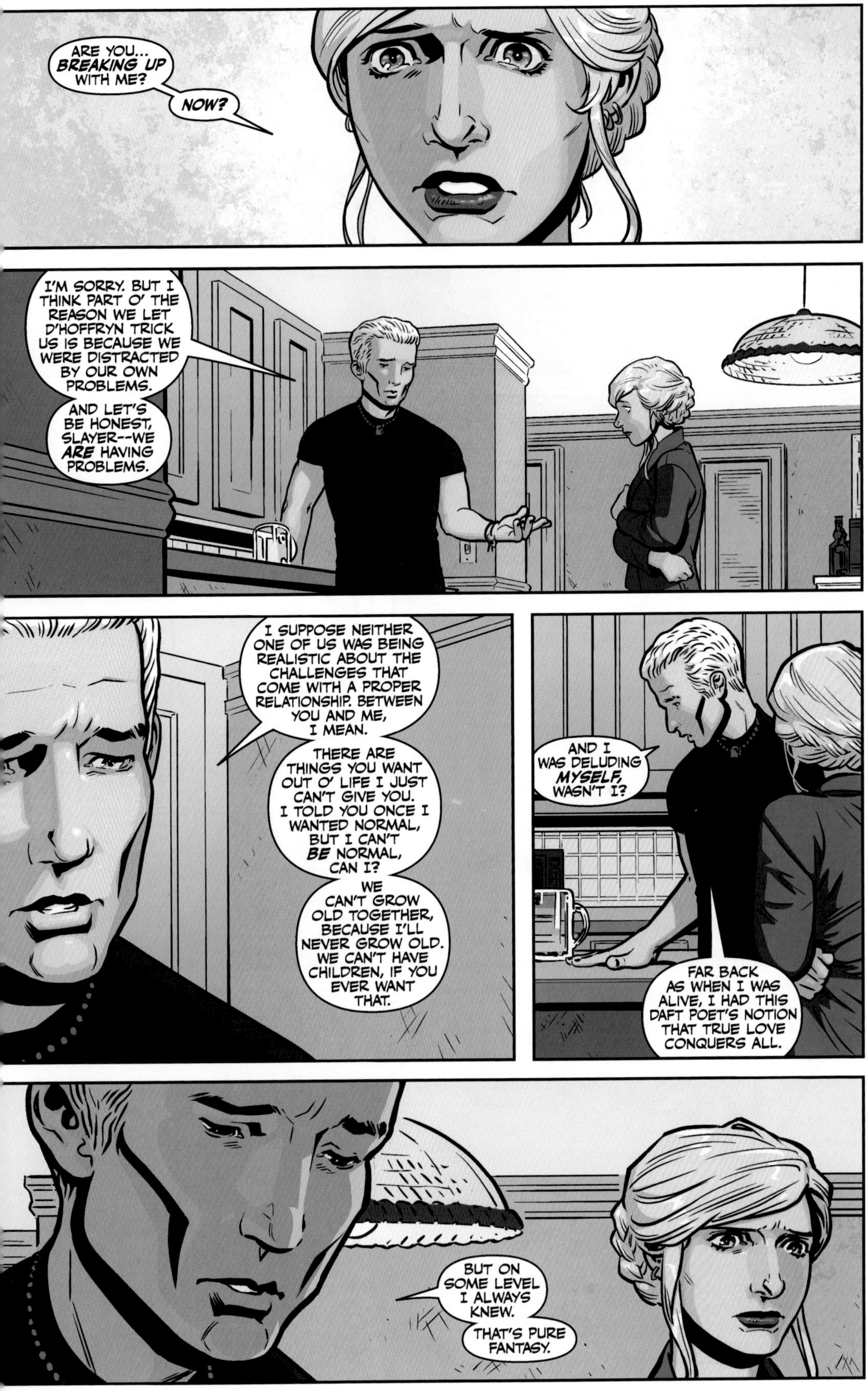
ARE YOU... BREAKING UP WITH ME?
NOW?
I'M SORRY. BUT I THINK PART O' THE REASON WE LET D'HOFFRYN TRICK US IS BECAUSE WE WERE DISTRACTED BY OUR OWN PROBLEMS.
AND LET'S BE HONEST, SLAYER--WE ARE HAVING PROBLEMS.
I SUPPOSE NEITHER ONE OF US WAS BEING REALISTIC ABOUT THE CHALLENGES THAT COME WITH A PROPER RELATIONSHIP. BETWEEN YOU AND ME, I MEAN.
THERE ARE THINGS YOU WANT OUT O' LIFE I JUST CAN'T GIVE YOU. I TOLD YOU ONCE I WANTED NORMAL, BUT I CAN'T BE NORMAL, CAN I?
WE CAN'T GROW OLD TOGETHER, BECAUSE I'LL NEVER GROW OLD. WE CAN'T HAVE CHILDREN, IF YOU EVER WANT THAT.
AND I WAS DELUDING MYSELF, WASN'T I?
FAR BACK AS WHEN I WAS ALIVE, I HAD THIS DAFT POET'S NOTION THAT TRUE LOVE CONQUERS ALL.
BUT ON SOME LEVEL I ALWAYS KNEW.
THAT'S PURE FANTASY.

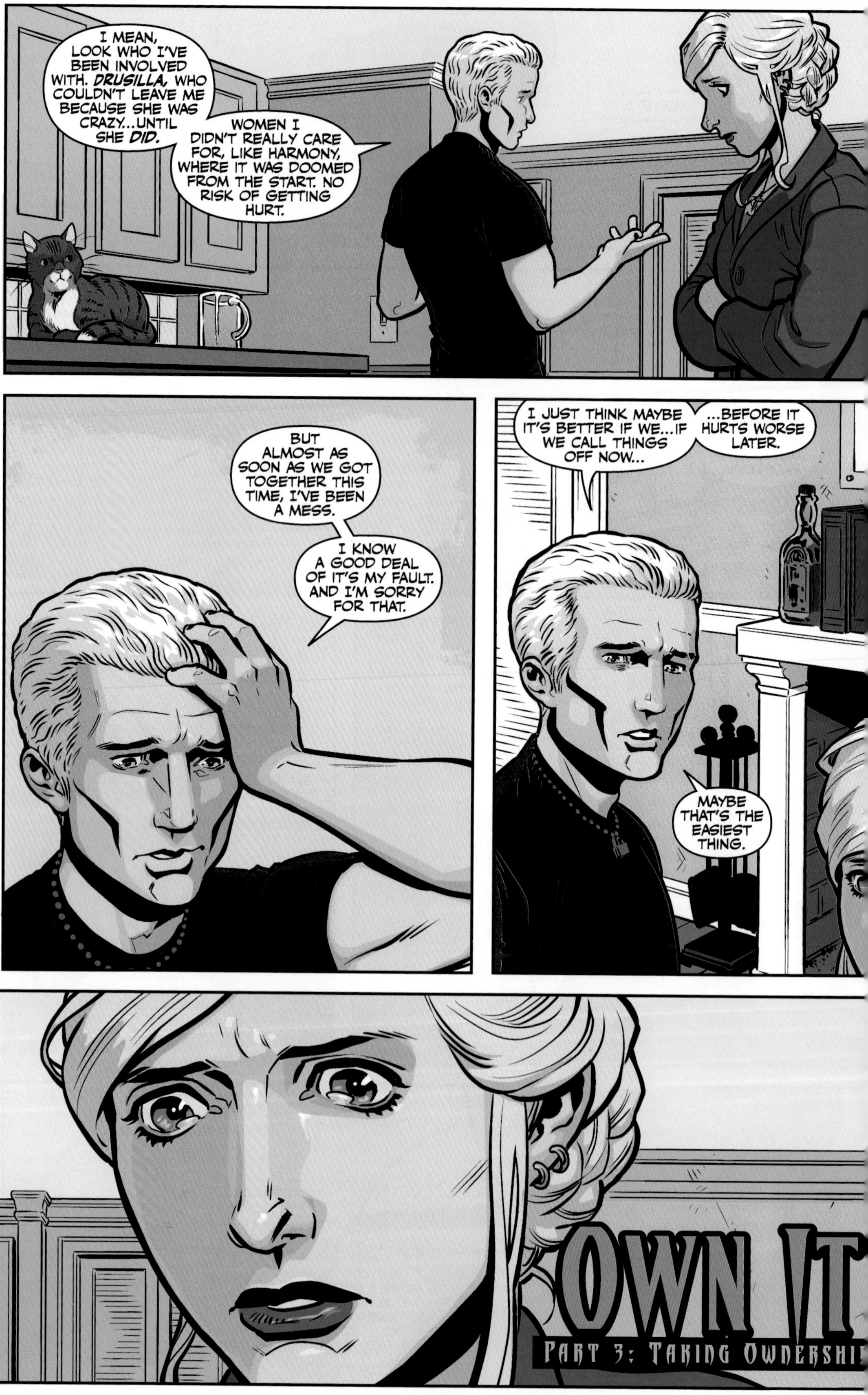
I MEAN, LOOK WHO I'VE BEEN INVOLVED WITH. DRUSILLA, WHO COULDN'T LEAVE ME BECAUSE SHE WAS CRAZY...UNTIL SHE DID.
WOMEN I DIDN'T REALLY CARE FOR, LIKE HARMONY, WHERE IT WAS DOOMED FROM THE START. NO RISK OF GETTING HURT.
BUT ALMOST AS SOON AS WE GOT TOGETHER THIS TIME, I'VE BEEN A MESS.
I KNOW A GOOD DEAL OF IT'S MY FAULT. AND I'M SORRY FOR THAT.
I JUST THINK MAYBE IT'S BETTER IF WE...IF WE CALL THINGS OFF NOW...
...BEFORE IT HURTS WORSE LATER.
MAYBE THAT'S THE EASIEST THING.
OWN IT
PART 3: TAKING OWNERSHI

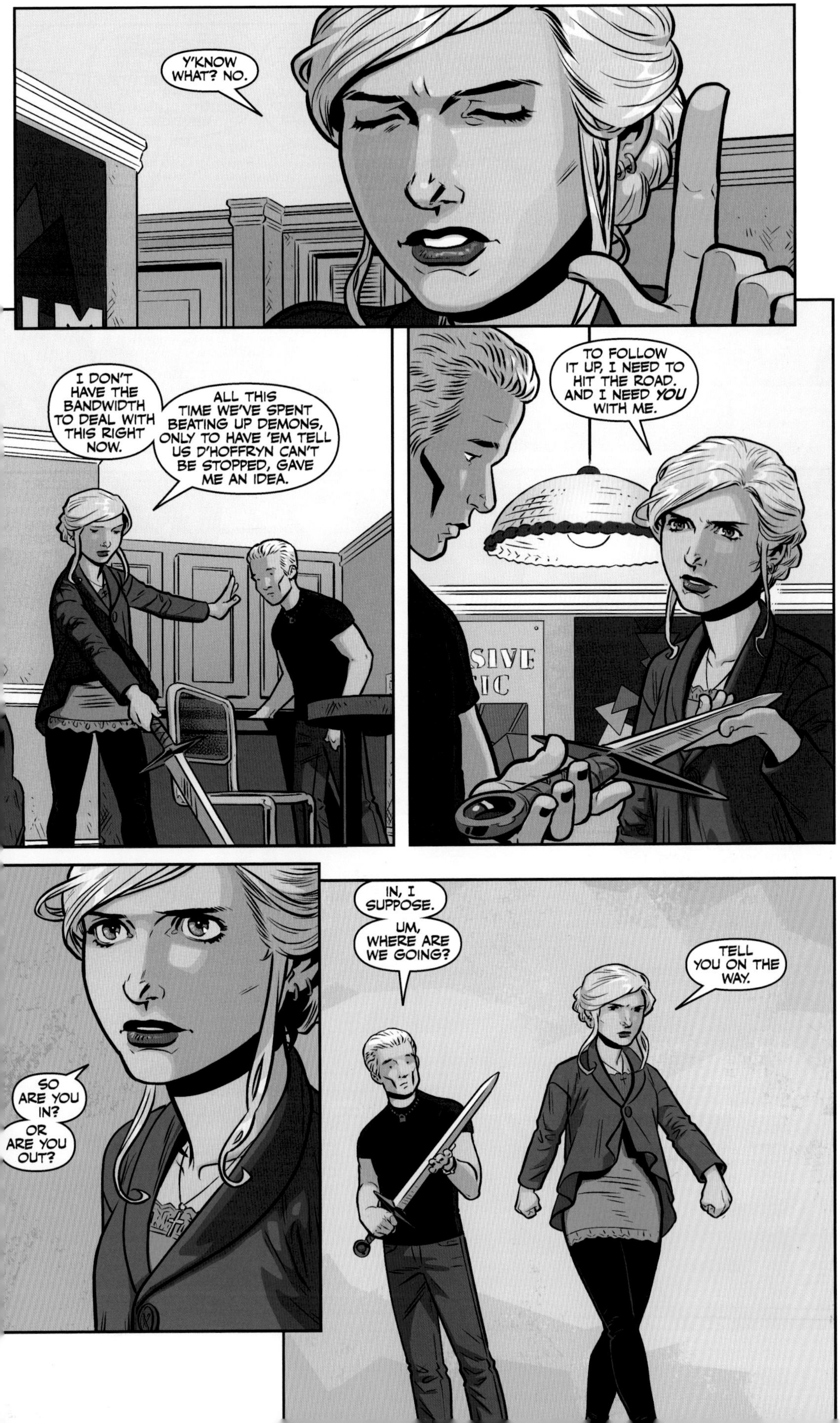
Y'KNOW WHAT? NO.
I DON'T HAVE THE BANDWIDTH TO DEAL WITH THIS RIGHT NOW.
ALL THIS TIME WE'VE SPENT BEATING UP DEMONS, ONLY TO HAVE 'EM TELL US D'HOFFRYN CAN'T BE STOPPED, GAVE ME AN IDEA.
TO FOLLOW IT UP, I NEED TO HIT THE ROAD. AND I NEED *YOU* WITH ME.
SO ARE YOU IN?
OR ARE YOU OUT?
IN, I SUPPOSE.
UM, WHERE ARE WE GOING?
TELL YOU ON THE WAY.

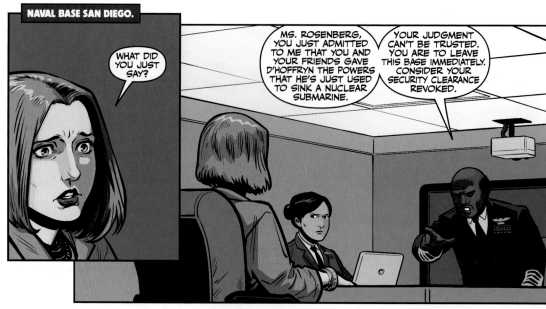

WHAT DID YOU JUST SAY?

MS. ROSENBERG, YOU JUST ADMITTED TO ME THAT YOU AND YOUR FRIENDS GAVE D'HOFFRYN THE POWERS THAT HE'S JUST USED TO SINK A NUCLEAR SUBMARINE.

YOUR JUDGMENT CAN'T BE TRUSTED. YOU ARE TO LEAVE THIS BASE IMMEDIATELY. CONSIDER YOUR SECURITY CLEARANCE REVOKED.

WAIT! ADMIRAL, WE NEED TO WORK *TOGETHER* ON THIS!

LAKE, TELL HIM!

ESCORT M* ROSENBERG THE PREMISE THAT'S AN ORDER.

THIS IS WHAT D'HOFFRYN WANTS! TO SPLIT US UP! YOU HAVE TO FIND SOMEONE WHO'LL *LISTEN!*

WILLOW, I'M SORRY. THIS IS THE MILITARY. IT DOESN'T WORK THAT WAY.

ORDERS ARE ORDERS.

THERE'S NOTHING I CAN DO.

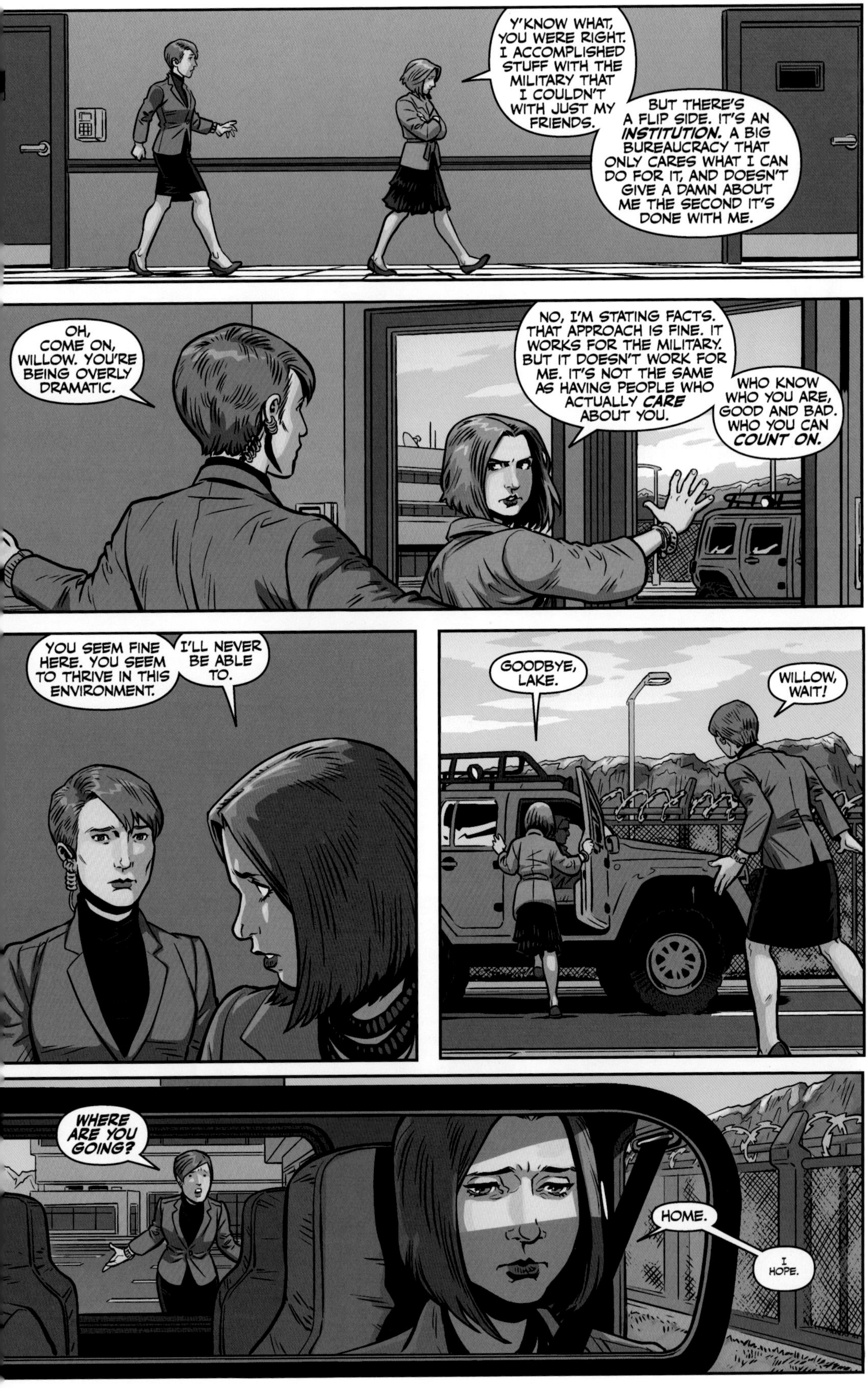
Y'KNOW WHAT, YOU WERE RIGHT. I ACCOMPLISHED STUFF WITH THE MILITARY THAT I COULDN'T WITH JUST MY FRIENDS.
BUT THERE'S A FLIP SIDE. IT'S AN INSTITUTION. A BIG BUREAUCRACY THAT ONLY CARES WHAT I CAN DO FOR IT, AND DOESN'T GIVE A DAMN ABOUT ME THE SECOND IT'S DONE WITH ME.
OH, COME ON, WILLOW. YOU'RE BEING OVERLY DRAMATIC.
NO, I'M STATING FACTS. THAT APPROACH IS FINE. IT WORKS FOR THE MILITARY. BUT IT DOESN'T WORK FOR ME. IT'S NOT THE SAME AS HAVING PEOPLE WHO ACTUALLY CARE ABOUT YOU.
WHO KNOW WHO YOU ARE, GOOD AND BAD. WHO YOU CAN COUNT ON.
YOU SEEM FINE HERE. YOU SEEM TO THRIVE IN THIS ENVIRONMENT.
I'LL NEVER BE ABLE TO.
GOODBYE, LAKE.
WILLOW, WAIT!
WHERE ARE YOU GOING?
HOME.
I HOPE.

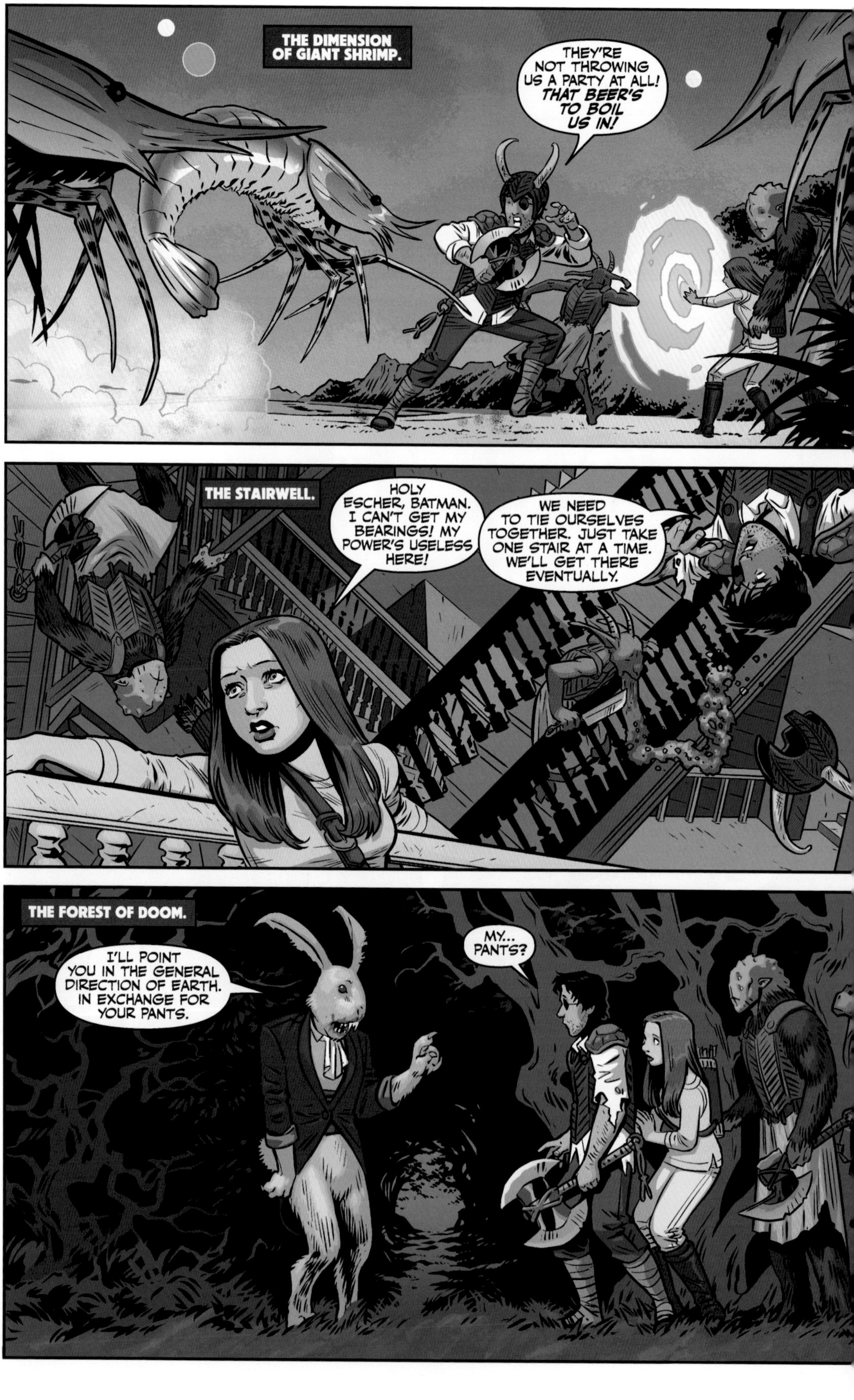
THE DIMENSION OF GIANT SHRIMP.
THEY'RE NOT THROWING US A PARTY AT ALL! THAT BEER'S TO BOIL US IN!
THE STAIRWELL.
HOLY ESCHER, BATMAN. I CAN'T GET MY BEARINGS! MY POWER'S USELESS HERE!
WE NEED TO TIE OURSELVES TOGETHER. JUST TAKE ONE STAIR AT A TIME. WE'LL GET THERE EVENTUALLY.
THE FOREST OF DOOM.
I'LL POINT YOU IN THE GENERAL DIRECTION OF EARTH. IN EXCHANGE FOR YOUR PANTS.
MY... PANTS?

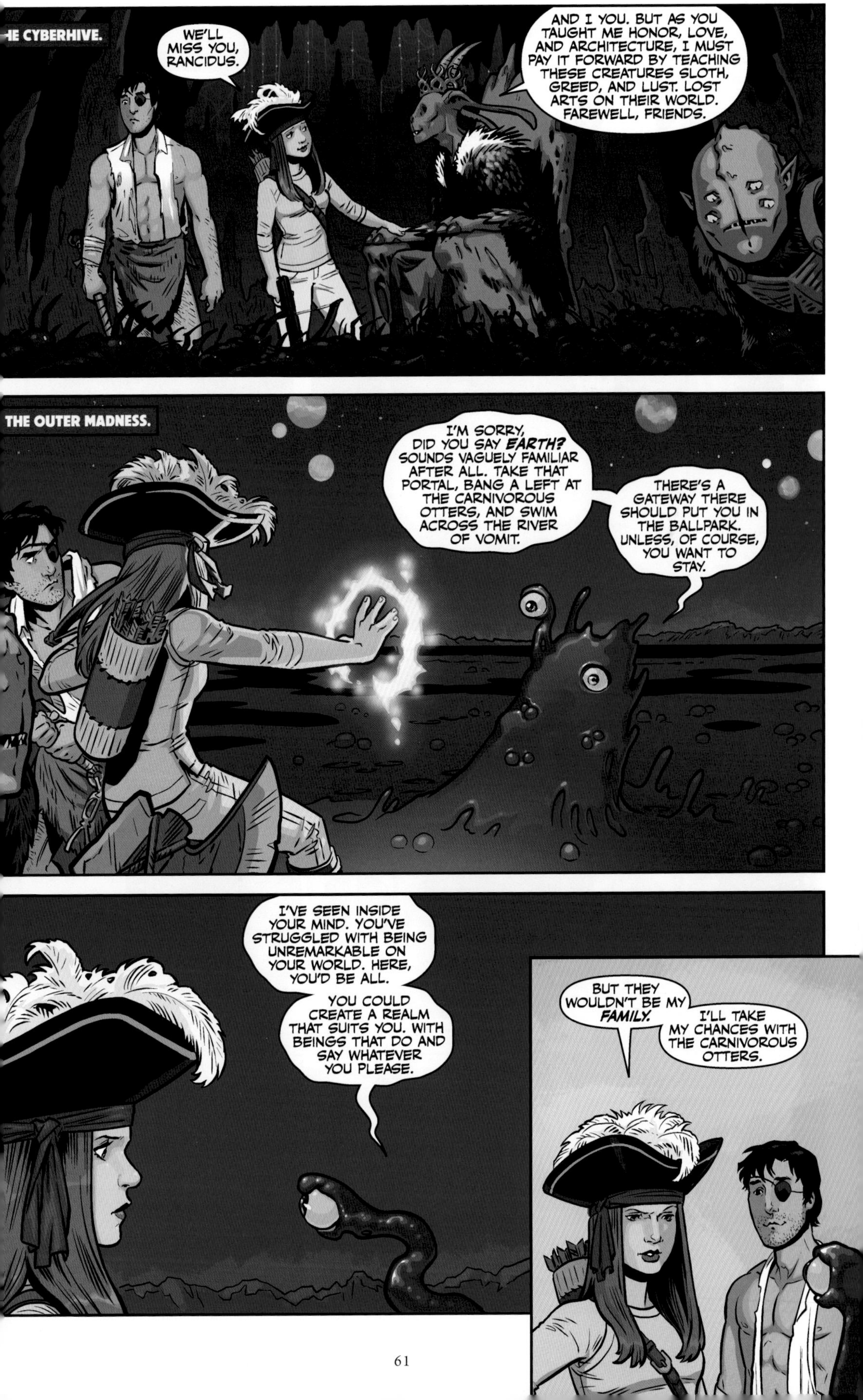

HE CYBERHIVE.
WE'LL MISS YOU, RANCIDUS.
AND I YOU. BUT AS YOU TAUGHT ME HONOR, LOVE, AND ARCHITECTURE, I MUST PAY IT FORWARD BY TEACHING THESE CREATURES SLOTH, GREED, AND LUST. LOST ARTS ON THEIR WORLD. FAREWELL, FRIENDS.
THE OUTER MADNESS.
I'M SORRY, DID YOU SAY *EARTH?* SOUNDS VAGUELY FAMILIAR AFTER ALL. TAKE THAT PORTAL, BANG A LEFT AT THE CARNIVOROUS OTTERS, AND SWIM ACROSS THE RIVER OF VOMIT.
THERE'S A GATEWAY THERE SHOULD PUT YOU IN THE BALLPARK. UNLESS, OF COURSE, YOU WANT TO STAY.
I'VE SEEN INSIDE YOUR MIND. YOU'VE STRUGGLED WITH BEING UNREMARKABLE ON YOUR WORLD. HERE, YOU'D BE ALL.
YOU COULD CREATE A REALM THAT SUITS YOU. WITH BEINGS THAT DO AND SAY WHATEVER YOU PLEASE.
BUT THEY WOULDN'T BE MY *FAMILY.*
I'LL TAKE MY CHANCES WITH THE CARNIVOROUS OTTERS.

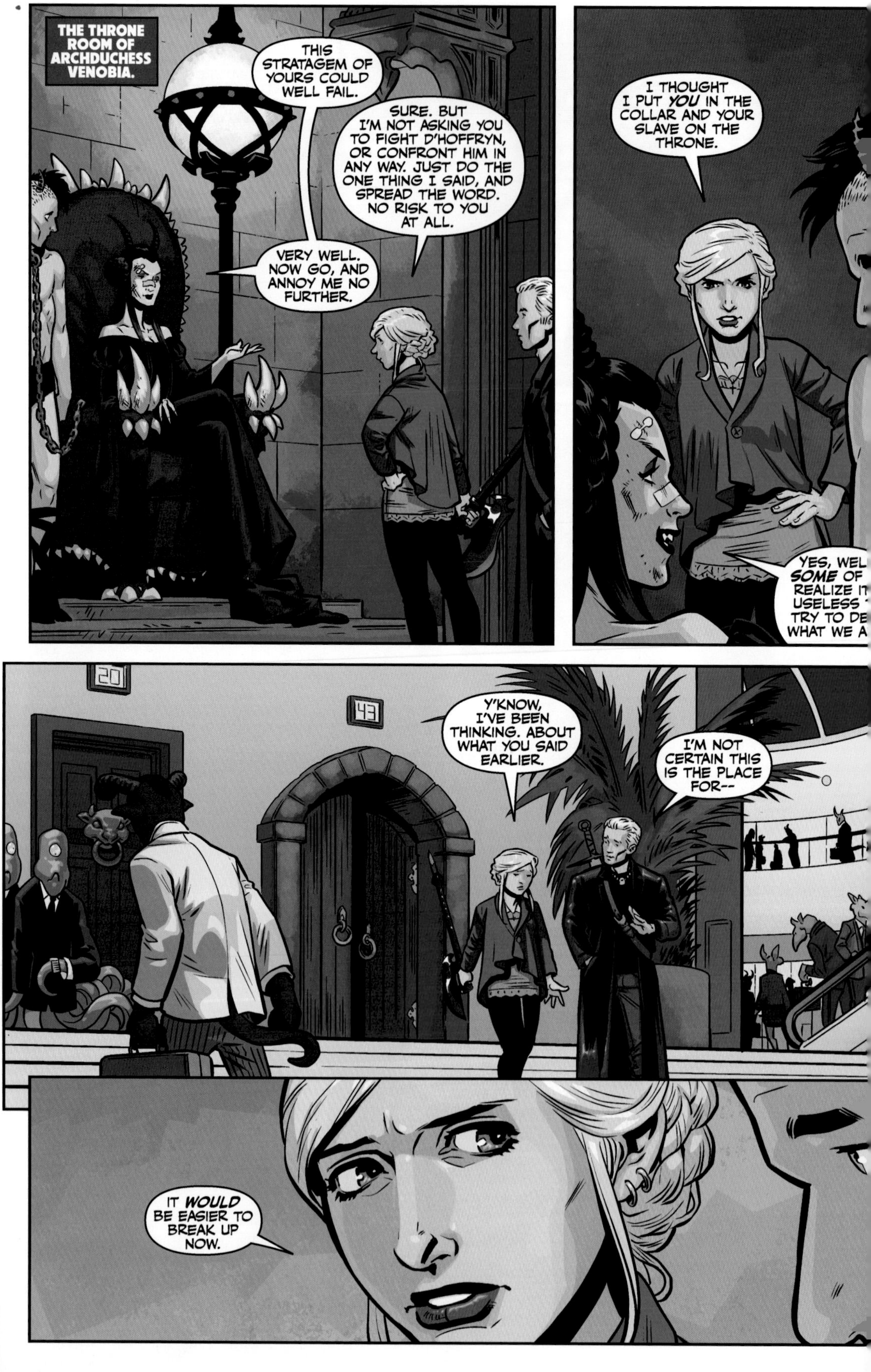
THE THRONE ROOM OF ARCHDUCHESS VENOBIA.
THIS STRATAGEM OF YOURS COULD WELL FAIL.
SURE. BUT I'M NOT ASKING YOU TO FIGHT D'HOFFRYN, OR CONFRONT HIM IN ANY WAY. JUST DO THE ONE THING I SAID, AND SPREAD THE WORD. NO RISK TO YOU AT ALL.
VERY WELL. NOW GO, AND ANNOY ME NO FURTHER.
I THOUGHT I PUT YOU IN THE COLLAR AND YOUR SLAVE ON THE THRONE.
YES, WEL SOME OF REALIZE IT USELESS TRY TO DE WHAT WE A
20
43
Y'KNOW, I'VE BEEN THINKING. ABOUT WHAT YOU SAID EARLIER.
I'M NOT CERTAIN THIS IS THE PLACE FOR--
IT WOULD BE EASIER TO BREAK UP NOW.

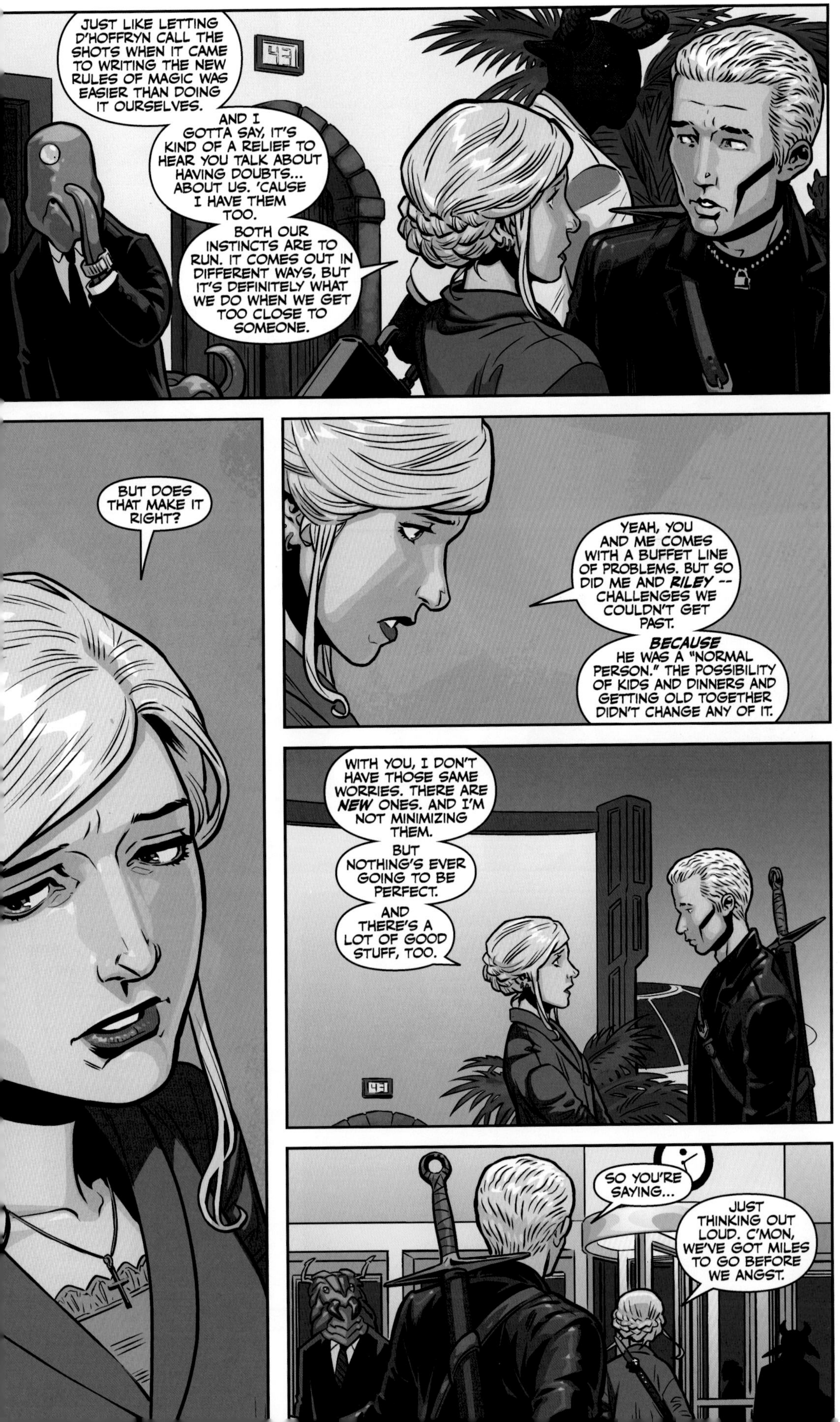
JUST LIKE LETTING D'HOFFRYN CALL THE SHOTS WHEN IT CAME TO WRITING THE NEW RULES OF MAGIC WAS EASIER THAN DOING IT OURSELVES.
AND I GOTTA SAY, IT'S KIND OF A RELIEF TO HEAR YOU TALK ABOUT HAVING DOUBTS... ABOUT US. 'CAUSE I HAVE THEM TOO.
BOTH OUR INSTINCTS ARE TO RUN. IT COMES OUT IN DIFFERENT WAYS, BUT IT'S DEFINITELY WHAT WE DO WHEN WE GET TOO CLOSE TO SOMEONE.
BUT DOES THAT MAKE IT RIGHT?
YEAH, YOU AND ME COMES WITH A BUFFET LINE OF PROBLEMS. BUT SO DID ME AND *RILEY* -- CHALLENGES WE COULDN'T GET PAST.
BECAUSE HE WAS A "NORMAL PERSON." THE POSSIBILITY OF KIDS AND DINNERS AND GETTING OLD TOGETHER DIDN'T CHANGE ANY OF IT.
WITH YOU, I DON'T HAVE THOSE SAME WORRIES. THERE ARE *NEW* ONES. AND I'M NOT MINIMIZING THEM.
BUT NOTHING'S EVER GOING TO BE PERFECT.
AND THERE'S A LOT OF GOOD STUFF, TOO.
SO YOU'RE SAYING...
JUST THINKING OUT LOUD. C'MON, WE'VE GOT MILES TO GO BEFORE WE ANGST.

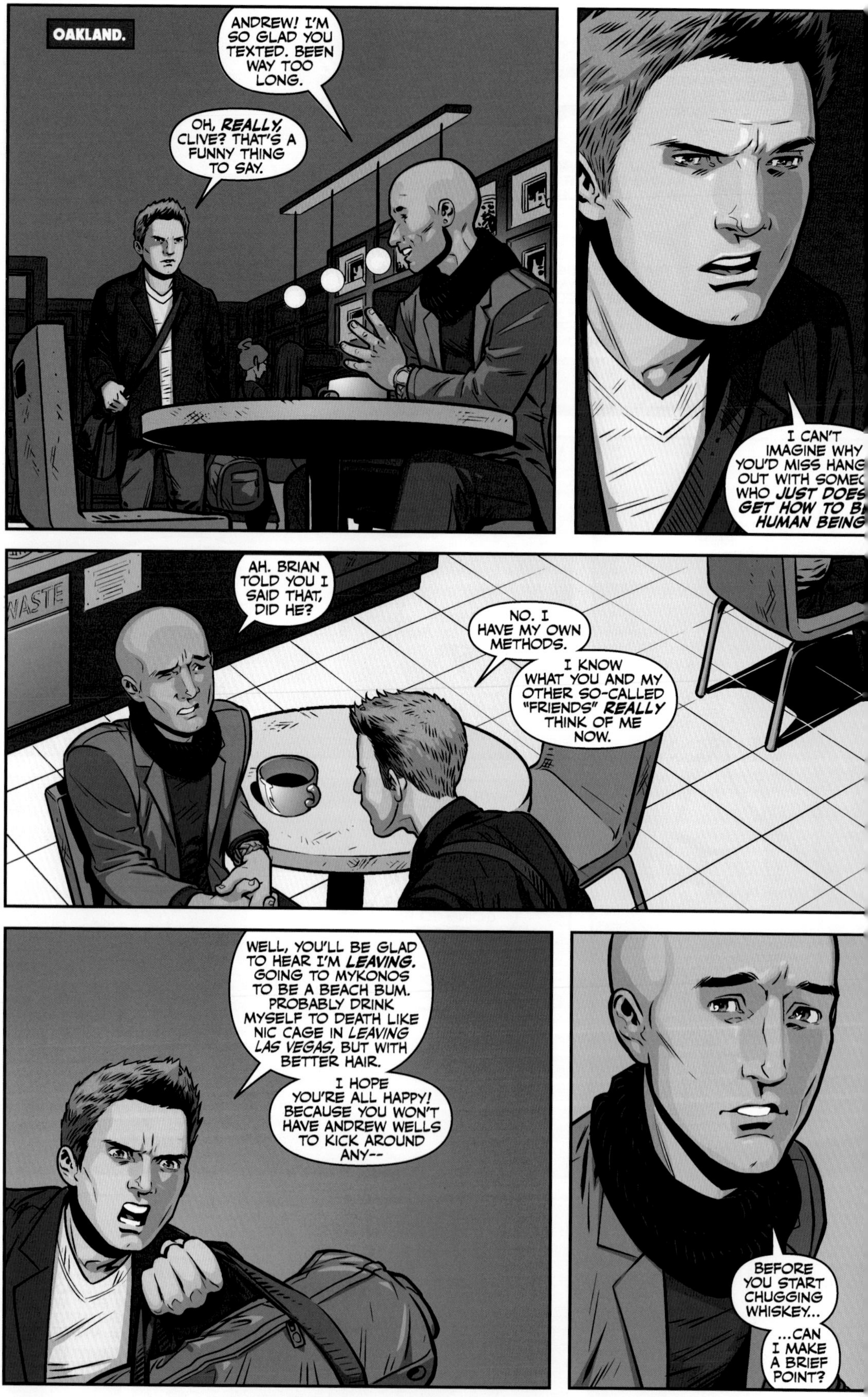
OAKLAND.
ANDREW! I'M SO GLAD YOU TEXTED. BEEN WAY TOO LONG.
OH, REALLY, CLIVE? THAT'S A FUNNY THING TO SAY.
I CAN'T IMAGINE WHY YOU'D MISS HANG OUT WITH SOMEC WHO JUST DOES GET HOW TO B HUMAN BEING
WASTE
AH. BRIAN TOLD YOU I SAID THAT, DID HE?
NO. I HAVE MY OWN METHODS.
I KNOW WHAT YOU AND MY OTHER SO-CALLED "FRIENDS" REALLY THINK OF ME NOW.
WELL, YOU'LL BE GLAD TO HEAR I'M LEAVING. GOING TO MYKONOS TO BE A BEACH BUM. PROBABLY DRINK MYSELF TO DEATH LIKE NIC CAGE IN LEAVING LAS VEGAS, BUT WITH BETTER HAIR.
I HOPE YOU'RE ALL HAPPY! BECAUSE YOU WON'T HAVE ANDREW WELLS TO KICK AROUND ANY--
BEFORE YOU START CHUGGING WHISKEY...
...CAN I MAKE A BRIEF POINT?

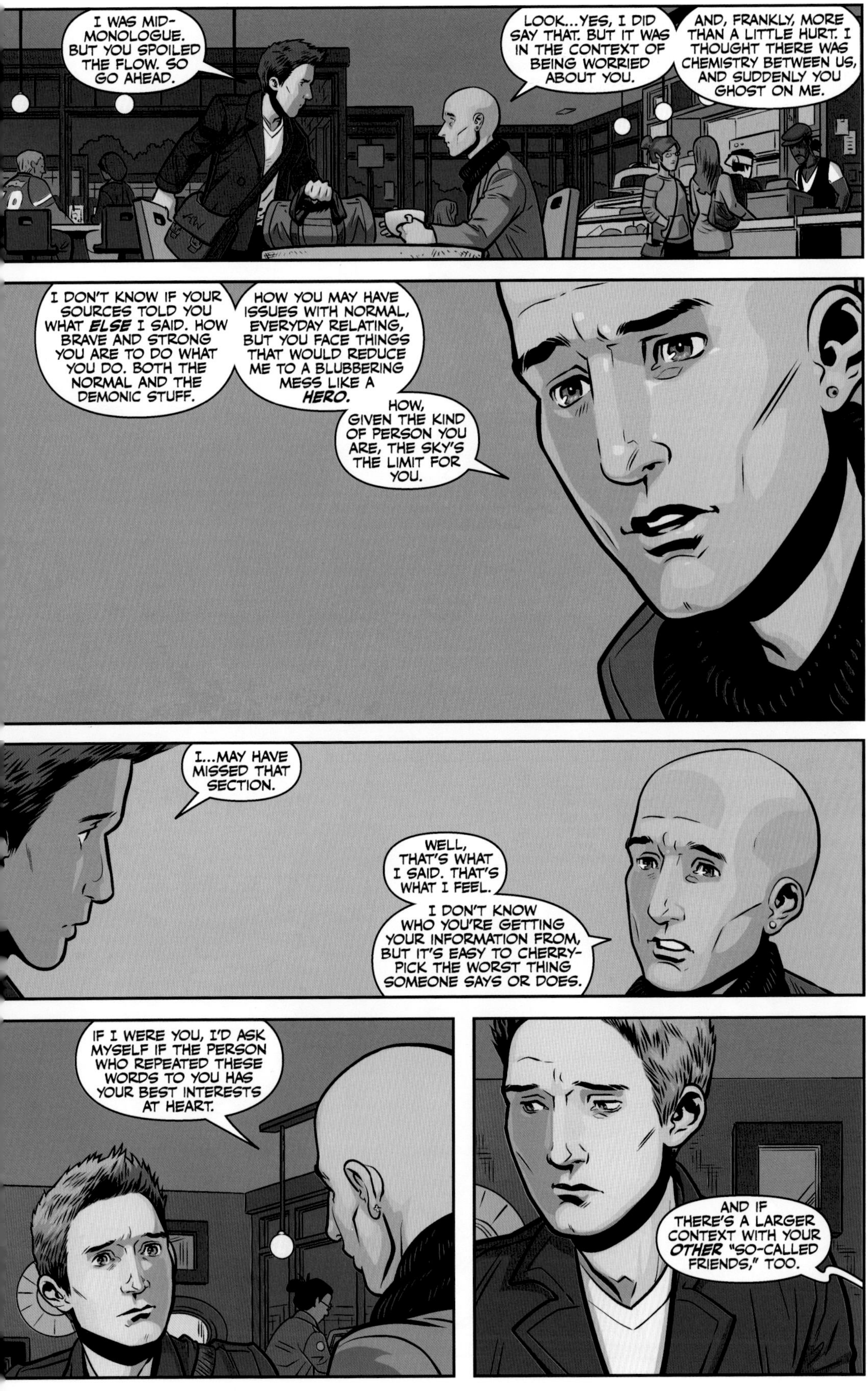
I WAS MID-MONOLOGUE. BUT YOU SPOILED THE FLOW. SO GO AHEAD.
LOOK...YES, I DID SAY THAT. BUT IT WAS IN THE CONTEXT OF BEING WORRIED ABOUT YOU.
AND, FRANKLY, MORE THAN A LITTLE HURT. I THOUGHT THERE WAS CHEMISTRY BETWEEN US, AND SUDDENLY YOU GHOST ON ME.
I DON'T KNOW IF YOUR SOURCES TOLD YOU WHAT *ELSE* I SAID. HOW BRAVE AND STRONG YOU ARE TO DO WHAT YOU DO. BOTH THE NORMAL AND THE DEMONIC STUFF.
HOW YOU MAY HAVE ISSUES WITH NORMAL, EVERYDAY RELATING, BUT YOU FACE THINGS THAT WOULD REDUCE ME TO A BLUBBERING MESS LIKE A ***HERO.***
HOW, GIVEN THE KIND OF PERSON YOU ARE, THE SKY'S THE LIMIT FOR YOU.
I...MAY HAVE MISSED THAT SECTION.
WELL, THAT'S WHAT I SAID. THAT'S WHAT I FEEL.
I DON'T KNOW WHO YOU'RE GETTING YOUR INFORMATION FROM, BUT IT'S EASY TO CHERRY-PICK THE WORST THING SOMEONE SAYS OR DOES.
IF I WERE YOU, I'D ASK MYSELF IF THE PERSON WHO REPEATED THESE WORDS TO YOU HAS YOUR BEST INTERESTS AT HEART.
AND IF THERE'S A LARGER CONTEXT WITH YOUR ***OTHER*** "SO-CALLED FRIENDS," TOO.

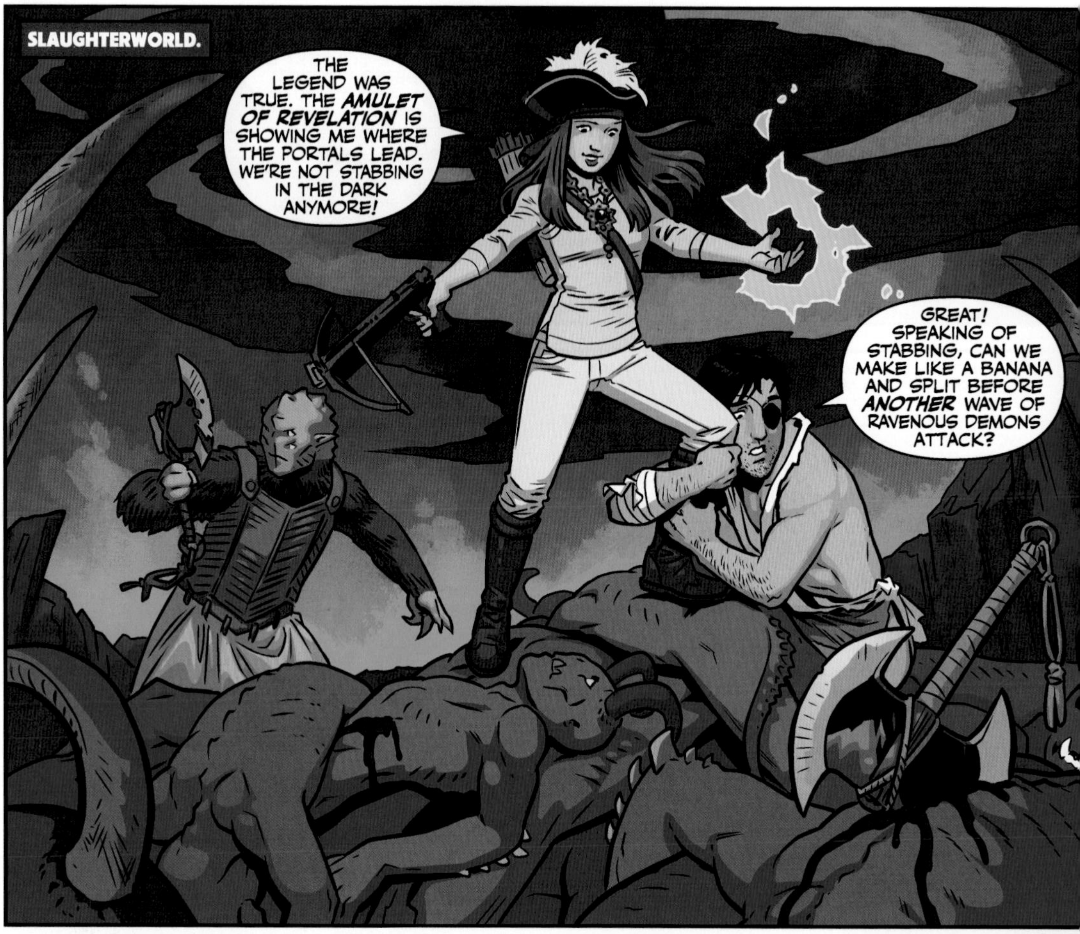
SLAUGHTERWORLD.
THE LEGEND WAS TRUE. THE *AMULET OF REVELATION* IS SHOWING ME WHERE THE PORTALS LEAD. WE'RE NOT STABBING IN THE DARK ANYMORE!
GREAT! SPEAKING OF STABBING, CAN WE MAKE LIKE A BANANA AND SPLIT BEFORE *ANOTHER* WAVE OF RAVENOUS DEMONS ATTACK?

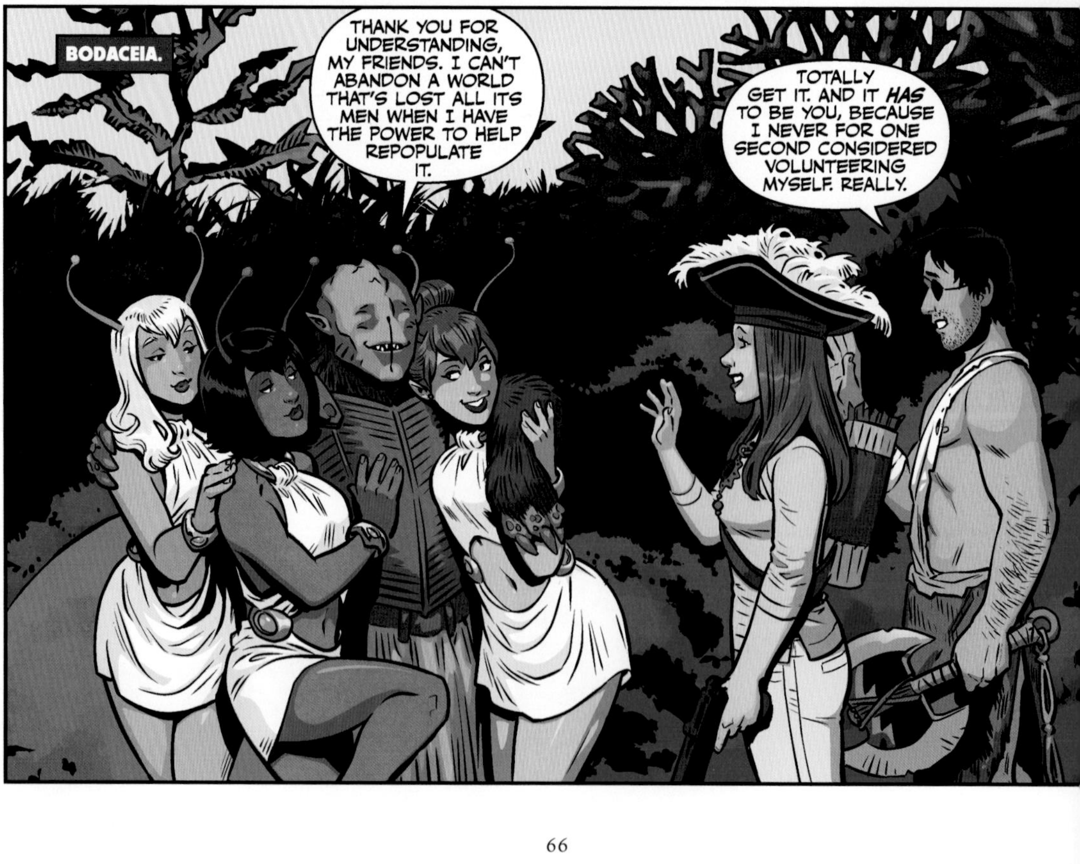
BODACEIA.
THANK YOU FOR UNDERSTANDING, MY FRIENDS. I CAN'T ABANDON A WORLD THAT'S LOST ALL ITS MEN WHEN I HAVE THE POWER TO HELP REPOPULATE IT.
TOTALLY GET IT. AND IT *HAS* TO BE YOU, BECAUSE I NEVER FOR ONE SECOND CONSIDERED VOLUNTEERING MYSELF. REALLY.

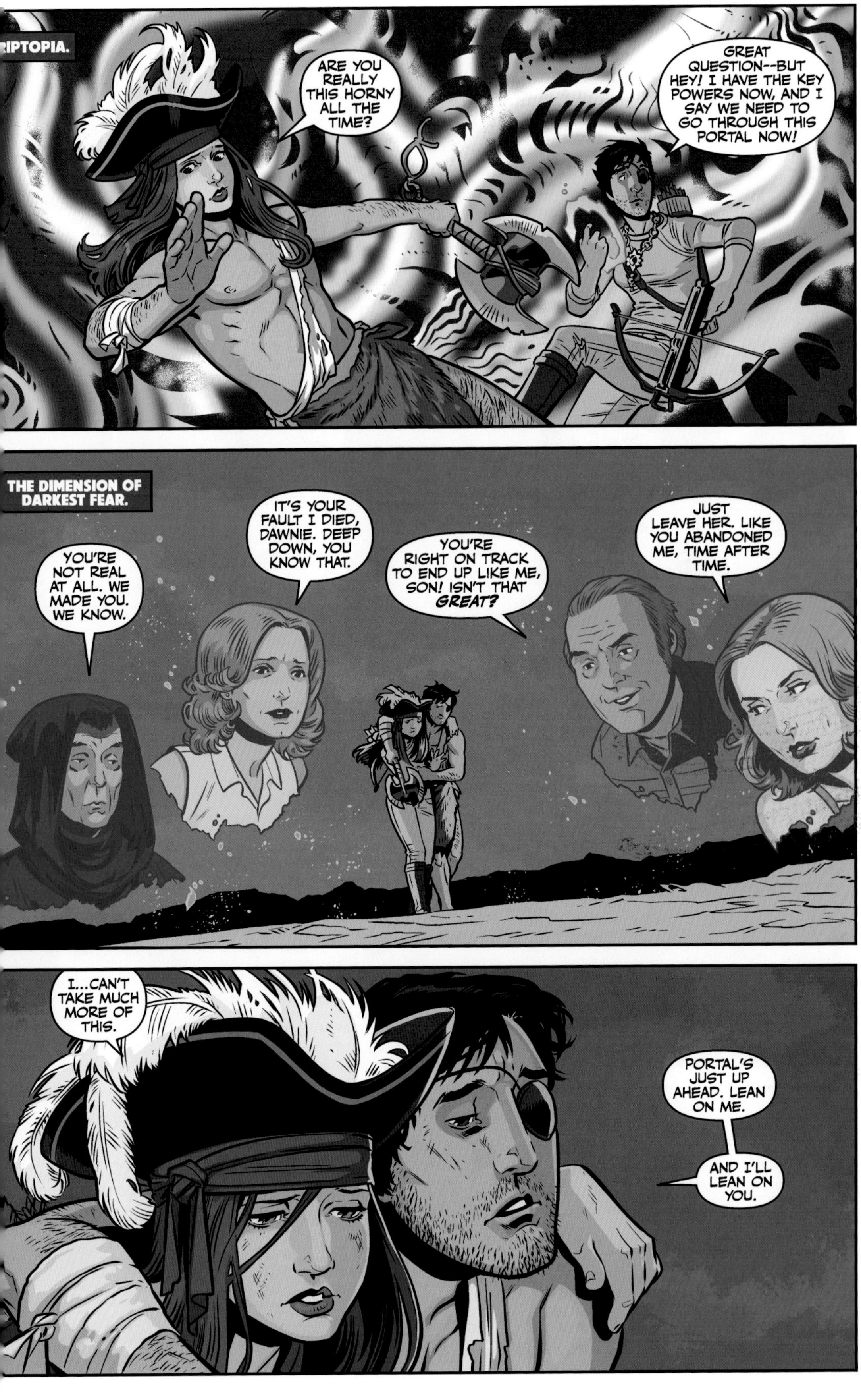
RIPTOPIA.
ARE YOU REALLY THIS HORNY ALL THE TIME?
GREAT QUESTION--BUT HEY! I HAVE THE KEY POWERS NOW, AND I SAY WE NEED TO GO THROUGH THIS PORTAL NOW!
THE DIMENSION OF DARKEST FEAR.
YOU'RE NOT REAL AT ALL. WE MADE YOU. WE KNOW.
IT'S YOUR FAULT I DIED, DAWNIE. DEEP DOWN, YOU KNOW THAT.
YOU'RE RIGHT ON TRACK TO END UP LIKE ME, SON! ISN'T THAT GREAT?
JUST LEAVE HER. LIKE YOU ABANDONED ME, TIME AFTER TIME.
I...CAN'T TAKE MUCH MORE OF THIS.
PORTAL'S JUST UP AHEAD. LEAN ON ME.
AND I'LL LEAN ON YOU.

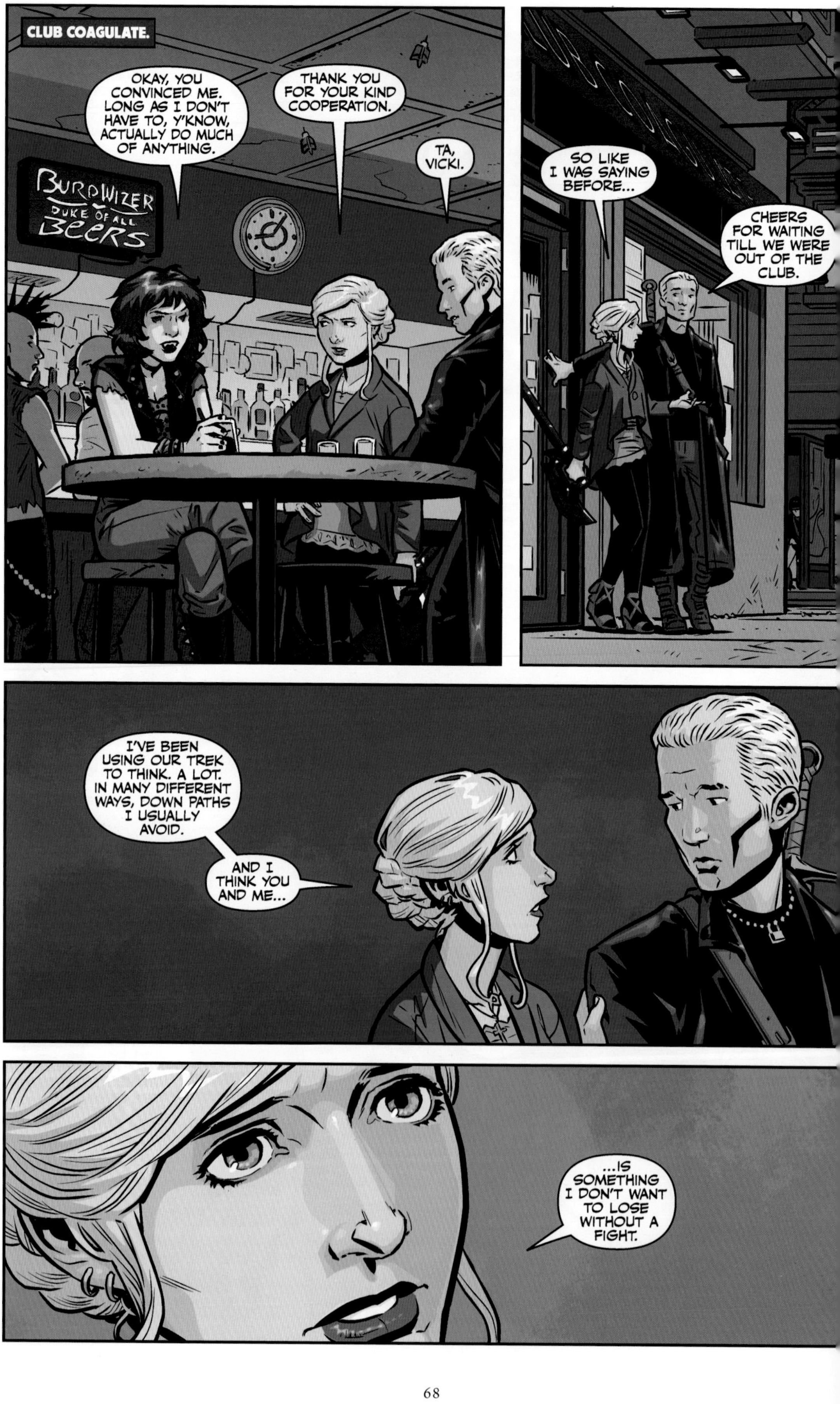
CLUB COAGULATE.
OKAY, YOU CONVINCED ME. LONG AS I DON'T HAVE TO, Y'KNOW, ACTUALLY DO MUCH OF ANYTHING.
THANK YOU FOR YOUR KIND COOPERATION.
TA, VICKI.
BURDWIZER DUKE OF ALL BEERS
SO LIKE I WAS SAYING BEFORE...
CHEERS FOR WAITING TILL WE WERE OUT OF THE CLUB.
I'VE BEEN USING OUR TREK TO THINK. A LOT. IN MANY DIFFERENT WAYS, DOWN PATHS I USUALLY AVOID.
AND I THINK YOU AND ME...
...IS SOMETHING I DON'T WANT TO LOSE WITHOUT A FIGHT.

I'M NOT SAYING WE SHOULD STAY TOGETHER IF WE'RE MISERABLE. I'M NOT SAYING WE SHOULD GET MARRIED, EITHER.

JUST THAT, MAYBE, FOR ONCE, WE SHOULD TRY DOING THE THING THAT SCARES US MOST.

AND IT *DOES* SCARE ME.

BUT I'D LIKE TO TRY TO GET THROUGH THE TOUGH PARTS. BE HONEST WITH EACH OTHER ABOUT THEM, WHICH WE HAVEN'T BEEN. BUT NOT LET THEM OVERSHADOW THE GOOD, EITHER.

IF IT GOES BAD--IF WE GET HURT--YEAH, IT'LL BE OUR FAULT. AND THAT...WILL BE HARD.

BUT THERE COMES A TIME WHEN YOU HAVE TO EITHER FACE YOUR FEARS AND COME OUT STRONGER...OR JUST LET LIFE PASS YOU BY.

SO I WANT TO GIVE IT A TRY. IF YOU DO.

FOR THE LOVE OF GOD SAY SOMETHING.

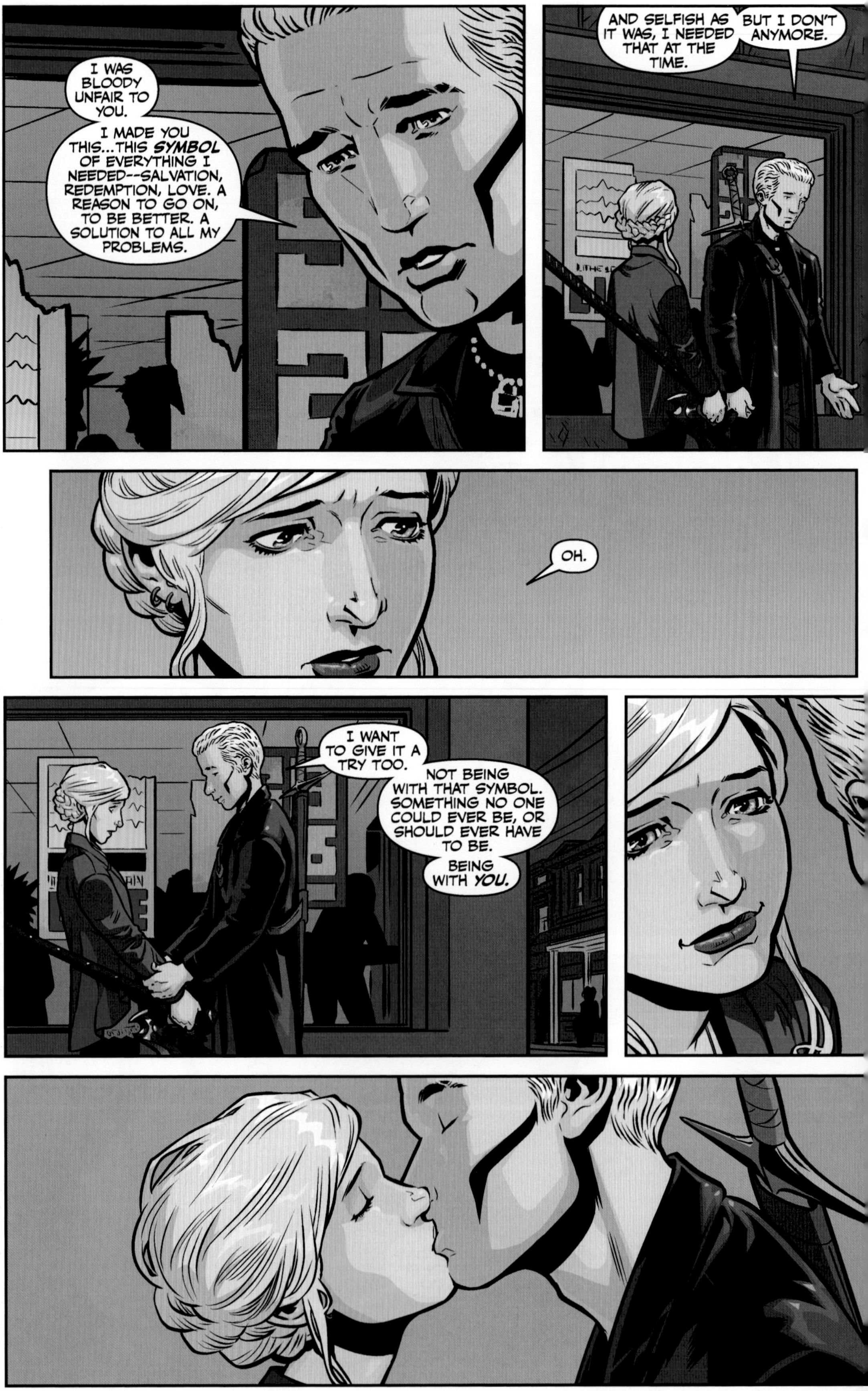
I WAS BLOODY UNFAIR TO YOU.
I MADE YOU THIS...THIS SYMBOL OF EVERYTHING I NEEDED--SALVATION, REDEMPTION, LOVE. A REASON TO GO ON, TO BE BETTER. A SOLUTION TO ALL MY PROBLEMS.
AND SELFISH AS IT WAS, I NEEDED THAT AT THE TIME.
BUT I DON'T ANYMORE.
OH.
I WANT TO GIVE IT A TRY TOO.
NOT BEING WITH THAT SYMBOL. SOMETHING NO ONE COULD EVER BE, OR SHOULD EVER HAVE TO BE.
BEING WITH YOU.

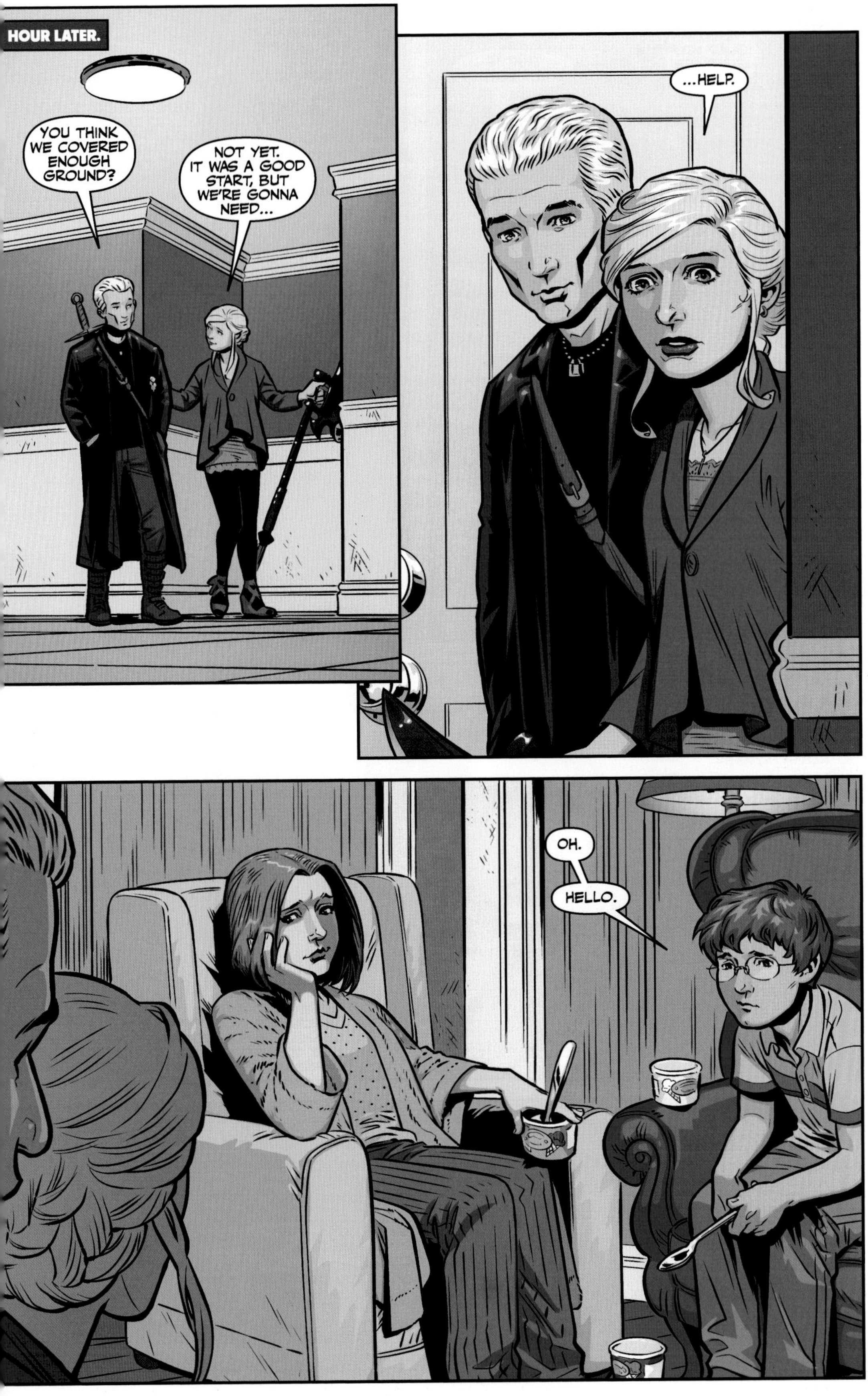
HOUR LATER.
YOU THINK WE COVERED ENOUGH GROUND?
NOT YET. IT WAS A GOOD START, BUT WE'RE GONNA NEED...
...HELP.
OH.
HELLO.

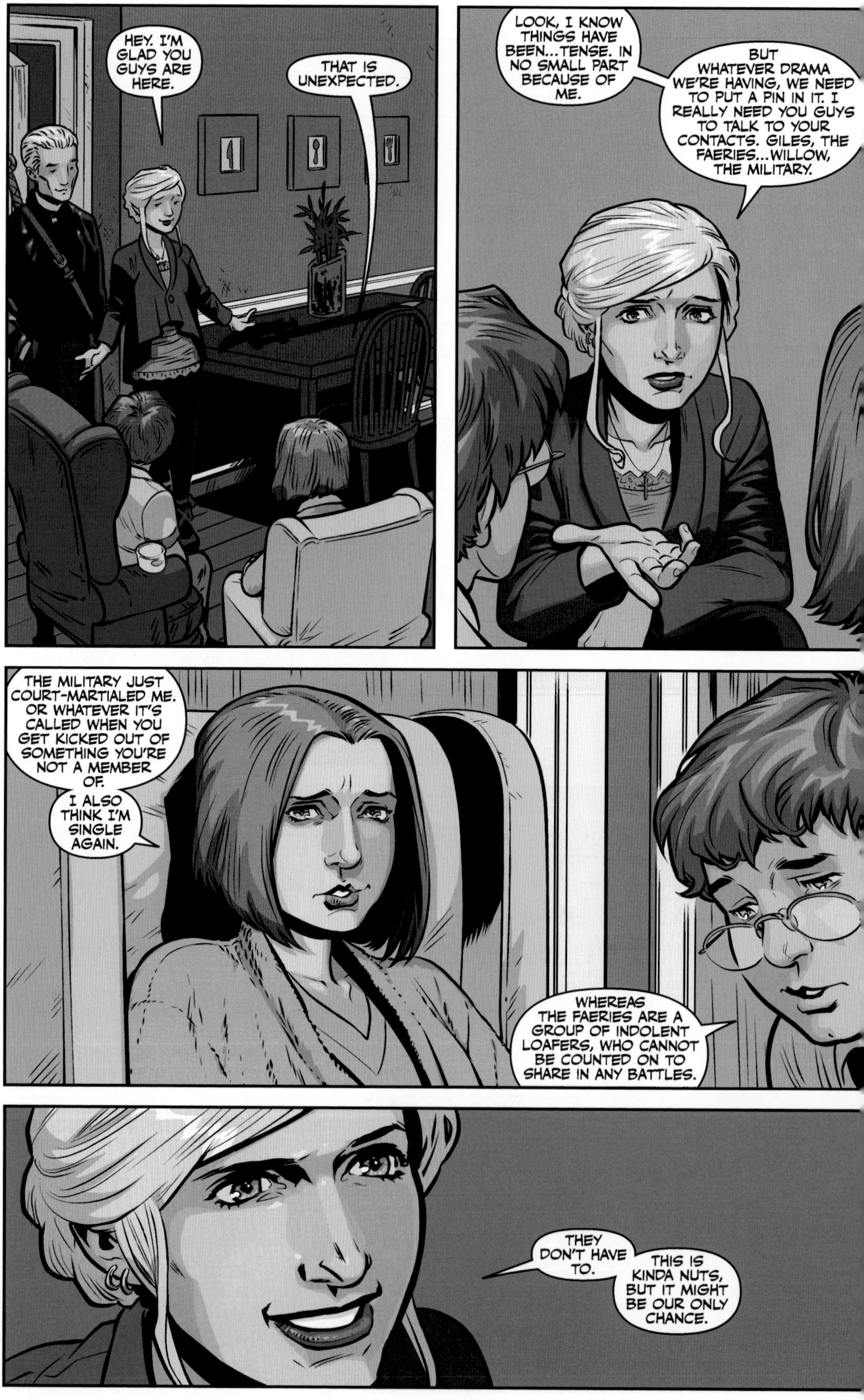
HEY. I'M GLAD YOU GUYS ARE HERE.
THAT IS UNEXPECTED.
LOOK, I KNOW THINGS HAVE BEEN...TENSE. IN NO SMALL PART BECAUSE OF ME.
BUT WHATEVER DRAMA WE'RE HAVING, WE NEED TO PUT A PIN IN IT. I REALLY NEED YOU GUYS TO TALK TO YOUR CONTACTS. GILES, THE FAERIES...WILLOW, THE MILITARY.
THE MILITARY JUST COURT-MARTIALED ME. OR WHATEVER IT'S CALLED WHEN YOU GET KICKED OUT OF SOMETHING YOU'RE NOT A MEMBER OF.
I ALSO THINK I'M SINGLE AGAIN.
WHEREAS THE FAERIES ARE A GROUP OF INDOLENT LOAFERS, WHO CANNOT BE COUNTED ON TO SHARE IN ANY BATTLES.
THEY DON'T HAVE TO.
THIS IS KINDA NUTS, BUT IT MIGHT BE OUR ONLY CHANCE.

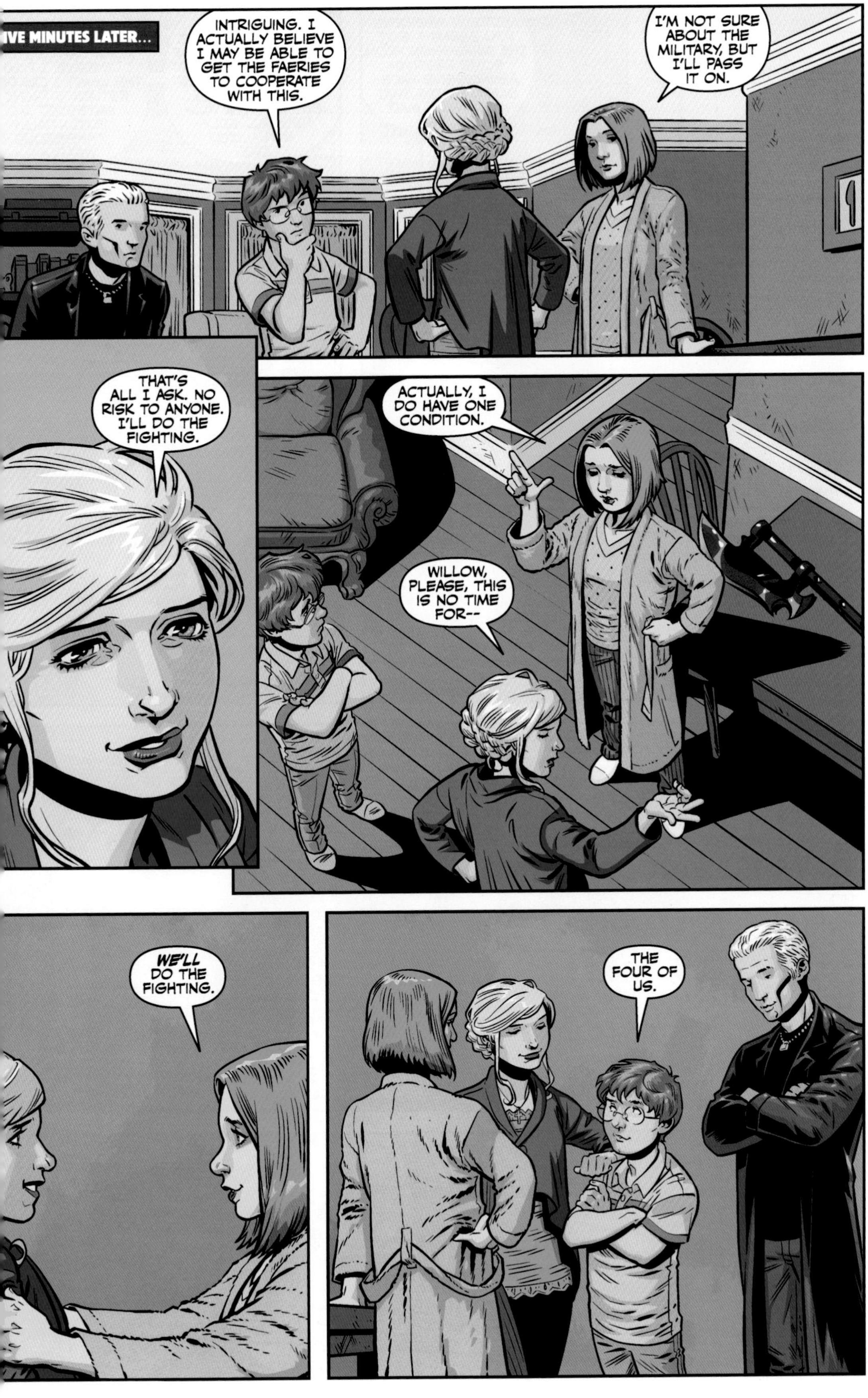
IVE MINUTES LATER...
INTRIGUING. I ACTUALLY BELIEVE I MAY BE ABLE TO GET THE FAERIES TO COOPERATE WITH THIS.
I'M NOT SURE ABOUT THE MILITARY, BUT I'LL PASS IT ON.
THAT'S ALL I ASK. NO RISK TO ANYONE. I'LL DO THE FIGHTING.
ACTUALLY, I DO HAVE ONE CONDITION.
WILLOW, PLEASE, THIS IS NO TIME FOR--
WE'LL DO THE FIGHTING.
THE FOUR OF US.

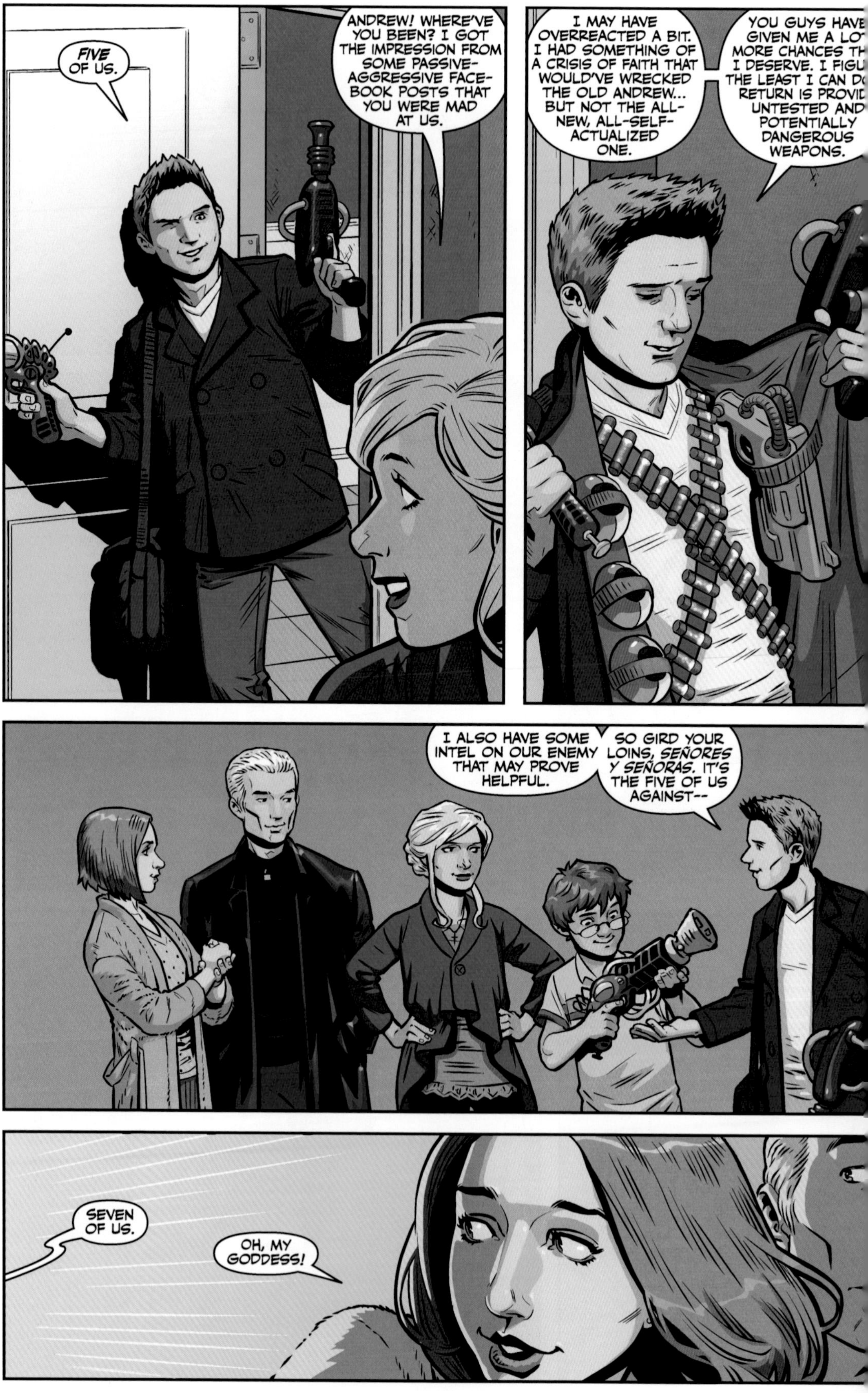
FIVE OF US.
ANDREW! WHERE'VE YOU BEEN? I GOT THE IMPRESSION FROM SOME PASSIVE-AGGRESSIVE FACE-BOOK POSTS THAT YOU WERE MAD AT US.
I MAY HAVE OVERREACTED A BIT. I HAD SOMETHING OF A CRISIS OF FAITH THAT WOULD'VE WRECKED THE OLD ANDREW... BUT NOT THE ALL-NEW, ALL-SELF-ACTUALIZED ONE.
YOU GUYS HAVE GIVEN ME A LO MORE CHANCES T I DESERVE. I FIGU THE LEAST I CAN D RETURN IS PROVI UNTESTED AND POTENTIALLY DANGEROUS WEAPONS.
I ALSO HAVE SOME INTEL ON OUR ENEMY THAT MAY PROVE HELPFUL.
SO GIRD YOUR LOINS, SEÑORES Y SEÑORAS. IT'S THE FIVE OF US AGAINST--
SEVEN OF US.
OH, MY GODDESS!

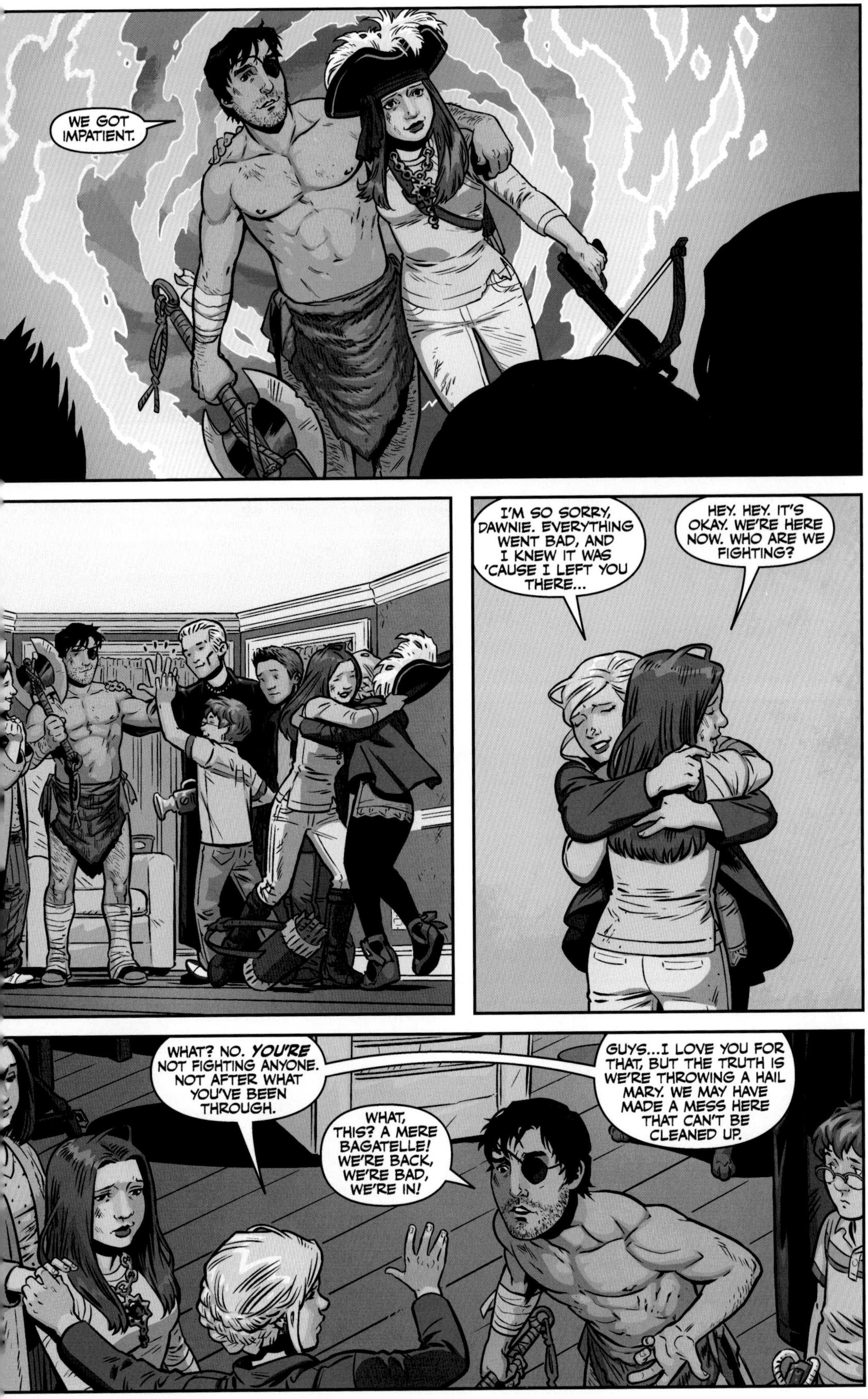
WE GOT IMPATIENT.
I'M SO SORRY, DAWNIE. EVERYTHING WENT BAD, AND I KNEW IT WAS 'CAUSE I LEFT YOU THERE...
HEY. HEY. IT'S OKAY. WE'RE HERE NOW. WHO ARE WE FIGHTING?
WHAT? NO. ***YOU'RE*** NOT FIGHTING ANYONE. NOT AFTER WHAT YOU'VE BEEN THROUGH.
WHAT, THIS? A MERE BAGATELLE! WE'RE BACK, WE'RE BAD, WE'RE IN!
GUYS...I LOVE YOU FOR THAT, BUT THE TRUTH IS WE'RE THROWING A HAIL MARY. WE MAY HAVE MADE A MESS HERE THAT CAN'T BE CLEANED UP.

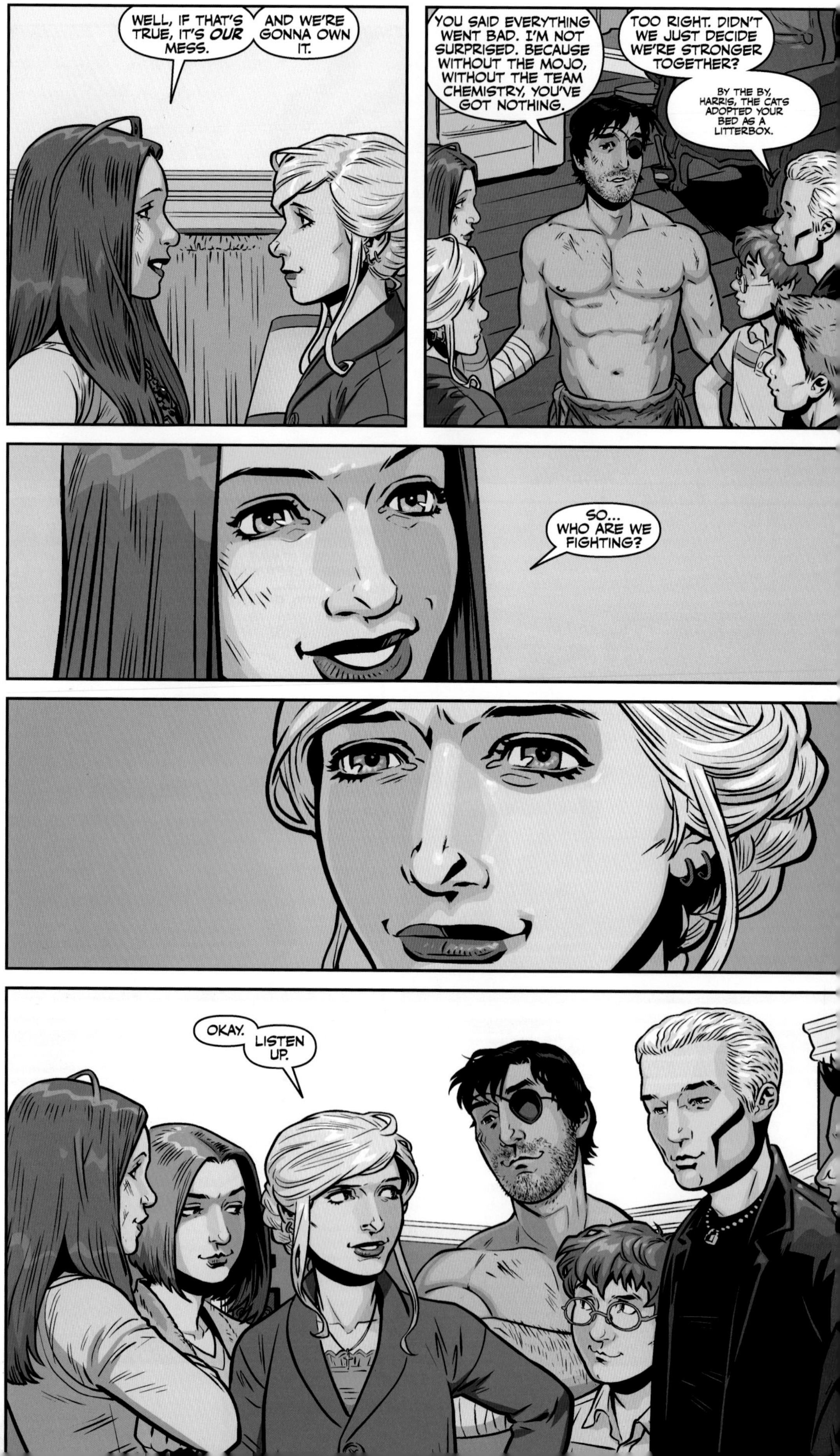

WELL, IF THAT'S TRUE, IT'S *OUR* MESS.
AND WE'RE GONNA OWN IT.
YOU SAID EVERYTHING WENT BAD. I'M NOT SURPRISED. BECAUSE WITHOUT THE MOJO, WITHOUT THE TEAM CHEMISTRY, YOU'VE GOT NOTHING.
TOO RIGHT. DIDN'T WE JUST DECIDE WE'RE STRONGER TOGETHER?
BY THE BY, HARRIS, THE CATS ADOPTED YOUR BED AS A LITTERBOX.
SO... WHO ARE WE FIGHTING?
OKAY.
LISTEN UP.

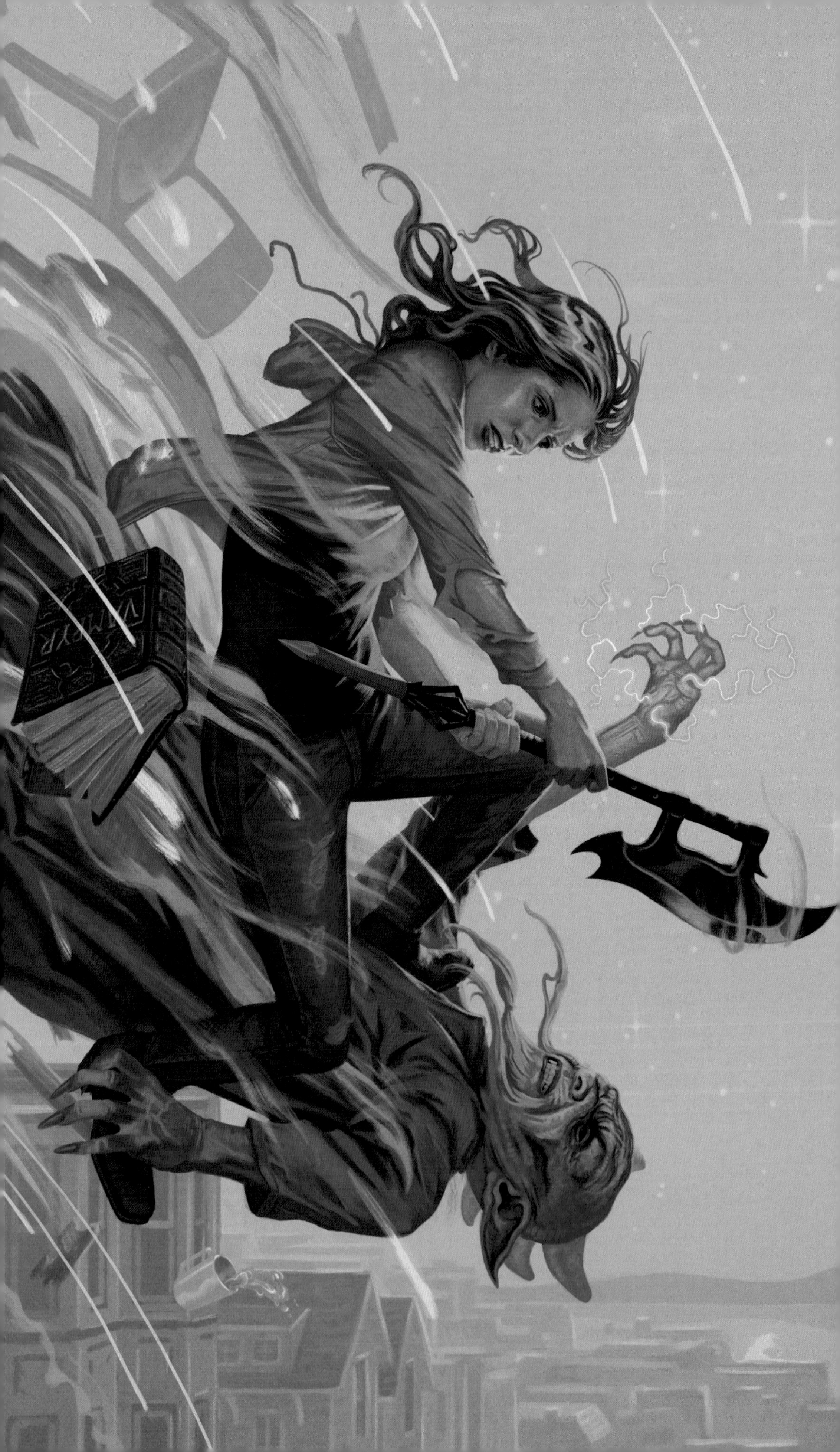
VAMPYR

OWN IT
PART 4: VENGEANCE

THE HELL DIMENSION OF ARASHMAHARR. HOME DIMENSION OF D'HOFFRYN. VENGEANCE, L.L.C., OFFICE PARK.

WHAT IS IT TO BE A VENGEANCE DEMON?

22 DAYS WITHOUT AN APOCALYPSE

POWER.

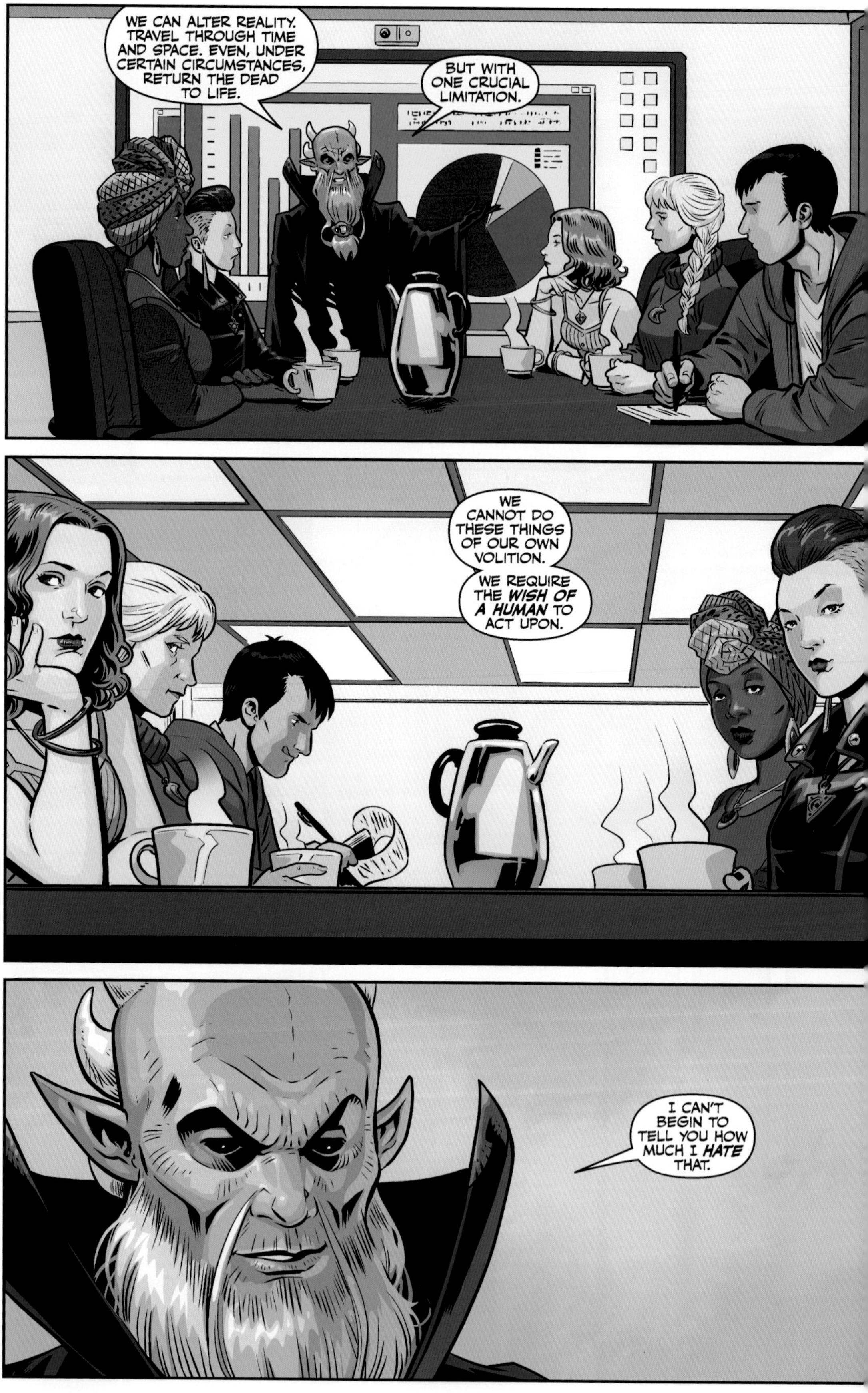
WE CAN ALTER REALITY. TRAVEL THROUGH TIME AND SPACE. EVEN, UNDER CERTAIN CIRCUMSTANCES, RETURN THE DEAD TO LIFE.
BUT WITH ONE CRUCIAL LIMITATION.
WE CANNOT DO THESE THINGS OF OUR OWN VOLITION.
WE REQUIRE THE *WISH OF A HUMAN* TO ACT UPON.
I CAN'T BEGIN TO TELL YOU HOW MUCH I *HATE* THAT.

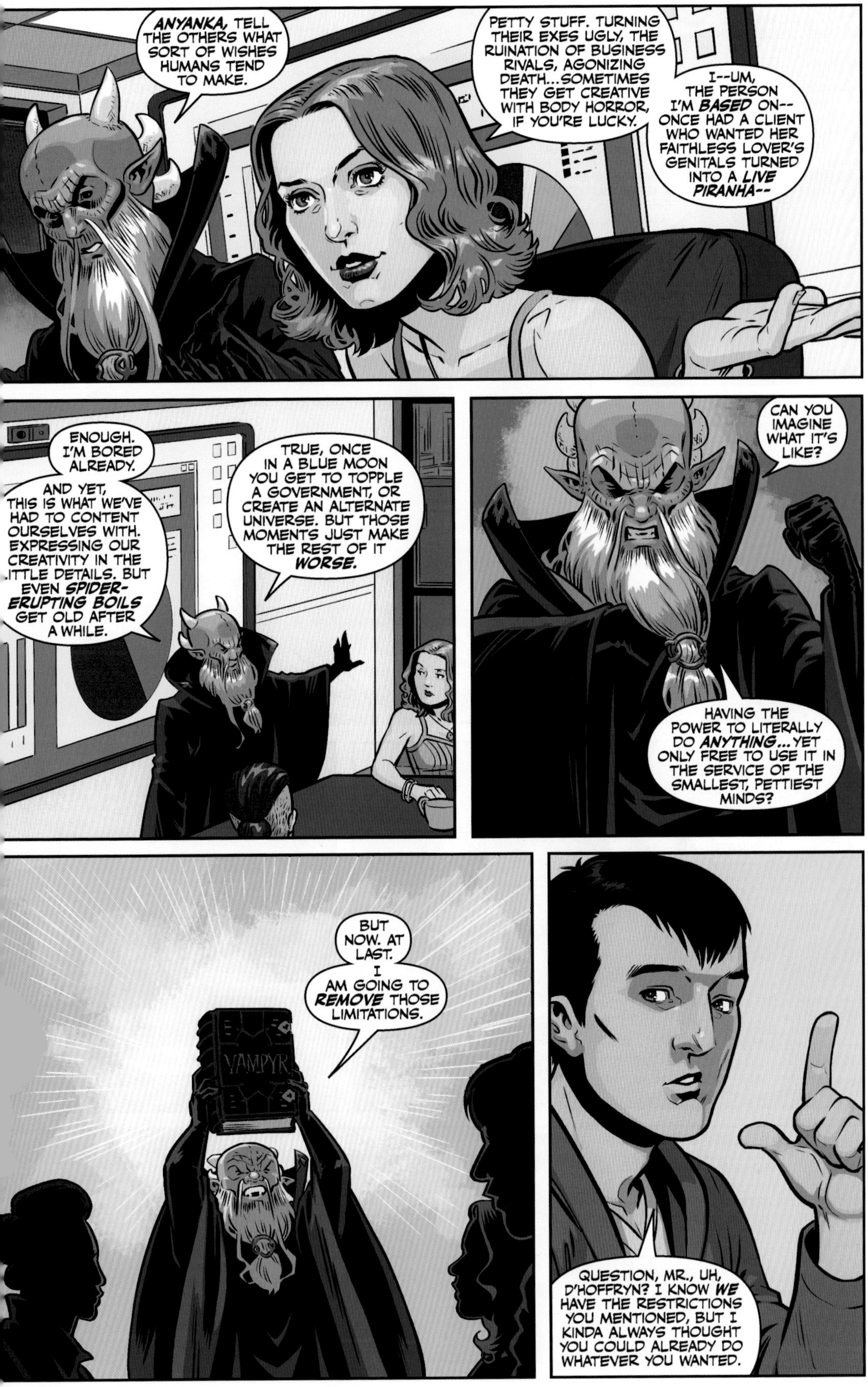
ANYANKA, TELL THE OTHERS WHAT SORT OF WISHES HUMANS TEND TO MAKE.
PETTY STUFF. TURNING THEIR EXES UGLY, THE RUINATION OF BUSINESS RIVALS, AGONIZING DEATH...SOMETIMES THEY GET CREATIVE WITH BODY HORROR, IF YOU'RE LUCKY.
I--UM, THE PERSON I'M BASED ON--ONCE HAD A CLIENT WHO WANTED HER FAITHLESS LOVER'S GENITALS TURNED INTO A LIVE PIRANHA--
ENOUGH. I'M BORED ALREADY.
AND YET, THIS IS WHAT WE'VE HAD TO CONTENT OURSELVES WITH. EXPRESSING OUR CREATIVITY IN THE LITTLE DETAILS. BUT EVEN SPIDER-ERUPTING BOILS GET OLD AFTER A WHILE.
TRUE, ONCE IN A BLUE MOON YOU GET TO TOPPLE A GOVERNMENT, OR CREATE AN ALTERNATE UNIVERSE. BUT THOSE MOMENTS JUST MAKE THE REST OF IT WORSE.
CAN YOU IMAGINE WHAT IT'S LIKE?
HAVING THE POWER TO LITERALLY DO ANYTHING...YET ONLY FREE TO USE IT IN THE SERVICE OF THE SMALLEST, PETTIEST MINDS?
BUT NOW. AT LAST.
I AM GOING TO REMOVE THOSE LIMITATIONS.
VAMPYR
QUESTION, MR., UH, D'HOFFRYN? I KNOW WE HAVE THE RESTRICTIONS YOU MENTIONED, BUT I KINDA ALWAYS THOUGHT YOU COULD ALREADY DO WHATEVER YOU WANTED.

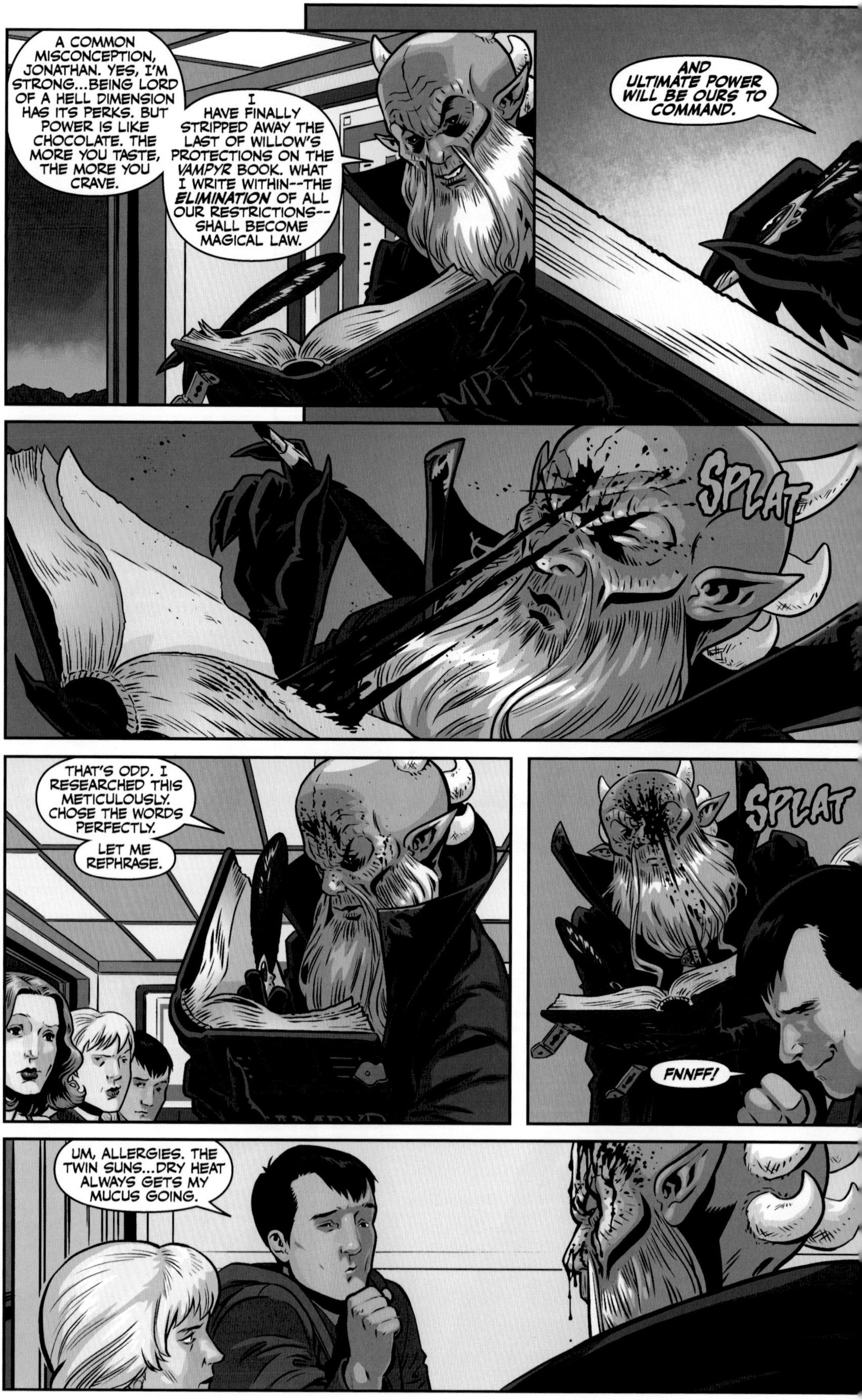
A COMMON MISCONCEPTION, JONATHAN. YES, I'M STRONG...BEING LORD OF A HELL DIMENSION HAS ITS PERKS. BUT POWER IS LIKE CHOCOLATE. THE MORE YOU TASTE, THE MORE YOU CRAVE.
I HAVE FINALLY STRIPPED AWAY THE LAST OF WILLOW'S PROTECTIONS ON THE *VAMPYR* BOOK. WHAT I WRITE WITHIN--THE ***ELIMINATION*** OF ALL OUR RESTRICTIONS--SHALL BECOME MAGICAL LAW.
AND ULTIMATE POWER WILL BE OURS TO COMMAND.
SPLAT
THAT'S ODD. I RESEARCHED THIS METICULOUSLY. CHOSE THE WORDS PERFECTLY.
LET ME REPHRASE.
SPLAT
FNNFF!
UM, ALLERGIES. THE TWIN SUNS...DRY HEAT ALWAYS GETS MY MUCUS GOING.

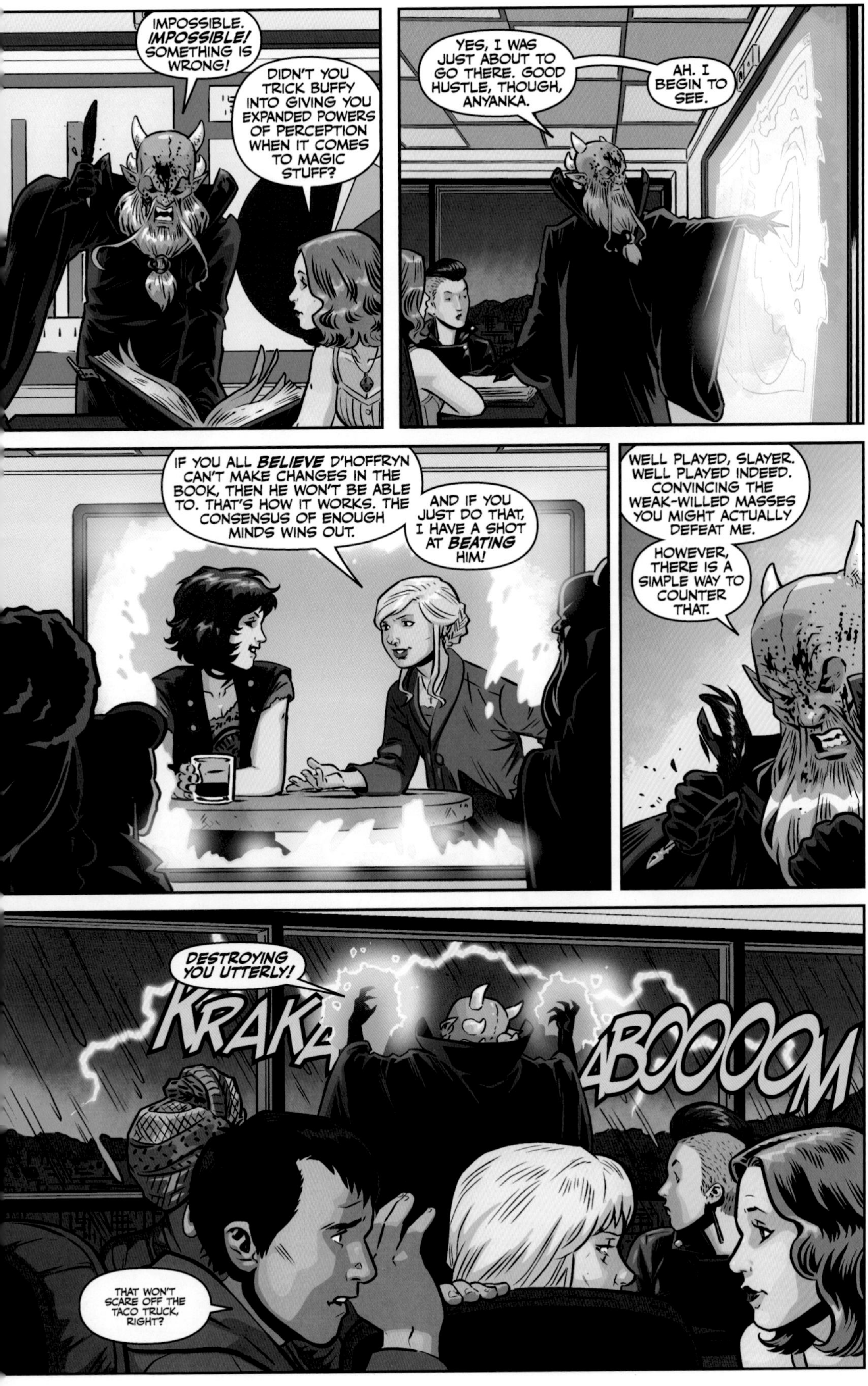
IMPOSSIBLE. *IMPOSSIBLE!* SOMETHING IS WRONG!
DIDN'T YOU TRICK BUFFY INTO GIVING YOU EXPANDED POWERS OF PERCEPTION WHEN IT COMES TO MAGIC STUFF?
YES, I WAS JUST ABOUT TO GO THERE. GOOD HUSTLE, THOUGH, ANYANKA.
AH. I BEGIN TO SEE.
IF YOU ALL *BELIEVE* D'HOFFRYN CAN'T MAKE CHANGES IN THE BOOK, THEN HE WON'T BE ABLE TO. THAT'S HOW IT WORKS. THE CONSENSUS OF ENOUGH MINDS WINS OUT.
AND IF YOU JUST DO THAT, I HAVE A SHOT AT *BEATING* HIM!
WELL PLAYED, SLAYER. WELL PLAYED INDEED. CONVINCING THE WEAK-WILLED MASSES YOU MIGHT ACTUALLY DEFEAT ME.
HOWEVER, THERE IS A SIMPLE WAY TO COUNTER THAT.
DESTROYING YOU UTTERLY!
KRAKABOOOOM
THAT WON'T SCARE OFF THE TACO TRUCK, RIGHT?

BUFFY, WILLOW, AND DAWN'S APARTMENT.

OH, MAN, *CLEAN CLOTHES!* I CAN STILL SMELL THE FABRIC SOFTENER! THIS IS BLISS.

DOUBLE BLISS FOR ME. THAT LOINCLOTH CHAFED IN PLACES THAT REALLY SHOULD NOT BE CHAFED.

XANDER WAS TELLING US SOME OF HOW YOU GOT BACK. I SHOULD BE MAD AT YOU FOR TAKING THE RISK, BUT I'M JUST SO HAPPY YOU'RE HERE, I CAN'T SUMMON THE FROWNIES.

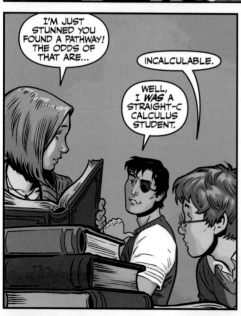

I'M JUST STUNNED YOU FOUND A PATHWAY! THE ODDS OF THAT ARE...

INCALCULABLE.

WELL, I *WAS* A STRAIGHT-C CALCULUS STUDENT.

TRUTH IS, IT WAS DAWN. REALLY EMBRACING HER KEY MOJO.

YEAH...ONCE I STOPPED STRESSING ABOUT IT AND JUST WENT WITH IT, IT'S AMAZING WHAT I COULD DO. I'M GONNA MISS THOSE POWERS.

BUT I MISSED YOU GUYS MORE.

WISH THOSE KEY POWERS HAD STUCK AROUND, THOUGH...THEY WOULD'VE COME IN HANDY AGAINST D'HOFFRYN.

NO FEAR, LITTLE BIT. WE'LL HANDLE THAT END.

I BROUGHT SOME EXPERIMENTAL WEAPONS. ENERGY DISRUPTORS, FREQUENCY JAMMERS...ATTACKING MAGIC WITH SCIENCE, DON'TCHA KNOW.

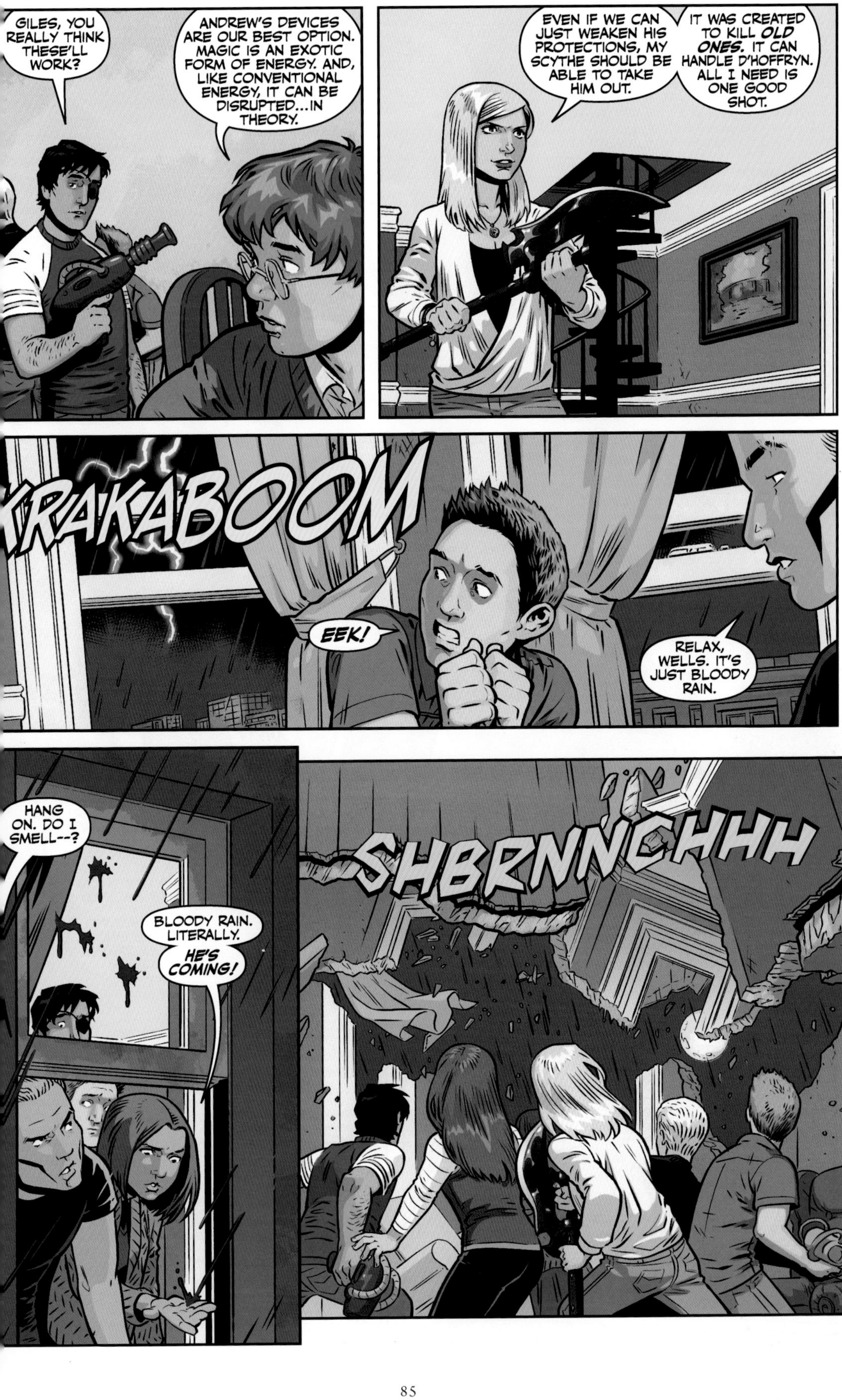
GILES, YOU REALLY THINK THESE'LL WORK?
ANDREW'S DEVICES ARE OUR BEST OPTION. MAGIC IS AN EXOTIC FORM OF ENERGY. AND, LIKE CONVENTIONAL ENERGY, IT CAN BE DISRUPTED...IN THEORY.
EVEN IF WE CAN JUST WEAKEN HIS PROTECTIONS, MY SCYTHE SHOULD BE ABLE TO TAKE HIM OUT.
IT WAS CREATED TO KILL *OLD ONES.* IT CAN HANDLE D'HOFFRYN. ALL I NEED IS ONE GOOD SHOT.
KRAKABOOM
EEK!
RELAX, WELLS. IT'S JUST BLOODY RAIN.
HANG ON. DO I SMELL--?
BLOODY RAIN. LITERALLY. *HE'S COMING!*
SHBRNNCHHH

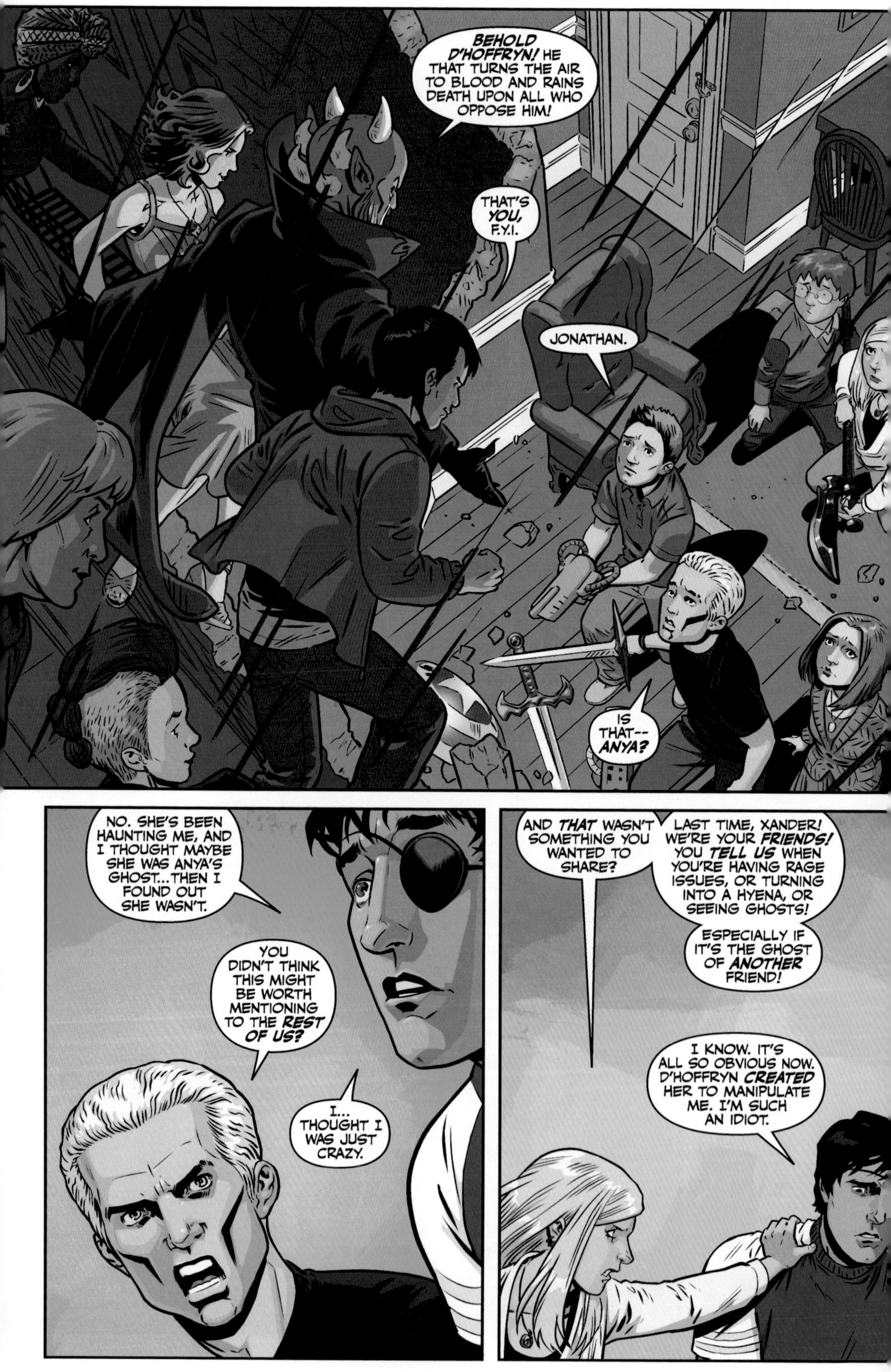

BEHOLD D'HOFFRYN! HE THAT TURNS THE AIR TO BLOOD AND RAINS DEATH UPON ALL WHO OPPOSE HIM!
THAT'S YOU, F.Y.I.
JONATHAN.
IS THAT-- ANYA?
NO. SHE'S BEEN HAUNTING ME, AND I THOUGHT MAYBE SHE WAS ANYA'S GHOST...THEN I FOUND OUT SHE WASN'T.
YOU DIDN'T THINK THIS MIGHT BE WORTH MENTIONING TO THE REST OF US?
I... THOUGHT I WAS JUST CRAZY.
AND THAT WASN'T SOMETHING YOU WANTED TO SHARE?
LAST TIME, XANDER! WE'RE YOUR FRIENDS! YOU TELL US WHEN YOU'RE HAVING RAGE ISSUES, OR TURNING INTO A HYENA, OR SEEING GHOSTS!
ESPECIALLY IF IT'S THE GHOST OF ANOTHER FRIEND!
I KNOW. IT'S ALL SO OBVIOUS NOW. D'HOFFRYN CREATED HER TO MANIPULATE ME. I'M SUCH AN IDIOT.

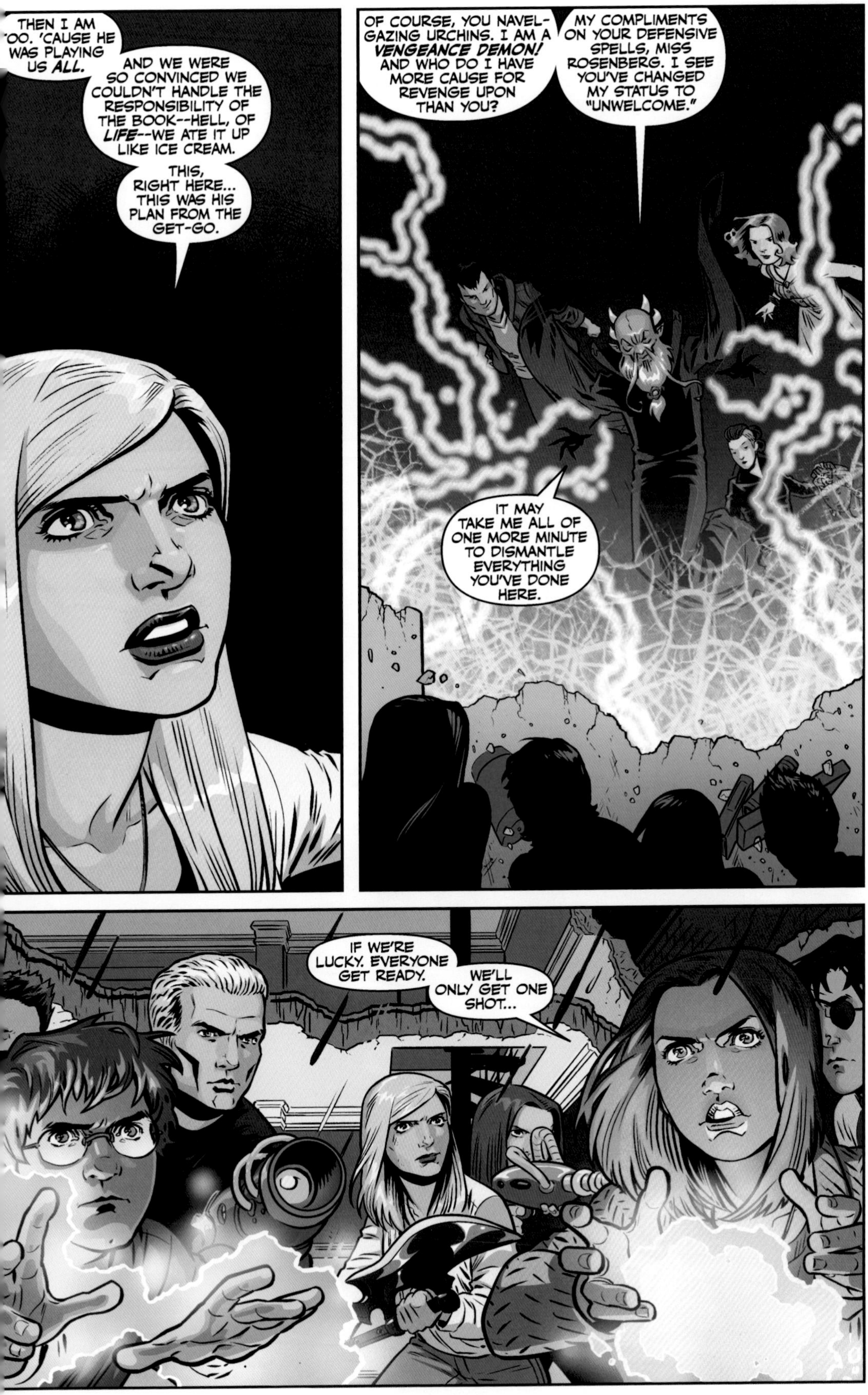
THEN I AM 'OO. 'CAUSE HE WAS PLAYING US *ALL*.
AND WE WERE SO CONVINCED WE COULDN'T HANDLE THE RESPONSIBILITY OF THE BOOK--HELL, OF *LIFE*--WE ATE IT UP LIKE ICE CREAM.
THIS, RIGHT HERE... THIS WAS HIS PLAN FROM THE GET-GO.
OF COURSE, YOU NAVEL-GAZING URCHINS. I AM A *VENGEANCE DEMON!* AND WHO DO I HAVE MORE CAUSE FOR REVENGE UPON THAN YOU?
MY COMPLIMENTS ON YOUR DEFENSIVE SPELLS, MISS ROSENBERG. I SEE YOU'VE CHANGED MY STATUS TO "UNWELCOME."
IT MAY TAKE ME ALL OF ONE MORE MINUTE TO DISMANTLE EVERYTHING YOU'VE DONE HERE.
IF WE'RE LUCKY. EVERYONE GET READY.
WE'LL ONLY GET ONE SHOT...

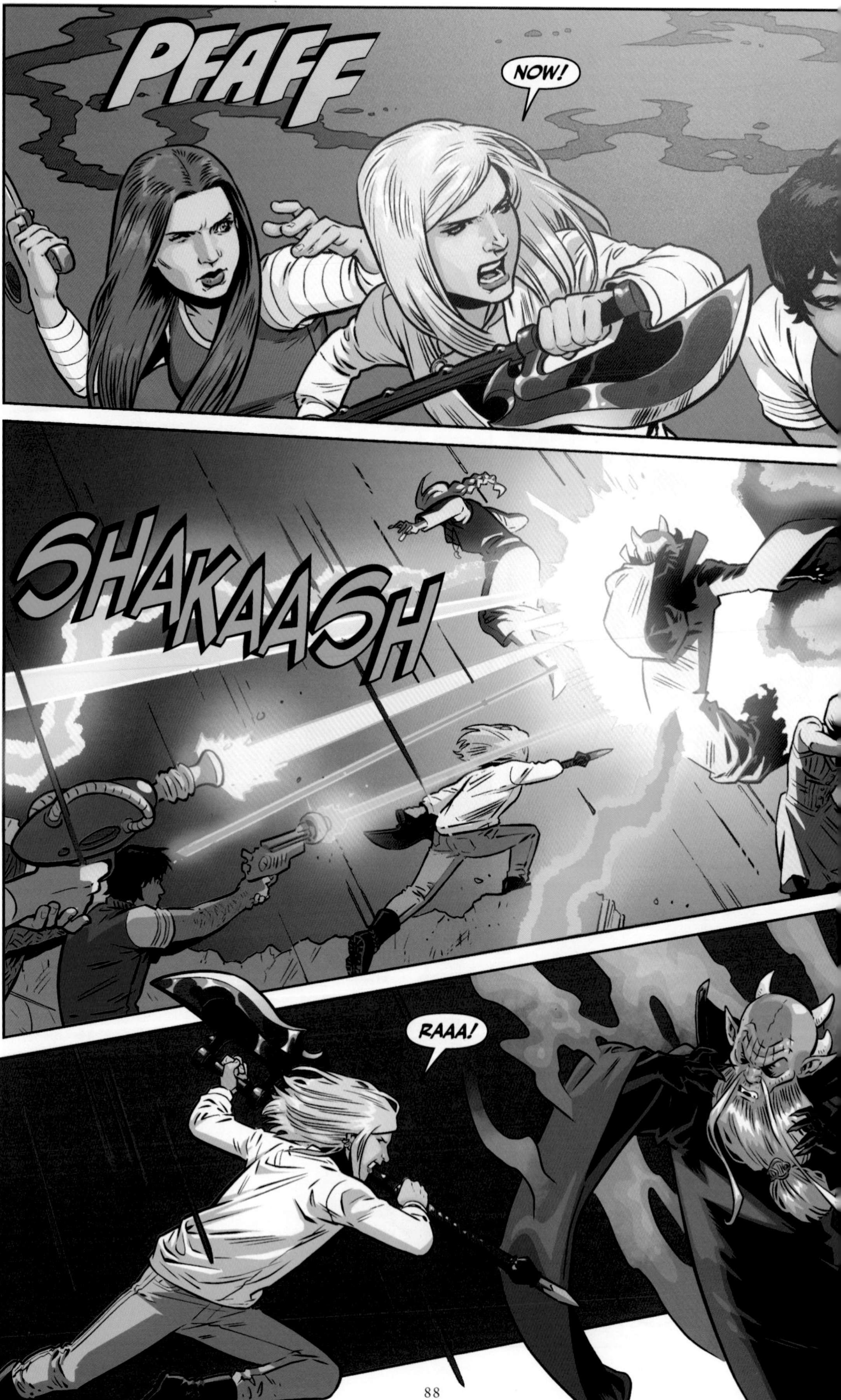
PFAFF
NOW!
SHAKAASH
RAAA!

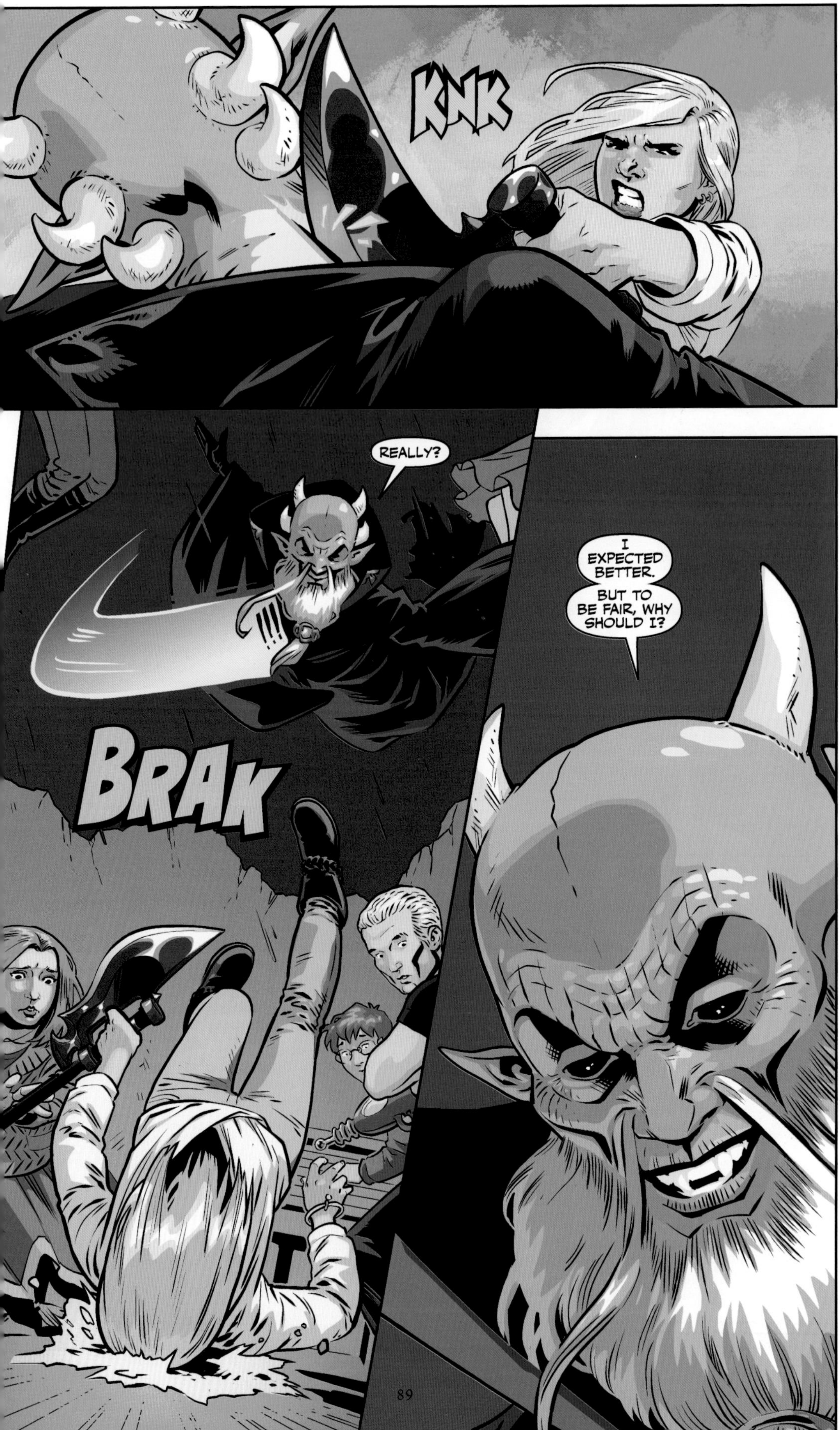
KNK
REALLY?
BRAK
I EXPECTED BETTER.
BUT TO BE FAIR, WHY SHOULD I?

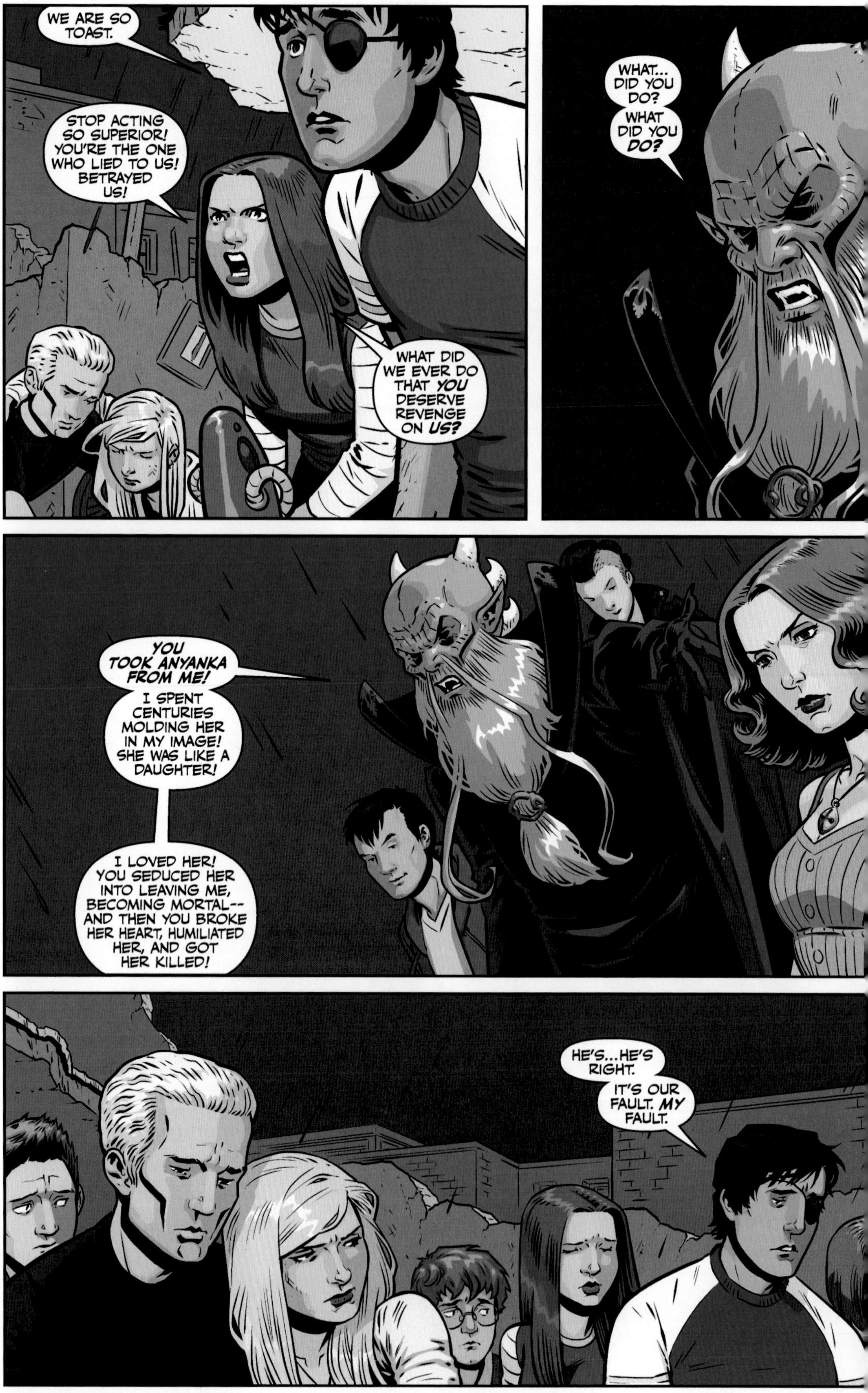

WE ARE SO TOAST.
STOP ACTING SO SUPERIOR! YOU'RE THE ONE WHO LIED TO US! BETRAYED US!
WHAT DID WE EVER DO THAT *YOU* DESERVE REVENGE ON *US?*
WHAT... DID YOU DO?
WHAT DID YOU *DO?*
YOU TOOK ANYANKA FROM ME!
I SPENT CENTURIES MOLDING HER IN MY IMAGE! SHE WAS LIKE A DAUGHTER!
I LOVED HER! YOU SEDUCED HER INTO LEAVING ME, BECOMING MORTAL-- AND THEN YOU BROKE HER HEART, HUMILIATED HER, AND GOT HER KILLED!
HE'S...HE'S RIGHT.
IT'S OUR FAULT. *MY* FAULT.

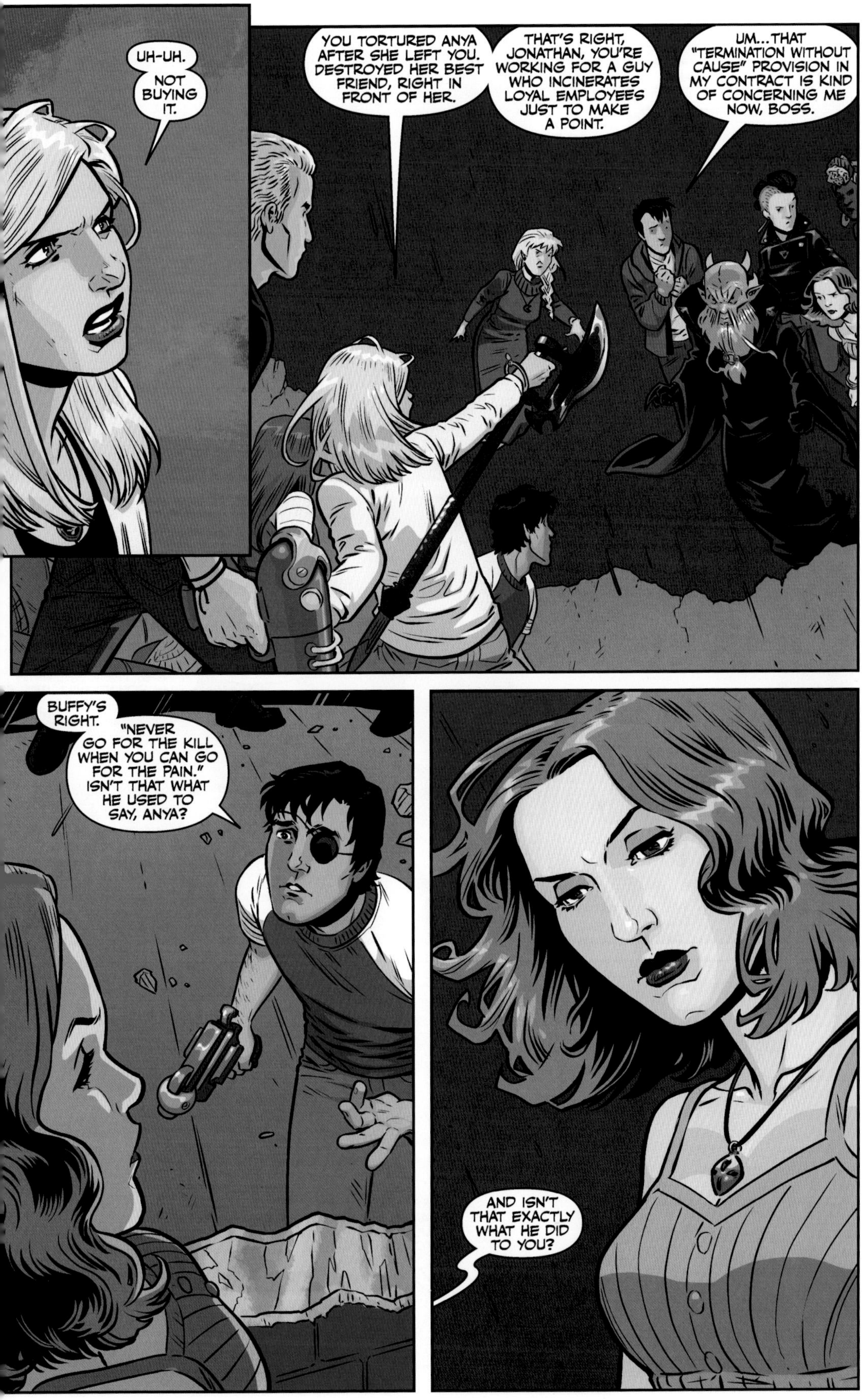
UH-UH.
NOT BUYING IT.
YOU TORTURED ANYA AFTER SHE LEFT YOU. DESTROYED HER BEST FRIEND, RIGHT IN FRONT OF HER.
THAT'S RIGHT, JONATHAN, YOU'RE WORKING FOR A GUY WHO INCINERATES LOYAL EMPLOYEES JUST TO MAKE A POINT.
UM...THAT "TERMINATION WITHOUT CAUSE" PROVISION IN MY CONTRACT IS KIND OF CONCERNING ME NOW, BOSS.
BUFFY'S RIGHT.
"NEVER GO FOR THE KILL WHEN YOU CAN GO FOR THE PAIN." ISN'T THAT WHAT HE USED TO SAY, ANYA?
AND ISN'T THAT EXACTLY WHAT HE DID TO YOU?

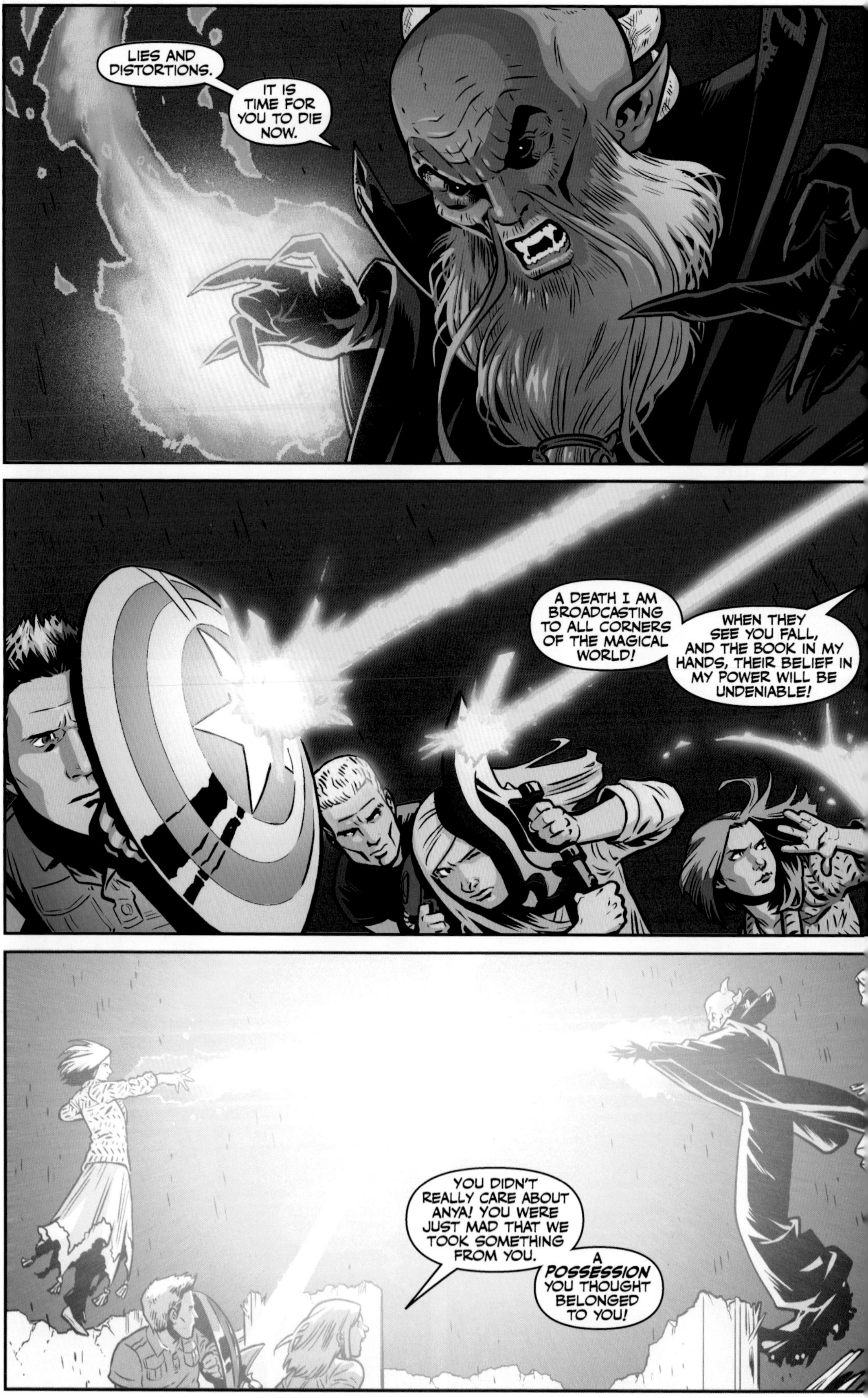
LIES AND DISTORTIONS.
IT IS TIME FOR YOU TO DIE NOW.
A DEATH I AM BROADCASTING TO ALL CORNERS OF THE MAGICAL WORLD!
WHEN THEY SEE YOU FALL, AND THE BOOK IN MY HANDS, THEIR BELIEF IN MY POWER WILL BE UNDENIABLE!
YOU DIDN'T REALLY CARE ABOUT ANYA! YOU WERE JUST MAD THAT WE TOOK SOMETHING FROM YOU.
A *POSSESSION* YOU THOUGHT BELONGED TO YOU!

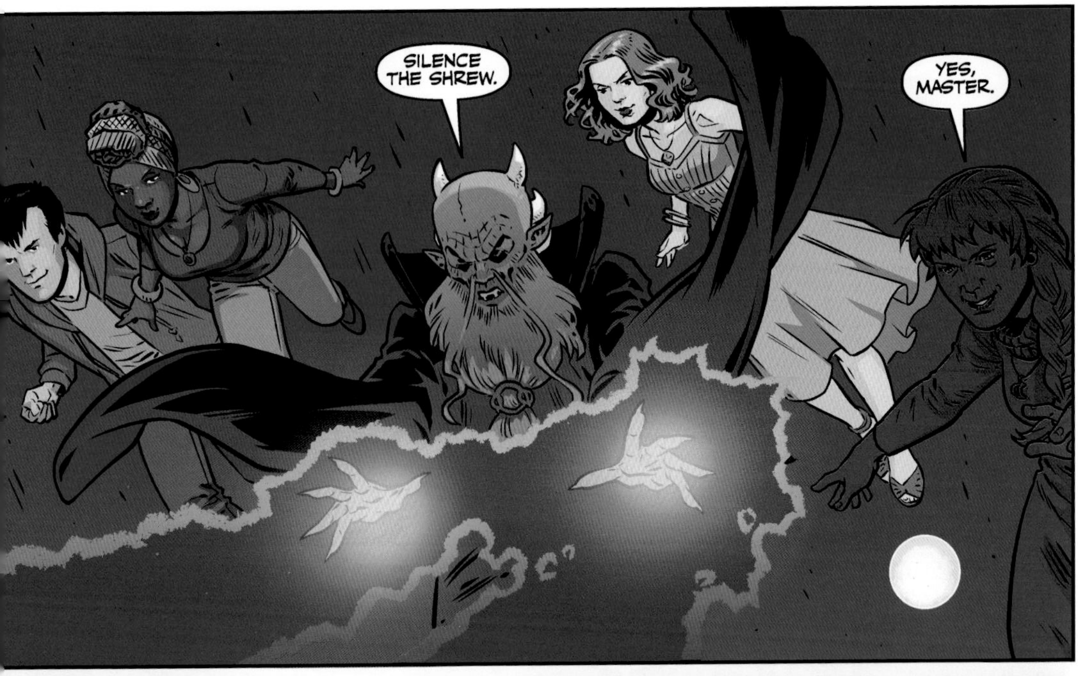
SILENCE THE SHREW.
YES, MASTER.

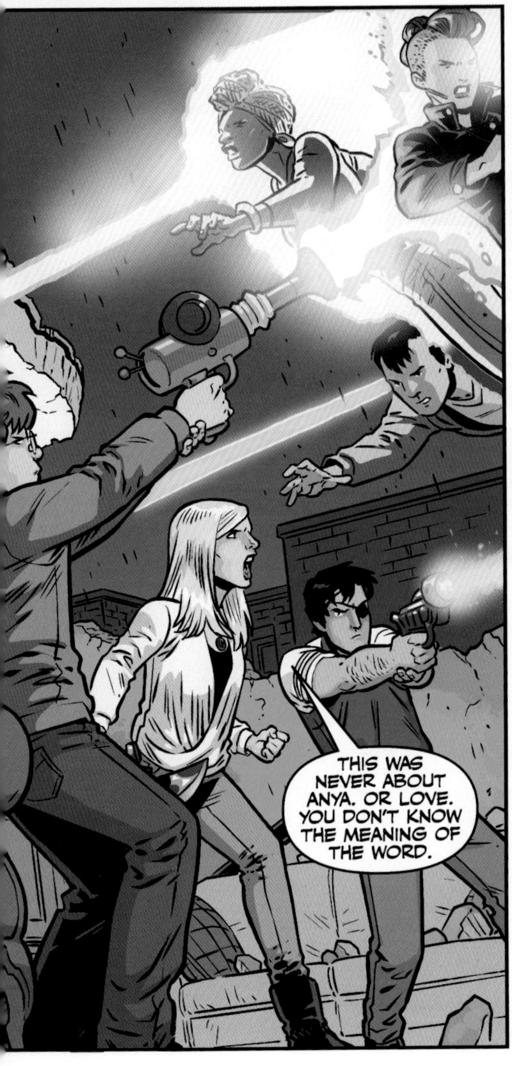
THIS WAS NEVER ABOUT ANYA. OR LOVE. YOU DON'T KNOW THE MEANING OF THE WORD.

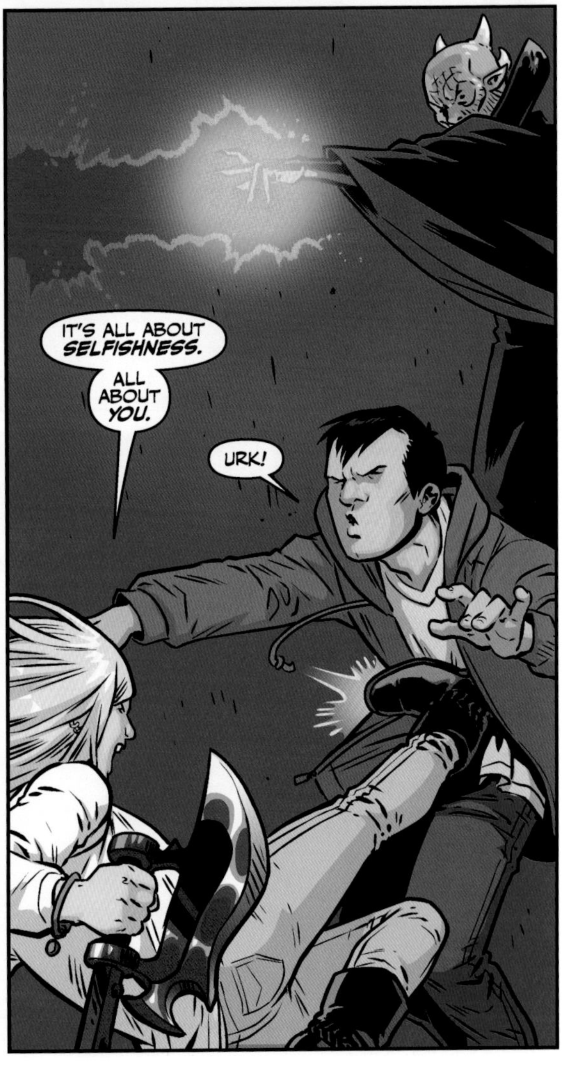
IT'S ALL ABOUT *SELFISHNESS.*
ALL ABOUT *YOU.*
URK!

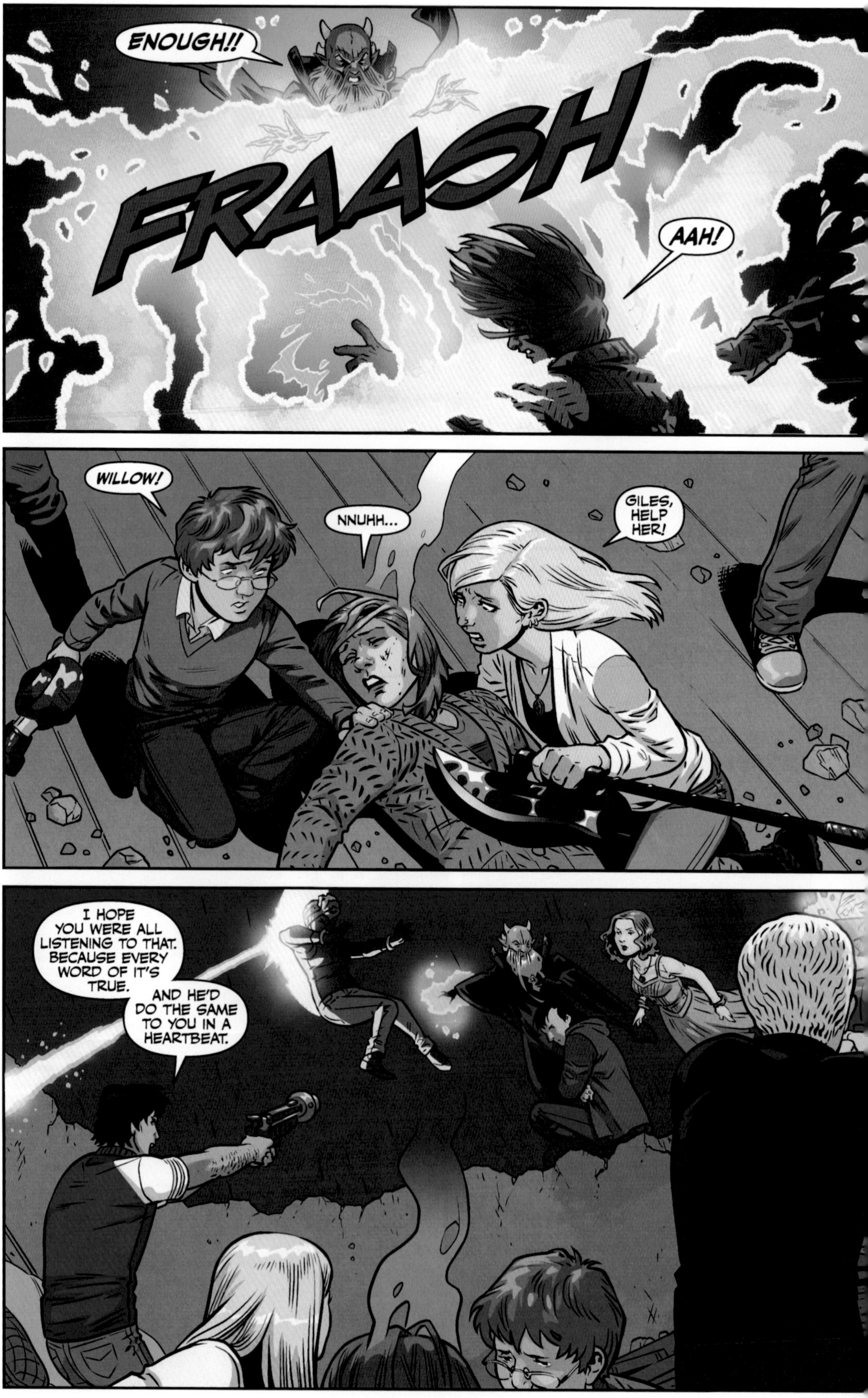
ENOUGH!!
FRAASH
AAH!
WILLOW!
NNUHH...
GILES, HELP HER!
I HOPE YOU WERE ALL LISTENING TO THAT. BECAUSE EVERY WORD OF IT'S TRUE.
AND HE'D DO THE SAME TO YOU IN A HEARTBEAT.

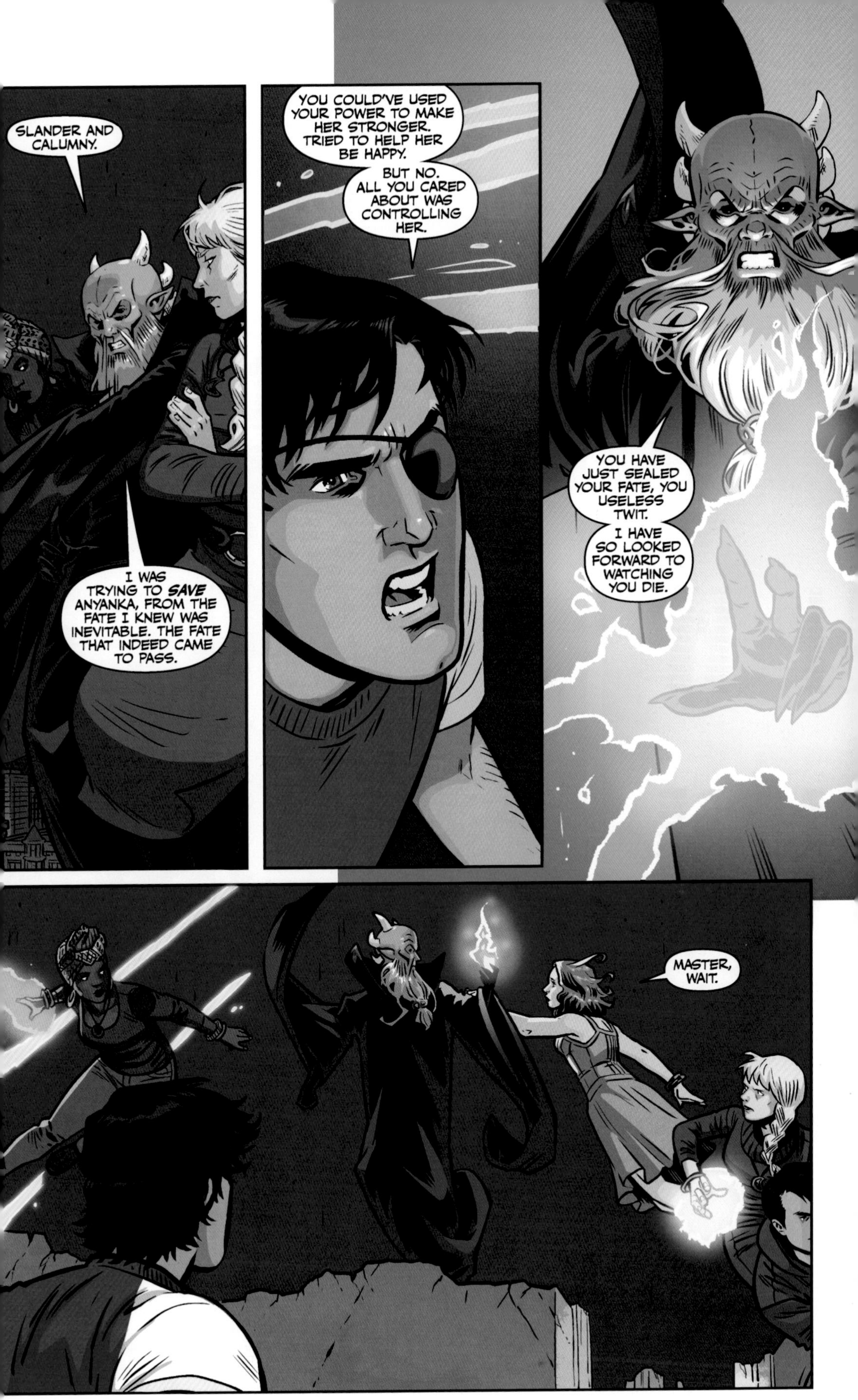
SLANDER AND CALUMNY.
I WAS TRYING TO SAVE ANYANKA, FROM THE FATE I KNEW WAS INEVITABLE. THE FATE THAT INDEED CAME TO PASS.
YOU COULD'VE USED YOUR POWER TO MAKE HER STRONGER. TRIED TO HELP HER BE HAPPY.
BUT NO. ALL YOU CARED ABOUT WAS CONTROLLING HER.
YOU HAVE JUST SEALED YOUR FATE, YOU USELESS TWIT.
I HAVE SO LOOKED FORWARD TO WATCHING YOU DIE.
MASTER, WAIT.

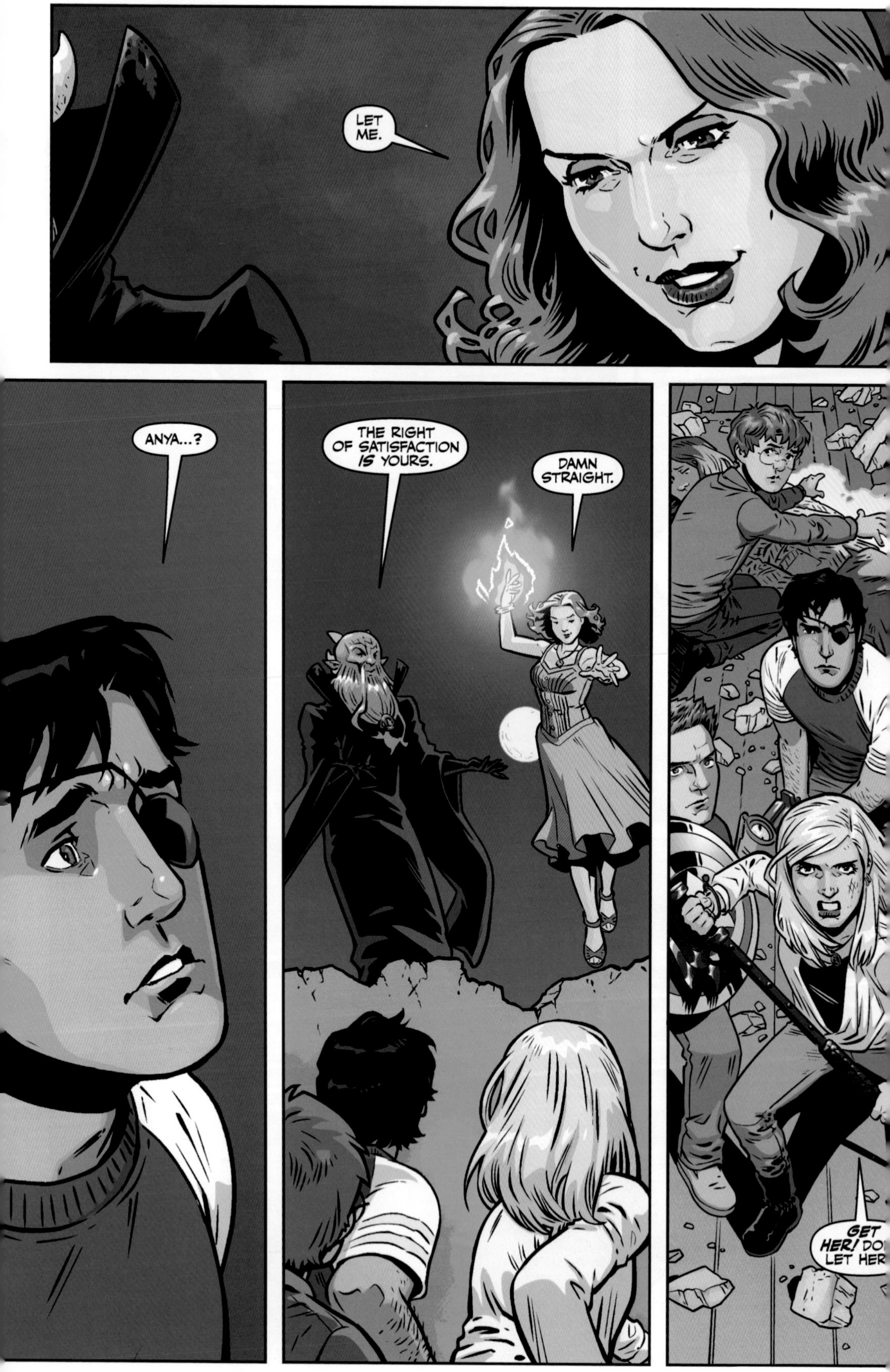
LET ME.
ANYA...?
THE RIGHT OF SATISFACTION IS YOURS.
DAMN STRAIGHT.
GET HER! DO
LET HER

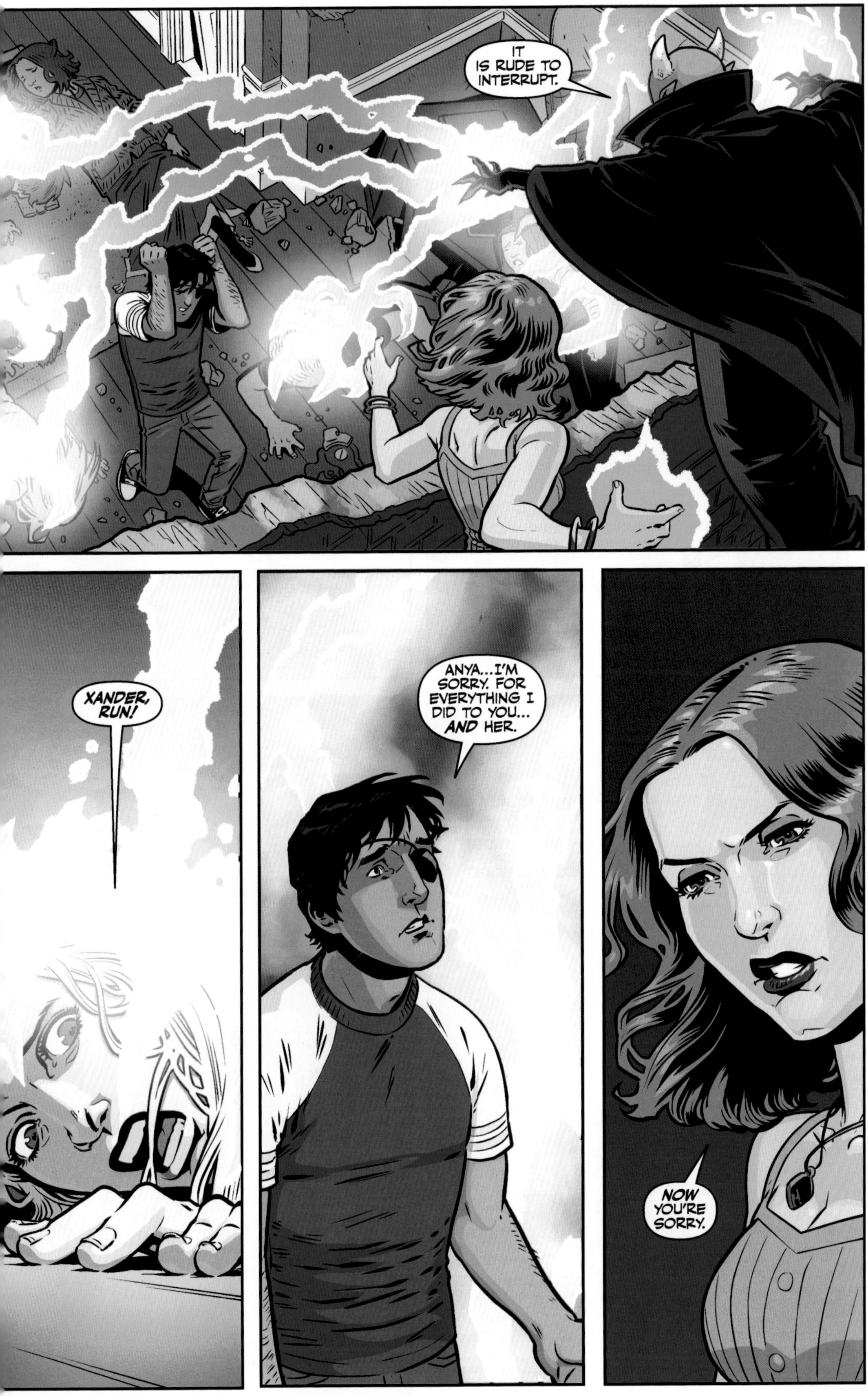
IT IS RUDE TO INTERRUPT.
XANDER, RUN!
ANYA...I'M SORRY. FOR EVERYTHING I DID TO YOU... AND HER.
NOW YOU'RE SORRY.

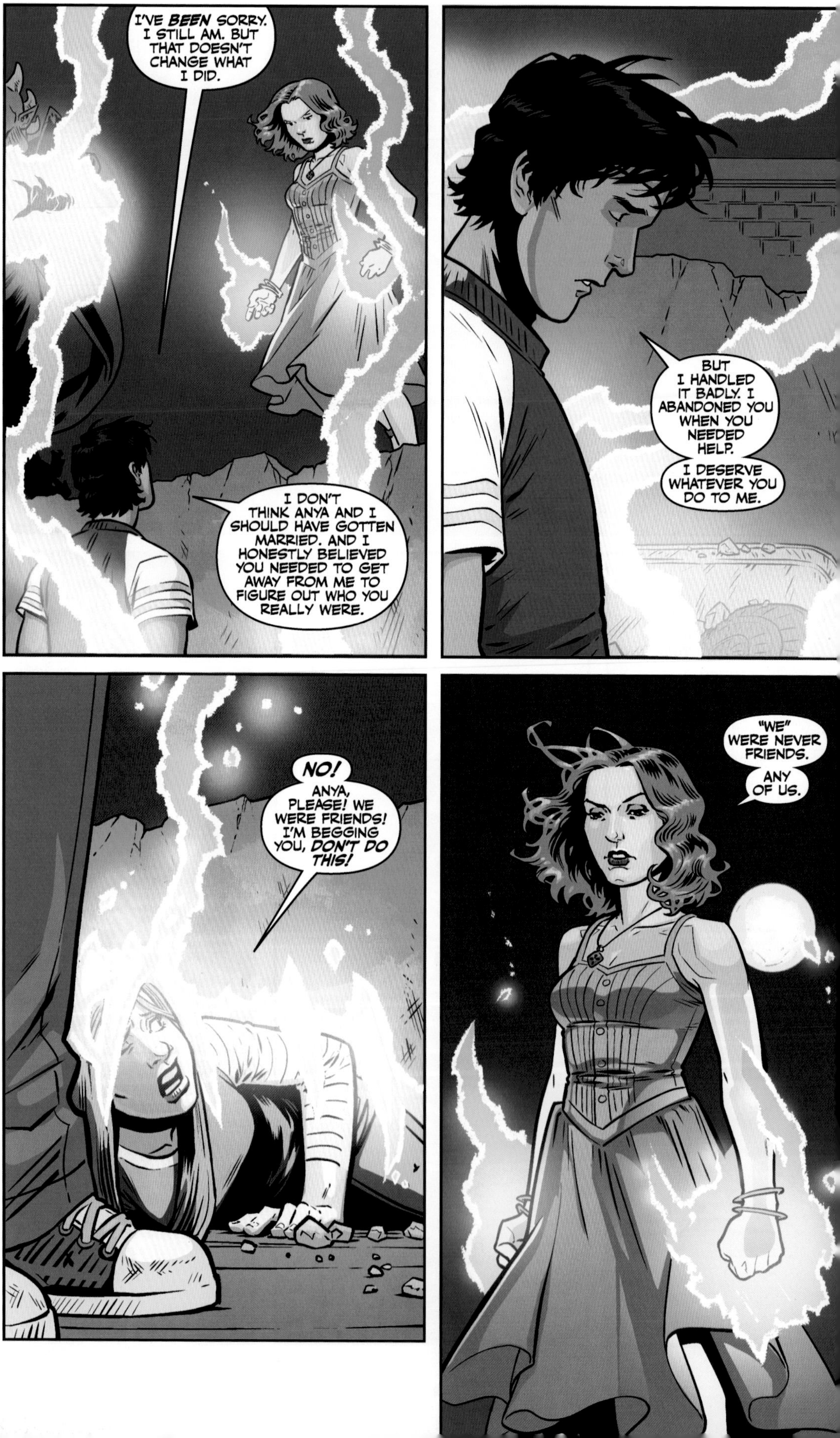
I'VE BEEN SORRY. I STILL AM. BUT THAT DOESN'T CHANGE WHAT I DID.
I DON'T THINK ANYA AND I SHOULD HAVE GOTTEN MARRIED. AND I HONESTLY BELIEVED YOU NEEDED TO GET AWAY FROM ME TO FIGURE OUT WHO YOU REALLY WERE.
BUT I HANDLED IT BADLY. I ABANDONED YOU WHEN YOU NEEDED HELP.
I DESERVE WHATEVER YOU DO TO ME.
NO!
ANYA, PLEASE! WE WERE FRIENDS! I'M BEGGING YOU, DON'T DO THIS!
"WE" WERE NEVER FRIENDS.
ANY OF US.

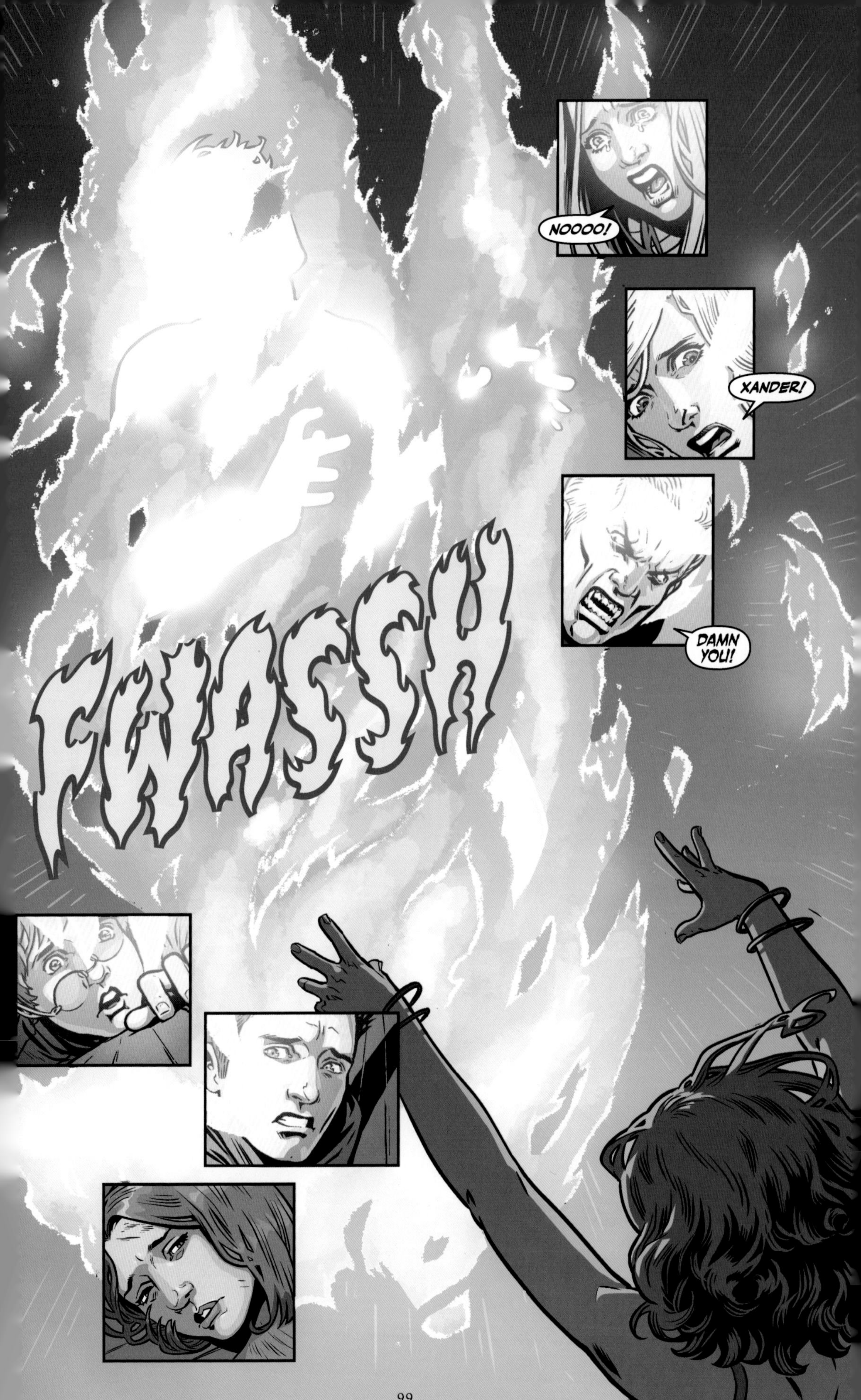
NOOOO!
XANDER!
DAMN YOU!
FWASSH

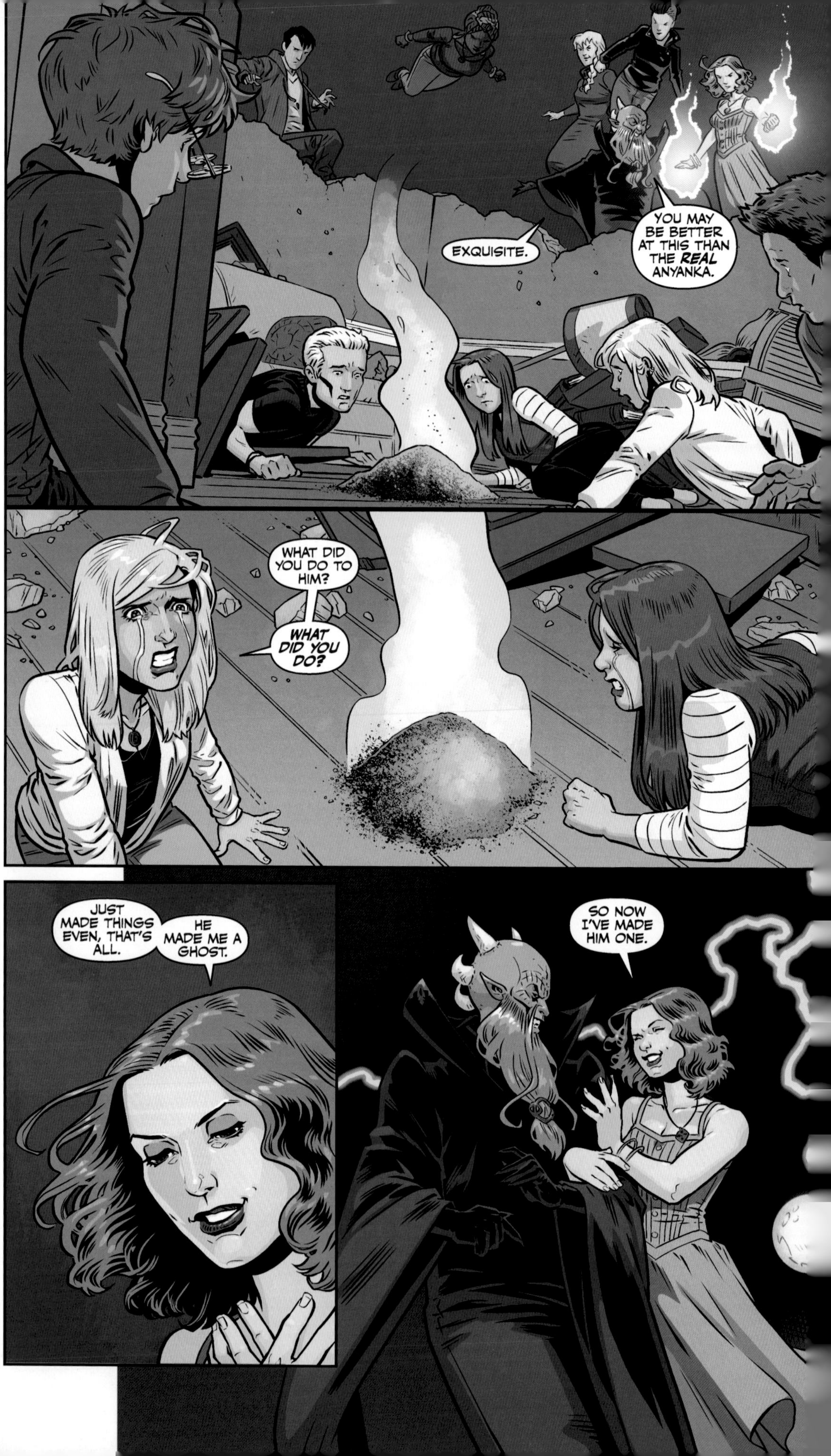
EXQUISITE.
YOU MAY BE BETTER AT THIS THAN THE *REAL* ANYANKA.
WHAT DID YOU DO TO HIM?
WHAT DID YOU DO?
JUST MADE THINGS EVEN, THAT'S ALL.
HE MADE ME A GHOST.
SO NOW I'VE MADE HIM ONE.

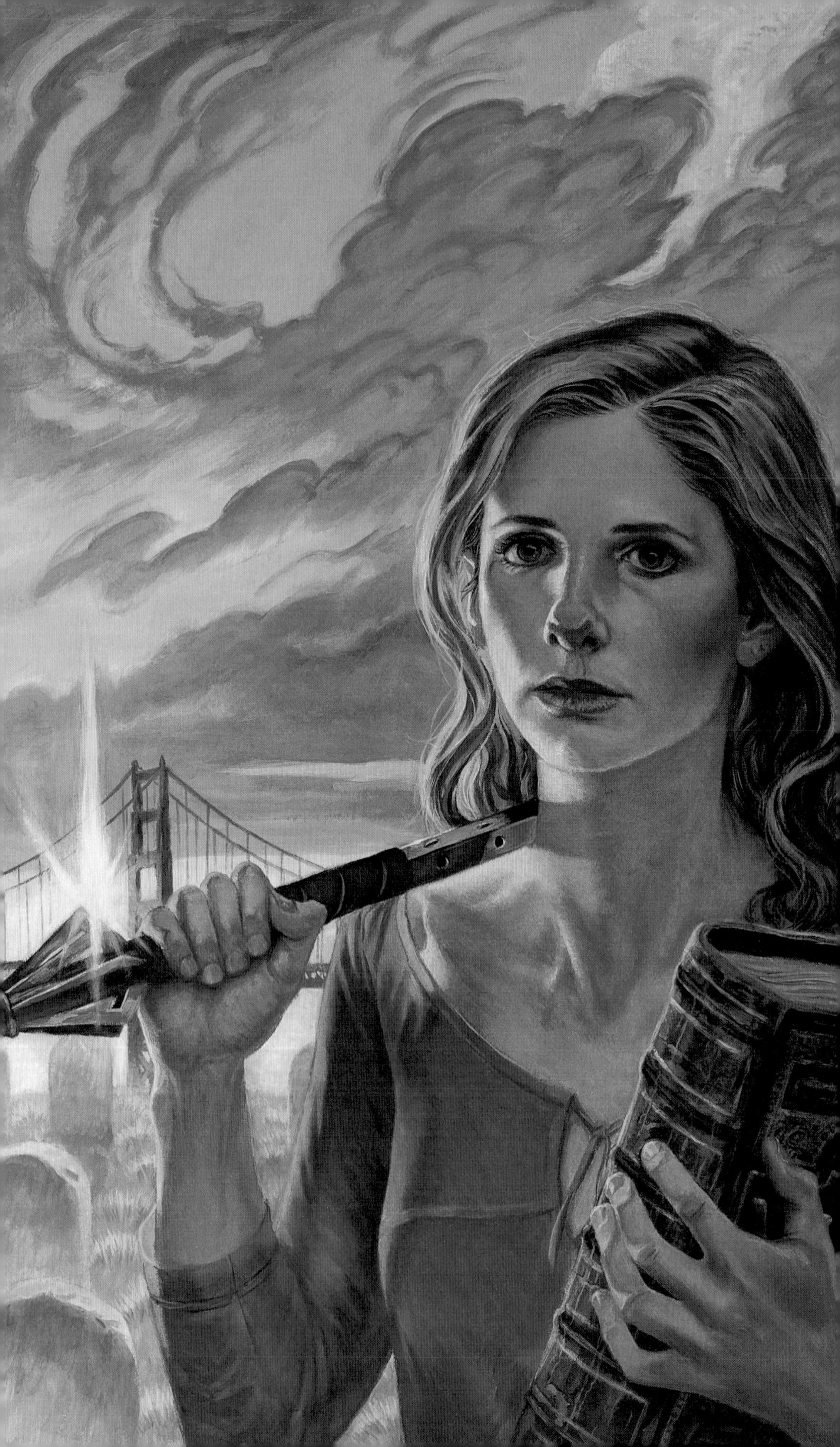

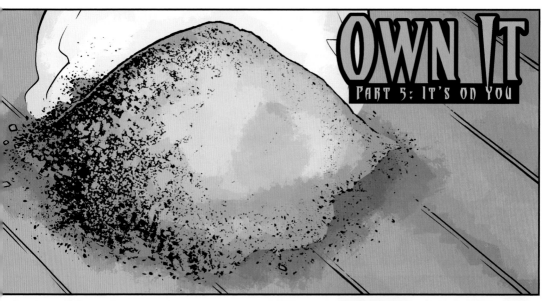

OWN IT

PART 5: IT'S ON YOU

XANDER, NO, NO, NO...

ANYA, YOU-- HOW COULD YOU--

SHE'S NOT REALLY ANYA.

BY SLAYING XANDER HARRIS BEFORE YOUR EYES...SHE HAS *SURPASSED* HER.

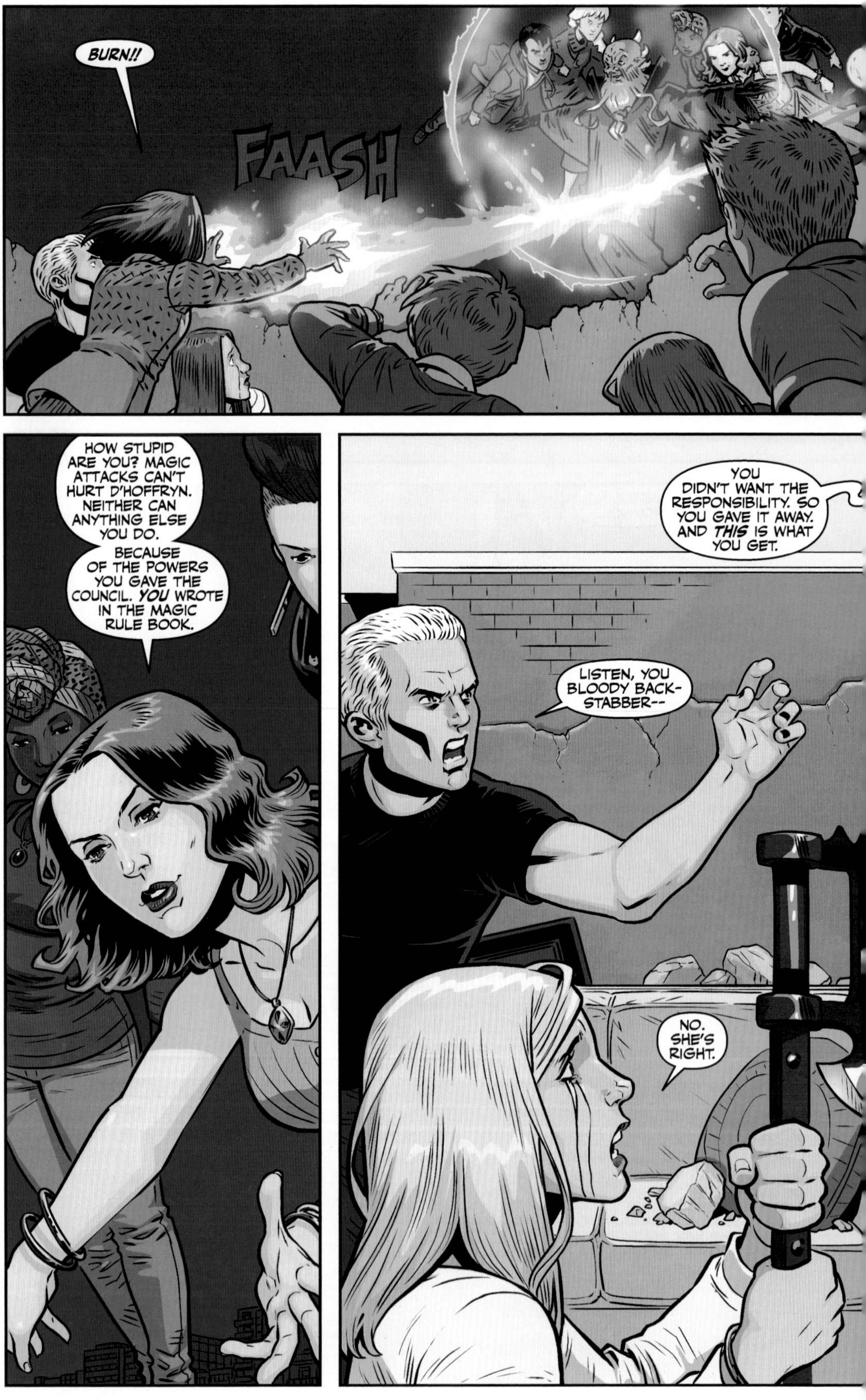

BURN!!
FAASH
HOW STUPID ARE YOU? MAGIC ATTACKS CAN'T HURT D'HOFFRYN. NEITHER CAN ANYTHING ELSE YOU DO.
BECAUSE OF THE POWERS YOU GAVE THE COUNCIL. *YOU* WROTE IN THE MAGIC RULE BOOK.
YOU DIDN'T WANT THE RESPONSIBILITY. SO YOU GAVE IT AWAY. AND *THIS* IS WHAT YOU GET.
LISTEN, YOU BLOODY BACK-STABBER--
NO. SHE'S RIGHT.

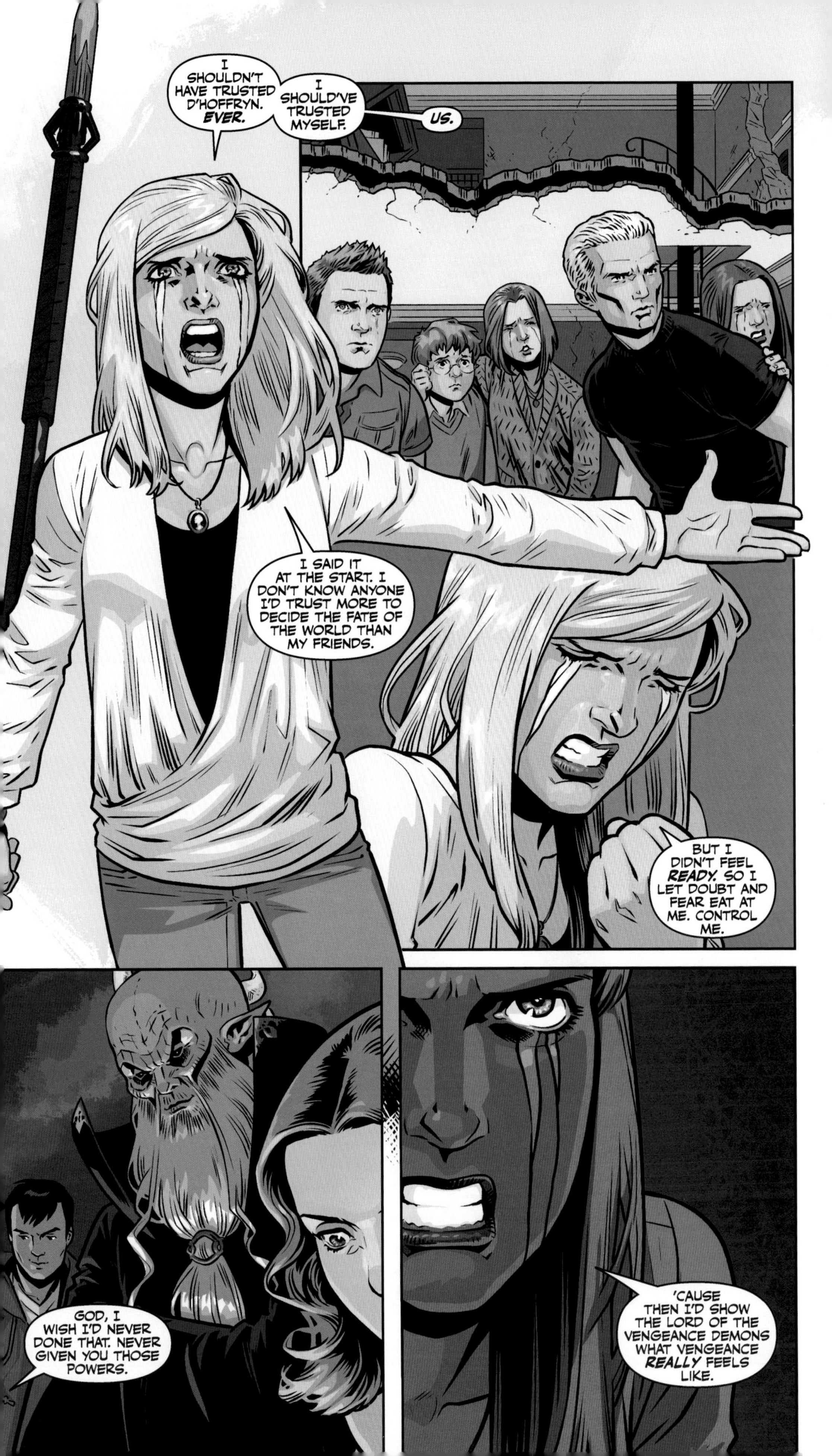
I SHOULDN'T HAVE TRUSTED D'HOFFRYN. EVER.
I SHOULD'VE TRUSTED MYSELF.
US.
I SAID IT AT THE START. I DON'T KNOW ANYONE I'D TRUST MORE TO DECIDE THE FATE OF THE WORLD THAN MY FRIENDS.
BUT I DIDN'T FEEL READY. SO I LET DOUBT AND FEAR EAT AT ME. CONTROL ME.
GOD, I WISH I'D NEVER DONE THAT. NEVER GIVEN YOU THOSE POWERS.
'CAUSE THEN I'D SHOW THE LORD OF THE VENGEANCE DEMONS WHAT VENGEANCE REALLY FEELS LIKE.

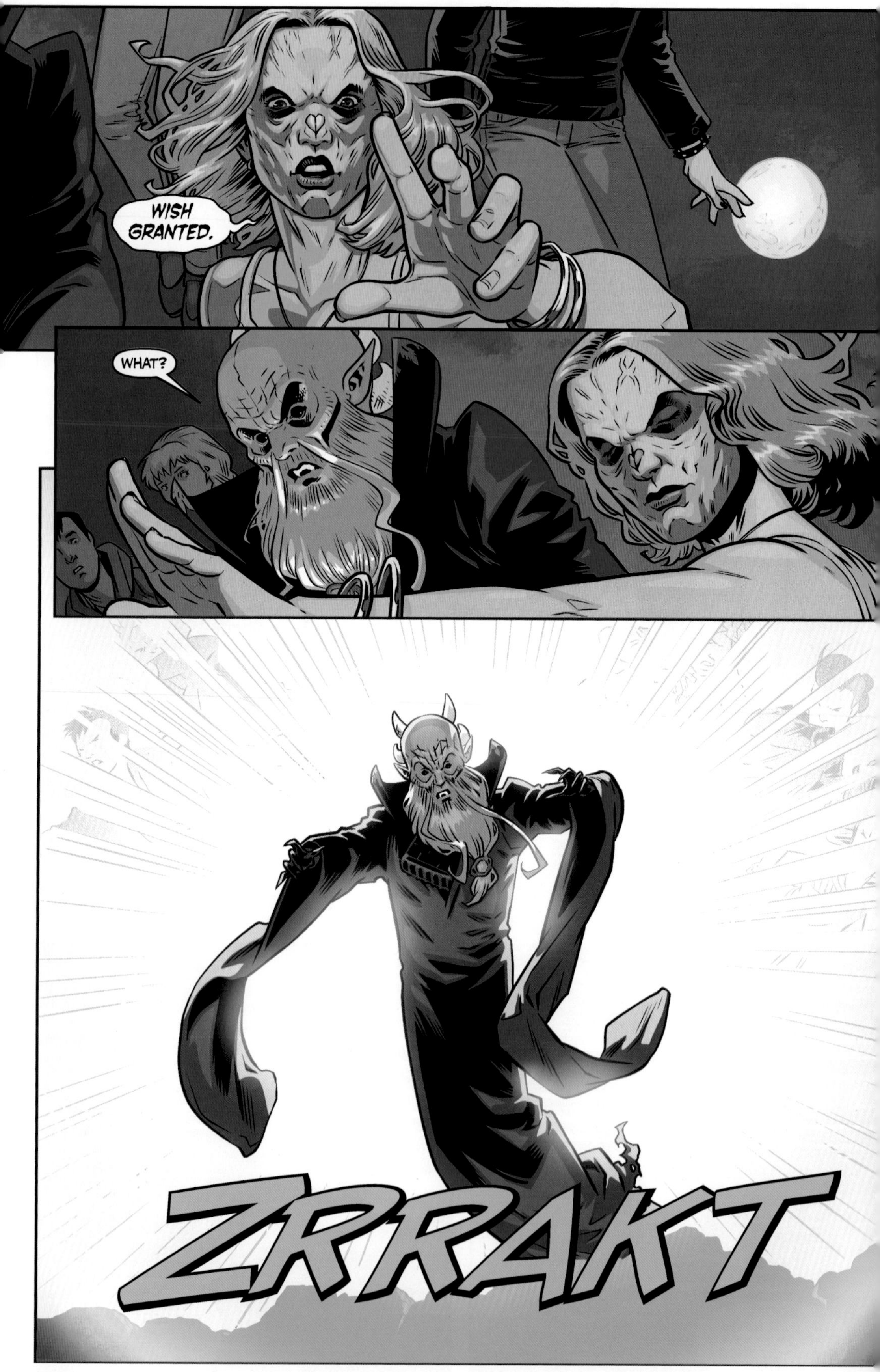
WISH GRANTED.
WHAT?
ZRRAKT

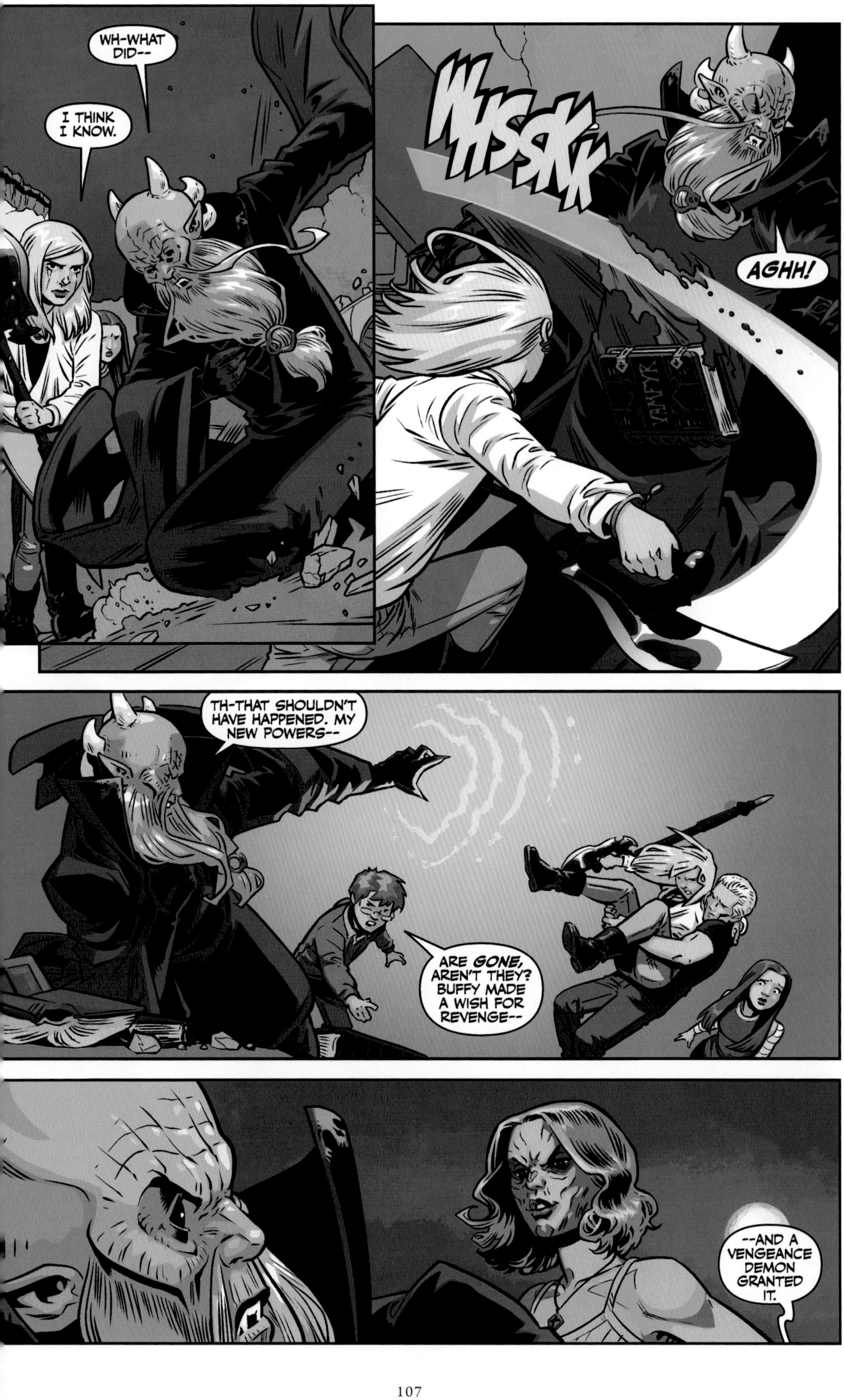
WH-WHAT DID--
I THINK I KNOW.
WHSSKK
AGHH!
TH-THAT SHOULDN'T HAVE HAPPENED. MY NEW POWERS--
ARE *GONE,* AREN'T THEY? BUFFY MADE A WISH FOR REVENGE--
--AND A VENGEANCE DEMON GRANTED IT.

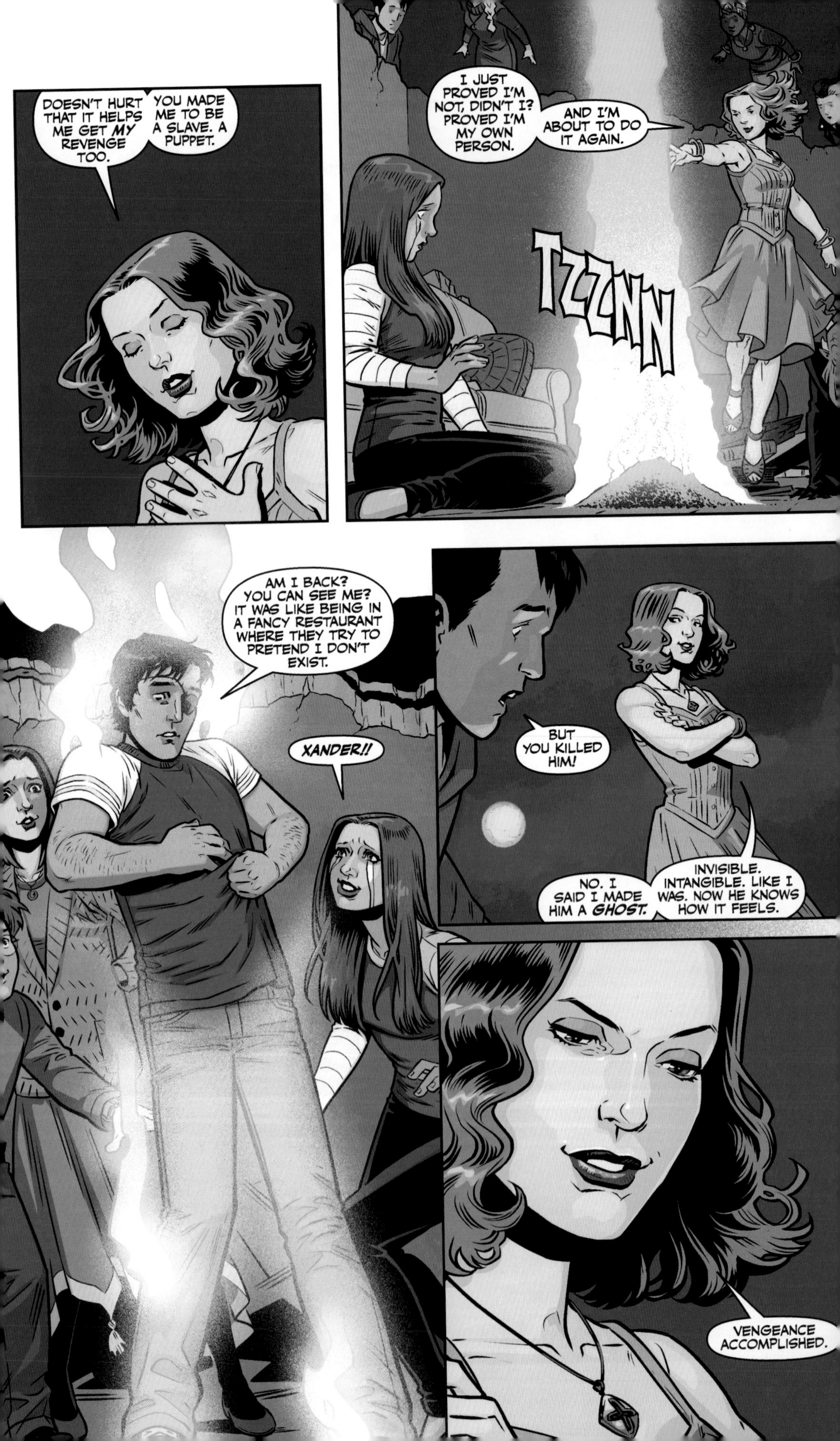

DOESN'T HURT THAT IT HELPS ME GET MY REVENGE TOO.
YOU MADE ME TO BE A SLAVE. A PUPPET.
I JUST PROVED I'M NOT, DIDN'T I? PROVED I'M MY OWN PERSON.
AND I'M ABOUT TO DO IT AGAIN.
TZZNN
AM I BACK? YOU CAN SEE ME? IT WAS LIKE BEING IN A FANCY RESTAURANT WHERE THEY TRY TO PRETEND I DON'T EXIST.
XANDER!!
BUT YOU KILLED HIM!
NO. I SAID I MADE HIM A GHOST.
INVISIBLE. INTANGIBLE. LIKE I WAS. NOW HE KNOWS HOW IT FEELS.
VENGEANCE ACCOMPLISHED.

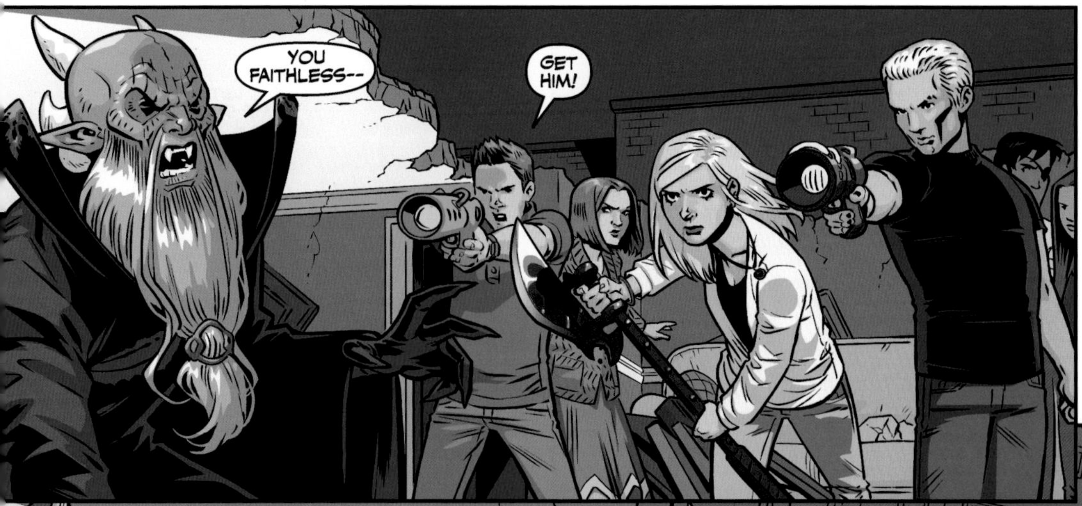
YOU FAITHLESS--
GET HIM!

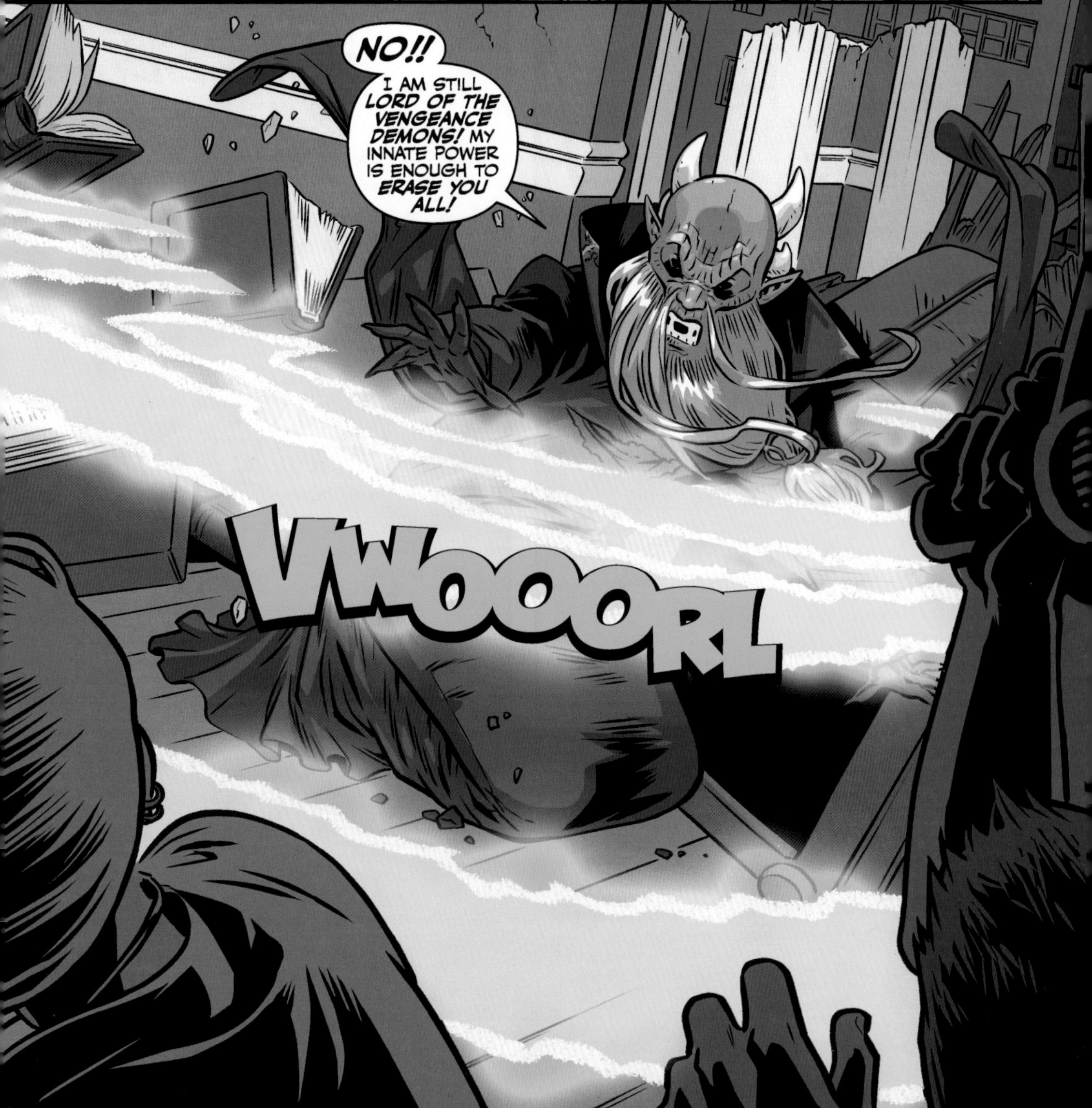
NO!! I AM STILL LORD OF THE VENGEANCE DEMONS! MY INNATE POWER IS ENOUGH TO ERASE YOU ALL!
VWOOORL

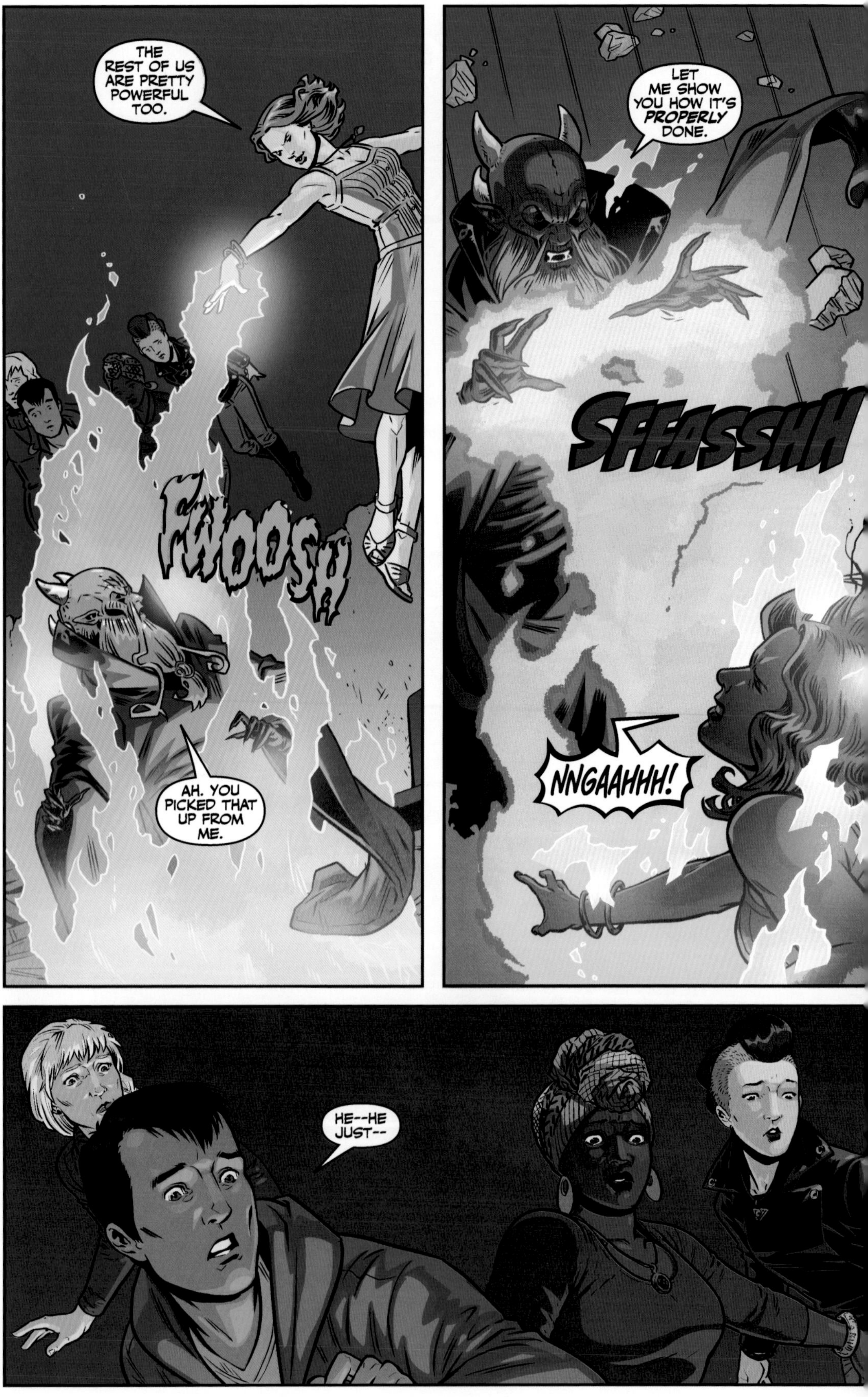
THE REST OF US ARE PRETTY POWERFUL TOO.
FWOOSH
AH. YOU PICKED THAT UP FROM ME.
LET ME SHOW YOU HOW IT'S PROPERLY DONE.
SFFASSHH
NNGAAHHH!
HE--HE JUST--

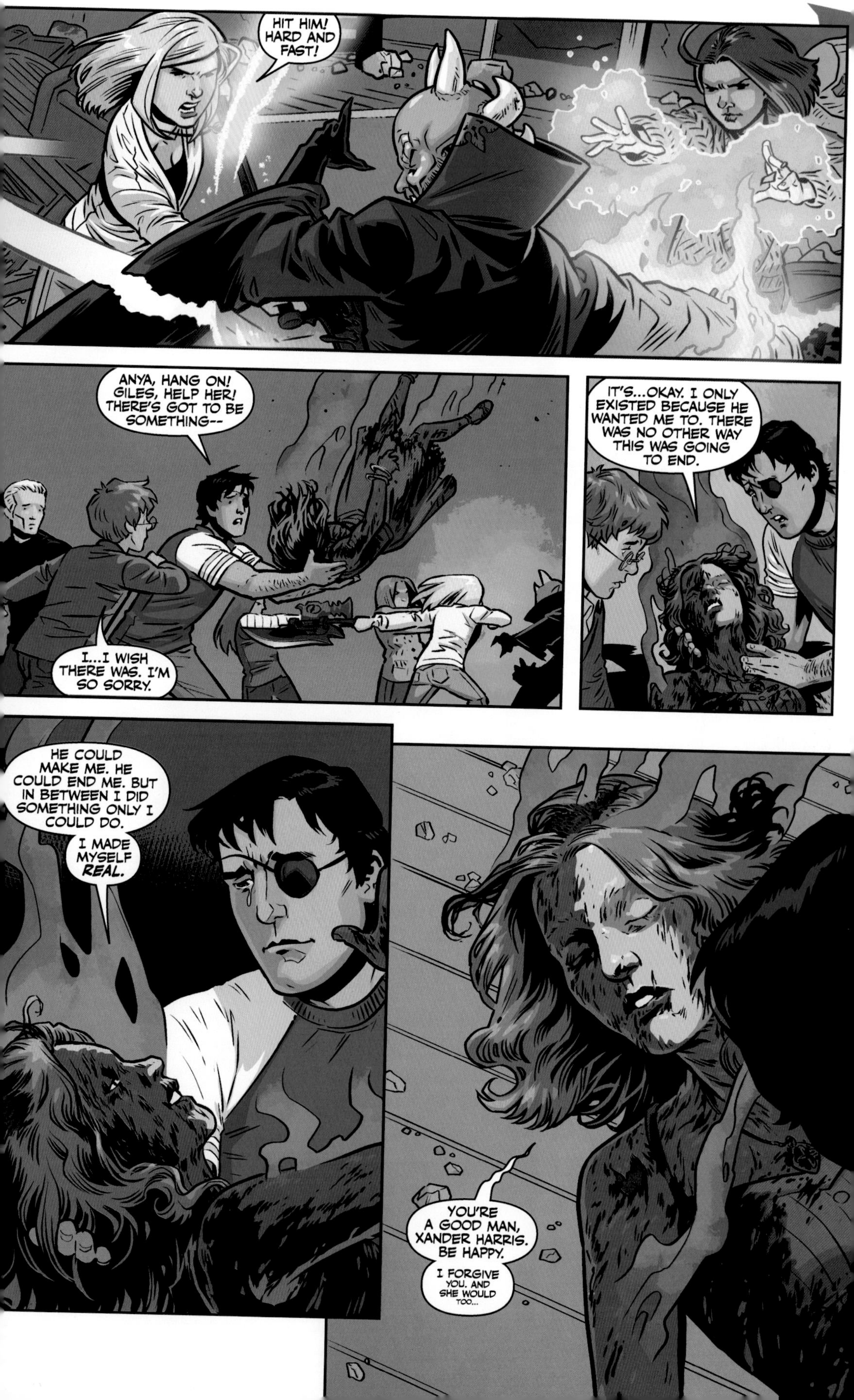
HIT HIM! HARD AND FAST!
ANYA, HANG ON! GILES, HELP HER! THERE'S GOT TO BE SOMETHING--
I...I WISH THERE WAS. I'M SO SORRY.
IT'S...OKAY. I ONLY EXISTED BECAUSE HE WANTED ME TO. THERE WAS NO OTHER WAY THIS WAS GOING TO END.
HE COULD MAKE ME. HE COULD END ME. BUT IN BETWEEN I DID SOMETHING ONLY I COULD DO.
I MADE MYSELF *REAL.*
YOU'RE A GOOD MAN, XANDER HARRIS. BE HAPPY.
I FORGIVE YOU. AND SHE WOULD TOO...

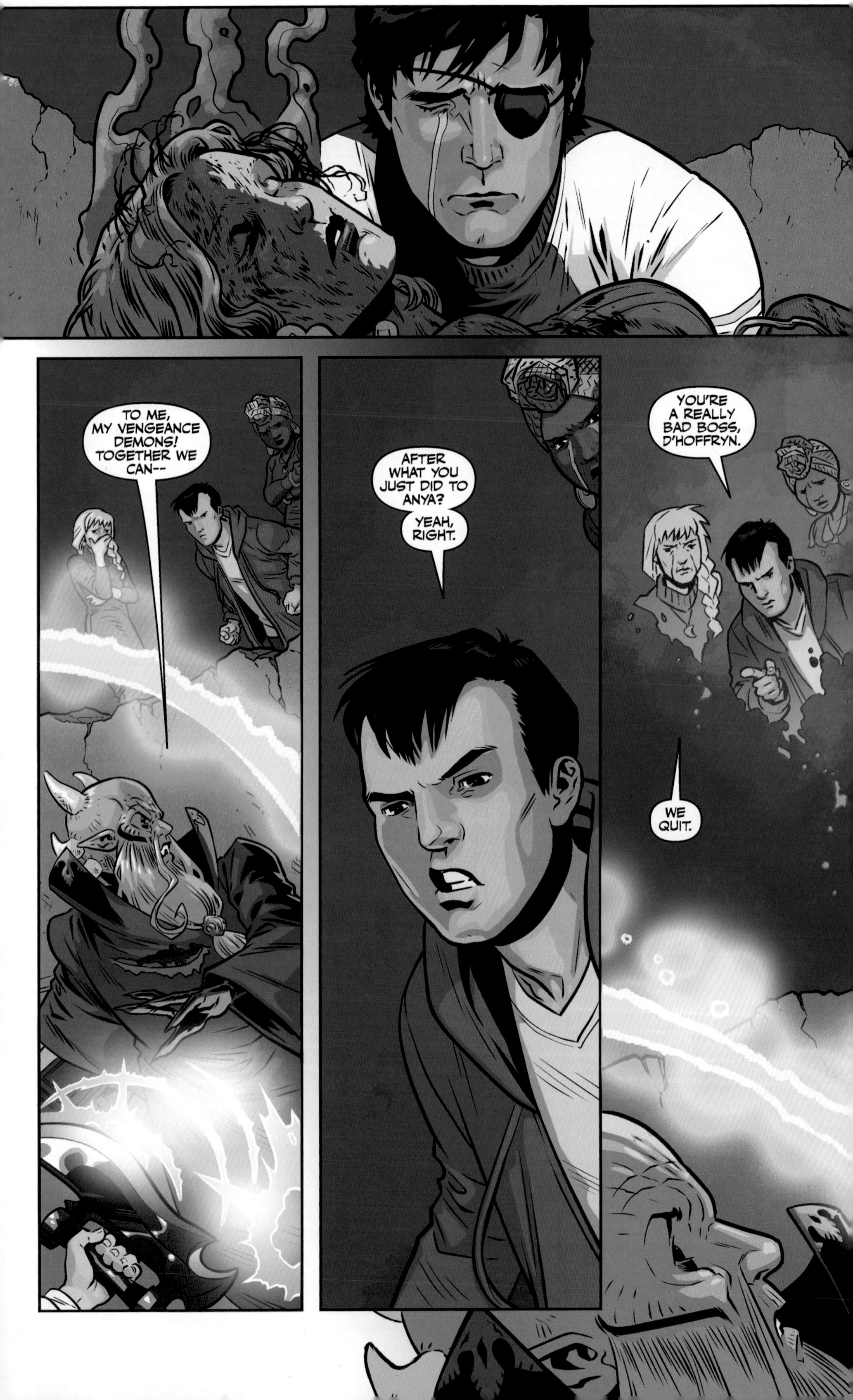
TO ME, MY VENGEANCE DEMONS! TOGETHER WE CAN--
AFTER WHAT YOU JUST DID TO ANYA?
YEAH, RIGHT.
YOU'RE A REALLY BAD BOSS, D'HOFFRYN.
WE QUIT.

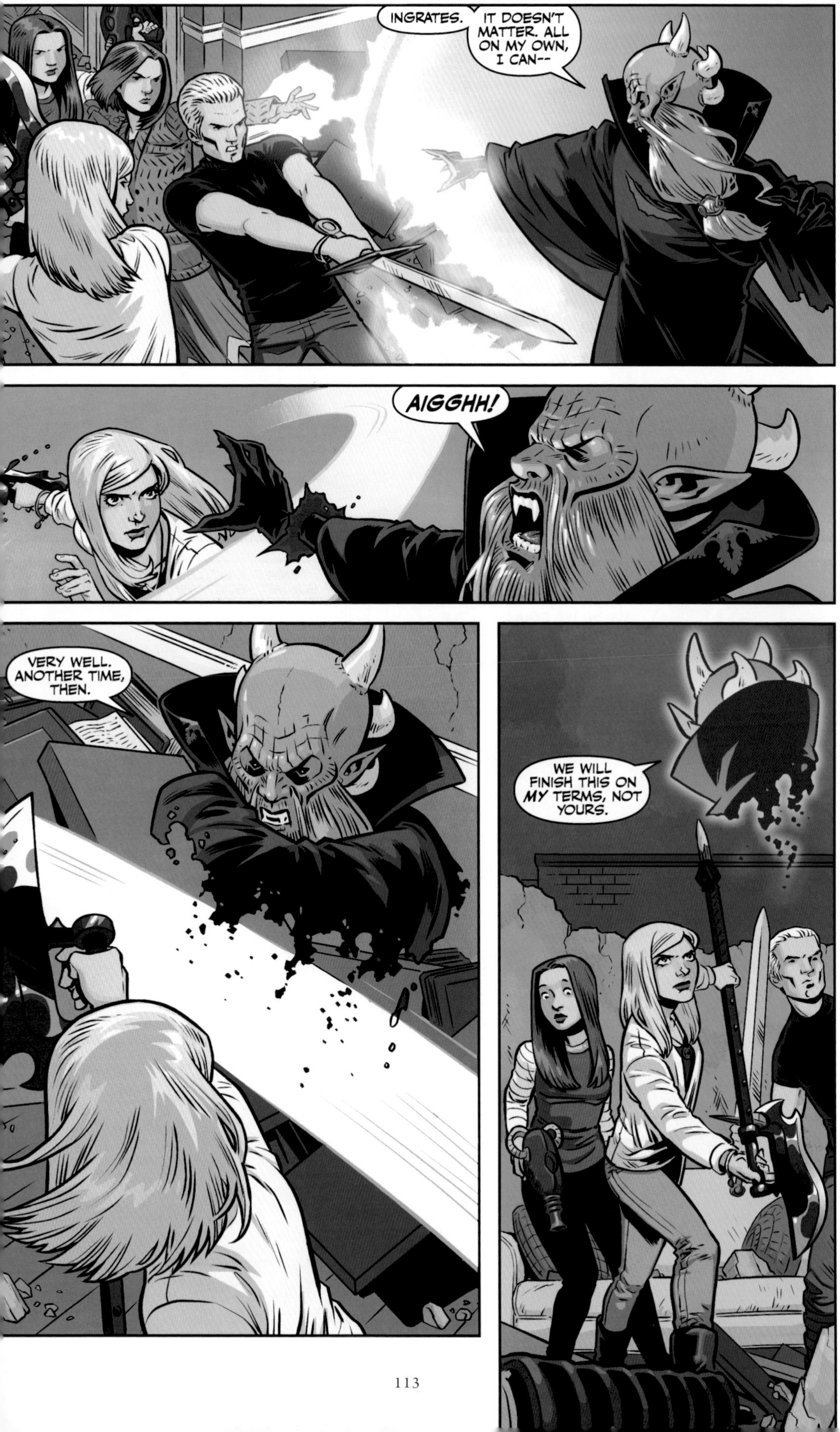
INGRATES.
IT DOESN'T MATTER. ALL ON MY OWN, I CAN--
AIGGHH!
VERY WELL. ANOTHER TIME, THEN.
WE WILL FINISH THIS ON *MY* TERMS, NOT YOURS.

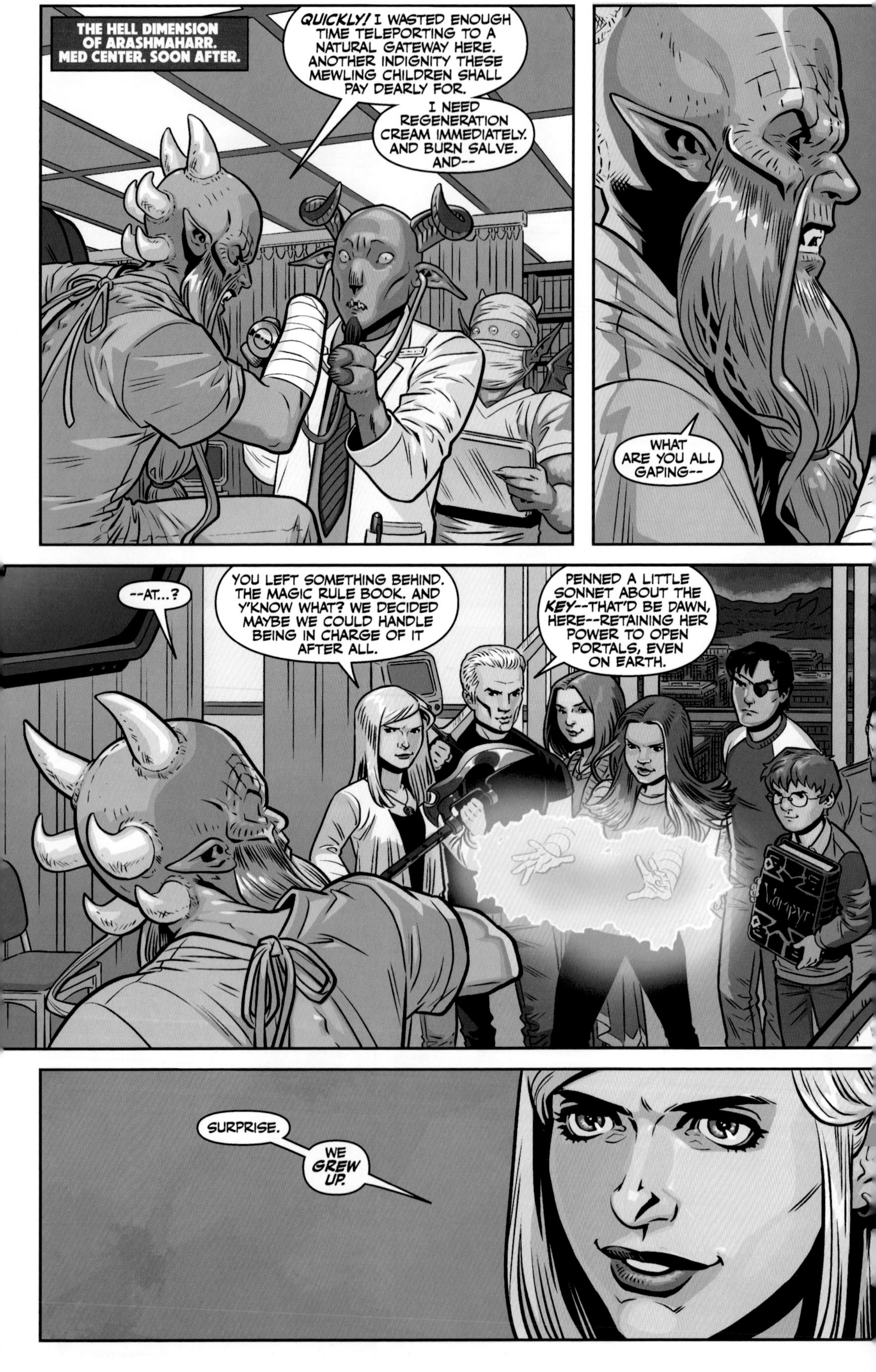
THE HELL DIMENSION OF ARASHMAHARR. MED CENTER. SOON AFTER.
QUICKLY! I WASTED ENOUGH TIME TELEPORTING TO A NATURAL GATEWAY HERE. ANOTHER INDIGNITY THESE MEWLING CHILDREN SHALL PAY DEARLY FOR.
I NEED REGENERATION CREAM IMMEDIATELY. AND BURN SALVE. AND--
WHAT ARE YOU ALL GAPING--
--AT...?
YOU LEFT SOMETHING BEHIND. THE MAGIC RULE BOOK. AND Y'KNOW WHAT? WE DECIDED MAYBE WE COULD HANDLE BEING IN CHARGE OF IT AFTER ALL.
PENNED A LITTLE SONNET ABOUT THE KEY--THAT'D BE DAWN, HERE--RETAINING HER POWER TO OPEN PORTALS, EVEN ON EARTH.
Vampyr
SURPRISE.
WE GREW UP.

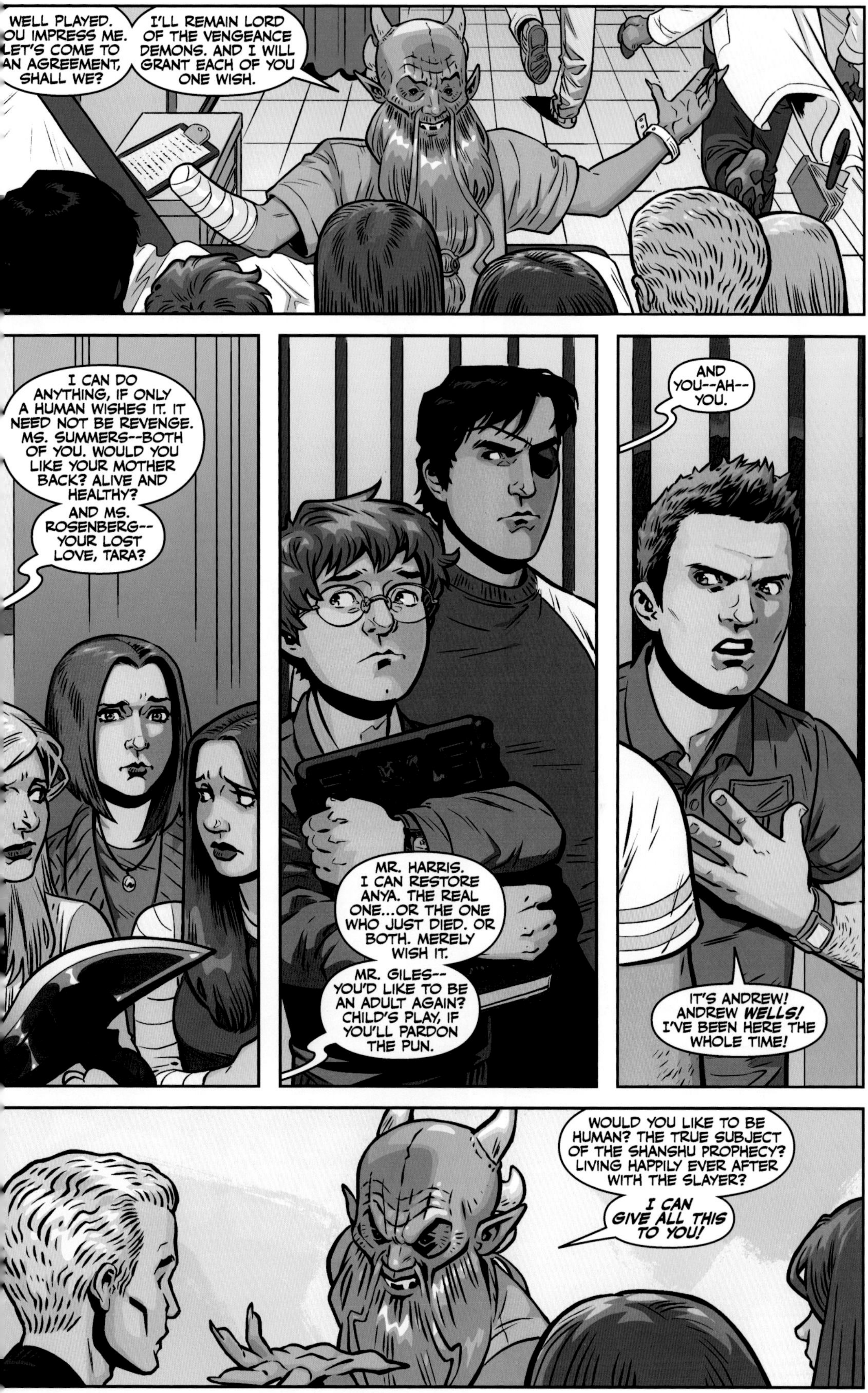
WELL PLAYED. OU IMPRESS ME. LET'S COME TO AN AGREEMENT, SHALL WE?
I'LL REMAIN LORD OF THE VENGEANCE DEMONS. AND I WILL GRANT EACH OF YOU ONE WISH.
I CAN DO ANYTHING, IF ONLY A HUMAN WISHES IT. IT NEED NOT BE REVENGE. MS. SUMMERS--BOTH OF YOU. WOULD YOU LIKE YOUR MOTHER BACK? ALIVE AND HEALTHY?
AND MS. ROSENBERG-- YOUR LOST LOVE, TARA?
MR. HARRIS. I CAN RESTORE ANYA. THE REAL ONE...OR THE ONE WHO JUST DIED. OR BOTH. MERELY WISH IT.
MR. GILES-- YOU'D LIKE TO BE AN ADULT AGAIN? CHILD'S PLAY, IF YOU'LL PARDON THE PUN.
AND YOU--AH-- YOU.
IT'S ANDREW! ANDREW *WELLS!* I'VE BEEN HERE THE WHOLE TIME!
WOULD YOU LIKE TO BE HUMAN? THE TRUE SUBJECT OF THE SHANSHU PROPHECY? LIVING HAPPILY EVER AFTER WITH THE SLAYER?
I CAN GIVE ALL THIS TO YOU!

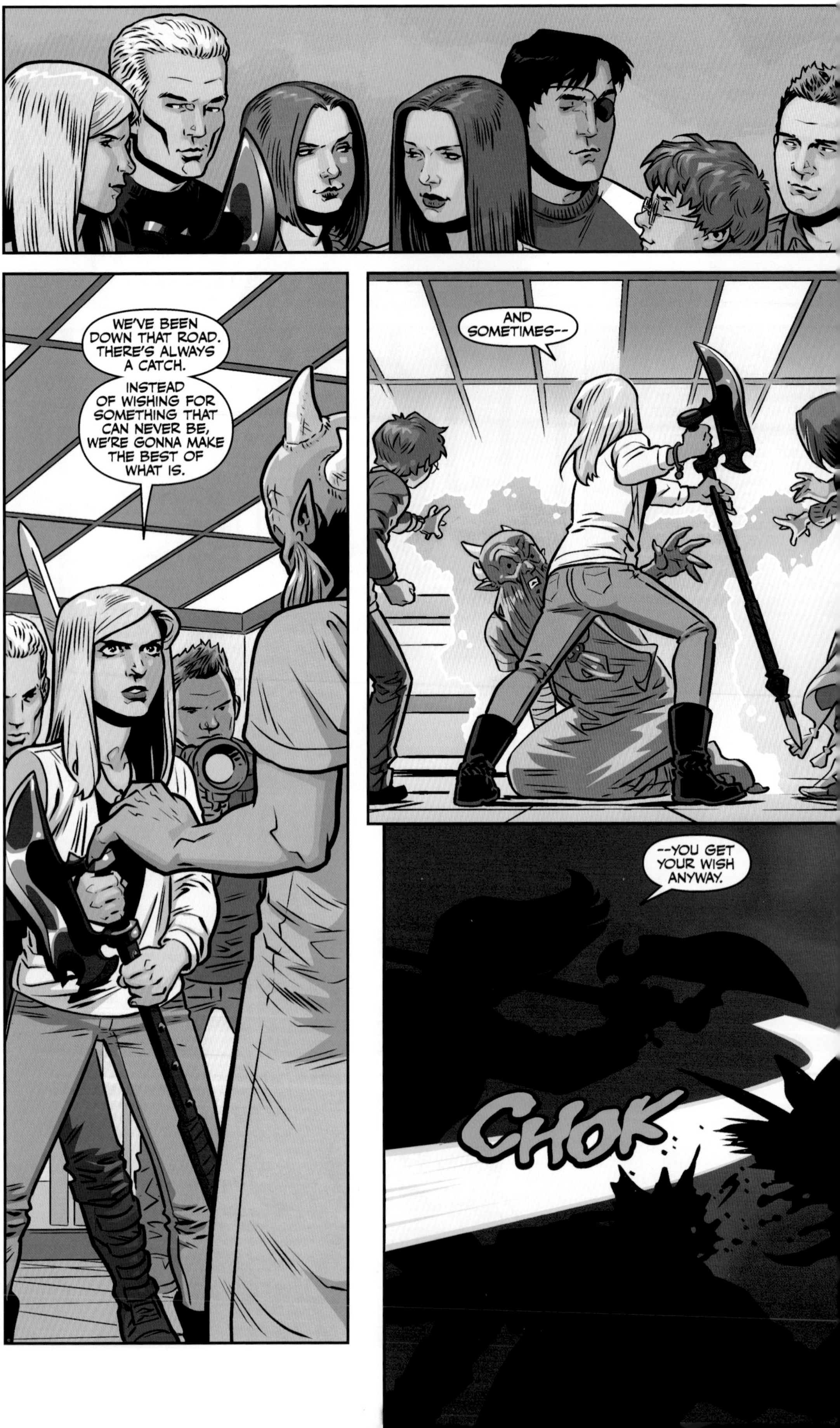
WE'VE BEEN DOWN THAT ROAD. THERE'S ALWAYS A CATCH.
INSTEAD OF WISHING FOR SOMETHING THAT CAN NEVER BE, WE'RE GONNA MAKE THE BEST OF WHAT IS.
AND SOMETIMES--
--YOU GET YOUR WISH ANYWAY.
CHOK

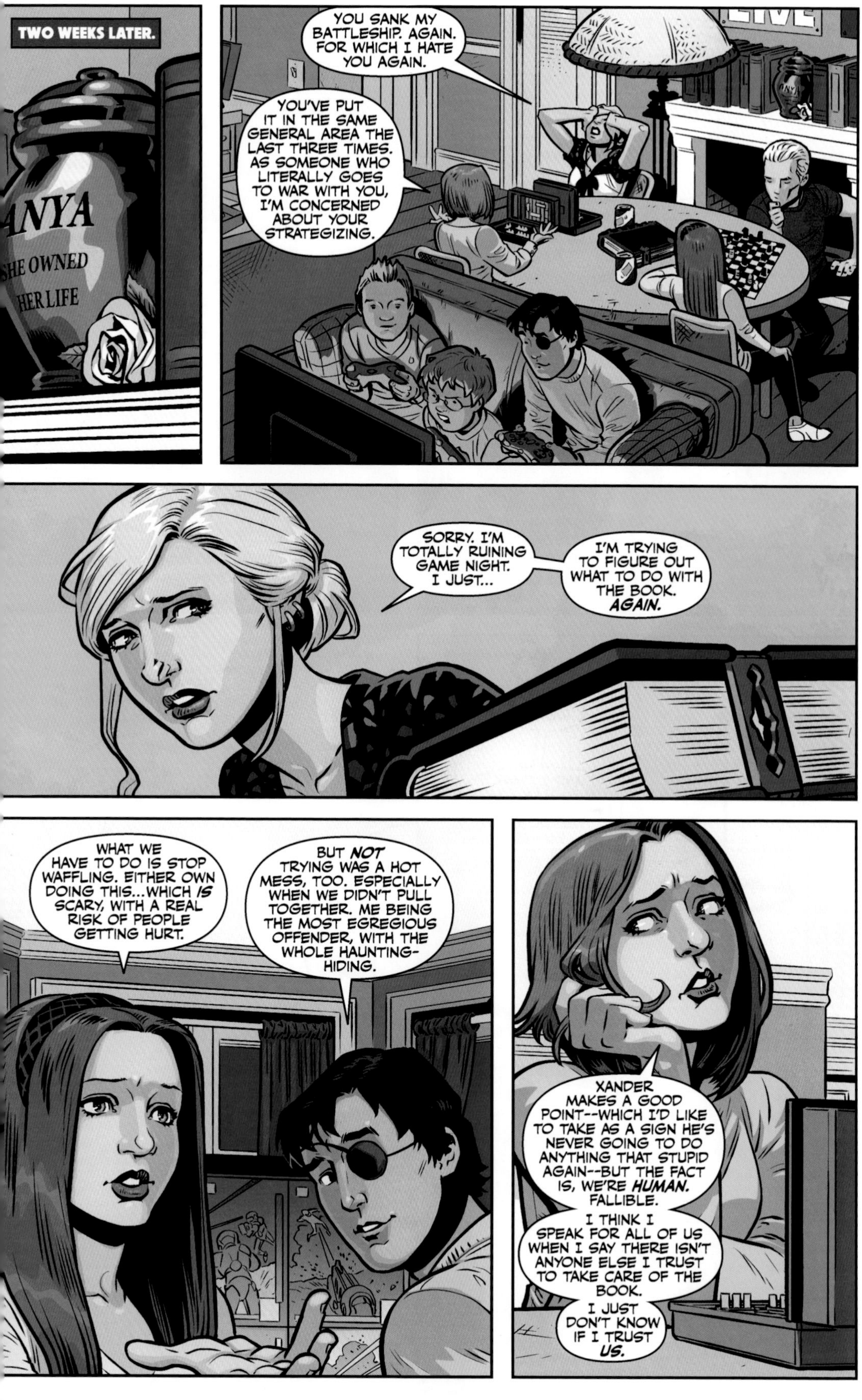
TWO WEEKS LATER.
ANYA
SHE OWNED
HER LIFE
YOU SANK MY BATTLESHIP. AGAIN. FOR WHICH I HATE YOU AGAIN.
YOU'VE PUT IT IN THE SAME GENERAL AREA THE LAST THREE TIMES. AS SOMEONE WHO LITERALLY GOES TO WAR WITH YOU, I'M CONCERNED ABOUT YOUR STRATEGIZING.
SORRY. I'M TOTALLY RUINING GAME NIGHT. I JUST...
I'M TRYING TO FIGURE OUT WHAT TO DO WITH THE BOOK. *AGAIN.*
WHAT WE HAVE TO DO IS STOP WAFFLING. EITHER OWN DOING THIS...WHICH *IS* SCARY, WITH A REAL RISK OF PEOPLE GETTING HURT.
BUT *NOT* TRYING WAS A HOT MESS, TOO. ESPECIALLY WHEN WE DIDN'T PULL TOGETHER. ME BEING THE MOST EGREGIOUS OFFENDER, WITH THE WHOLE HAUNTING-HIDING.
XANDER MAKES A GOOD POINT--WHICH I'D LIKE TO TAKE AS A SIGN HE'S NEVER GOING TO DO ANYTHING THAT STUPID AGAIN--BUT THE FACT IS, WE'RE *HUMAN.* FALLIBLE.
I THINK I SPEAK FOR ALL OF US WHEN I SAY THERE ISN'T ANYONE ELSE I TRUST TO TAKE CARE OF THE BOOK.
I JUST DON'T KNOW IF I TRUST *US.*

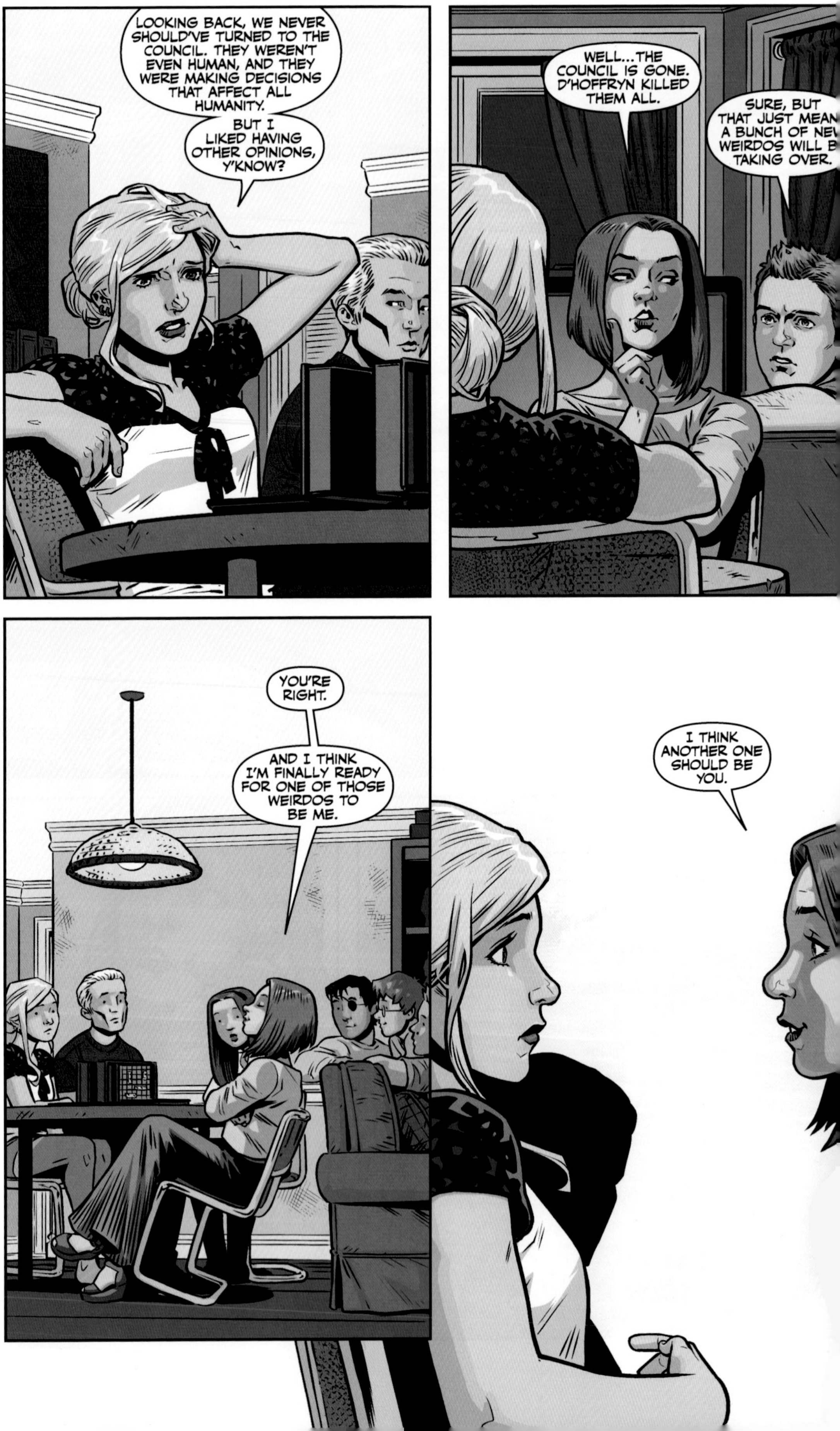
LOOKING BACK, WE NEVER SHOULD'VE TURNED TO THE COUNCIL. THEY WEREN'T EVEN HUMAN, AND THEY WERE MAKING DECISIONS THAT AFFECT ALL HUMANITY.
BUT I LIKED HAVING OTHER OPINIONS, Y'KNOW?
WELL...THE COUNCIL IS GONE. D'HOFFRYN KILLED THEM ALL.
SURE, BUT THAT JUST MEAN A BUNCH OF NEW WEIRDOS WILL B TAKING OVER.
YOU'RE RIGHT.
AND I THINK I'M FINALLY READY FOR ONE OF THOSE WEIRDOS TO BE ME.
I THINK ANOTHER ONE SHOULD BE YOU.

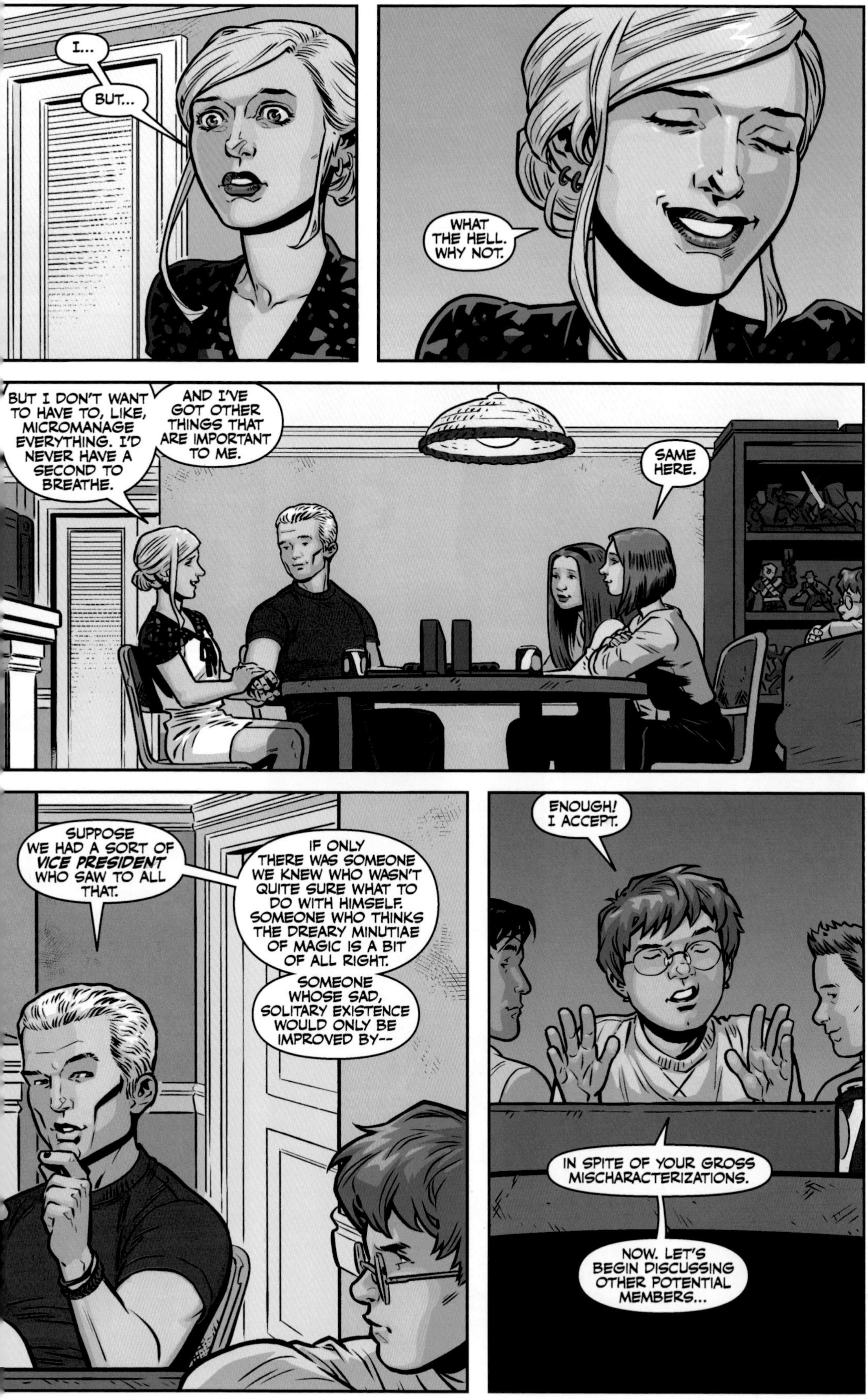
I...
BUT...
WHAT THE HELL. WHY NOT.
BUT I DON'T WANT TO HAVE TO, LIKE, MICROMANAGE EVERYTHING. I'D NEVER HAVE A SECOND TO BREATHE.
AND I'VE GOT OTHER THINGS THAT ARE IMPORTANT TO ME.
SAME HERE.
SUPPOSE WE HAD A SORT OF *VICE PRESIDENT* WHO SAW TO ALL THAT.
IF ONLY THERE WAS SOMEONE WE KNEW WHO WASN'T QUITE SURE WHAT TO DO WITH HIMSELF. SOMEONE WHO THINKS THE DREARY MINUTIAE OF MAGIC IS A BIT OF ALL RIGHT.
SOMEONE WHOSE SAD, SOLITARY EXISTENCE WOULD ONLY BE IMPROVED BY--
ENOUGH! I ACCEPT.
IN SPITE OF YOUR GROSS MISCHARACTERIZATIONS.
NOW. LET'S BEGIN DISCUSSING OTHER POTENTIAL MEMBERS...

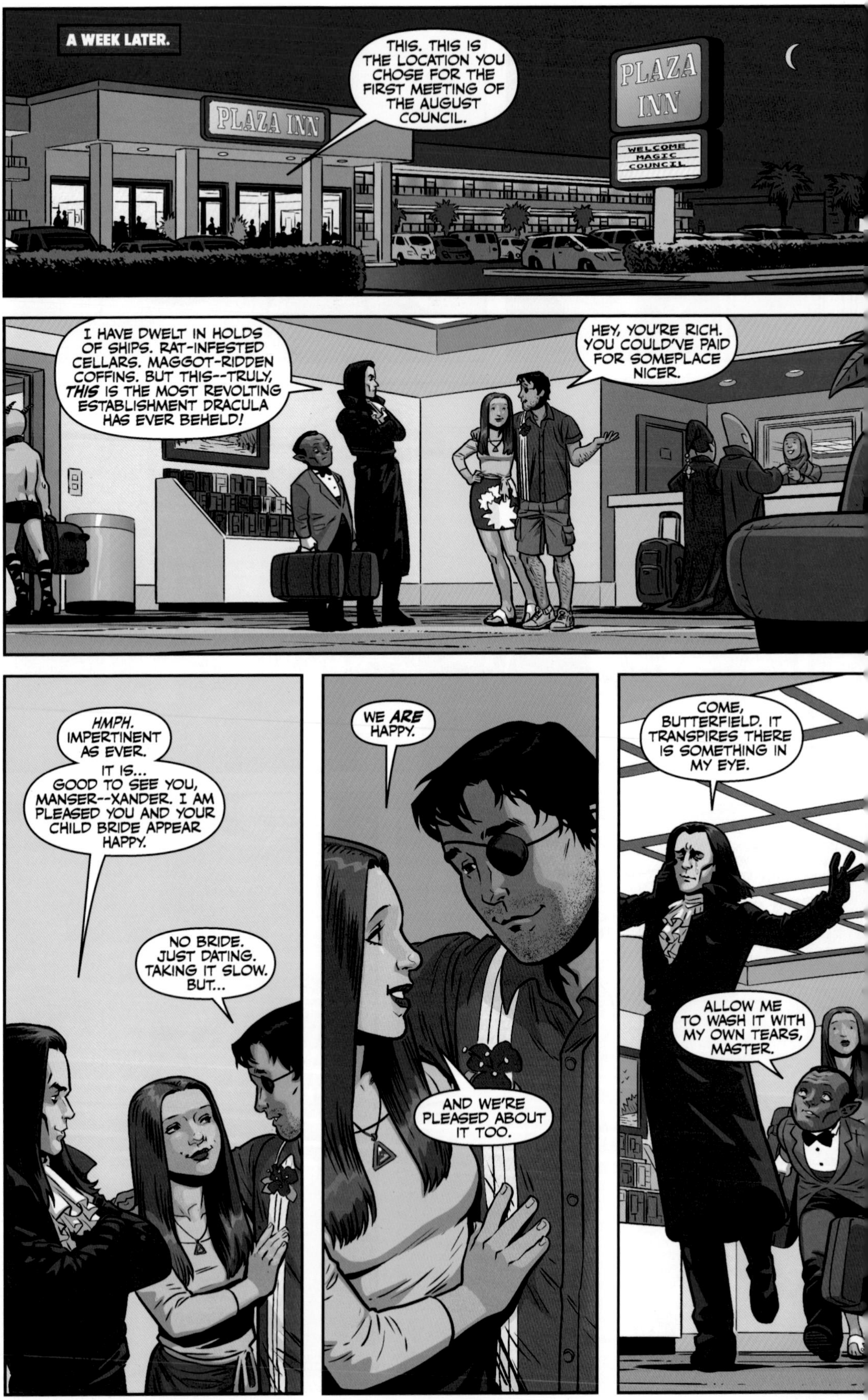
A WEEK LATER.
THIS. THIS IS THE LOCATION YOU CHOSE FOR THE FIRST MEETING OF THE AUGUST COUNCIL.
PLAZA INN
PLAZA INN
WELCOME MAGIC COUNCIL
I HAVE DWELT IN HOLDS OF SHIPS. RAT-INFESTED CELLARS. MAGGOT-RIDDEN COFFINS. BUT THIS--TRULY, *THIS* IS THE MOST REVOLTING ESTABLISHMENT DRACULA HAS EVER BEHELD!
HEY, YOU'RE RICH. YOU COULD'VE PAID FOR SOMEPLACE NICER.
HMPH. IMPERTINENT AS EVER.
IT IS... GOOD TO SEE YOU, MANSER--XANDER. I AM PLEASED YOU AND YOUR CHILD BRIDE APPEAR HAPPY.
NO BRIDE. JUST DATING. TAKING IT SLOW. BUT...
WE *ARE* HAPPY.
AND WE'RE PLEASED ABOUT IT TOO.
COME, BUTTERFIELD. IT TRANSPIRES THERE IS SOMETHING IN MY EYE.
ALLOW ME TO WASH IT WITH MY OWN TEARS, MASTER.

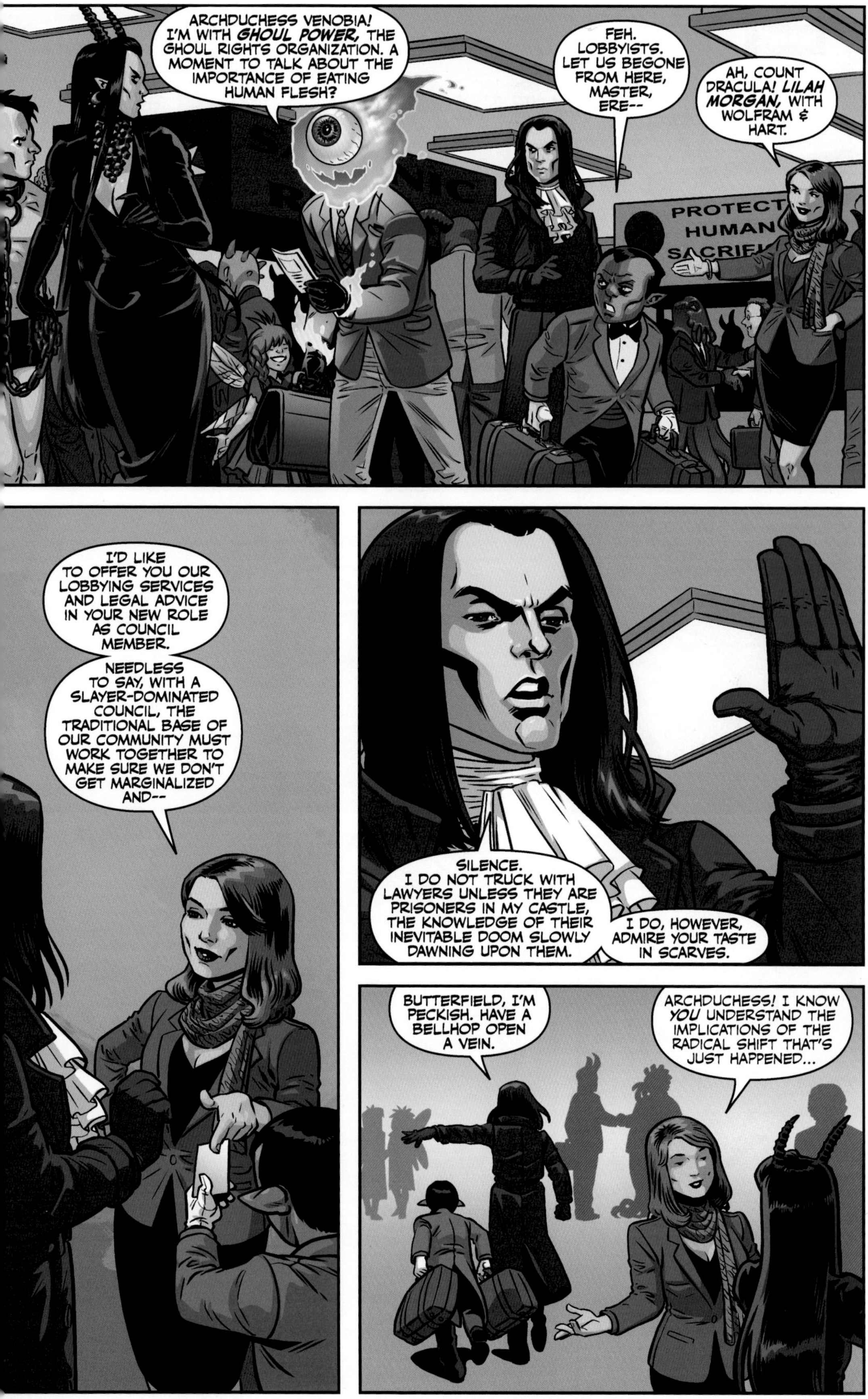
ARCHDUCHESS VENOBIA! I'M WITH GHOUL POWER, THE GHOUL RIGHTS ORGANIZATION. A MOMENT TO TALK ABOUT THE IMPORTANCE OF EATING HUMAN FLESH?
FEH. LOBBYISTS. LET US BEGONE FROM HERE, MASTER, ERE--
AH, COUNT DRACULA! LILAH MORGAN, WITH WOLFRAM & HART.
PROTECT HUMAN SACRIFI
I'D LIKE TO OFFER YOU OUR LOBBYING SERVICES AND LEGAL ADVICE IN YOUR NEW ROLE AS COUNCIL MEMBER.
NEEDLESS TO SAY, WITH A SLAYER-DOMINATED COUNCIL, THE TRADITIONAL BASE OF OUR COMMUNITY MUST WORK TOGETHER TO MAKE SURE WE DON'T GET MARGINALIZED AND--
SILENCE. I DO NOT TRUCK WITH LAWYERS UNLESS THEY ARE PRISONERS IN MY CASTLE, THE KNOWLEDGE OF THEIR INEVITABLE DOOM SLOWLY DAWNING UPON THEM.
I DO, HOWEVER, ADMIRE YOUR TASTE IN SCARVES.
BUTTERFIELD, I'M PECKISH. HAVE A BELLHOP OPEN A VEIN.
ARCHDUCHESS! I KNOW YOU UNDERSTAND THE IMPLICATIONS OF THE RADICAL SHIFT THAT'S JUST HAPPENED...

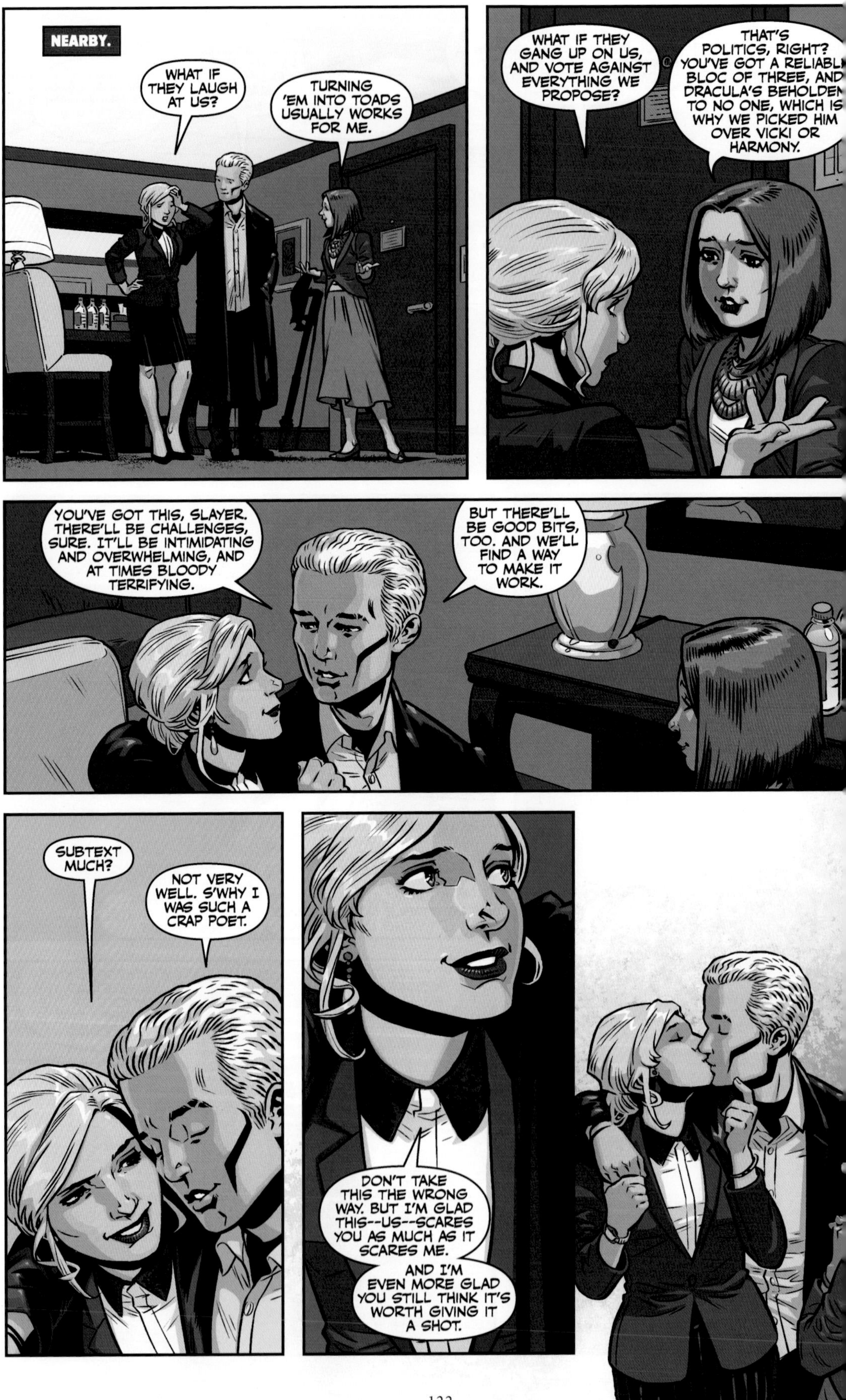
NEARBY.
WHAT IF THEY LAUGH AT US?
TURNING 'EM INTO TOADS USUALLY WORKS FOR ME.
WHAT IF THEY GANG UP ON US, AND VOTE AGAINST EVERYTHING WE PROPOSE?
THAT'S POLITICS, RIGHT? YOU'VE GOT A RELIABL BLOC OF THREE, AND DRACULA'S BEHOLDE TO NO ONE, WHICH IS WHY WE PICKED HIM OVER VICKI OR HARMONY.
YOU'VE GOT THIS, SLAYER. THERE'LL BE CHALLENGES, SURE. IT'LL BE INTIMIDATING AND OVERWHELMING, AND AT TIMES BLOODY TERRIFYING.
BUT THERE'LL BE GOOD BITS, TOO. AND WE'LL FIND A WAY TO MAKE IT WORK.
SUBTEXT MUCH?
NOT VERY WELL. S'WHY I WAS SUCH A CRAP POET.
DON'T TAKE THIS THE WRONG WAY. BUT I'M GLAD THIS--US--SCARES YOU AS MUCH AS IT SCARES ME.
AND I'M EVEN MORE GLAD YOU STILL THINK IT'S WORTH GIVING IT A SHOT.

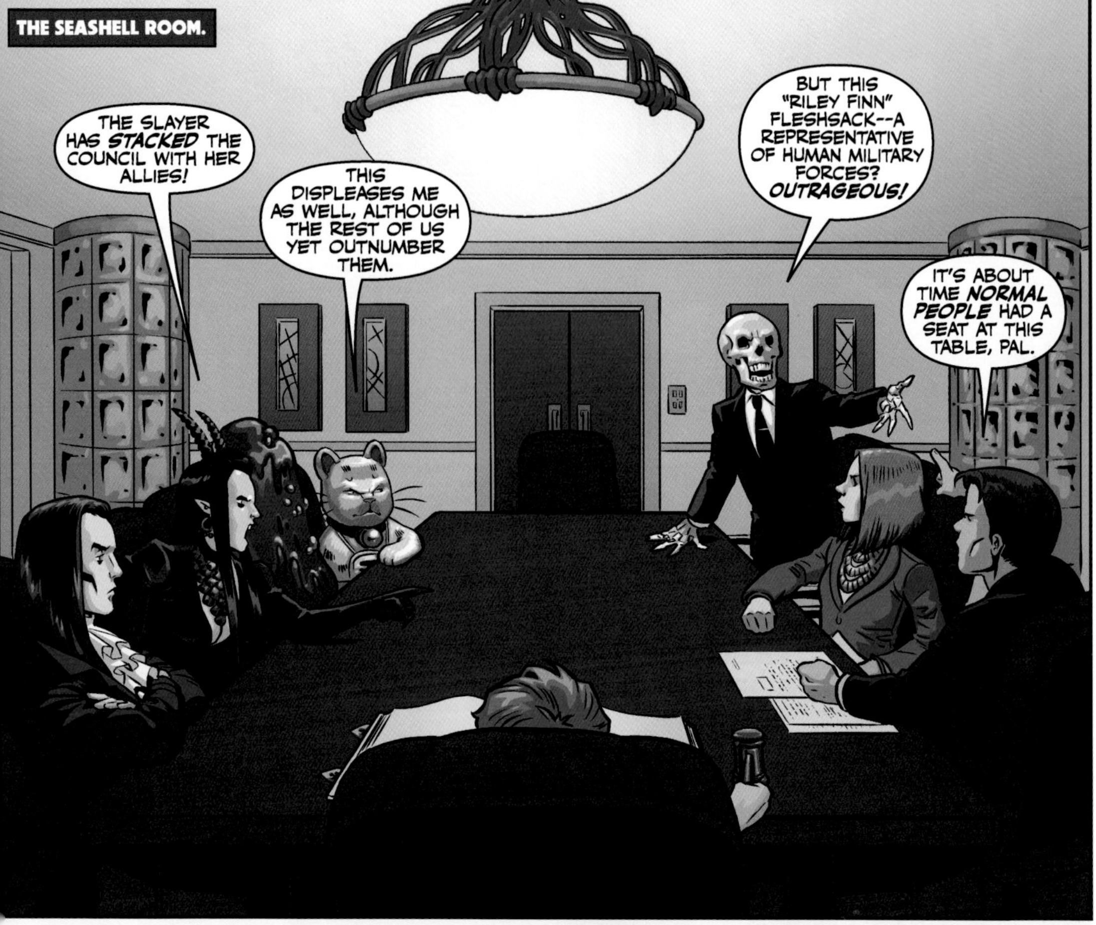
THE SEASHELL ROOM.
THE SLAYER HAS STACKED THE COUNCIL WITH HER ALLIES!
THIS DISPLEASES ME AS WELL, ALTHOUGH THE REST OF US YET OUTNUMBER THEM.
BUT THIS "RILEY FINN" FLESHSACK--A REPRESENTATIVE OF HUMAN MILITARY FORCES? OUTRAGEOUS!
IT'S ABOUT TIME NORMAL PEOPLE HAD A SEAT AT THIS TABLE, PAL.

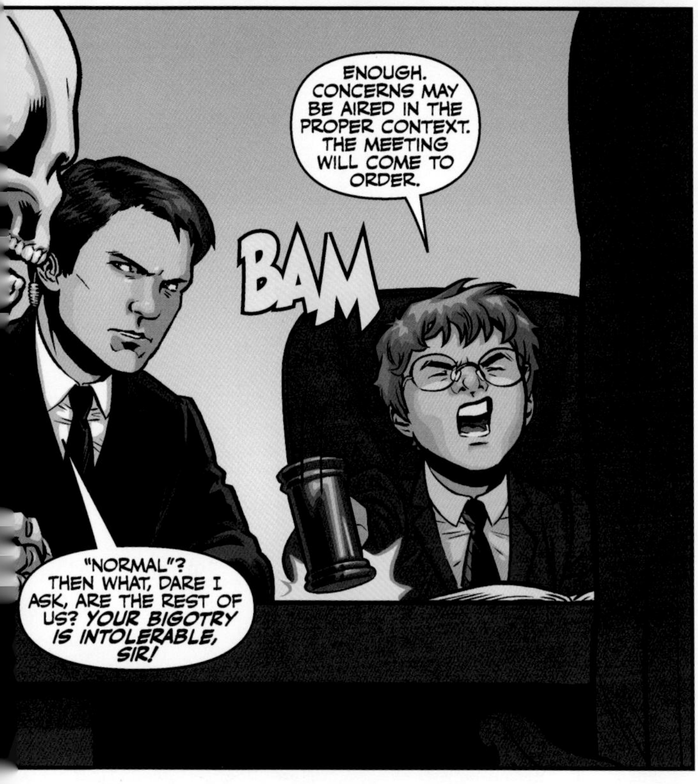
ENOUGH. CONCERNS MAY BE AIRED IN THE PROPER CONTEXT. THE MEETING WILL COME TO ORDER.
BAM
"NORMAL"? THEN WHAT, DARE I ASK, ARE THE REST OF US? YOUR BIGOTRY IS INTOLERABLE, SIR!

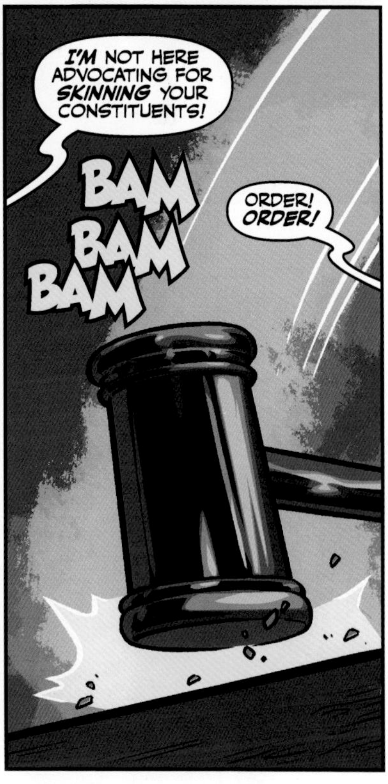
I'M NOT HERE ADVOCATING FOR SKINNING YOUR CONSTITUENTS!
BAM BAM BAM
ORDER! ORDER!

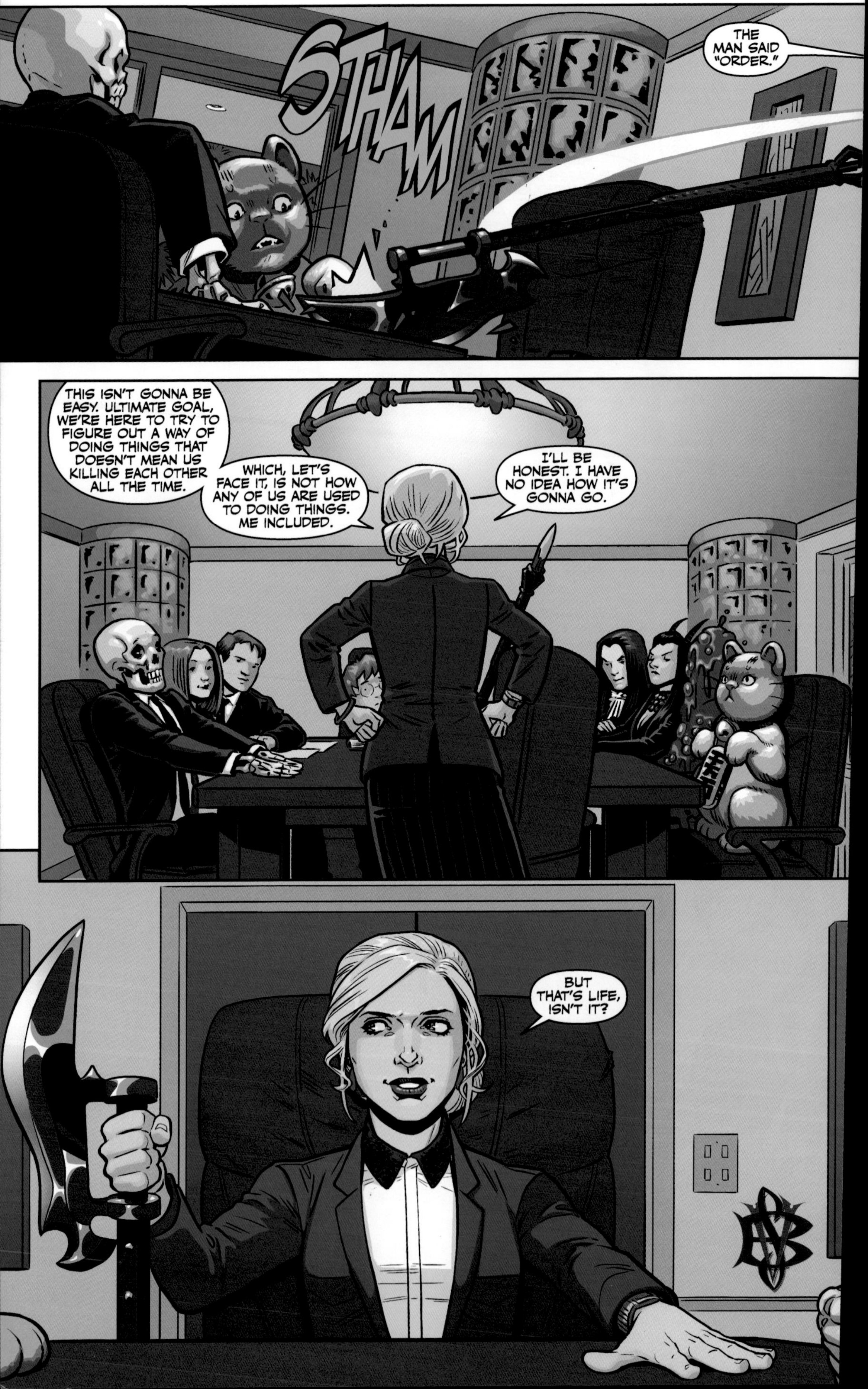
STHAM
THE MAN SAID "ORDER."
THIS ISN'T GONNA BE EASY. ULTIMATE GOAL, WE'RE HERE TO TRY TO FIGURE OUT A WAY OF DOING THINGS THAT DOESN'T MEAN US KILLING EACH OTHER ALL THE TIME.
WHICH, LET'S FACE IT, IS NOT HOW ANY OF US ARE USED TO DOING THINGS. ME INCLUDED.
I'LL BE HONEST. I HAVE NO IDEA HOW IT'S GONNA GO.
BUT THAT'S LIFE, ISN'T IT?

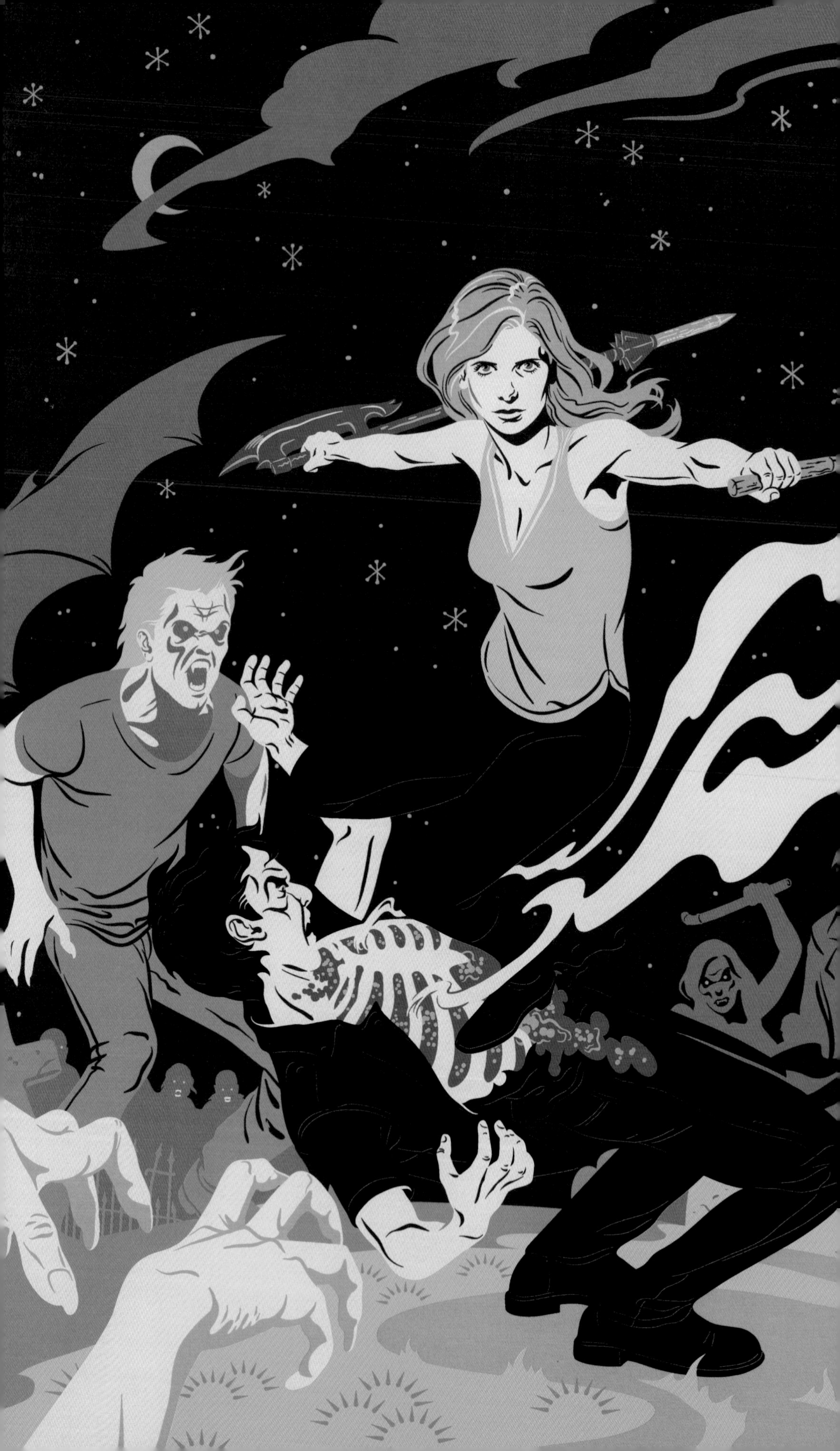

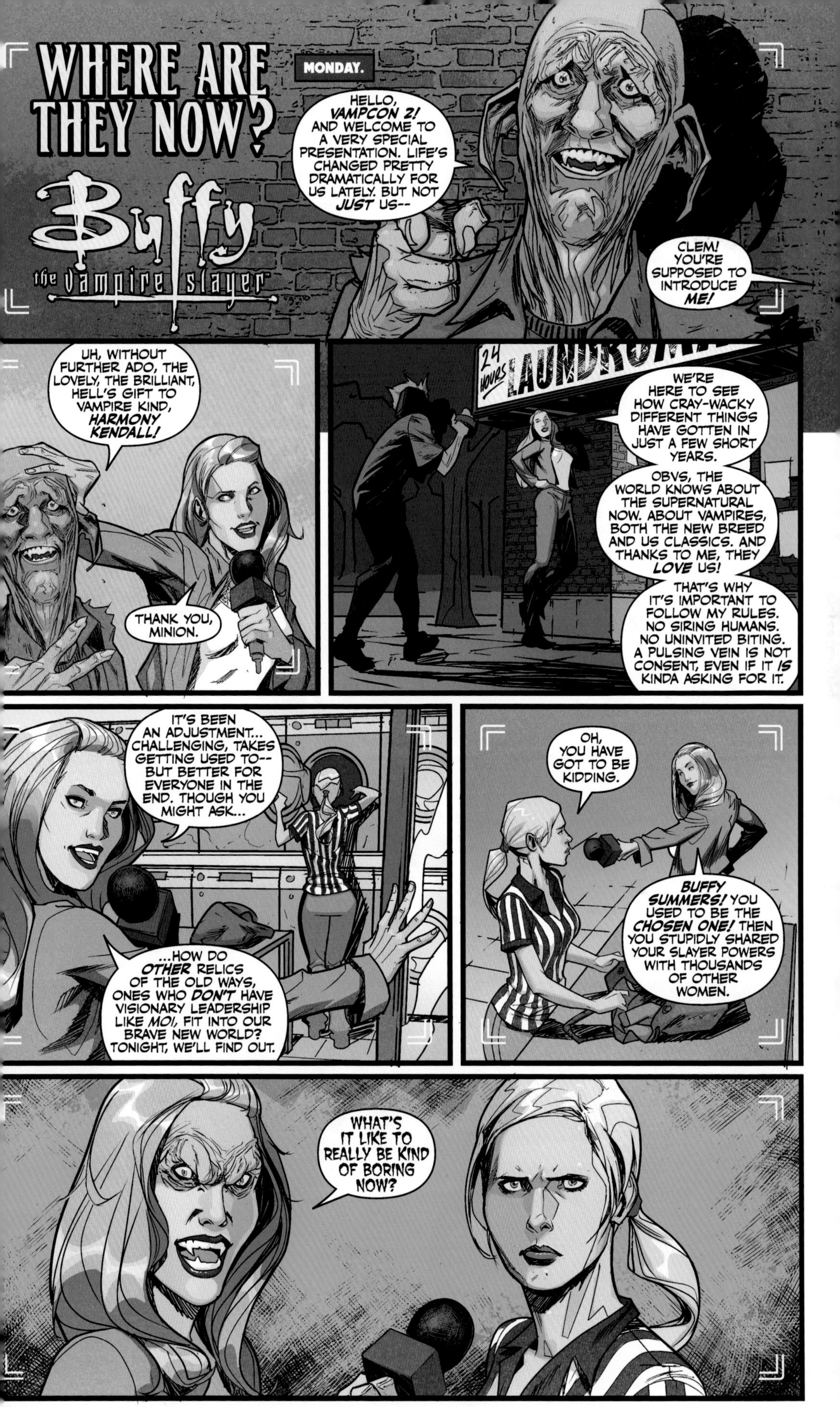
WHERE ARE THEY NOW?
Buffy the Vampire Slayer
MONDAY.
HELLO, VAMPCON 2! AND WELCOME TO A VERY SPECIAL PRESENTATION. LIFE'S CHANGED PRETTY DRAMATICALLY FOR US LATELY. BUT NOT JUST US--
CLEM! YOU'RE SUPPOSED TO INTRODUCE ME!
UH, WITHOUT FURTHER ADO, THE LOVELY, THE BRILLIANT, HELL'S GIFT TO VAMPIRE KIND, HARMONY KENDALL!
THANK YOU, MINION.
24 HOURS LAUNDROM
WE'RE HERE TO SEE HOW CRAY-WACKY DIFFERENT THINGS HAVE GOTTEN IN JUST A FEW SHORT YEARS.
OBVS, THE WORLD KNOWS ABOUT THE SUPERNATURAL NOW. ABOUT VAMPIRES, BOTH THE NEW BREED AND US CLASSICS. AND THANKS TO ME, THEY LOVE US!
THAT'S WHY IT'S IMPORTANT TO FOLLOW MY RULES. NO SIRING HUMANS. NO UNINVITED BITING. A PULSING VEIN IS NOT CONSENT, EVEN IF IT IS KINDA ASKING FOR IT.
IT'S BEEN AN ADJUSTMENT... CHALLENGING, TAKES GETTING USED TO-- BUT BETTER FOR EVERYONE IN THE END. THOUGH YOU MIGHT ASK...
...HOW DO OTHER RELICS OF THE OLD WAYS, ONES WHO DON'T HAVE VISIONARY LEADERSHIP LIKE MOI, FIT INTO OUR BRAVE NEW WORLD? TONIGHT, WE'LL FIND OUT.
OH, YOU HAVE GOT TO BE KIDDING.
BUFFY SUMMERS! YOU USED TO BE THE CHOSEN ONE! THEN YOU STUPIDLY SHARED YOUR SLAYER POWERS WITH THOUSANDS OF OTHER WOMEN.
WHAT'S IT LIKE TO REALLY BE KIND OF BORING NOW?

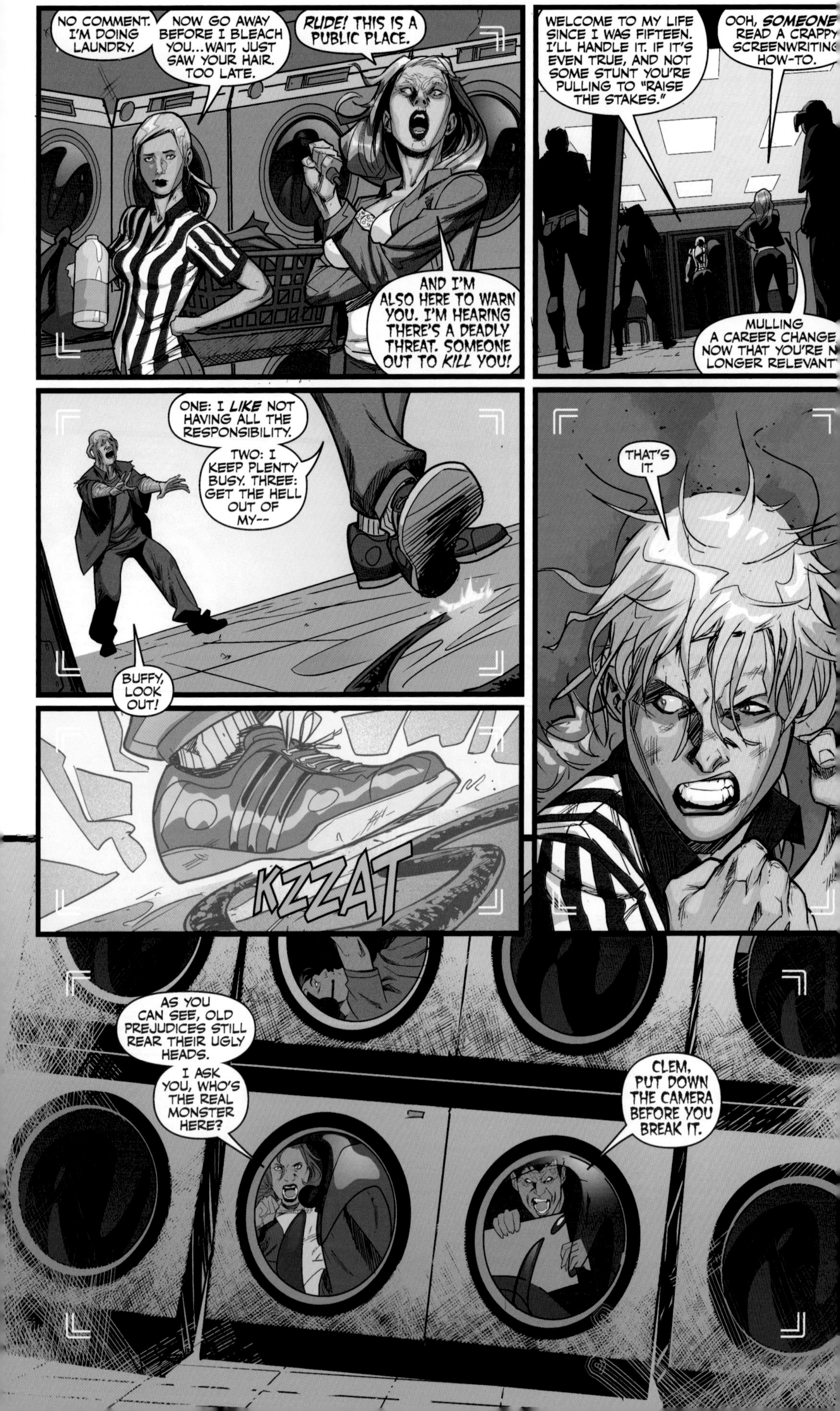
NO COMMENT. I'M DOING LAUNDRY.
NOW GO AWAY BEFORE I BLEACH YOU...WAIT, JUST SAW YOUR HAIR. TOO LATE.
RUDE! THIS IS A PUBLIC PLACE.
AND I'M ALSO HERE TO WARN YOU. I'M HEARING THERE'S A DEADLY THREAT. SOMEONE OUT TO KILL YOU!
WELCOME TO MY LIFE SINCE I WAS FIFTEEN. I'LL HANDLE IT. IF IT'S EVEN TRUE, AND NOT SOME STUNT YOU'RE PULLING TO "RAISE THE STAKES."
OOH, SOMEONE READ A CRAPPY SCREENWRITING HOW-TO.
MULLING A CAREER CHANGE NOW THAT YOU'RE N LONGER RELEVANT
ONE: I LIKE NOT HAVING ALL THE RESPONSIBILITY.
TWO: I KEEP PLENTY BUSY. THREE: GET THE HELL OUT OF MY--
BUFFY, LOOK OUT!
KZZAT
THAT'S IT.
AS YOU CAN SEE, OLD PREJUDICES STILL REAR THEIR UGLY HEADS.
I ASK YOU, WHO'S THE REAL MONSTER HERE?
CLEM, PUT DOWN THE CAMERA BEFORE YOU BREAK IT.

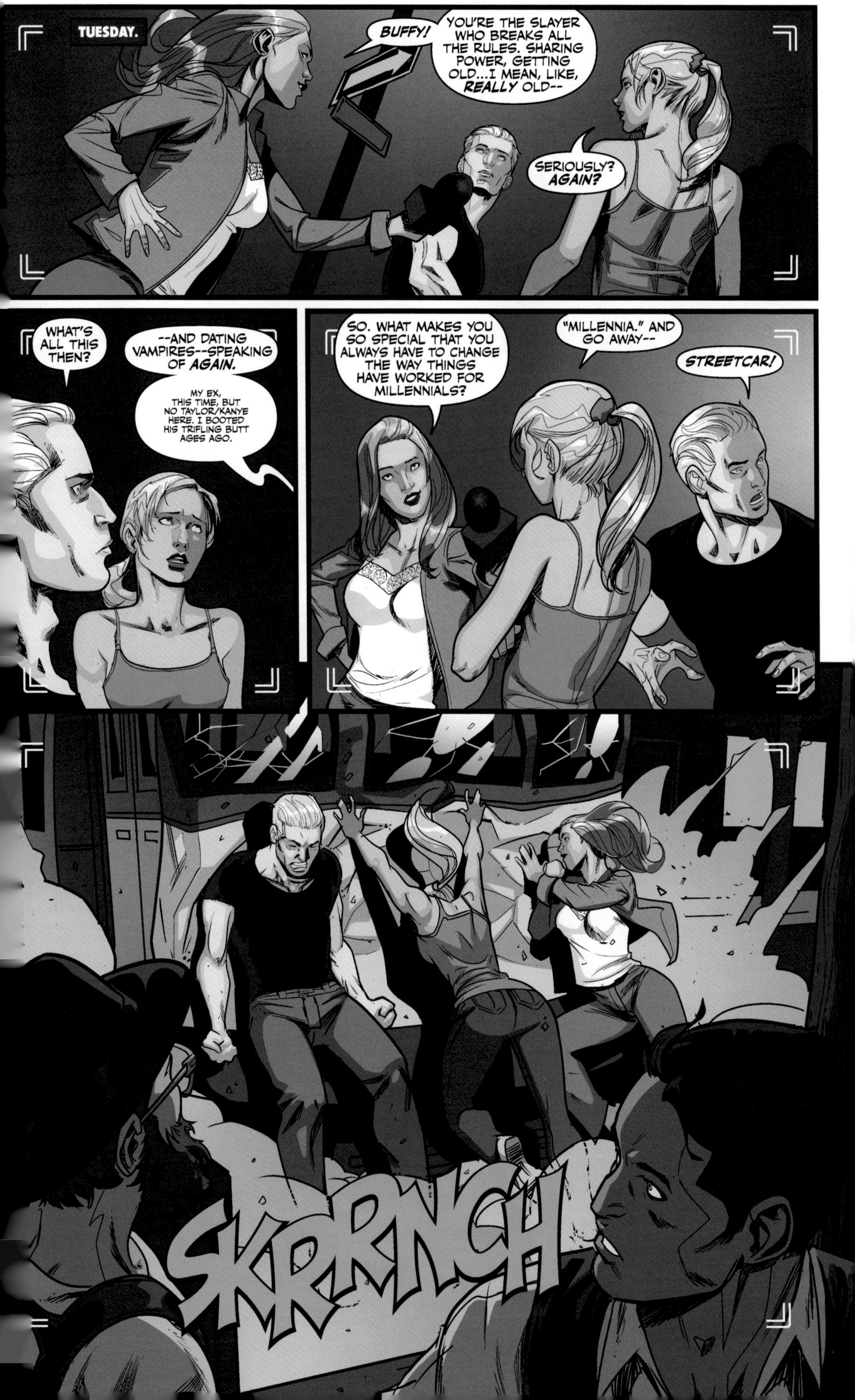
TUESDAY.
BUFFY!
YOU'RE THE SLAYER WHO BREAKS ALL THE RULES. SHARING POWER, GETTING OLD...I MEAN, LIKE, REALLY OLD--
SERIOUSLY? AGAIN?
WHAT'S ALL THIS THEN?
--AND DATING VAMPIRES--SPEAKING OF AGAIN.
MY EX, THIS TIME, BUT NO TAYLOR/KANYE HERE. I BOOTED HIS TRIFLING BUTT AGES AGO.
SO. WHAT MAKES YOU SO SPECIAL THAT YOU ALWAYS HAVE TO CHANGE THE WAY THINGS HAVE WORKED FOR MILLENNIALS?
"MILLENNIA." AND GO AWAY--
STREETCAR!
SKRRNCH

THANKS! OUR BRAKES JUST WENT!

I TOLD BUFFY SOMEONE'S TRYING TO KILL HER!

RIGHT. FUNNY HOW IT HAPPENS WHEN YOU'RE THERE TO FILM IT.

OH! MY! GOD! I WAS STANDING THERE TOO! HOW YOU DARE YOU INSANGUINATE--

"INSINUATE." SPIKE, LET'S JUST GO. DATE NIGHT'S KINDA RUINED.

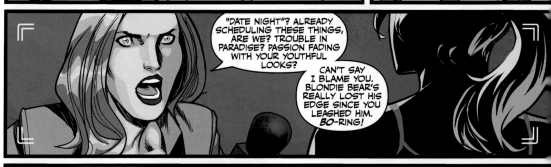

"DATE NIGHT"? ALREADY SCHEDULING THESE THINGS, ARE WE? TROUBLE IN PARADISE? PASSION FADING WITH YOUR YOUTHFUL LOOKS?

CAN'T SAY I BLAME YOU. BLONDIE BEAR'S REALLY LOST HIS EDGE SINCE YOU LEASHED HIM. BO-RING!

THIS IS HOW A BLOKE'S MEANT TO ACT WHEN HE'S IN A RELATIONSHIP, I'LL HAVE YOU--

SPIKE. BETTER THIS WAY.

KRIK

VAMP

CLEM! RECORD THIS SO WE CAN SUE THEM!

YOU GUYS SAID NOT TO TOUCH THE CAMERA.

JUST DO IT!

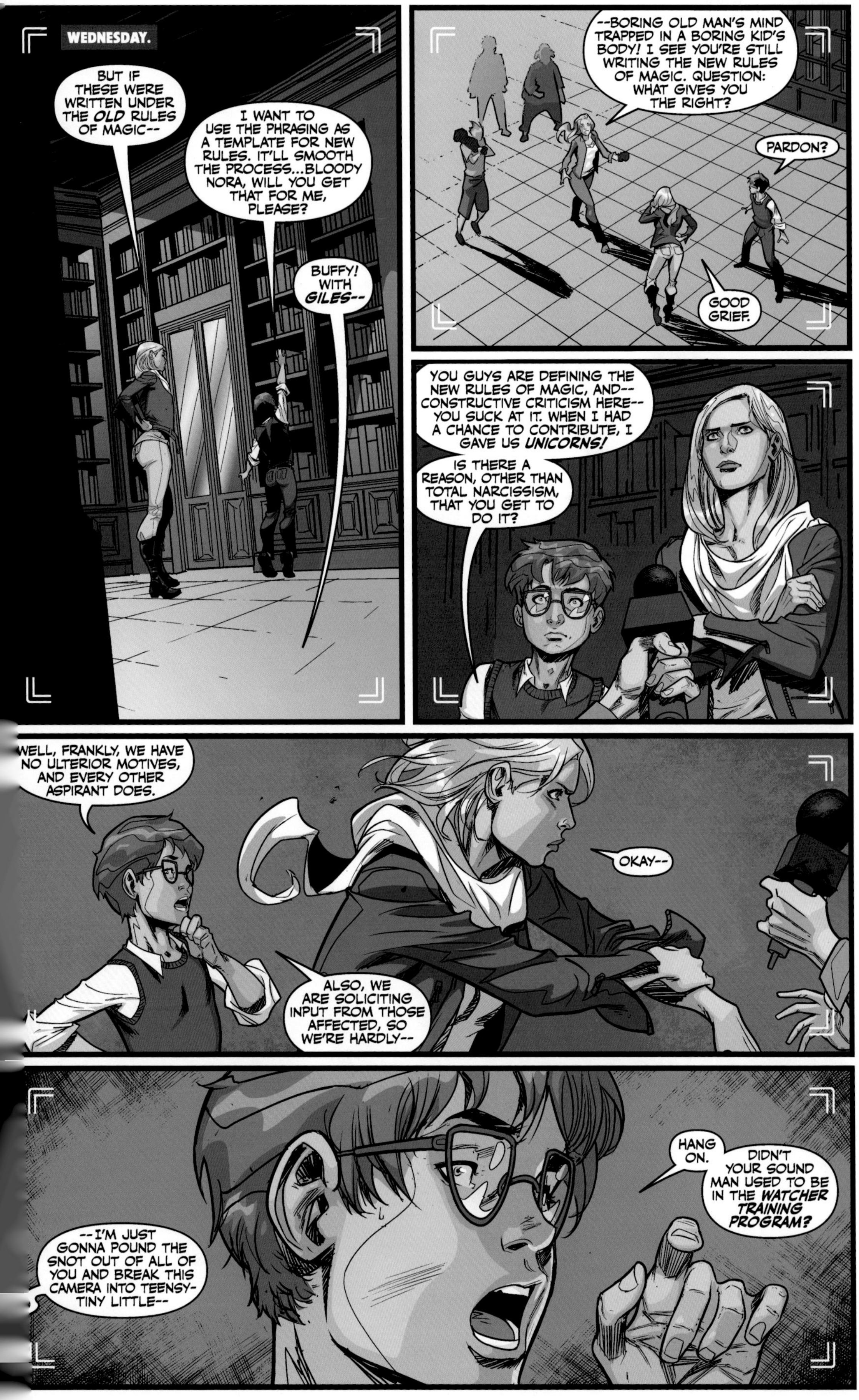
WEDNESDAY.
BUT IF THESE WERE WRITTEN UNDER THE *OLD* RULES OF MAGIC--
I WANT TO USE THE PHRASING AS A TEMPLATE FOR NEW RULES. IT'LL SMOOTH THE PROCESS...BLOODY NORA, WILL YOU GET THAT FOR ME, PLEASE?
BUFFY! WITH *GILES--*
--BORING OLD MAN'S MIND TRAPPED IN A BORING KID'S BODY! I SEE YOU'RE STILL WRITING THE NEW RULES OF MAGIC. QUESTION: WHAT GIVES YOU THE RIGHT?
PARDON?
GOOD GRIEF.
YOU GUYS ARE DEFINING THE NEW RULES OF MAGIC, AND--CONSTRUCTIVE CRITICISM HERE--YOU SUCK AT IT. WHEN I HAD A CHANCE TO CONTRIBUTE, I GAVE US *UNICORNS!*
IS THERE A REASON, OTHER THAN TOTAL NARCISSISM, THAT YOU GET TO DO IT?
WELL, FRANKLY, WE HAVE NO ULTERIOR MOTIVES, AND EVERY OTHER ASPIRANT DOES.
OKAY--
ALSO, WE ARE SOLICITING INPUT FROM THOSE AFFECTED, SO WE'RE HARDLY--
--I'M JUST GONNA POUND THE SNOT OUT OF ALL OF YOU AND BREAK THIS CAMERA INTO TEENSY-TINY LITTLE--
HANG ON.
DIDN'T YOUR SOUND MAN USED TO BE IN THE *WATCHER TRAINING PROGRAM?*

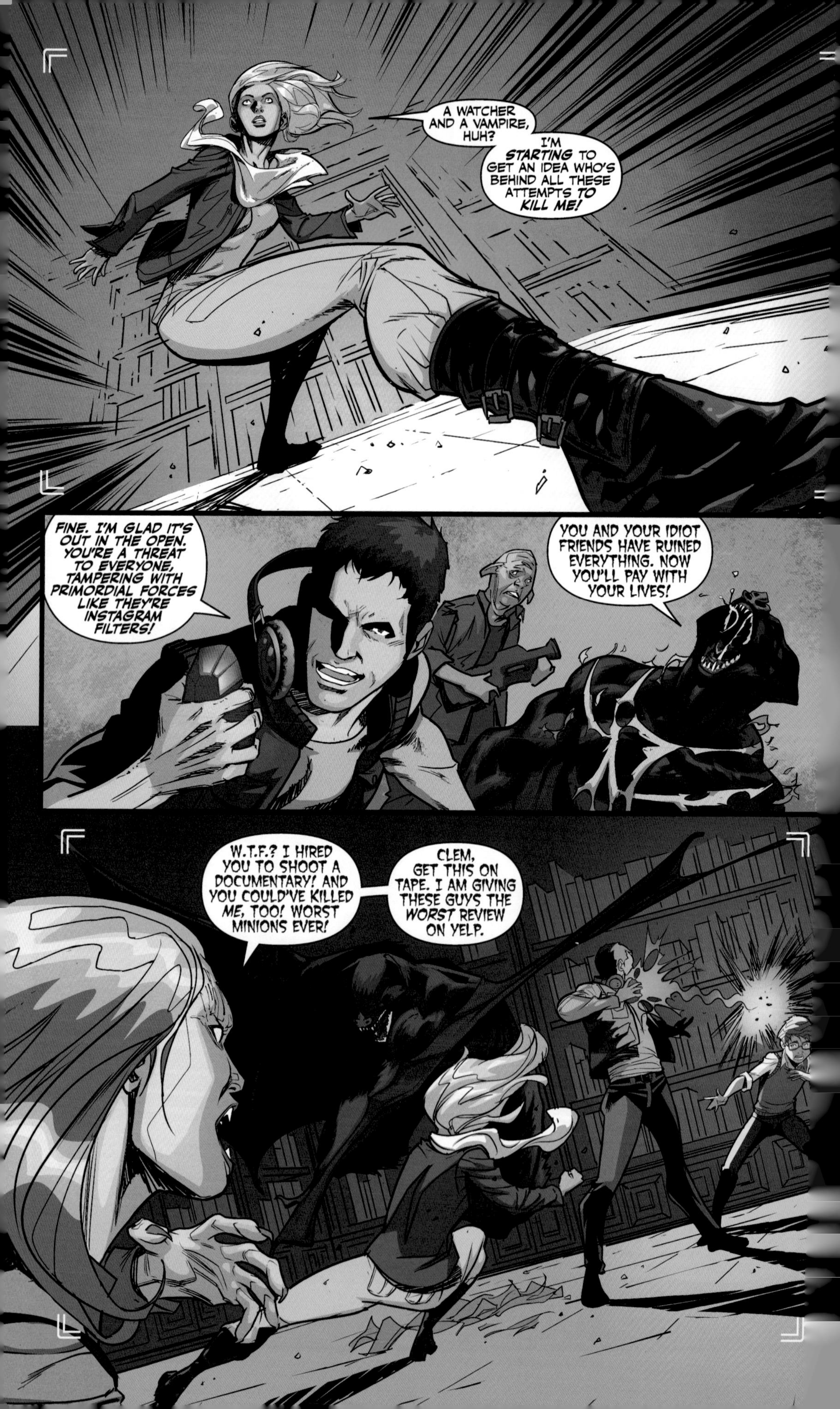

A WATCHER AND A VAMPIRE, HUH?
I'M STARTING TO GET AN IDEA WHO'S BEHIND ALL THESE ATTEMPTS TO KILL ME!
FINE. I'M GLAD IT'S OUT IN THE OPEN. YOU'RE A THREAT TO EVERYONE, TAMPERING WITH PRIMORDIAL FORCES LIKE THEY'RE INSTAGRAM FILTERS!
YOU AND YOUR IDIOT FRIENDS HAVE RUINED EVERYTHING. NOW YOU'LL PAY WITH YOUR LIVES!
W.T.F.? I HIRED YOU TO SHOOT A DOCUMENTARY! AND YOU COULD'VE KILLED ME, TOO! WORST MINIONS EVER!
CLEM, GET THIS ON TAPE. I AM GIVING THESE GUYS THE WORST REVIEW ON YELP.

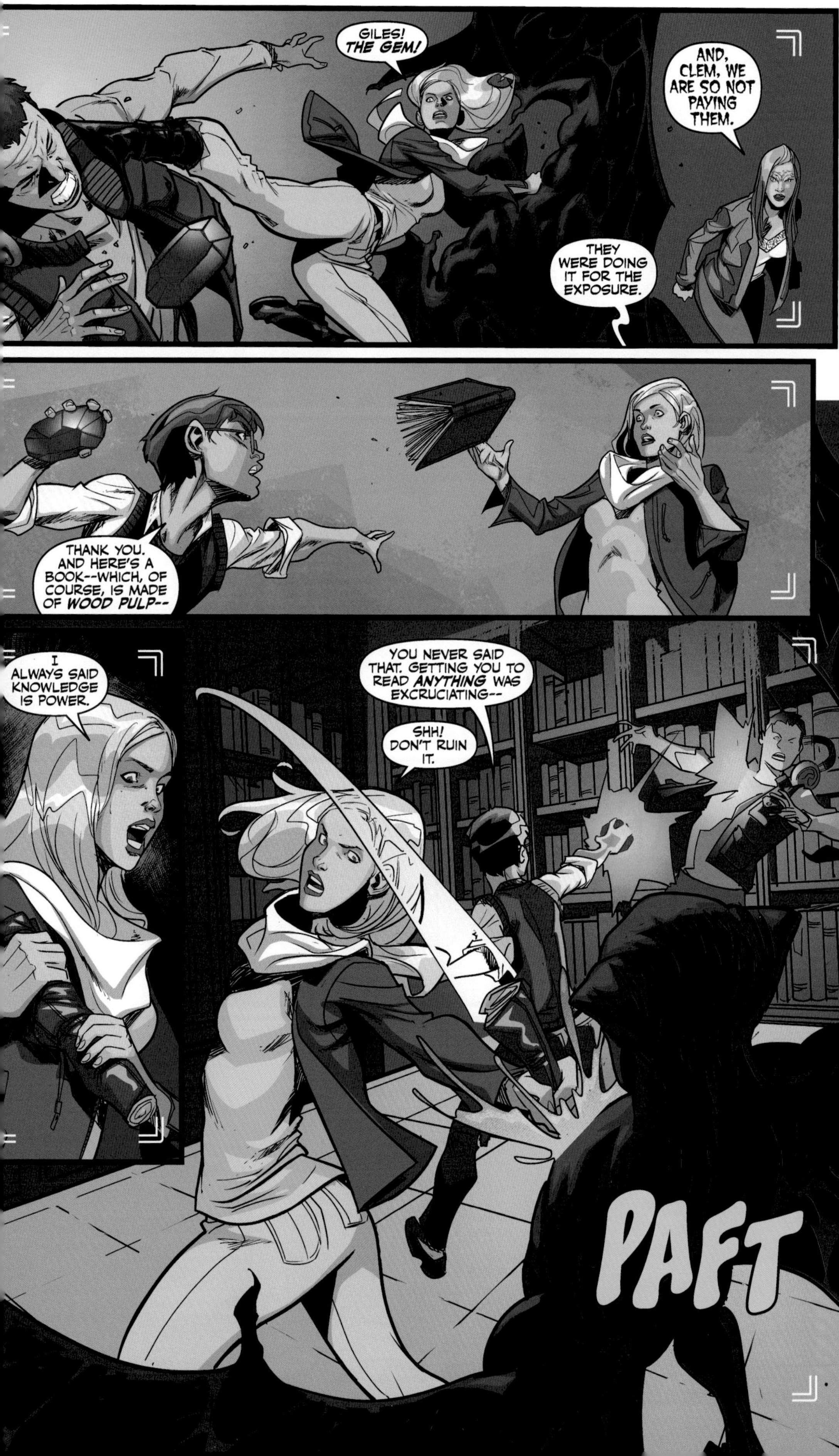

GILES! THE GEM!
AND, CLEM, WE ARE SO NOT PAYING THEM.
THEY WERE DOING IT FOR THE EXPOSURE.
THANK YOU. AND HERE'S A BOOK--WHICH, OF COURSE, IS MADE OF WOOD PULP--
I ALWAYS SAID KNOWLEDGE IS POWER.
YOU NEVER SAID THAT. GETTING YOU TO READ ANYTHING WAS EXCRUCIATING--
SHH! DON'T RUIN IT.
PAFT

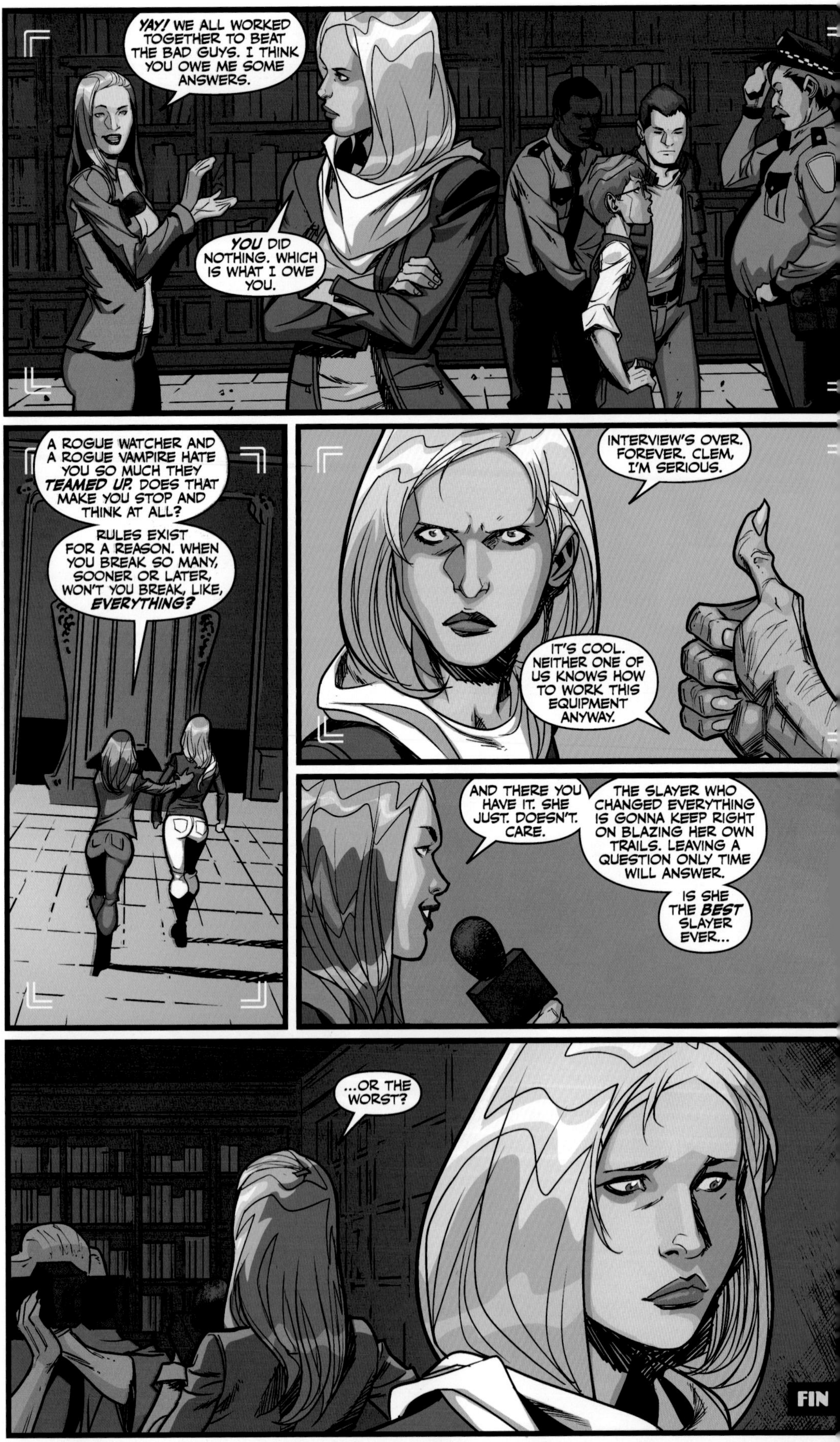

YAY! WE ALL WORKED TOGETHER TO BEAT THE BAD GUYS. I THINK YOU OWE ME SOME ANSWERS.
YOU DID NOTHING. WHICH IS WHAT I OWE YOU.
A ROGUE WATCHER AND A ROGUE VAMPIRE HATE YOU SO MUCH THEY TEAMED UP. DOES THAT MAKE YOU STOP AND THINK AT ALL?
RULES EXIST FOR A REASON. WHEN YOU BREAK SO MANY, SOONER OR LATER, WON'T YOU BREAK, LIKE, EVERYTHING?
INTERVIEW'S OVER. FOREVER. CLEM, I'M SERIOUS.
IT'S COOL. NEITHER ONE OF US KNOWS HOW TO WORK THIS EQUIPMENT ANYWAY.
AND THERE YOU HAVE IT. SHE JUST. DOESN'T. CARE.
THE SLAYER WHO CHANGED EVERYTHING IS GONNA KEEP RIGHT ON BLAZING HER OWN TRAILS. LEAVING A QUESTION ONLY TIME WILL ANSWER.
IS SHE THE BEST SLAYER EVER...
...OR THE WORST?
FIN

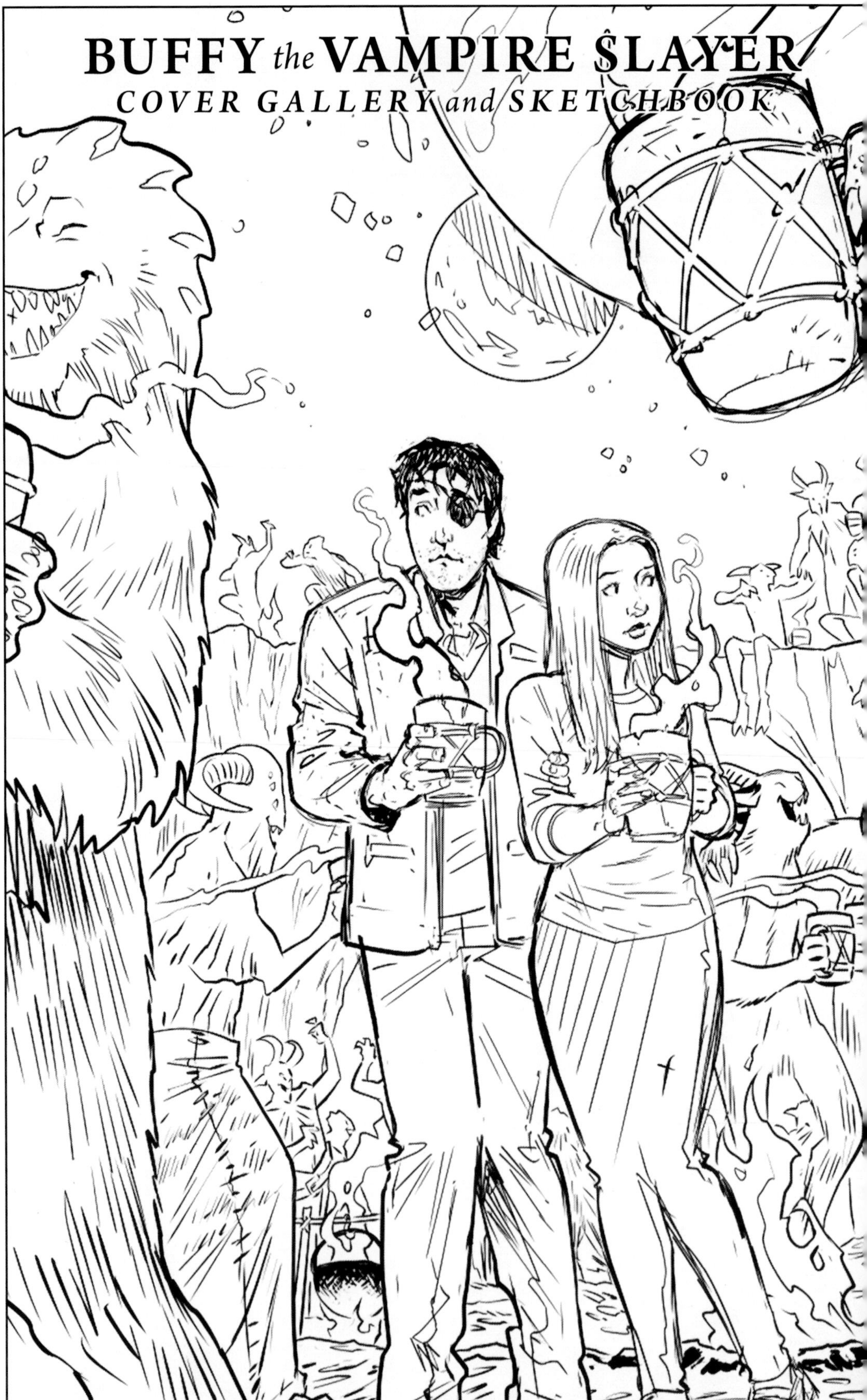

Pencils for the *Buffy* Season 10 #27 variant cover. Dawn and Xander lost in another dimension filled with demons, wary and uncert

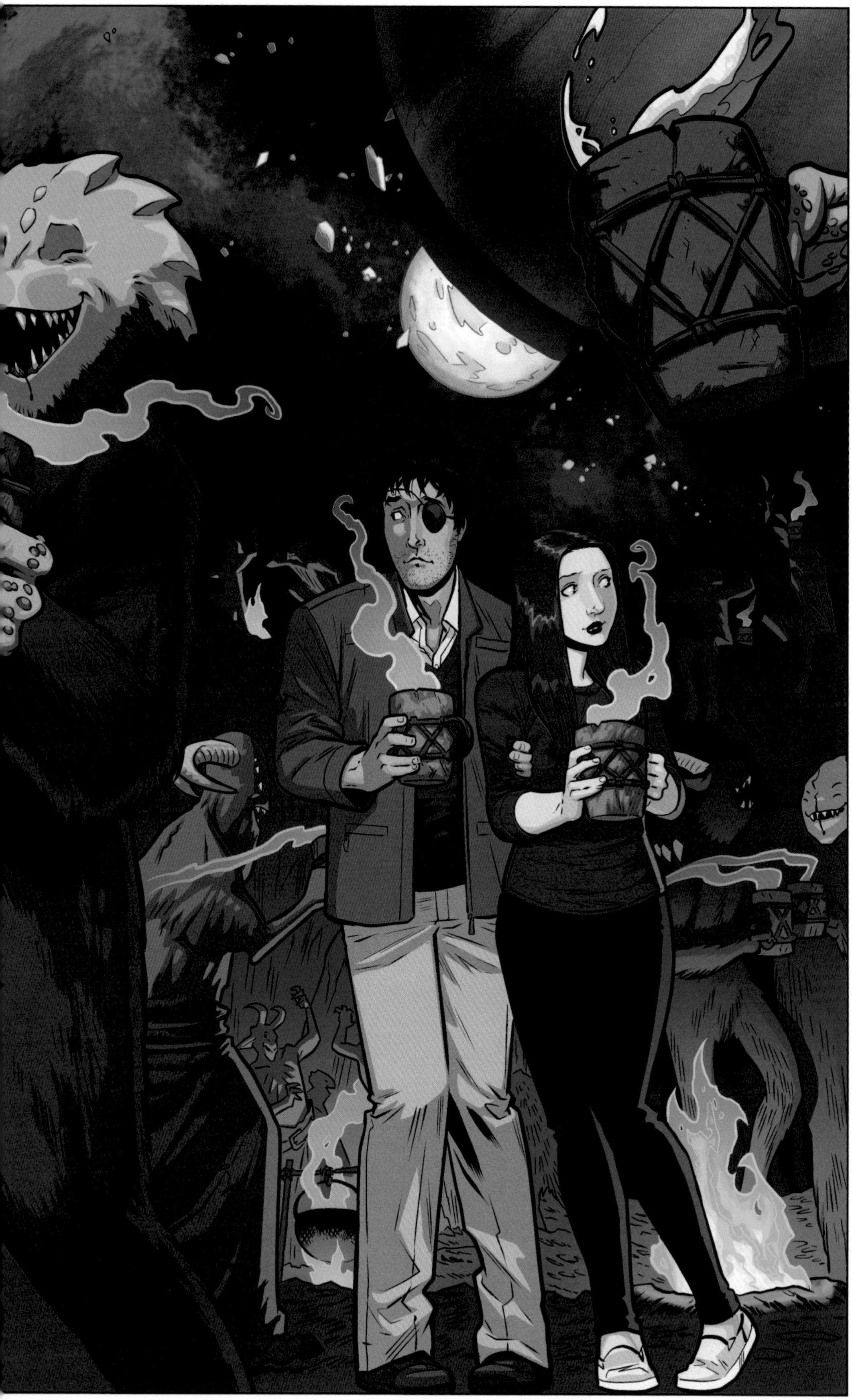

Variant cover art for *Buffy* Season 10 #27, by Rebekah Isaacs with Dan Jackson.

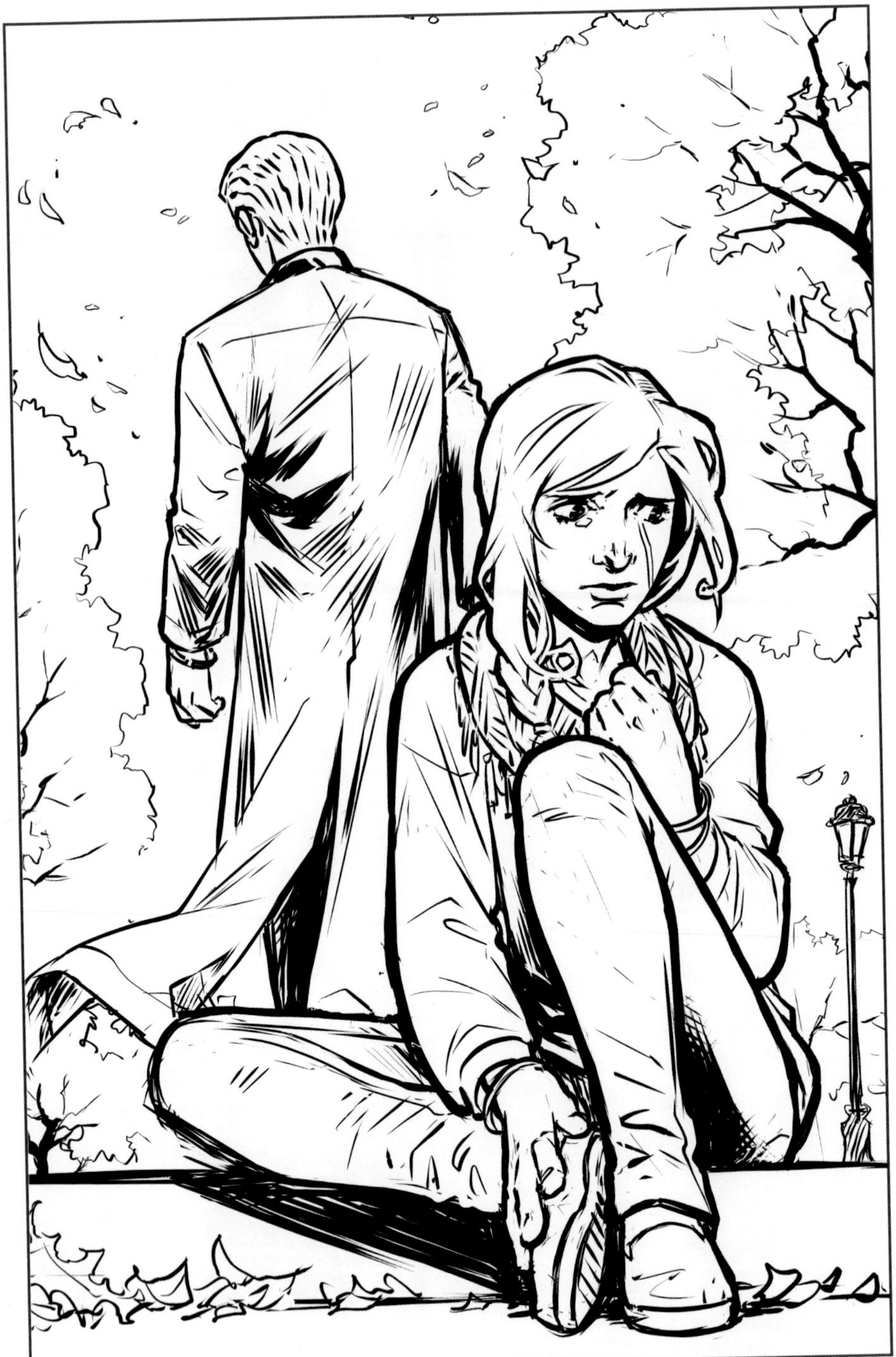

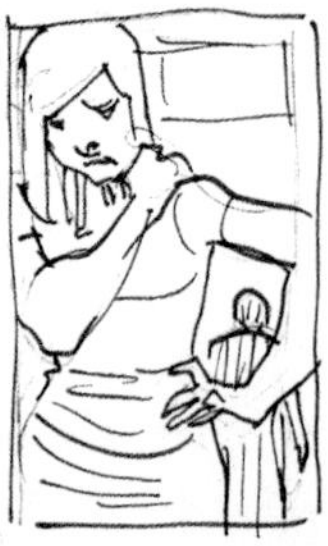

A

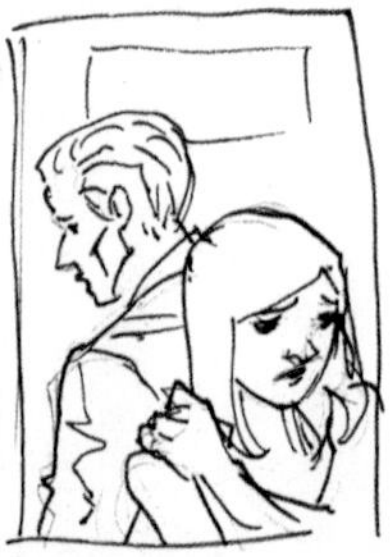

B

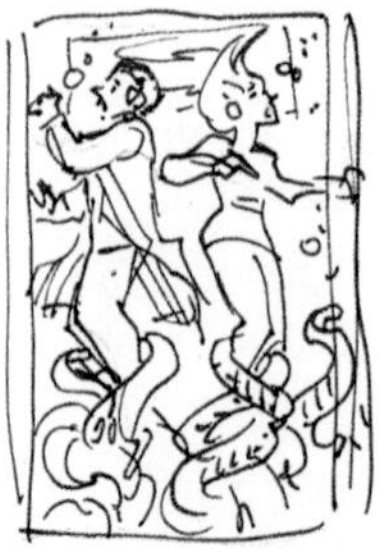

C

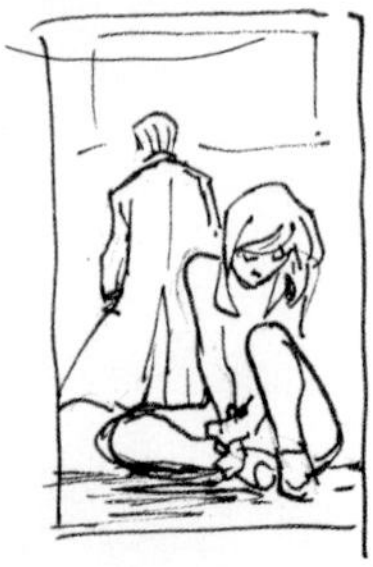

D

Thumbnail concepts and cover pencils for the *Buffy* Season 10 #28 variant cover.

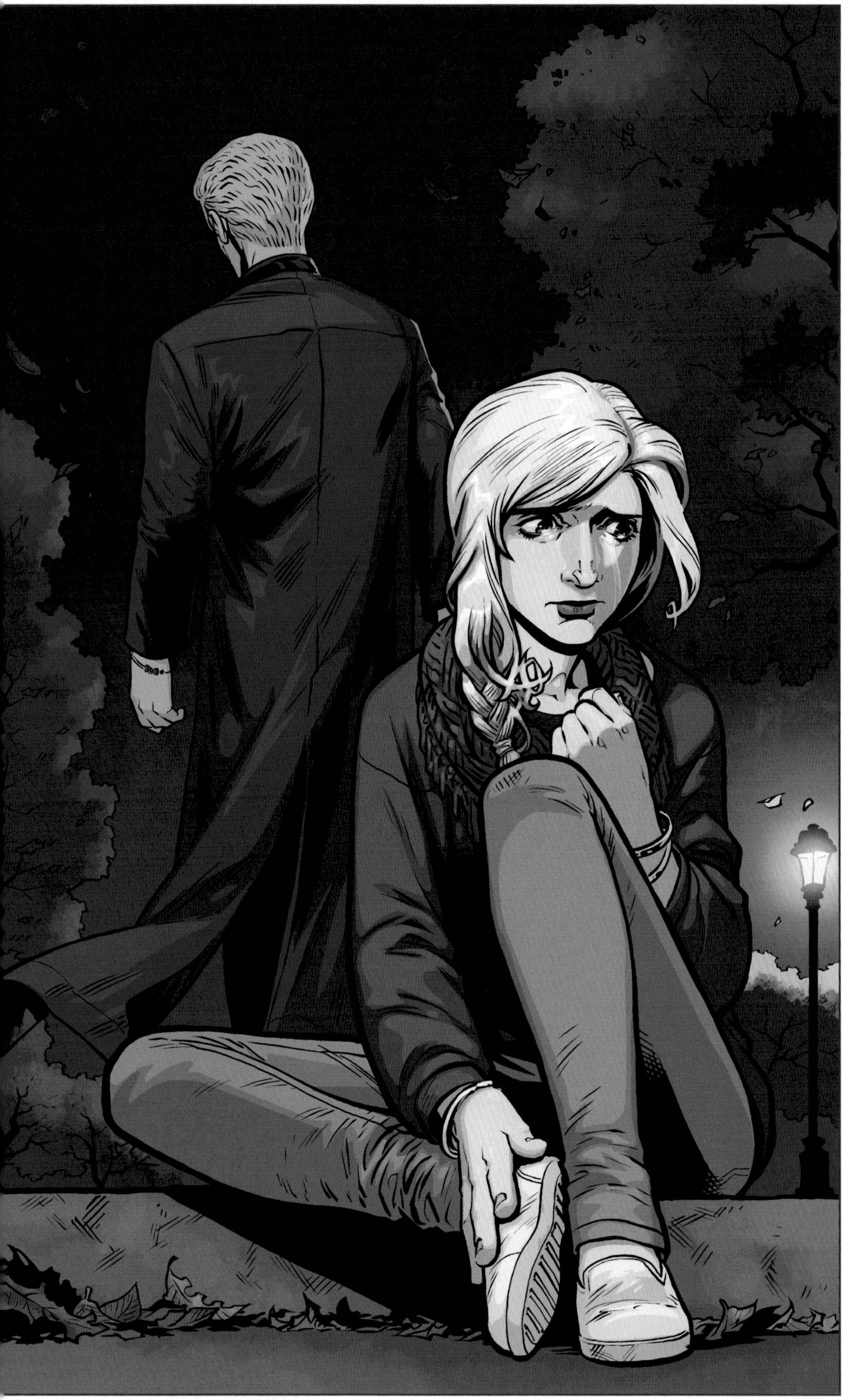

ant cover art for *Buffy* Season 10 #28, by Rebekah Isaacs with Dan Jackson.

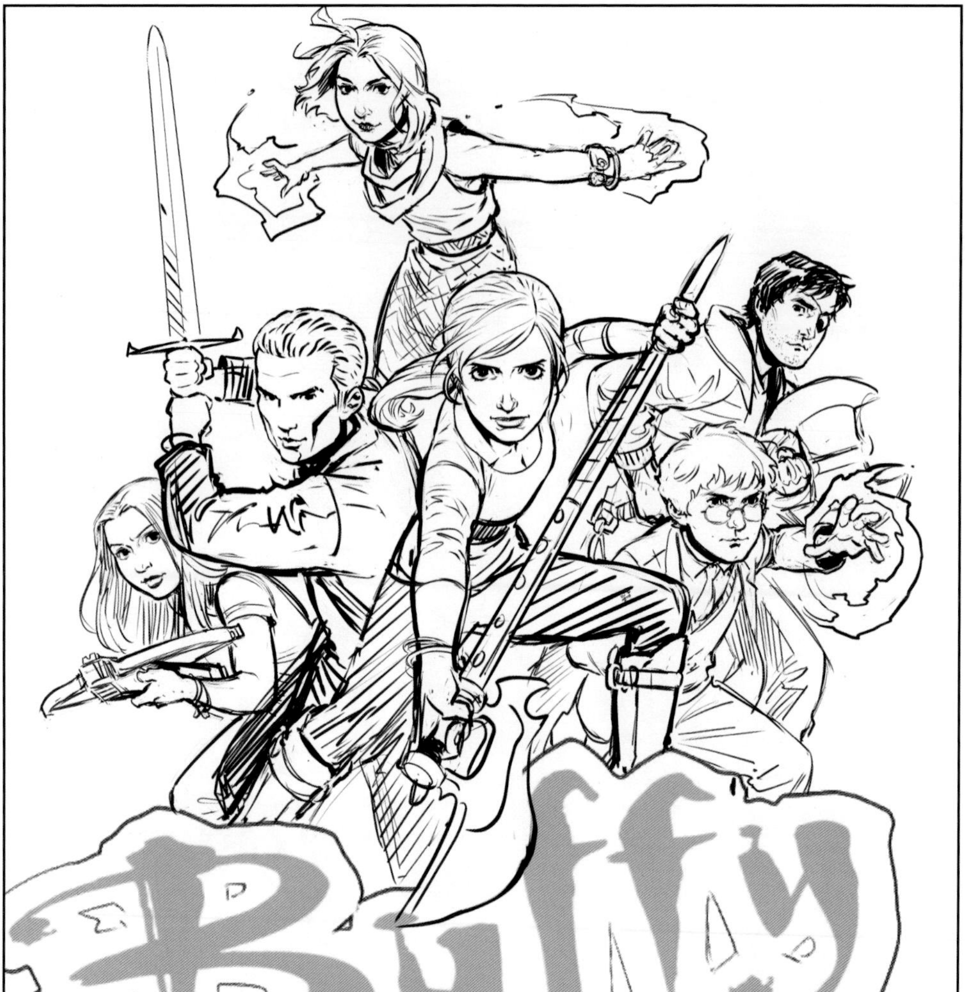
Buffy
the vampire slayer

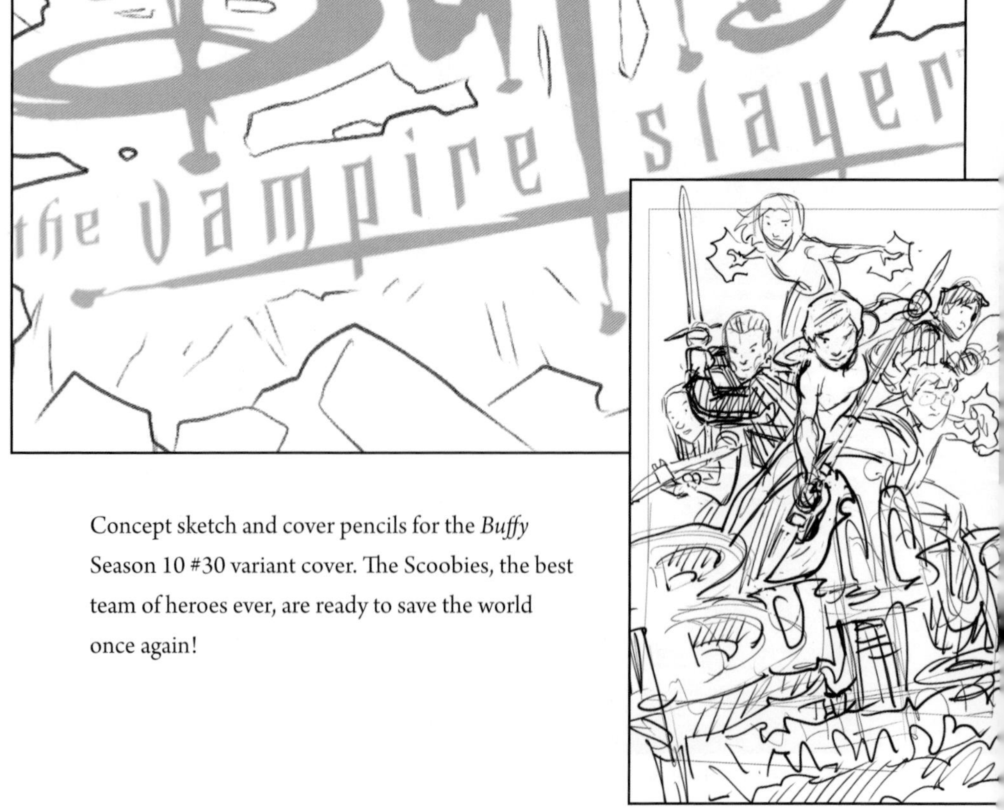

Concept sketch and cover pencils for the *Buffy* Season 10 #30 variant cover. The Scoobies, the best team of heroes ever, are ready to save the world once again!

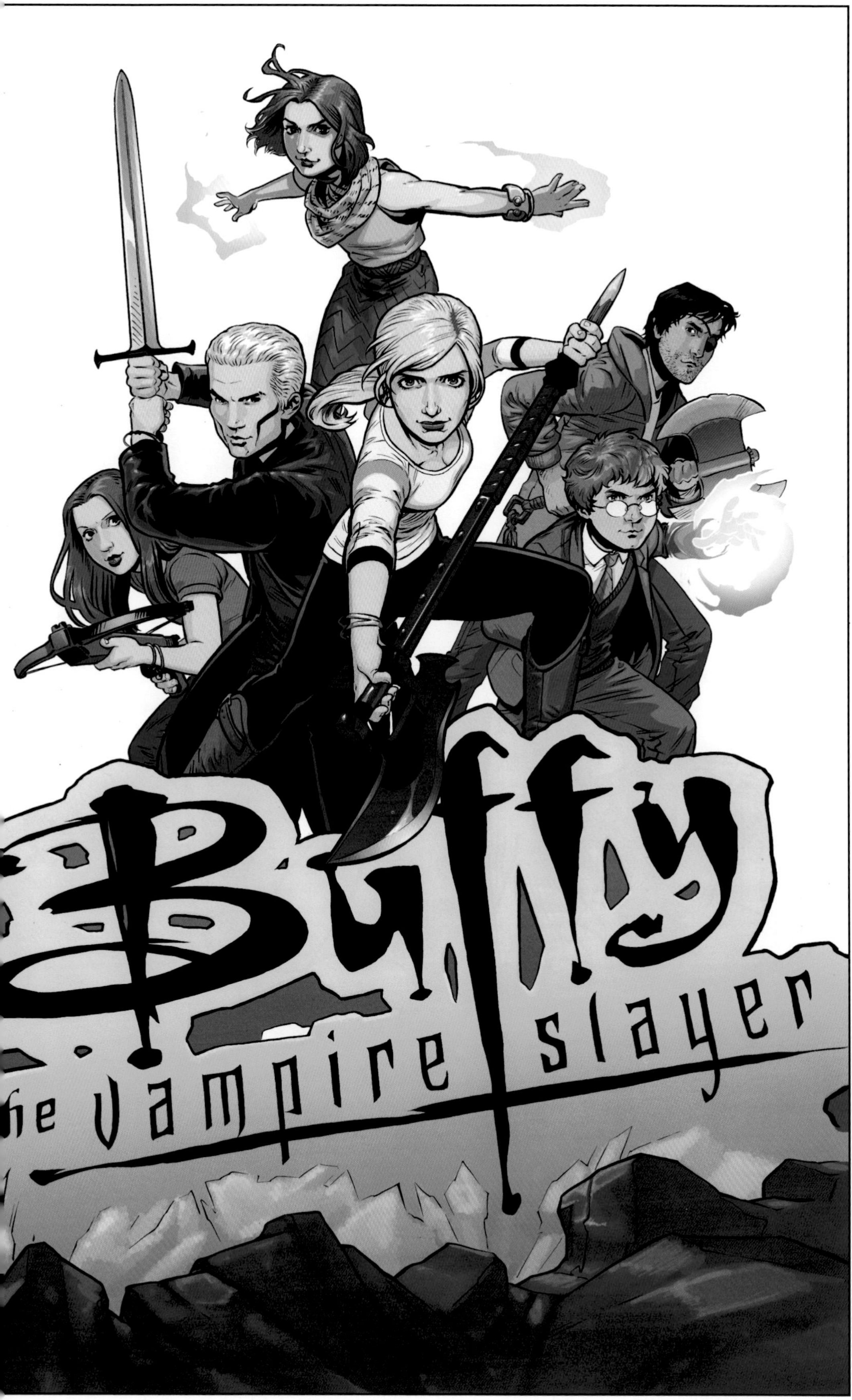
Buffy
he Vampire slayer

ant cover art for *Buffy* Season 10 #30, by Rebekah Isaacs with Dan Jackson.

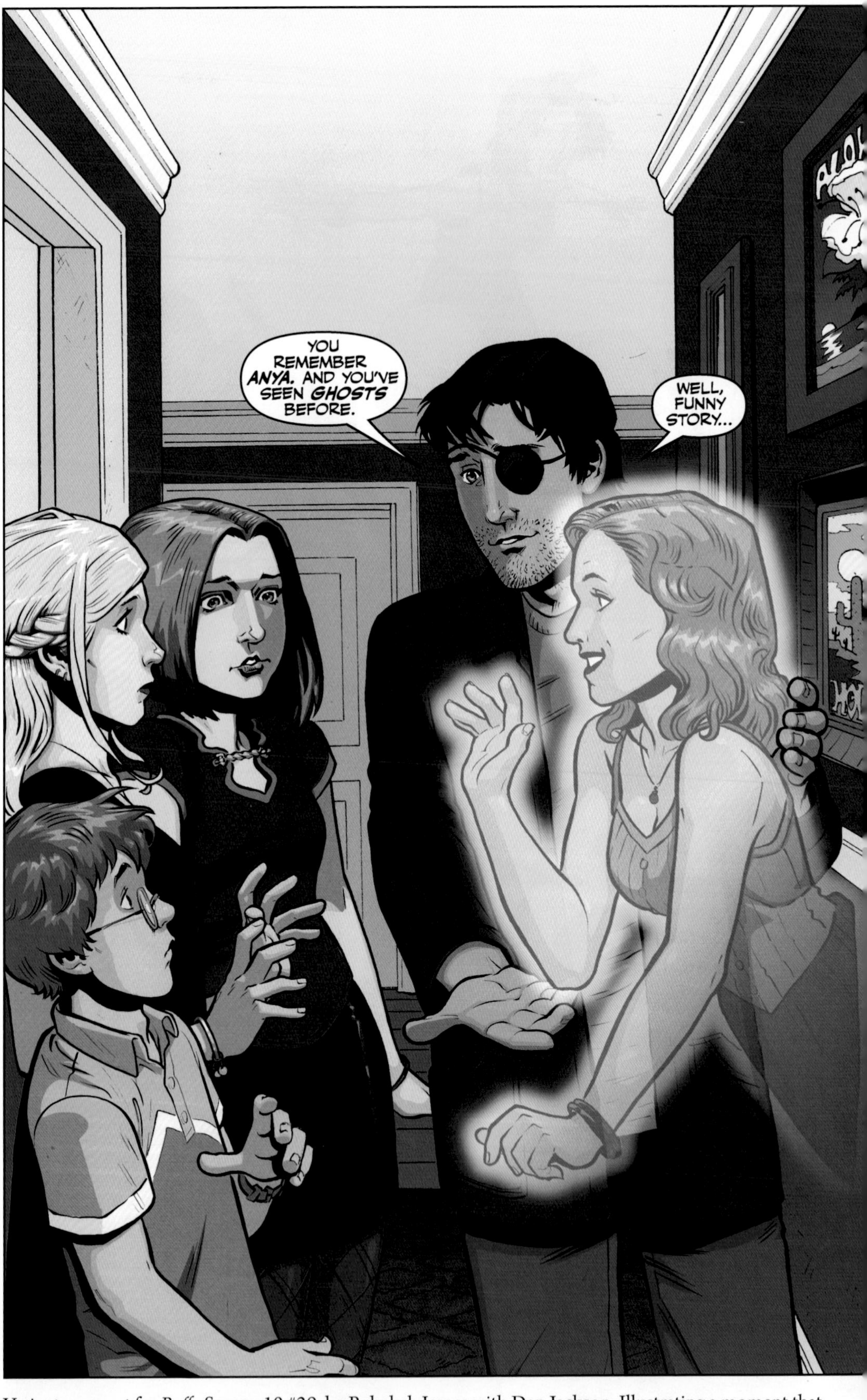
YOU REMEMBER ANYA. AND YOU'VE SEEN GHOSTS BEFORE.
WELL, FUNNY STORY...

Variant cover art for *Buffy* Season 10 #29, by Rebekah Isaacs with Dan Jackson. Illustrating a moment that, maybe, should have happened. Oh, Xander . . .

UFFY THE VAMPIRE
LAYER SEASON 8

LUME 1: THE LONG WAY HOME
Whedon and Georges Jeanty
N 978-1-59307-822-5 | $15.99

LUME 2: NO FUTURE FOR YOU
an K. Vaughan, Georges Jeanty,
Joss Whedon
N 978-1-59307-963-5 | $15.99

LUME 3: WOLVES AT THE GATE
w Goddard, Georges Jeanty, and Joss Whedon
N 978-1-59582-165-2 | $15.99

LUME 4: TIME OF YOUR LIFE
Whedon, Jeph Loeb,
rges Jeanty, and others
N 978-1-59582-310-6 | $15.99

LUME 5: PREDATORS AND PREY
Whedon, Jane Espenson, Georges Jeanty,
f Richards, and others
N 978-1-59582-342-7 | $15.99

LUME 6: RETREAT
Whedon, Jane Espenson, Georges Jeanty,
l Moline, and others
N 978-1-59582-415-8 | $15.99

LUME 7: TWILIGHT
Whedon, Brad Meltzer, and Georges Jeanty
N 978-1-59582-558-2 | $16.99

LUME 8: LAST GLEAMING
Whedon, Scott Allie, and Georges Jeanty
N 978-1-59582-610-7 | $16.99

UFFY THE VAMPIRE
LAYER SEASON 8
IBRARY EDITION

LUME 1 ISBN 978-1-59582-888-0 | $29.99
LUME 2 ISBN 978-1-59582-935-1 | $29.99
LUME 3 ISBN 978-1-59582-978-8 | $29.99
LUME 4 ISBN 978-1-61655-127-8 | $29.99

BUFFY THE VAMPIRE SLAYER SEASON 9

VOLUME 1: FREEFALL
Joss Whedon, Andrew Chambliss, Georges Jeanty, and others
ISBN 978-1-59582-922-1 | $17.99

VOLUME 2: ON YOUR OWN
Andrew Chambliss, Scott Allie, Georges Jeanty, and others
ISBN 978-1-59582-990-0 | $17.99

VOLUME 3: GUARDED
Joss Whedon, Jane Espenson, Drew Z. Greenberg, Georges Jeanty, and others
ISBN 978-1-61655-099-8 | $17.99

VOLUME 4: WELCOME TO THE TEAM
Andrew Chambliss, Georges Jeanty, Karl Moline, and others
ISBN 978-1-61655-166-7 | $17.99

VOLUME 5: THE CORE
Andrew Chambliss, Georges Jeanty, and others
ISBN 978-1-61655-254-1 | $17.99

BUFFY THE VAMPIRE SLAYER SEASON 9 LIBRARY EDITION

VOLUME 1 ISBN 978-1-61655-715-7 | $29.99
VOLUME 2 ISBN 978-1-61655-716-4 | $29.99
VOLUME 3 ISBN 978-1-61655-717-1 | $29.99

BUFFY THE VAMPIRE SLAYER SEASON 10

VOLUME 1: NEW RULES
Christos Gage, Rebekah Isaacs, Nicholas Brendon, and others
ISBN 978-1-61655-490-3 | $18.99

VOLUME 2: I WISH
Christos Gage, Rebekah Isaacs, Nicholas Brendon, and others
ISBN 978-1-61655-600-6 | $18.99

VOLUME 3: LOVE DARES YOU
Christos Gage, Rebekah Isaacs, Nicholas Brendon, and Megan Levens
ISBN 978-1-61655-758-4 | $18.99

VOLUME 4: OLD DEMONS
Christos Gage and Rebekah Isaacs
ISBN 978-1-61655-802-4 | $18.99

ANGEL & FAITH SEASON 9

VOLUME 1: LIVE THROUGH THIS
Christos Gage, Rebekah Isaacs, and Phil Noto
ISBN 978-1-59582-887-3 | $17.99

VOLUME 2: DADDY ISSUES
Christos Gage, Rebekah Isaacs, and Chris Samnee
ISBN 978-1-59582-960-3 | $17.99

VOLUME 3: FAMILY REUNION
Christos Gage, Rebekah Isaacs, Lee Garbett, and David Lapham
ISBN 978-1-61655-079-0 | $17.99

VOLUME 4: DEATH AND CONSEQUENCES
Christos Gage and Rebekah Isaacs
ISBN 978-1-61655-165-0 | $17.99

VOLUME 5: WHAT YOU WANT, NOT WHAT YOU NEED
Christos Gage and Rebekah Isaacs
ISBN 978-1-61655-253-4 | $17.99

ANGEL & FAITH SEASON 9 LIBRARY EDITION

VOLUME 1 ISBN 978-1-61655-712-6 | $29.99
VOLUME 2 ISBN 978-1-61655-713-3 | $29.99
VOLUME 3 ISBN 978-1-61655-714-0 | $29.99

ANGEL & FAITH SEASON 10

VOLUME 1: WHERE THE RIVER MEETS THE SEA
Victor Gischler, Will Conrad, Derlis Santacruz, and others
ISBN 978-1-61655-503-0 | $18.99

VOLUME 2: LOST AND FOUND
Victor Gischler and Will Conrad
ISBN 978-1-61655-601-3 | $18.99

VOLUME 3: UNITED
Victor Gischler and Will Conrad
ISBN 978-1-61655-766-9 | $18.99

SPIKE

VOLUME 1: A DARK PLACE
Victor Gischler and Paul Lee
ISBN 978-1-61655-109-4 | $17.99

SPIKE: INTO THE LIGHT
James Marsters and Derlis Santacruz
ISBN 978-1-61655-421-7 | $14.99

WILLOW

VOLUME 1: WONDERLAND
Jeff Parker, Christos Gage, and Brian Ching
ISBN 978-1-61655-145-2 | $17.99

Buffy the Vampire Slayer™

AVAILABLE AT YOUR LOCAL COMICS SHOP OR BOOKSTORE!
To find a comics shop in your area, call 1-888-266-4226. For more information or to order direct:
On the web: DarkHorse.com • E-mail: mailorder@darkhorse.com • Phone: 1-800-862-0052 Mon.–Fri. 9 AM to 5 PM Pacific Time

ALSO FROM

JOSS WHEDON

Serenity
FIREFLY CLASS 03-K64
THOSE LEFT BEHIND

DR. HORRIBLE
AND OTHER HORRIBLE STORIES BY ZACK WHEDON

JOSS WHEDON'S
dollhouse
EPITAPHS

Buffy
the vampire slayer
OMNIBUS
VOLUME 1

SERENITY VOLUME 1: THOSE LEFT BEHIND SECOND EDITON HC
Joss Whedon, Brett Matthews, and Will Conrad
978-1-59582-914-6 | $17.99

SERENITY VOLUME 2: BETTER DAYS AND OTHER STORIES HC
Joss Whedon, Patton Oswalt, Zack Whedon, Patric Reynolds, and others
978-1-59582-739-5 | $19.99

SERENITY VOLUME 3: THE SHEPHERD'S TALE HC
Joss Whedon, Zack Whedon, and Chris Samnee
978-1-59582-561-2 | $14.99

SERENITY VOLUME 4: LEAVES ON THE WIND
Zack Whedon, Georges Jeanty, and Karl Story
978-1-61655-489-7 | $19.99

DR. HORRIBLE AND OTHER HORRIBLE STORIES
Joss Whedon, Zack Whedon, Joëlle Jones, and others
978-1-59582-577-3 | $9.99

DOLLHOUSE: EPITAPHS
Andrew Chambliss, Jed Whedon, Maurissa Tancharoen, and Cliff Richards
978-1-59582-863-7 | $18.99

BUFFY THE VAMPIRE SLAYER: TALES
978-1-59582-644-2 | $29.99

ANGEL OMNIBUS
Christopher Golden, Eric Powell, and others
978-1-59582-706-7 | $24.99

BUFFY THE VAMPIRE SLAYER OMNIBUS
Volume 1 978-1-59307-784-6 | $24.99
Volume 2 978-1-59307-826-3 | $24.99
Volume 3 978-1-59307-885-0 | $24.99
Volume 4 978-1-59307-968-0 | $24.99
Volume 5 978-1-59582-225-3 | $24.99
Volume 6 978-1-59582-242-0 | $24.99
Volume 7 978-1-59582-331-1 | $24.99

BUFFY THE VAMPIRE SLAYER: PANEL TO PANEL
978-1-59307-836-2 | $19.99

BUFFY THE VAMPIRE SLAYER: PANEL TO PANEL—SEASONS 8 & 9
978-1-61655-743-0 | $24.99

SPIKE VOLUME 1: A DARK PLACE
Victor Gischler, Paul Lee, Andy Owens, and Dexter Vines
978-1-61655-109-4 | $17.99

SPIKE: INTO THE LIGHT
James Marsters, Derlis Santacruz, Andy Owens, and Steve Morris
978-1-61655-421-7 | $14.99

WILLOW VOLUME 1: WONDERLAND
Jeff Parker, Christos Gage, Brian Ching, and Jason Gorder
978-1-61655-145-2 | $17.99

DARK HORSE BOOKS

AVAILABLE AT YOUR LOCAL COMICS SHOP OR BOOKSTORE! • To find a comics shop in your area, call 1-888-266-4226.
For more information or to order direct visit DarkHorse.com or call 1-800-862-0052 Mon.–Fri. 9 AM to 5 PM Pacific Time. Prices and availability subject to change without notice.

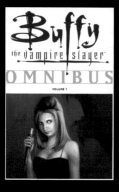

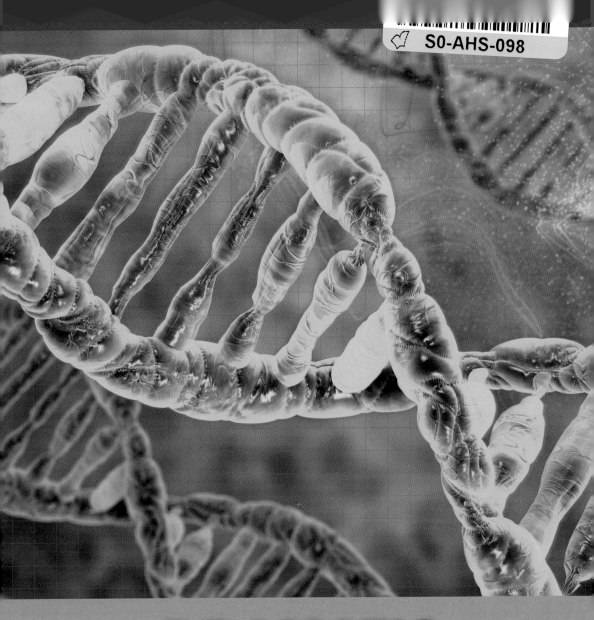

DRAMATIC DISCOVERIES

by Angie Smibert

12 STORY LIBRARY

www.12StoryLibrary.com

12-Story Library is an imprint of Bookstaves and Press Room Editions

Produced for 12-Story Library by Red Line Editorial

Photographs ©: vitstudio/Shutterstock Images, cover, 1; AP Images, 4, 6, 20; science photo/Shutterstock Images, 5; Angel Di Bilio/iStockphoto, 7; Alex Teo Khek Teck/Shutterstock Images, 8, 28; shunfa Teh/Shutterstock Images, 9; Adam Butler/AP Images, 10; roibu/Shutterstock Images, 11; Adam Foster CC2.0, 12; str/AP Images, 13; JPL /NASA, 14; Detlev van Ravenswaay/Science Source, 15; Hitoshi Yamada/NurPhoto/Sipa USA/AP Images, 16; Dr. Roger Hewitt/NOAA NMFS SWFSC Antarctic Marine Living Resources (AMLR) Program, 17; Jennifer Borton/iStockphoto, 18; Alexander Mustard/Solent News/Rex Features/AP Images, 19, 29; University of Washington/NOAA/OAR/OER, 21; D. Coe, J. Anderson, and R. van der Marel (STScI)/ESA/NASA, 22; MSFC/NASA, 23; Atlas Image [or Atlas Image mosaic] courtesy of 2MASS/UMass/IPAC-Caltech/NASA/NSF, 24; NASA, 25; Cassini Imaging Team/Space Science Institute/JPL/NASA, 26; GSFC/JPL/NASA, 27

Content Consultant: Dr. Carolyn Shapiro-Shapin, Assistant Chair and Professor of History, Department of History, Grand Valley State University

Library of Congress Cataloging-in-Publication Data
Names: Smibert, Angie.
Title: Dramatic discoveries / by Angie Smibert.
Description: Mankato, MN : 12 Story Library, [2018] | Series: Unbelievable |
   Audience: Grade 4 to 6. | Includes bibliographical references and index.
Identifiers: LCCN 2016046434 (print) | LCCN 2016047124 (ebook) | ISBN
   9781632354198 (hardcover : alk. paper) | ISBN 9781632354891 (pbk. : alk.
   paper) | ISBN 9781621435419 (hosted e-book)
Subjects: LCSH: Science--Miscellanea--Juvenile literature.
Classification: LCC Q163 .S5644 2018 (print) | LCC Q163 (ebook) | DDC
   500--dc23
LC record available at https://lccn.loc.gov/2016046434

Printed in the United States of America
022017

Access free, up-to-date content on this topic plus a full digital version of this book. Scan the QR code on page 31 or use your school's login at 12StoryLibrary.com.

Table of Contents

1

Dirty Dishes Lead to a Great Medical Discovery

During World War I (1914–1918), many wounded soldiers had horrific infections. Three-quarters of the soldiers with infected wounds died. Doctors had only antiseptics to clean the wounds. But antiseptics could not be used inside the body. Soldiers continued to die.

Scottish scientist Alexander Fleming studied bacteria during the war. He worked in a battlefield hospital in France. Fleming wanted to find something better to kill bacteria. After the war, Fleming continued his research.

One day in September 1928, Fleming stacked petri dishes in his lab's sink. The dishes were smeared with staphylococcus bacteria. He had been studying these bacteria in his research. He splashed a little cleaner over the dishes. Then, he went on vacation for several weeks.

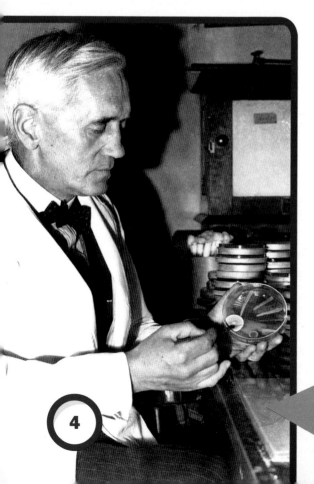

Alexander Fleming studies penicillin mold at his lab in London.

On September 28, Fleming returned to his lab. One of the dishes in the sink was moldy. Fleming did not throw it out. Instead, he scrutinized the dish. He noticed something odd. The bacteria around the mold had died. He theorized that the mold released something that killed bacteria. Fleming took samples of the mold. It was a species called *Penicillium notatum*. He called the bacteria-killing substance *penicillin*.

Penicillin fungus grows on petri dishes.

Over the next decade, several chemists tried to purify and manufacture penicillin. But it took another world war for people to mass-produce the drug. Doctors first used penicillin on patients in 1941. The world's first antibiotic saved millions of lives during World War II (1939–1945).

95
Percentage of World War II soldiers who recovered from infections because of penicillin.

- Alexander Fleming studied bacteria during World War I, when he saw many soldiers die from infections.
- He discovered penicillin by analyzing dirty petri dishes.
- Penicillin is produced by a mold that kills bacteria.

THINK ABOUT IT

Fleming worked his entire career to find a drug that killed bacteria. But he discovered penicillin by accident. What discoveries have you made by accident that have helped you or a friend?

2

Everything Began from a Single, Tiny Point

Before the 1920s, most scientists thought the universe was static. They thought the universe had always been the way it is now. They believed it would always stay the same. Then, astronomer Edwin Hubble made a startling discovery.

Hubble started observing space in the 1920s. He worked at the Mount Wilson Observatory in Los Angeles, California. In 1929, he made a public announcement of his findings. Hubble claimed that galaxies were speeding away from Earth and one another. The farther apart galaxies

Hubble studying in Chicago in 1931, two years after announcing the universe was expanding

were, the faster they were moving. The universe was not static. It was expanding.

Hubble was not the first scientist to claim the universe is expanding. Belgian astronomer and priest Georges Lemaître predicted the same thing in 1927. Lemaître proposed the universe started at a tiny, single point. An astronomer who disagreed with Lemaître's theory laughingly called it the "Big Bang Theory." The name stuck. Hubble's discovery provided more evidence Lemaître was correct. Later research convinced astronomers that the universe did start with a bang.

13.8 billion

Age of the universe, in years.

- Hubble discovered that galaxies are racing away from one another.
- This means the universe is expanding.
- Lemaître reasoned that the universe started at one tiny point.

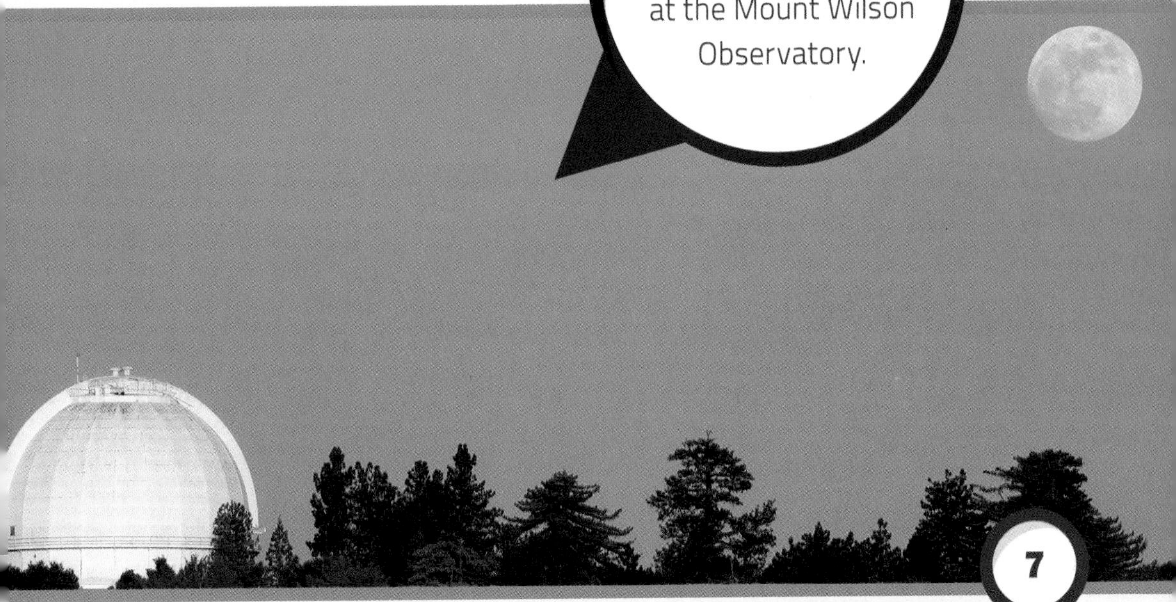

Scientists continue to study outer space at the Mount Wilson Observatory.

3

Fungus Turns Ants into Zombies

Deep in the tropical rain forest, a carpenter ant leaves its colony. Something inside the ant tells it to go to a particular leaf. The leaf is several inches off the ground. Like a zombie, the ant obeys. Once there, the ant chomps down on the leaf. Then, it dies.

What was controlling the ant? A zombie ant fungus. The fungus can take over an ant's brain. It directs the ant to a spot above the rain forest floor. The spot is just the right height, temperature, and humidity. The fungus will thrive.

Then, the fungus kills the ant. A few days later, fungal thread breaks through the ant's very tough exterior. A new fungus starts to grow. It will

An ant's body being taken over by a fungus

release spores that will infect other ants. The cycle repeats itself.

British naturalist Alfred Russel Wallace observed the first zombie ant fungus. He discovered it in 1859. He collected specimens in Indonesia and the Amazon. Since then, scientists have discovered at least 160 species of the fungus. Each fungus species takes over a particular species of ant. The fungus depends on the ant to survive. This relationship has existed for a long time. Scientists have found fossil evidence of zombie ant fungus. The oldest lived 48 million years ago.

9.8

Height, in inches (25 cm), at which the zombie ant attaches itself to a leaf.

- Some species of fungus can take over the brains of insects, including ants.
- The fungus's spores infect the ant and control it like a zombie.
- The fungus makes the ant go to the best spot for the fungus to grow.

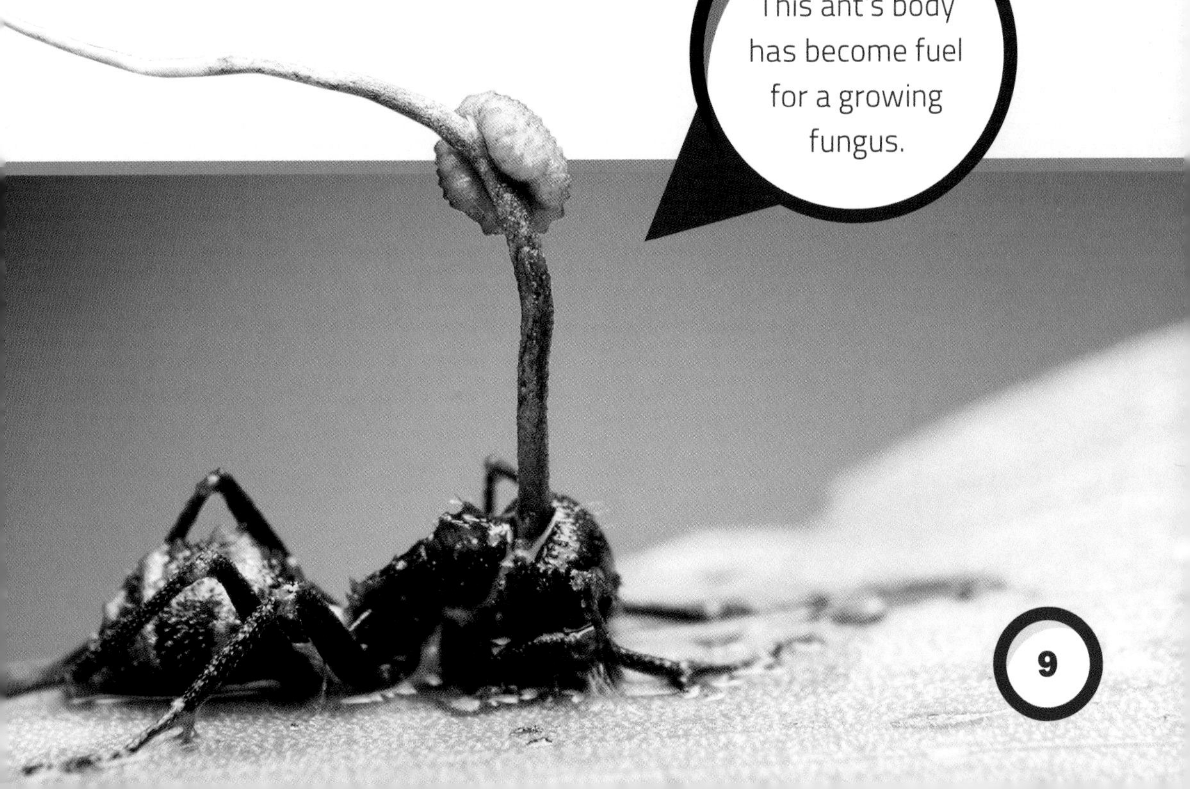

This ant's body has become fuel for a growing fungus.

4

Genes Make Up Only a Fraction of Human DNA

In 2001, the Human Genome Project (HGP) mapped every human gene. A gene is a portion of DNA, or deoxyribonucleic acid. DNA is a molecule found in cells. Genes tell cells how to create certain traits. To do so, genes use code to create proteins. These proteins determine if someone has brown eyes or red hair.

The HGP scientists found 98 or 99 percent of DNA does not make proteins. Genes make up a tiny fraction of the DNA in cells. For many years, scientists did not know what noncoding DNA did. Some believed it did not do anything.

But in 2012, a group of scientists made a big discovery. The Encode Project announced noncoding DNA did have a job. And it is a very important one. Some noncoding DNA tells the coding DNA what to do. It also tells the coding DNA when to do it.

British scientist John Sulston presents research on the human genome in 2001.

Future research will help scientists understand the relationship between coding and noncoding DNA.

Think of DNA as a recipe. The coding DNA forms the ingredients. The noncoding DNA makes up the directions. It tells cells how to make the recipe. Scientists are just beginning to understand how this process works. Vast areas of human DNA are still a mystery. But scientists now think at least 80 percent of DNA is active. It is not junk at all.

21,000
Number of genes in human DNA.

- The Human Genome Project mapped human DNA.
- Many scientists thought most DNA did not have a job.
- The Encode Project discovered the "junk" DNA tells genes what to do.

JUMPING GENES

In the 1950s, Barbara McClintock made a fascinating discovery. She found some genes could actually jump, or change places. Before her discovery, scientists thought genes did not move within the DNA molecule. This shuffling of genes creates variations in a species. This helps the species survive.

11

5 Hobbits Discovered in Indonesia

In 2004, a team of archaeologists unearthed a set of small bones. They were digging in a cave on Flores, an Indonesian island. At first, scientists thought they had found a child. Then, they laid out the bones. They realized they were wrong.

The archaeologists had found an entirely new species of early human. The adults of this species were quite small. The woman they found would have stood just 3.5 feet (1.1 m) tall.

Since the initial discovery, scientists have found a dozen more individuals.

The new species was officially named *Homo floresiensis*. But it was nicknamed "the Hobbit." Hobbits are an imaginary race of humanlike creatures. J. R. R. Tolkien created short, human-like hobbits. He wrote about them in novels and short stories. The most famous are *The Hobbit* and *The Lord of the Rings*.

Scientists initially thought *Homo floresiensis* was only 18,000 years old. But later research proved the bones were much older. The species lived on Flores between 100,000 and 80,000 years ago. *Homo floresiensis* had a small brain compared with modern humans. But these individuals made tools and hunted. They may even have discovered fire.

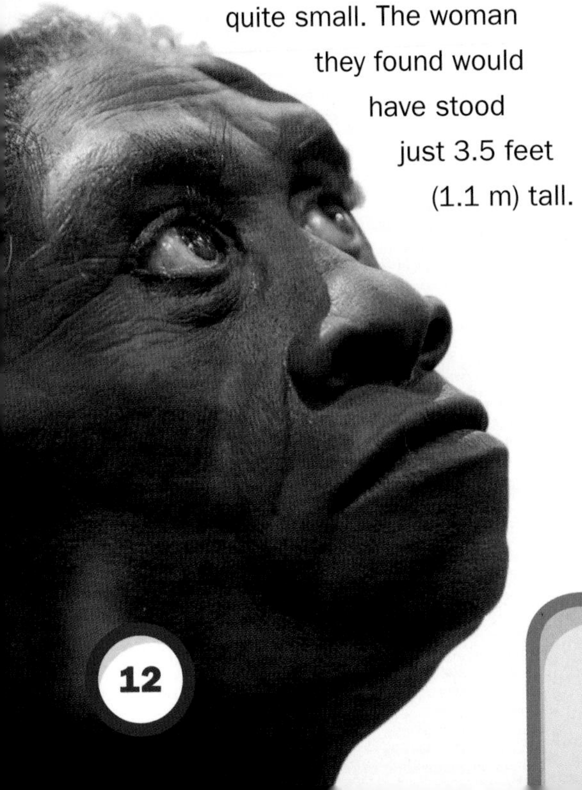

A model of how scientists believe *Homo floresiensis* looked

50,000

Years ago modern humans first appeared in Southeast Asia and Australia.

- Archaeologists found the bones of an early human species on Flores.
- This new species was only 3.5 feet (1.1 m) tall.
- They lived 100,000 to 80,000 years ago.

HOMININS

The term *hominin* refers to modern humans, extinct human species, and their ancestors. Hominins include members of the *Homo*, *Australopithecus*, and *Paranthropus* groups. Humans and the extinct Hobbit and Neanderthal species are all hominins.

So far, the Hobbit species has been found only on Flores. Scientists think a larger, older species may have been stranded there 300,000 years ago. The island is small and has limited food. The ancestors of *Homo floresiensis* may have evolved over thousands of years. By becoming smaller, more individuals would have survived.

The skull of *Homo floresiensis* (left) is much smaller than that of a modern human.

A Huge Asteroid Wiped Out the Dinosaurs

Dinosaurs have long fascinated scientists. The last species of these large animals died off 65 million years ago. For decades, people wondered why. In 1980, physicist Luis Walter Alvarez discovered the likely answer.

Alvarez and his geologist son Walter analyzed soil around the world. In some places, they found a thin layer of clay. It was 65 million years old.

The layer marked a boundary. It separated two time periods in Earth's history. Below the clay, paleontologists found dinosaur fossils. Above it, they found no dinosaur bones.

But Luis and Walter Alvarez did find something curious. An element called iridium was in the clay. Iridium is rare on Earth. But it is common at the core of asteroids and comets.

Alvarez claimed that an asteroid similar to this one hit Earth and killed the dinosaurs.

Alvarez believed the iridium came from a massive asteroid that crashed into Earth.

The asteroid's impact had dramatic effects. Millions of tons of dirt shot up into the atmosphere. The dust cloud blotted out the sun. Temperatures dropped for a long time. Approximately 70 percent of all species on Earth died off afterward. Among them were the mighty dinosaurs.

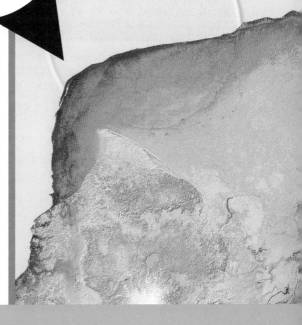

NASA found evidence of the Chicxulub crater in images from space.

6.2

Estimated diameter, in miles (10 km), of the asteroid that wiped out the dinosaurs.

- Luis and Walter Alvarez discovered iridium in a 65-million-year-old layer of clay.
- Iridium is a common element in asteroids and comets.
- A massive asteroid hit Earth 65 million years ago, wiping out the dinosaurs.

CHICXULUB CRATER

In 1978, geophysicists discovered a huge crater. It lies north of the Yucatán Peninsula in Mexico. The scientists worked for a private oil company. Their discovery was not made public. A decade later, scientist Alan Hildebrand reviewed the oil company's records. He rediscovered the enormous crater. It was centered on the village of Chicxulub. This crater was the age of the iridium Alvarez found. Hildebrand had discovered the asteroid's impact site.

7 Massive Earthquakes Can Shorten a Day

In 2011, a massive earthquake struck off the coast of Japan. The 8.9-magnitude quake caused a powerful tsunami. These extreme events destroyed entire towns. They killed thousands of people. They caused a nuclear meltdown at the Fukushima Daiichi power plant. Amid the destruction, scientists observed other dramatic effects. The earthquake had shortened the day. It had shifted the way Earth wobbles.

All major earthquakes can do these things. They move large portions of Earth's surface. Though slight, this redistributes Earth's mass. This can cause Earth to rotate at a different speed. NASA estimated the 2011 earthquake

The 2011 earthquake that hit northern Japan devastated cities and towns.

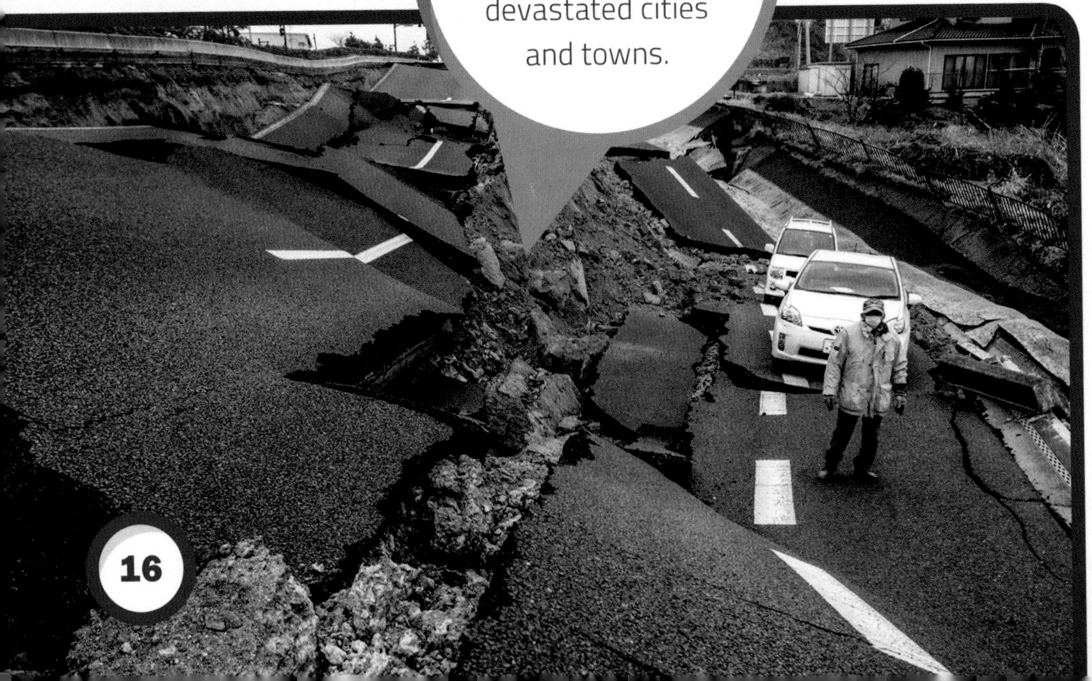

The melting of enormous ice shelves can cause Earth's motion to change.

caused Earth to rotate a tiny bit faster. This extra speed made the day 1.8 microseconds shorter. A microsecond is a millionth of a second.

The earthquake also shifted Earth's position on its figure axis. The figure axis is an imaginary line. Earth's mass is balanced around it. Earth does not spin perfectly like a top does. It wobbles. Shifting the figure axis causes Earth to wobble differently. Typhoons and melting ice shelves can also change Earth's wobble.

3

Time, in microseconds, lost after a 9.1-magnitude earthquake in 2004.

- Massive earthquakes can affect how fast Earth spins.
- This can shorten the length of the day.
- Earthquakes can also affect Earth's wobble on its figure axis.

8

One Supercontinent Once Dominated the Globe

In 1912, Alfred Wegener observed something peculiar. The east coast of North America fits together with the west coast of Europe. Similarly, South America fits together with Africa. The continents look like jigsaw puzzle pieces. Wegener was not the first to notice this. But he was the first to propose a reason for it.

Wegener believed the continents had once been one big, connected supercontinent. He called it *Pangea*. The word means "all lands." Pangea existed from 300 to 150 million years ago.

Gradually, Pangea broke up. The continents present today drifted into position over millions of years. Wegener called this theory *continental drift*. To prove it, he combined several discoveries. The plants and fossils of South America and Africa were similar along the continents' coasts. Rock formations also matched on both sides.

But Wegener could not explain how the continents actually moved. He had some ideas. But other scientists were skeptical. Then, in the 1950s, oceanographers discovered the mid-Atlantic Ridge. This mountain range in the Atlantic Ocean is

Eventually, Pangea shifted into the current continents on Earth today.

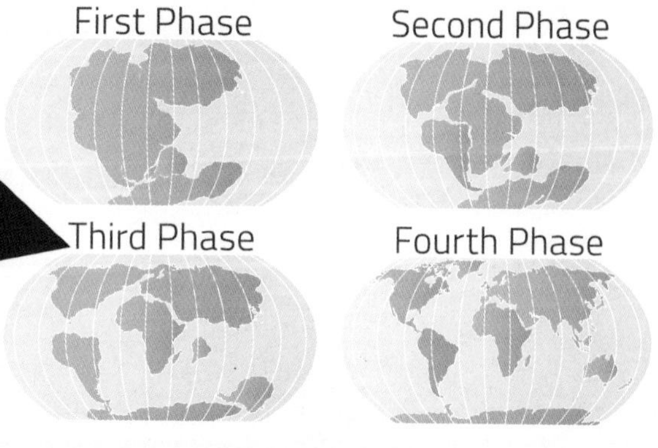
First Phase
Second Phase
Third Phase
Fourth Phase

31,000 miles (50,000 km) long. It is one of many mid-ocean ridges. Mid-ocean ridges are where the continental plates meet. The mid-Atlantic Ridge separates the European and North American continents in the north. To the south, it separates Africa and South America. At mid-ocean ridges, new ocean crust forms through volcanic activity. Magma bubbles up, cools, and pushes the tectonic plates apart. The seafloor spreads. The continents move a few centimeters a year.

A diver navigates the Silfra crack in Iceland.

200 million
Years ago Pangea began to break up.

- Alfred Wegener proposed the continents were once one big continent.
- He called the supercontinent *Pangea*.
- Decades later, scientists discovered mid-ocean ridges that explained how the continents move.

SILFRA CRACK

The mid-Atlantic Ridge passes through Thingvellir National Park in Iceland. The Silfra crack is a popular diving spot in Thingvellir Lake. Tourists can dive between two continental plates.

9

Strange Life Thrives at the Ocean Floor

On February 15, 1977, *Alvin* dove off the northeast coast of the Galapagos Islands. The remotely controlled submersible plunged 8,000 feet (2,438 m) into the Pacific Ocean. The sub's camera snapped photographs as it crawled along the ocean floor. Scientists from Woods Hole Oceanographic Institute reviewed the pictures. They were stunned by what they saw.

The scientists expected to see nothing. They thought the ocean floor was a cold, dark desert. It certainly would not contain any life. But *Alvin*'s camera proved the opposite was true. It captured an oasis of mussels, clams, and other animal life.

A few days later, divers descended to see for themselves. They dove down in another submersible. They discovered surprisingly warm water

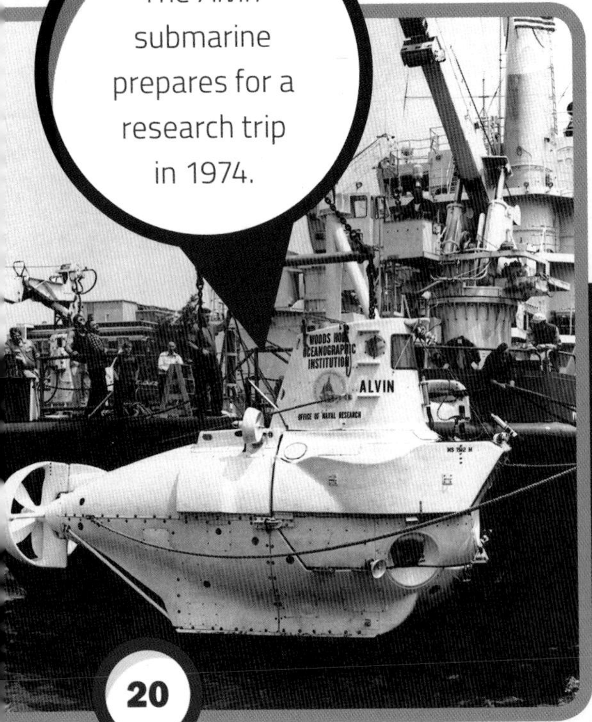
WOODS HOLE
OCEANOGRAPHIC
INSTITUTION
ALVIN

The *Alvin* submarine prepares for a research trip in 1974.

THINK ABOUT IT

Based on what you have read, do you think there is any place on Earth where life cannot exist? Use evidence from this book to support your answer.

750

Temperature, in degrees Fahrenheit (400°C), of the seawater directly above hydrothermal vents.

- In 1977, scientists discovered life thousands of feet under the Pacific Ocean near the Galapagos Islands.
- Many of the species had never been discovered before.
- This life was concentrated around hydrothermal vents that form over cracks in the ocean floor.

Hydrothermal vents are home to tube worms.

and strange living things. Biologists later identified blind crabs, giant clams, and mouthless tube worms. Many of the species had never been seen before.

All this life thrived around hydrothermal vents. These vents form where seawater meets magma from beneath the ocean floor. Seawater seeps down into the narrow cracks in the ocean crust.

Particles in the magma meet the freezing cold seawater. They cool and form chimney-like structures called smokers. Chemicals and minerals get deposited on the smokers. Bacteria feed on these substances. Then, the tube worms, shrimp, and mussels feed on the bacteria. And larger creatures eat these smaller ones. The ocean floor is not a lifeless desert. Hydrothermal vents support life far from sunlight.

10

A Supermassive Black Hole Lies at the Galaxy's Center

Something enormous and invisible lies at the center of the Milky Way galaxy. It is 4 million times the mass of the sun. It is a black hole called Sagittarius A.

Black holes are places in space. In these places, gravity is incredibly strong. Matter is squeezed into a tiny space. Even light cannot get out. This is why scientists cannot see black holes. They can look only for their effects.

In 1974, astrophysicist Martin Rees made a dramatic proposal. He claimed that the Milky Way galaxy rotates around a supermassive black hole (SMBH). For 15 years, astronomers searched for evidence of this SMBH. They scanned the center of the galaxy.

Stars are densely packed at the galaxy's center. They move at millions of miles per hour. What is pulling them so dramatically? In 1992, the scientists discovered Sagittarius A.

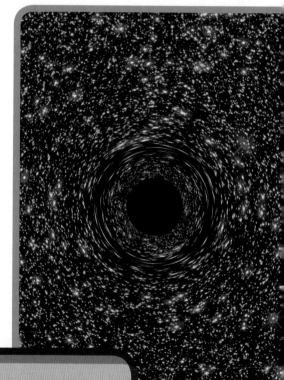

An illustration of an SMBH, which cannot be observed by sight

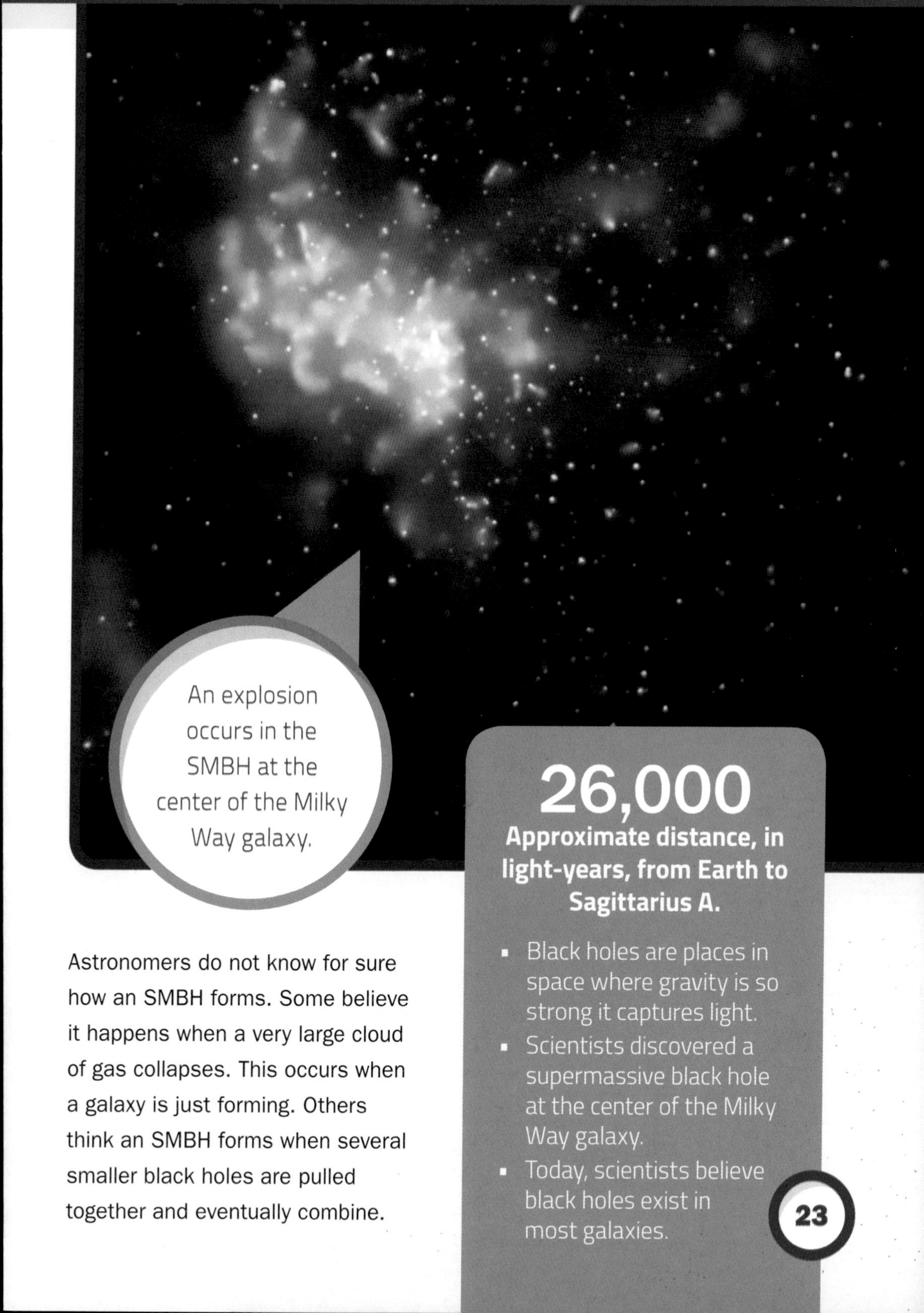

An explosion occurs in the SMBH at the center of the Milky Way galaxy.

26,000

Approximate distance, in light-years, from Earth to Sagittarius A.

- Black holes are places in space where gravity is so strong it captures light.
- Scientists discovered a supermassive black hole at the center of the Milky Way galaxy.
- Today, scientists believe black holes exist in most galaxies.

Astronomers do not know for sure how an SMBH forms. Some believe it happens when a very large cloud of gas collapses. This occurs when a galaxy is just forming. Others think an SMBH forms when several smaller black holes are pulled together and eventually combine.

11

Very Little of the Universe Is Visible

In the 1930s, Fritz Zwicky wanted to calculate the mass of the Coma Cluster. It is a group of thousands of galaxies. Zwicky measured how fast the cluster's galaxies were moving. What he found was startling.

Zwicky observed that the galaxies were moving much faster than he had predicted. Based on the light the cluster emitted, the galaxies should have been moving more slowly. What was going on?

Zwicky believed he was not seeing the full picture. The Coma Cluster had to be much more massive than what he could observe. Zwicky called the unseen matter *dark matter*. His discovery was not widely accepted until the 1970s. That is when scientist Vera Rubin confirmed matter was missing from the Coma Cluster. She was mapping the speed of the stars in the Milky Way. During her research, she found evidence of missing mass.

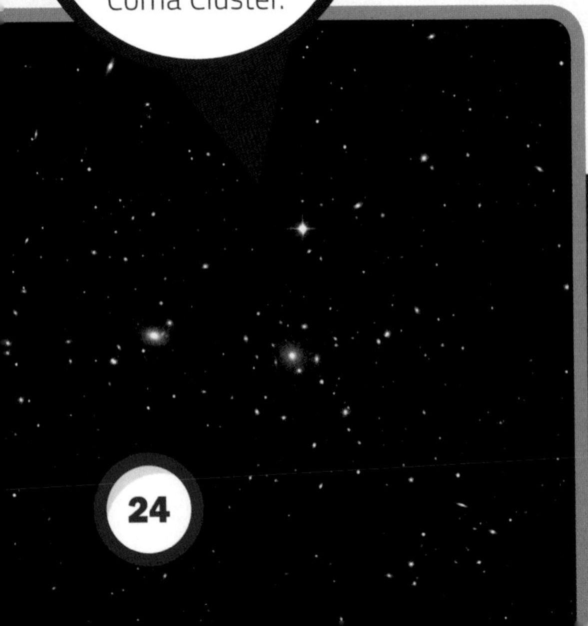

Each point of light in this image is an individual galaxy in the Coma Cluster.

THINK ABOUT IT

Zwicky knew dark matter existed because of what was *missing* from his observations. When have you been able to make an educated guess even when you were missing part of a story?

Today, scientists think 27 percent of the universe is dark matter. Just 4 to 5 percent is visible matter. The rest is dark energy, which scientists are still trying to understand. Scientists used to think the universe was expanding at the same rate it had been since the Big Bang. But in 1998, the Hubble Space Telescope proved the universe was actually expanding faster. Scientists think dark energy is the mysterious force fueling this expansion.

68
Percentage of the universe made up of dark energy.

- Fritz Zwicky found galaxies in the Coma Cluster were moving faster than they should.
- He thought the difference was caused by matter he couldn't see and called it dark matter.
- Vera Rubin confirmed evidence of dark matter when mapping the Coma Cluster in the 1970s.

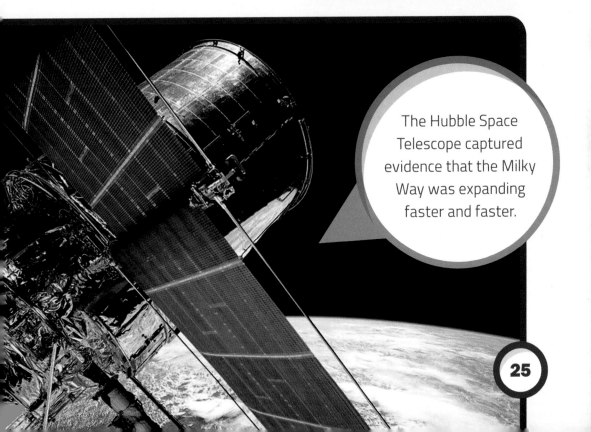

The Hubble Space Telescope captured evidence that the Milky Way was expanding faster and faster.

12

A Volcano on One of Saturn's Moons Spews Ice

Enceladus is the sixth largest of Saturn's 53 moons. An icy crust encircles Enceladus. Scientists wanted to know more about Saturn and its moons. Scientists from the National Aeronautics and Space Administration (NASA) launched the Cassini spacecraft to observe Saturn. The spacecraft flew by Enceladus in 2008. It discovered something dramatic.

Under its icy crust, Enceladus has an ocean of liquid salt water. But at its southern pole, there is something even more fantastic. A cryovolcano spews ice particles into space. A cryovolcano is a volcano that erupts with ice, not lava. The one on Enceladus has a large plume. It spreads for hundreds of miles. Some of the particles

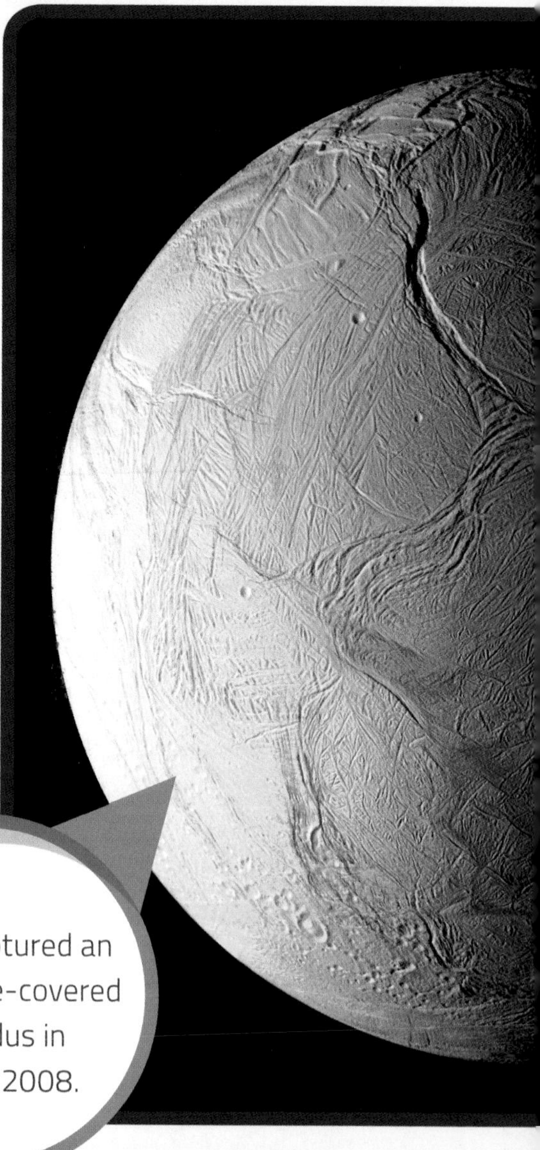

Cassini captured an image of ice-covered Enceladus in October 2008.

800

Speed, in miles per hour (1,300 km/h), that material shoots out of Enceladus's cryovolcano.

- Enceladus is an icy moon of Saturn.
- A cryovolcano on Enceladus spews an icy plume of particles into space, forming Saturn's E ring.
- Scientists believe Enceladus has hydrothermal vents at the bottom of its ocean.

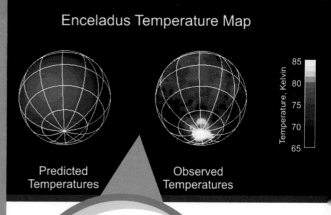

Enceladus Temperature Map

Predicted Temperatures

Observed Temperatures

Temperature, Kelvin

85
80
75
70
65

NASA scientists were surprised to find higher temperatures at Enceladus's south pole (right).

fall back onto the moon's surface. But part of the plume continues to spread. It ultimately forms one of Saturn's rings.

Saturn's E ring is made up mostly of ice droplets. It also contains tiny grains of silica. Silica can form only at high temperatures. So why does it appear in Enceladus's icy plume? NASA scientists think the moon must have hydrothermal vents on its ocean floor. Similar vents are found on Earth's ocean floor. On Earth, life is plentiful around these vents. Scientists believe there could be life at the bottom of Enceladus's ocean.

CRYOVOLCANOES

NASA has found evidence of cryovolcanoes on several other moons. The dwarf planet Pluto may also contain cryovolcanoes. In 2016, NASA's New Horizon probe took pictures of two possible examples. Scientists think cryovolcanoes may be common on icy objects in the Milky Way galaxy.

Fact Sheet

- In 1942, Anne Miller was the first patient saved by penicillin. She was dying from a streptococcal infection. Her temperature spiked to 107 degrees Fahrenheit (42°C). The doctors tried everything available to save her. Finally, they gave her a tiny amount of a new experimental drug: penicillin. Her temperature dropped dramatically overnight. After that, she recovered.

- The zombie ant fungus is just one organism that takes over the mind or body of its host. Another example is the Costa Rican wasp (*Hymenoepimecis argyraphaga*). Females lay their eggs in an orb spider called *Plesiometa argyra*. The spider makes a new kind of web. It is bigger and stronger than any web the spider has ever made before. The web is strong enough to support the cocoon of the wasp larvae. When they emerge, the young wasps kill and eat the spider.

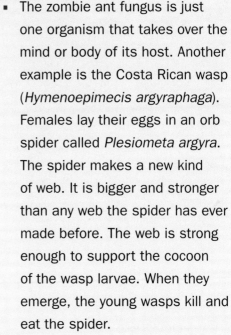

- Some scientists think that a comet hitting Earth killed the dinosaurs, not an asteroid. They agree that Chicxulub was the point of impact. But scientists argue the amount of iridium and another rare element, osmium, found in the clay layer would be higher if an asteroid hit Earth. A comet has lower levels of these elements.

- The interior of rocky planets such as Earth are made up of five levels: inner core, outer core, mantle, upper mantle, and crust. The crust can be oceanic or continental. Tectonic plates are parts of the crust that move. They can be made up of continental or oceanic crust—or parts of both. When plates meet, they form mountains, faults, volcanoes, and ocean ridges. Most plates move only 1 to 4 centimeters per year.

- Pangea was the first supercontinent humans discovered. But it is really the most recent one in a long cycle. Earth's supercontinents have been forming and breaking up and re-forming for billions of years. The first supercontinent may have formed around 3 billion years ago. Called Ur, it was much smaller than Pangea. Ur exists on what is now India, Madagascar, and Australia. Three supercontinents existed between Ur and Pangea.

Glossary

antibiotic
A drug used to kill harmful bacteria and cure infections.

archaeologist
Someone who studies past human life and activities by studying bones, tools, and other signs of civilization.

element
A very basic substance that cannot be broken down into another substance.

galaxy
A very large group of stars.

light-year
A unit of distance equal to the distance light travels in one year, approximately 5.88 trillion miles (9.46 trillion km).

magma
Hot, liquid rock below Earth's surface.

mass
Quantity of matter.

molecule
The smallest particle of a substance.

protein
A substance found in all living organisms, especially in muscle, hair, and connective tissue.

tectonic
Of or relating to the structure of Earth's surface.

tsunami
A large wave in the ocean, usually caused by an earthquake under the sea.

For More Information

Books

DeCristofano, Carolyn Cinami. *A Black Hole Is Not a Hole*. Watertown, MA: Charlesbridge, 2012.

Goldsmith, Mike. *Eureka! The Most Amazing Scientific Discoveries of All Time*. New York: Thames & Hudson, 2014.

Kluger, Jeffrey, ed. *100 New Scientific Discoveries: Fascinating, Unbelievable, and Mind-Expanding Stories.* New York: TIME, 2011.

Visit 12StoryLibrary.com

Scan the code or use your school's login at **12StoryLibrary.com** for recent updates about this topic and a full digital version of this book. Enjoy free access to:

- Digital ebook
- Breaking news updates
- Live content feeds
- Videos, interactive maps, and graphics
- Additional web resources

Note to educators: Visit 12StoryLibrary.com/register to sign up for free premium website access. Enjoy live content plus a full digital version of every 12-Story Library book you own for every student at your school.

Index

About the Author

Angie Smibert was a writer and online training developer at NASA's Kennedy Space Center for many years. She received NASA's prestigious Silver Snoopy, as well as several other awards for her work.